The Fish and Rice Chronicles

The Fish and Rice Chronicles

My Extraordinary Adventures in Palau and Micronesia

PG Bryan

Copyright © 2011 by PG Bryan.

Library of Congress Control Number: 2011911995
ISBN: Hardcover   978-1-4628-9097-2
        Softcover   978-1-4628-9096-5
        Ebook   978-1-4628-9098-9

All rights reserved. This manuscript or parts thereof may not be reproduced without the explicit permission of the author. The names of some characters in this story are fictitious, but the events depicted were real. No part of this book may be reproduced or transmitted in any form or by any means, electronic or mechanical, including photocopying, recording, or by any information storage and retrieval system, without permission in writing from the copyright owner.

This book was printed in the United States of America.

Cover design by Harvey Reed
www.pacificaphoto.com

To order additional copies of this book, contact:
Xlibris Corporation
1-888-795-4274
www.Xlibris.com
Orders@Xlibris.com
99596

CONTENTS

Part I

The Pacific

Chapter 1-Group VI 11
Chapter 2-To the Carolines 24
Chapter 3-In Palau 37
Chapter 4-More Training 59
Chapter 5-The "Ax" 75
Chapter 6-Life in Koror 89
Chapter 7-The *Emeraech* 119
Chapter 8-Helen Reef 146
Chapter 9-A Bird, a Bomb, and Camping Out 164

Part II

Only in Palau

Chapter 10-Hollywood Comes to Palau 191
Chapter 11-Palau Graffiti 203
Chapter 12-Voyages 225
Chapter 13-Wildness 240
Chapter 14-Underwater 256
Chapter 15-Wildlife 274
Chapter 16-California 290
Chapter 17-And Polynesia 307

Index 329

About the Author

PG (Patrick) Bryan spent three years ('67-'70) in a Peace Corps fisheries program in Palau, Western Caroline Islands.

After Peace Corps, Patrick earned his MS in marine biology at the University of Guam Marine Laboratory and returned to Palau to work on rabbit fish culture at the Micronesian Mariculture Demonstration Center. He and his co-workers were the first in the world to successfully spawn and rear *Siganus lineatus* and *S. canaliculatus* from hatching through metamorphosis.

Patrick was the first "fisheries specialist" for the Marshall Islands. In Samoa, he ran a successful mariculture project propagating topminnows as bait for pole-and-line tuna fishing. In addition, he was instrumental in establishing 1st and 2nd generation FAD (fish aggregating device) systems in Samoa.

He worked for the Commonwealth of the Northern Mariana Islands planning and implementing the initial marine projects program for Division of Marine Resources; and he developed a marine monitoring program for Division of Environmental Quality.

In 1990, Patrick relocated to Hawaii and purchased a fishing vessel which later bankrupted him. He returned to the CNMI under government contract for two years and subsequently worked as a private environmental consultant before returning to Hawaii in 2000. He currently resides on the Big Island, near Hilo.

"I'm going for it!" he yelled, throwing me his spear gun.

"Don't do it," I said. But he was gone.

The wind whipped at the water, turning the placid surface of thirty minutes ago into white froth. Rain angled from the sky as darkness closed in. A *mengerenger* meandered by, one of thousands out there for some sort of serpent convention.

Groping with my fins, I stood on a coral head and looked out over the breakers for Bob and the boat—the boat sailing toward New Guinea, Bob stroking hard to catch her. I saw neither. Forty-knot winds, ripping currents, sea snakes, sharks. No use, I thought and wondered if I'd ever see Bob again.

A half mile away, at the end of the reef, lay a tiny spit of coral rubble. Ditching the spear guns and stringers, I swam for it.

—

PART I

The Pacific

Chapter 1

Group VI

Years ago, when the gods inhabited the earth, a raised plate of limestone several square miles in area sat far out in the Pacific. Its white cliffs burst up from the clear tropical waters, and its hills and plateaus were covered with lush green jungle and rain forest. The guano-rich island of Ngaur lay isolated, an island alone, a playground for the gods—fat jovial folks, with big elephant-like legs, bigger appetites, and clever minds.

One of the gods, called Uab, possessed an insatiable appetite, eating everything he could find. As he grew, so too did his food obsession, and the island's crops alarmingly disappeared. When Uab had grown higher than the trees and into the clouds, the other gods decided they must kill Uab or they themselves would perish in the famine. They built a huge fire around Uab's feet, the heat causing Uab to expand like a giant balloon. Uab finally burst, his body parts falling into the ocean to form the islands of Belau (Palau).

But that happened long before my time. I never heard of Palau until after college.

I grew up in a small coastal California town called Lompoc. We had a nice private backyard with a brick fence around it, and I kept it stocked with wildlife: lizards, horned toads, snakes, mice, rats, opossums, rabbits, squirrels, sparrows, blackbirds, hawks; and the tiny pond stocked with various fishes, turtles, frogs, salamanders, and ducks. Whatever I caught, I brought home. And I caught a lot.

Fishing always fascinated me. When I was in the third grade, my sister's boyfriend told me that if I filled up the bathtub I might catch a fish. I took a safety pin, hung it from a stick on some line, and sat near the tub, but away so the fish couldn't see me. One time the pin hung up in the drain, and I thought I had a strike. I peed in my pants.

My dad hunted all the time, and I always tagged along. As soon as I was old enough, I started hunting. I loved it. Mostly I liked getting out in the wild, getting close to nature, away from people, observing.

In high school, a group of us palled around, good friends. Some of us had grown up together, from kindergarten. There was Eddie Brooks, tall, athletic, handsome. His parents and mine were best friends. They had a boat, and we vacationed together summers at a lake in the Sierras, waterskiing all day long. R. B. Lilley, his father a prominent outspoken civic statesman, was of the same mold. Smart, often loudly obnoxious, he was destined for law school. Rennie Adam was from a literary family, owners of the *Lompoc Record*, an award-winning small-town newspaper which Rennie would someday run. And Tony Centeno, a short, muscular, athletic Mexican-Indian, the only person in high school who could do twenty legitimate pull-ups nonstop.

All of us played high school football. I loved football but was too small and fragile for the sport. I got beat up, should have played tennis instead. We did the normal things—drank, smoked, dated, fought, vandalized, cheated, stole, lied, cried.

In our sophomore year, 1958, Rennie went away to Los Angeles to attend Harvard Preparatory Academy. He brought a surfboard back that Christmas break. We learned how to surf during those two weeks, taking turns on his board. Stoked, I begged fifty dollars from my mom so Rennie could buy me a used board in LA. When Rennie returned with my board that summer, we really came into our own. We were the only surfers in Lompoc in 1959. Respect.

Rennie would borrow his mom and dad's Lincoln Continental, a real boat, and we'd put the boards on the racks and drive 101 to Refugio, El Capitan, Rincon, Ventura, sometimes as far as Malibu. We'd take my dad's 1944 jeep, boards strapped to the windshield and roll bar, on four-wheel drive roads into Coho Bay at Point Conception, a spectacular area, untouched, with wonderful waves. When I graduated from high school in 1961, my father bought my first car—a 1957 Chevy 210, two-door hard top, red and white. I had a good job that summer and bought myself a new 327 V8 engine for my car and a new board, a 9'6" IKE from Santa Barbara. Surfing, girls, cruising; what else was there? Never heard of Viet Nam, Cambodia, any place like that. That first year in my '57 Chevy, I scored five moving violations and nearly lost my license.

Both my parents worked, hard. Blue-collar hard. My dad was unschooled. Retired army, he was determined that I be educated. My older sister had shown little interest in college, preferring marriage and work instead. I entered Allan Hancock Junior College in Santa Maria, twenty-five miles north of Lompoc, that September 1961. Eddie Brooks and I would alternate driving our cars, ferrying our friends the fifty mile round trip each day. If the weather was good, I'd ditch and go surfing. After the first semester, Hancock gave me a warning. Hancock kicked me out after the second. My dad was upset and angry. "What's wrong with you," he'd say. Was there something wrong? He threatened to take away my surfboard. I always threw him the curveball: "Surfing is healthy," I'd say. "I'll do well when I go back, honest." I think he empathized with my immaturity, but he really wanted me to get serious, to get the education that he lacked.

Sitting out that semester was good for me. I had a good job at a sheet metal company in Lompoc, but I watched all my friends go back to school, and it left me feeling as if I might be missing out. I resolved to go back, to do good.

That summer I fell in love with Gail. She was still in high school, and her parents despised me. Too old, perhaps, or too unpolished for their daughter. Gail was tall, slender, blond, and lovely; a Lauren Bacall, I thought. Gail, with a prominent scar on her lower lip—running down a bit, then back toward her jaw—the result of a walk through a sliding glass door. I liked the way it looked.

Back in college again, I did good. I moved into the dormitory with Eddie Brooks who was playing football for Hancock. I made a lot of friends. Freddie Buss, from Cuyama, a tiny desert settlement, was one. Eileen Engle, from Santa Maria, was another. Eileen's parents had a cabin with a dock and jet boat for waterskiing at Naciamento Lake up near Paso Robles. A gang of us, boys and girls, would go up there on weekends and ski, party, play, go crazy. Her folks loved it. So did we.

From Hancock, I transferred to Humboldt State in Northern California. Eddie married his high school girlfriend and went to San Jose State. RB was at Santa Clara. Rennie had just flunked out of USC; too much time with his board. Tony Centeno was navy, on a carrier somewhere in the Pacific. Most of my other friends from Hancock had gone to San Francisco State. I was still madly in love with Gail.

The war in Viet Nam was heating up. On campus, Viet Nam was the hot topic; that and the draft. I wasn't exactly on the honor role at Humboldt, and I feared getting yanked and sent to Viet Nam. Always having liked airplanes, I tried to enlist in OCS as a pilot. Flying over as a lieutenant behind the controls of an F-4 Phantom would be okay. I talked with navy and air force campus recruiters, but my medical history included an ulcer out of high school. They would put me in in the cockpit as an engineer or navigator, but not as a pilot. "Pilots don't need stomachaches," they told me.

That year, 1965, they bussed students from Humblodt State down to San Francisco for physical examinations. I was on the same bus with a guy named Tony Keel, the outstanding defensive linebacker for the Humboldt State Lumberjacks. A senior, he had several pro offers and was slated for the National Football League draft after graduation. But he missed the physical; they sidelined him during the preliminary paperwork, gave him a 1-Y. The rest of us had to suffer the indignities of bending over, body odor, bad breath, and insolent sergeants.

The last part of the exercise was an interview with a medical doctor and psychologist. Learning of my teenage bout with a duodenal ulcer, they told me to go home over Christmas, get a letter from my doctor documenting my case, and send it to my draft board. I said okay.

My family doctor was a retired army major. I grew up with his son Bruce. This was an embarrassment for me to approach Dr. Holloway concerning my need for a letter so that I might avoid the draft. He seemed willing enough, but I sensed he thought badly of me for evading Viet Nam. Avoiding the military had become very important to me since I found out they wouldn't accept me as a pilot. If they wouldn't let me fly, then I wasn't going to walk. I was 1-Y, just like Tony Keel; only he was NFL-draft material.

Humboldt State was slow. The campus had one small chapter of Students for a Democratic Society with several long-haired members. No one took them seriously. Humboldt county was redwood country, and redneck country. Folks up there were serious Americans. The outdoor life, hunting and fishing, had no equal. The country was beautiful, despite what Governor Reagan said about it: "You seen one redwood, you seen 'em all," or something close to that. But little else was happening up there. The boy-girl ratio was about five to one, and the biggest thing to hit the campus was a Kingston Trio concert one Friday night in early December of 1966. But although Humboldt State may not have been a social mecca during those years, it was academically tough.

I started driving down to San Francisco on weekends to see my friends and sample the action that I felt Humboldt lacked. Fred Buss and the rest of the Hancock bunch resided in a flat near Golden Gate Park. The influential antiwar faction at San Francisco State had turned them against the war. We had rarely mentioned the war at Hancock; now Viet Nam dominated any conversation at their house. I had mixed feelings about the war, and when I visited they worked on me, trying to convert me. Fred and I struck up silly arguments. Fred was short and stocky with a square face and big white front teeth that glistened when he smiled. He talked fast and always grinned after he'd made a statement, funny or not.

"Those people don't want us over there. They want to be left alone, that's all. We've got no business over there. We don't even know who we're shooting. Who're the commies? We're killing everyone. It's screwed. Stupid. It's criminal. Yeah, Peege?"

"I don't know, Fred. Communism is no good. That's all I know."

"Oh shit, Peege. You're stupid."

"Probably."[1]

---

[1] I grew up with my initials as my first name. I was P. G. Bryan. Peege was the short version. Of course I put up with the usual amount of verbal abuse from my peers; anyone who disliked me or who acted smart called

We marched in the anti-Vietnam war parades in trend in the Bay Area. Marching in a human parade with twenty-five thousand young people from UC Berkeley, SF State, USF, and other Bay Area colleges and universities inspired me; and I was impressed that everyone was so serious about it. Resisters, college jocks mostly, heckled us along the way. One time, a group of us marched in letterman's jackets just to harass the jocks and hecklers. My hair was cut crew cut length, and I looked suspiciously misplaced as I marched alongside my long-haired companions carrying a placard which read "U.S. Get Out Now!" As we walked through an intersection, about twenty jocks from Stanford, all wearing letterman's garb, shouted at me to quit marching, to break off from the rest of those commie hippies. Organizers had warned us to ignore hecklers. "Just march in good faith," they had said. One of my friends, an outspoken long-haired ex-Hancock athlete, traded comments with them, which set them off. The Stanford jocks waded alongside, pushing and shoving and shouting obscenities. For a few seconds things got tense and ugly, but the police rushed in and the jocks fell out. By the summer of 1966, I had turned steadfastly against the war in Viet Nam.

My San Francisco State friends smoked grass and occasionally dropped acid. I kept trying marijuana but never got high. One night my friend and I were at a girl's house in South San Francisco. Someone passed a joint, and suddenly I was stoned, really stoned. Then two Stanford Ivy Leaguers dressed in button-down shirts, V-neck sweaters, and wing-tip shoes, came in. Ronald Reagan was on TV, giving his inaugural address as the new governor of California. Helplessly stoned and petrified, I sat staring at Reagan. I was immobilized, as if I'd been glued to my chair by a pint of DuPont all-purpose cement. Unable to speak, I sat there, convinced the two Ivy Leaguers were talking about me. My eyes flickered back and forth between them and the TV. A ticker-tape flowed slowly through my head, entering my right ear and exiting my left ear, carrying obscure, unintelligible messages I could not

---

me pregnant. When I joined Peace Corps, and all my friends were new, I decided to go by Patrick or Pat, just for the change. So anyone who met me during Peace Corps or after knows me as Patrick. My older friends and family, those who knew me before I joined Peace Corps, call me Peege.

decipher. My friend's girlfriend kept coming over and whispering in my ear, "Are you all right?" I wasn't, but I'd nod I was.

After several hours, when the dope finally wore off, I felt euphoric, as if I'd just recovered from some terminal illness. That initiation tainted any further desire to smoke marijuana. I never tried LSD, but I watched my friends drop it—then get weird. It scared me.

The summer of 1966, before my last year at Humboldt, Gail and I broke up. It devastated me. I struggled at school, unable to concentrate. My stomach bothered me again. Figuring I'd better grow up, I sold my '57 Chevy and bought a Volkswagen. By the time graduation came around, I was eager for something new. I wanted to get away, but not to Viet Nam. Then just before graduation, I read of a Peace Corps program in Micronesia which would start in August 1967. Perfect timing for me. I could go overseas, forget about Gail and all the rest, do something good, perhaps.

In June 1967, I graduated from Humboldt with a degree in fisheries biology. My father had been convinced I'd never do it. But I always squeaked through, no matter how tough. My father was elated. So was I.

My friend Freddie Buss graduated from San Francisco State and wanted to drive down to Mexico. I borrowed my dad's new Scout, which he reluctantly loaned me, and Fred and I headed south with our surfboards. In Mazatlan, we rented a dingy little shack with a dirt floor and two bare canvas cots for fifty cents a night. Big green geckos hung out in the rafters, bombing us with lizard turds at night. We surfed a few days, then went back up to Lompoc, returned the Scout, and left for San Francisco.

I was offered a job as a swimming instructor at the San Francisco Olympic Club but decided instead to go with Freddie to Lake Tahoe and then out to the Mojave Desert where his folks lived. I wanted to goof off until Peace Corps training started in August. But insufficient funds presented a problem. We had a VW bug which was cheap enough to operate, and we slept on lawns or anywhere convenient, hitting motel swimming pools for showers and entertainment. At the Reno casinos we played Keno because it was cheap, and we got free drinks now and then. Then we ran into some friends from Humboldt working for the Forest Service who told us about some jobs planting trees over near Truckee as part of a reforestation project. Good way to pick up some spending money, we thought.

It was killer work.

After the second day, I told Fred, "Listen, Fred. I'm a college graduate—this is the shits, and I'm not going to do it."

I had a real attitude problem. I figured if I could just make it through the summer without starving to death, Peace Corps would take care of me. But the college grads weren't clever enough to inquire as to method of payment at the outset, assuming the man would pay up on the spot for services rendered. Ha! When we quit, the boss smiled and asked us where he could send our checks in several weeks. Our two days of hard labor were no help, and that ended the Keno.

—

Sometime around 1964, on the steps of the Capitol, a Washington reporter asked a senator a question regarding America's relationship with Micronesia. "Mike who?" the senator answered. When I first heard of the announcement for the Peace Corps program in Micronesia, I responded in similar fashion: "Micro what?" I was familiar with microscopy; had never heard of Micronesia, ever.

Micronesia, "small islands," is a Western Pacific group of some two thousand islands comprising a land area of only a few hundred square miles. On a globe, the islands looked as if an artist had squinted and dabbed here and there with a petite paintbrush. Micronesia covers an extensive piece of ocean real estate ranging in latitude from just south of the equator to 20 degrees north and in longitude from 175 degrees east (west of Honolulu) to 135 degrees east (600 miles east of the Philippines). In 1967, Micronesia consisted of the Caroline, Mariana, and Marshall islands (also the Gilberts, although the Gilberts were not part of the Trust Territory). For over 350 years after Magellan landed in the Marianas (Guam), Spain occupied the islands, eventually losing interest and selling them to Germany in 1899. That same year, the United States acquired Guam. Then, in 1914, Japan ousted the Germans and ruled Micronesia under mandate conjectured by the League of Nations. At the beginning of World War II, Japan forcibly took Guam from the U.S. But the United States recaptured the islands during the war, and in 1947 the United Nations entrusted the U.S. as caretakers of Micronesia. Known as the Trust Territory of the Pacific Islands, the Trust was, at that time, composed of six districts: Palau, in the Western Carolines; Truk, in the Central Carolines; Yap, also in the Central Carolines; Ponape, in the Eastern Carolines; the Northern Marianas; and the Marshall Islands. Guam, geographically part of the Mariana archipelago, became a politically discrete U.S. territory. The distinct culture and language of each district made for differing politics with each other as well as with the U.S.

It was a "strategic trust," the only one of its kind. The U.S. disallowed visitors and ran the islands with a low-keyed, low-budgeted navy administration intent on maintaining the status quo. Some called it the "zoo" theory. Although the Japanese had ruled with an iron hand, their rule had been based on order and infrastructure. After the war, the navy destroyed everything that had been built by the Japanese and rebuilt nothing. When the navy relinquished control to the Department of Interior in 1951, Interior acted as a preoccupied caretaker, running the TT on a crackerjack budget and maintaining only what the navy had established, doing little for ten years except to reduce its scale and protect the isolationism the Japanese had begun and which the navy had continued.

In the early 1960s, the Kennedy administration removed the Trust Territory solitude by opening it for tourism. Congress flooded the territorial government with money, laying the American Christmas diplomacy on the people; if nothing else, America might buy the hearts of the Micronesians. Several years later, Peace Corps became an extension of this initiative. As trustee, the United States bore the responsibility of preparing the Micronesians for self-government and self-reliance. And because of the Trust Territory's strategic significance, the United States desired that the districts choose the same political status, one amenable to the wishes of the United States.

I was excited about joining an elite organization. Not like the SEALs or the Green Berets. Not like Army Intelligence or CIA. Peace Corps offered no killer training, no guns, no covert activities, no spying. No flag raising, no propaganda. Just learn the language and do what you can. I read *The Zin Zin Road* and

Letters from the Peace Corps, and everything else I could find about the Peace Corps. By summer's end, I could think only of Peace Corps. I envisioned myself doing things such as building a water distribution system out of split bamboo for some remote island village as the natives looked on, or building fish ponds and raising fish. Things like that.

But I was tentative. Peace Corps required a training program which decided whether or not one reached the status of volunteer. Peace Corps had its share of buzz words: culture shock, cultural sensitivity, readjustment, terminate, axed, deselection. To Peace Corps trainees, deselection held fearful connotations. To be deselected was to disappear. One became a nonperson—never heard of again.

I took a physical exam, got inoculated with antiserums, secured a passport and all the other documentation needed to go overseas, said goodbye to friends and family, and flew off to San Francisco where Group VI Micronesia was meeting. When I left the house, I shall never forget my father's face as we shook hands. His sincere, profound smile radiated joy. It said I had finally found myself. I think my father was also extremely happy that now someone else could worry about me.

Staging for the 135 or so Group VI applicants took place on the campus of San Francisco State College, where they put us up in the dormitories. Most of the trainees had just graduated from college, the majority holding degrees in education. A few had degrees in health, others in business. I was part of a fisheries group. We got our teeth fixed, attended meetings, and ate in the cafeteria with the football team.

Peace Corps wanted to weed out as many applicants as possible in San Francisco, saving time, money, and embarrassment. Each trainee had two sessions with psychologists. I interviewed first with an older psychologist who loved fishing. When he learned I was from Humboldt, he started talking salmon. We drank coffee, puffed on Marlboros, and talked fish stories over time. He never got to his stock questions.

My second interviewer was a young, balding, starry-eyed swisher who wore white shoes, smiled excessively, and asked farcical questions in his coolest colloquials: "Have you ever smoked *weed*?" And "what do you expect to get out of this *far-out* experience?" I wanted to tell him to stuff his interview, but I sat through it and consequently survived the prefatory Peace Corps head game in San Francisco.

My roommate, a teacher, was rejoining Peace Corps for a second time, having already spent two years in Africa. He liked Africa, he told me, and looked forward to two more years as a volunteer in Micronesia. He was an elite; a professional volunteer.

I met a fisheries trainee from Long Beach named Norman Vas as he sat in the hallway playing his banjo. He looked like anything but a banjo player. His wide, angular jaw seemed steeped by gravity, and his nose mimicked Jimmy Durante's as if bolted on. A pair of unfashionable glasses perched cockeyed on its bridge. Norman had white hair, even at twenty-three.

"I don't sing," he said, "just strum a few chords to relax."

Thank God, I thought.

One night Norman and I took a trolley downtown and drank beer at a bar and sandwich joint called Tommy's just off Market Street. Later, while riding on a crowded cable car, we met two young ladies from Denver who were staying in the downtown Hilton. We rode the cable cars with them, had some drinks, and made arrangements to meet them in their room in half an hour. We arrived at the hotel drunk, and unable to recall their room number, banged on several doors. The hotel security manager escorted us out, leaving us standing on the streets of downtown San Francisco at 1:00 a.m. Since the buses had quit running and a taxi was cost prohibitive, we struck out across town on foot. Several hours later we hurried across campus to our dorm, where an 11:00 p.m. curfew was in force. Finding the front door locked, we made our way around the building to a side door.

"Keep your eyes peeled," Norman whispered as he tickled the mechanism with a pocketknife and strand of wire.

Five minutes later, we were inside. I stared at Vas as he walked down the hall. He could pick locks, as well as banjos, and could probably pick a whole lot more. And he wanted to join the Peace Corps.

—

Sixteen of us composed the fisheries group. We came from various parts of the country, and our backgrounds were diverse. I was the only one from Humboldt State. Some came from colleges on the East Coast and held degrees in biology or zoology. But Norman, with only two years of college, showed the most talent among us.

Forty-year-old Chet Wadsworth, a builder of down-easter wooden boats, was the oldest at forty-six. Always smoking a pipe, he held his glasses together with white medical tape. Chet couldn't swim and made it clear that his niche would be on shore. A young woodsman from upstate New York named Woody wore heavy flannel shirts, Levi's, and a wide leather belt which held a large holstered jackknife for skinning animals, I presumed. John Rupp and John Ives were both blond-haired Californians from the Los Angeles area. Scott Smouse was the clown of the group. Of medium height and build, Scott had curly brown hair and poor vision. Gene Helfman, short and cocky but with a fairly large brain, was always overeager to demonstrate his adeptness at whatever. The minstrel Dave Hodges, a spectacled, nervous, Harvard graduate, carried his guitar everywhere, presuming everyone was delighted by his music. And cute Dick Doughty, with an unwhiskered baby face, light blue eyes, and brown hair which grew prominently over his forehead, always appeared to be pleased with himself.

The group contained three married couples: the Learies, Imes, and Fuchs. Dan Leary was an ex-marine lieutenant. His broad face sported a permanent smirk, an inverted smile, the ends of his elongated lips pointing toward his feet. Norman once turned Leary's passport picture upside down, and we marveled at the transformation—a real smiling Leary. Dan didn't smoke or drink, and he and his wife attended church on Sundays. The Imes—Dave and Jan—were newlyweds, having joined Peace Corps in search of the great adventure. She was an introvert, he was an extrovert. The other couple was Bud Fuchs and his wife Cally. Cally was a bubbly girl, a tomboy who yelled when she talked. She laughed at everything she said, and everything she said came out funny. During training in Palau, she enjoyed hanging out in the dorm with the rest of us, talking story and telling jokes, until Bud would haul her off. Bud, like some of the other trainees, suffered a vision problem. He wore fire starter glasses and was inoperable without them. Bud, built like a bowling ball at age twenty-three, talked with a slight lisp, fine drops of spittle flying out from his mouth; best to stand back when engaged in conversation with Bud. In the water, Bud could do little more than dog paddle, provided he was bound securely in his Peace Corps issue Mae West.

And there was myself; average height and build, blond hair, blue eyes, light skin. The shy, quiet, introverted type. I was excited.

The fisheries program was unique because it was the first truly specialized effort in the history of Peace Corps Micronesia. Our group of sixteen fisheries people would train in Palau. The other 120 members of Group VI would train in Truk, on the island of Udot.

Chapter 2

To the Carolines

The Peace Corps staff person in charge of our training program was Don Bourne. Bourne was in his midthirties, married, with a small child. His wife prided Don's roll as our mentor. Tall and thin, Don had rosy cheeks and always dressed salty Ivy League, like a Kennedy, ready to step onto the yacht at Hyannis Port. He held a master's degree in marine science from one of those trendy eastern colleges, and he talked about seamanship and marlinespike methodology as if this were a Boy Scout camp. His favorite boats? Boston Whalers, and he plugged them constantly. I figured he probably motored a Boston Whaler once or twice on the Chesapeake, giving him all that experience. Bourne was presumptive and difficult to talk to. In San Francisco, he pushed each of us to make a commitment as to which island group we wished to work in. I scarcely knew where Micronesia was, let alone understood which island groups were involved. I knew only that if we survived the screening process at San Francisco State, then we would enter into a three-month training program in Palau, somewhere out there, wherever that was.

Bourne would guide us through training, but the real kingpin was Peter Wilson. Wilson was the head of Marine Resources for the Trust Territory, and as fisheries volunteers, we would be working under his supervision. We kept hearing bits and pieces about him, imposing tales which built him up in our minds.

After staging in San Francisco, we were to fly to Hawaii and spend a few days getting oriented to Hawaiian fisheries. Sometime during our stay, Bourne had planned a barbecue for us at the family house of Peter's wife in Honolulu. I figured all the Peace Corps stuff would be worth it if I could just get to Hawaii, even if I got no further. Hawaii; how impressive that seemed to me in August 1967.

My previous flight experience had been the flight from Santa Maria up to San Francisco for staging on a propeller driven DC-3, which thrilled me. The five-hour flight to Hawaii on a chartered World Airways Boeing 707 was grand. When we landed in Honolulu, our group of sixteen fisheries people deboarded the aircraft and headed out toward Waikiki, rubbing it in as we said goodbye to the others of Group VI. They would not get the Hawaii break, instead would continue on to Guam and Truk. The heat and humidity seemed stifling that late August night, and I wondered what the tropics would be like if the weather was this oppressive in subtropical Hawaii.

Peace Corps put us up in the Honolulu YMCA located across from the newly completed Ala Moana shopping center, proclaimed as the largest shopping center in the United States. The very next evening I walked outside the Y with Norman. Pausing under a coconut tree, he pulled out a flask of scotch. We passed the bottle back and forth, until I suddenly wretched on the front lawn of the Honolulu YMCA.

Later, Bourne took us all up to meet Ann Wilson at her family's house. She was startlingly beautiful, and Dick Doughty wasted no time dallying over her. Meeting Ann only helped to intensify the Peter Wilson aura. She explained that Peter was on a business trip to the mainland and that they would be back in Palau in a few weeks. Eyeballing her gave me visions of Peter as some herculean Greek god.

While in Hawaii, Bourne held a private interview with each of us. He wanted to feel us out, find out what each of us was about (I suppose). I told him the truth; I wanted to see the tropics and the islands, but I had little idea about what I might contribute to Micronesia in fisheries or otherwise. He looked at me funnylike, as if he might be thinking: just along for a free ride, Bryan? Perhaps I was. But I had every intention of staying.

The morning of our departure, Don Bourne marched into the YMCA cafeteria waving a Honolulu newspaper.

"Look at this," he said. "Peace Corps is hip, ha ha."

He dropped the paper on the table. A front page block was headlined, "Peace Corps Sends Hippies to Micronesia." Beneath the headline was a photograph of Matt Mix, a Group VI hippie. When the Peace Corps chartered 707 had landed in Guam early the previous morning, a sleepy-eyed *Pacific Daily News* photographer had photographed the long-haired, full-bearded Mix as he passed through customs. After the wire services picked it up, the photograph had inspired forty-six newspaper editorials across the United States, most of them expounding Peace Corps as a vehicle for draft dodging hippies. But Peace Corps was hip, not hippie. Matt had miraculously hurdled screening in San Francisco. Everyone in Group VI knew Matt, or at least knew of him, and he was well liked. Peace Corps liked him too, until, after he became a volunteer in Kusaie, they found a field of marijuana growing behind his house; then they axed him.

We left Hawaii in a Pan Am 707 that afternoon, flying counter to the rotation of the earth and arriving over Guam about 1:00 a.m. I looked out the cabin windows through rain and saw lights appear every now and then between thunder clouds. For over an hour we circled, the plane buffeting its way through the clouds. Perhaps the captain couldn't see the runway, I thought. My hands sweated. We landed.

The new, bright white Guam terminal seemed all business. Hardly the tropical setting I had envisioned, it reminded me of something out of an old science fiction movie. Too much pavement, cement, and tile; not enough green stuff—ferns, flowers, coconut trees. But the weather felt tropical. Even that early in the morning the air was sauna-like; instant sweat, damp clothes, and body odor.

Guam is a small island, a little over thirty miles in length, the southernmost island in the Mariana chain. It acted as the transportation hub of Micronesia through which all air and ship traffic entered. The navy owned a large portion of the southern end while Anderson Air Force Base occupied the northern end. B-52s launched from Anderson Air Force Base relentlessly bombed Viet Nam and Cambodia.

Peace Corps again put us up in exquisite style, this time in the lobby of the Micronesian Hotel.[2] The hotel was comprised of several old Quonsets, each partitioned into rooms, sitting randomly on several acres of land. The girl at the desk had little idea that seventeen new bodies would be arriving at 3:00 a.m. We lounged around and slept on the lobby floor until late morning when they finally gave us beds. The bed springs and mattresses were so broken down and full of bugs, I slept on the floor.

Just down the road from the hotel was Agana, the capital of Guam. The hotel road met Marine Drive at Town House department store, a white stuccoed monstrosity and dominant structure of downtown Agana. We spent two rainy days in Guam wandering around. Guam seemed strangely ugly to me. An agglomeration of stucco, cement, wood, and Quonsets interspersed with mud holes sat along Marine Drive. Up north toward Dededo, Marine Drive appeared as overkill, a wide, four-lane expressway nearly devoid of traffic. Guam boasted a college, the College of Guam (later to become the University of Guam) which was situated on the eastern side of the island. Overlooking the Pacific, the campus sat on a barren plateau, an outpost grossly naked of landscaping except for several nominal coconut palms.

—

Pan Am operated the Trust Territory Air Service (TTAS) in the islands. The TTAS owned two Douglas DC-4s, both of which had participated in the Berlin airlift, and two fourteen-passenger SA-16 Grumman Albatrosses for making lagoon landings.

Several years earlier, a third SA-16 had crash landed in Palau, severely injuring Palau's district administrator, Boyd Mackenzie. Just before the plane sank, a public works M-boat had rescued crew and passengers. Soon afterward, Peter Wilson arrived with SCUBA gear. He and his assistant dove on the plane, recovering the luggage, and, most importantly, the mail. Don Bourne told us

---

[2] In the late 1970s, police and escaped murderers from the Guam penitentiary staged a grisly and bloody shootout at the Micronesian Hotel. The aged hotel was demolished shortly thereafter.

this story in the Guam terminal just before we departed for Yap in one of the DC-4s. After hearing that story, I figured Peter Wilson had to be Superman.

It seemed to me the further west we travelled, the aircraft got older and smaller, and the runways loomed shorter. It was standard practice in the islands to circle the airfield at least once to make certain the runway was devoid of cars, people, dogs, pigs, goats, lizards, whatever. I peered out the window as we circled Yap International Airport. Here was an old World War II strip hacked out of the jungle by the Japanese to accommodate their Zeros. It sat smack in the middle of a dense coconut forest, and it seemed probable that we would shear off the tops of the trees as we landed. We got lucky. These white knuckle landings took a lot out of me and as we deplaned I reconsidered going on. Palau was even further west; therefore, it must have a shorter runway, I thought. That's the way things were out here. Yap's runway was at least nominally paved; Palau's probably was dirt.[3]

Several derelict Japanese Zeros sat in the brush off to the side of the runway, and a couple of us wandered over to have a look. The earth was pocked with craters, scars from American bombs dropped on these Zeros during the war, and the planes were riddled with strafed bullet holes. But after all the years of exposure to sun and moisture, the aluminum on the Zeros remained unoxidized and shiny.

Sweating in the hot tropical sun, we made our way back to the terminal, a plywood shack with a thatched roof. Inside, we got our first peek at a bare breasted Yapese woman dressed in a traditional grass skirt. The men wore red *thus* (loincloths). They flashed red teeth when they smiled and now and then spat red juice, a byproduct of the betel nut they chewed. Two Peace Corps girls, on standby, sat on a bench, waiting for boarding to begin. One of the girls had large, ugly, open sores on her legs. I asked her where they were from.

---

[3] In later years, Continental Air Micronesia flew Boeing 727s throughout Micronesia, gunning the engines in reverse on touchdown. About 1978, an Air Mike 727 crashed and burned on the Yap runway. The plane incinerated, but no deaths occurred, the flight crew miraculously getting everyone out.

"Yap," she answered, bleakly.

"What happened," I said, gawking at the gang of flies feasting on her wounds.

"Mosquito bites; they always get infected. How many people are on the flight?" she asked.

"Not sure, but there're seventeen of us going to Palau. Is that where you're going?"

"Palau, then Guam. We have to fly to Palau and book to Guam because the Yap-Guam segment is all taken," she explained.

Strange. "What?" I didn't get it.

"Yeah. That's the way it works out here."

"But Palau's west; Guam's east. You mean you can't catch the plane to Guam on its return trip?"

"Uh uh. All booked up."

"Oh, I get it. When it turns around in Palau it flies straight through to Guam."

"Oh no. It stops in Yap."

"Oh, so you just want to go to Palau?"

"No, Guam. But we have to go to Palau first."

"To get to Guam?"

"Yeah."

When we finally boarded the airplane, the two volunteers sat directly behind me. I watched the stewardess drift down the aisle making the head count. The inside of the plane smoldered, and everyone sweated as the plane taxied down the strip. But something was amiss. We sat at the end of the runway for fifteen or twenty minutes, the engines idling. The stewardesses took another head count. Then the plane taxied back toward the terminal, and the captain came on over the intercom, informing us the aircraft was overweight and the head count defied the manifest. At the terminal, the captain shut down the port engines and spoke again over the intercom: "Will the two hitchhikers please depart the aircraft." The two Peace Corps girls dejectedly left the airplane.

Now one of the engines refused to start. We sweated inside the aircraft while the captain cranked the port outboard engine. Not even a sputter. The captain shut down the other engines and we deboarded, making our way into the shade under the thatch roof. Tense and nervous, I watched incredulously as the cockpit crew rolled up their sleeves, got up on step ladders, removed the cowling, and went to work on the engine with what looked like hammers and screwdrivers.

"Hey, Norman. Can they really fix that thing with a hammer?" I asked seriously.

He shrugged. "Hope they have some nails," he said.

An hour later, we were back on board with three engines running; but now a starboard engine refused to start. Like the other one, it would turn over but failed to fire. The pilots had an onboard solution to the problem. They taxied out and then ran the plane up and down the runway a few times until wind friction wound it up enough to start it. Woody, sitting next to me in the window seat, beckoned me to look out the window. I gazed out at several *thu*-clad, betel nut-crazed Yapese jumping up and down, pointing and laughing, their red-stained mouths glowing in the afternoon sun. I saw little humor in all this. To me, this was intense drama. I sweated; fear sweat. My hands gripped the ends of the armrests, squeezed tightly as we raced down the runway on takeoff. I looked up the aisle at the stewardess, a Micronesian, sitting in the forward jump seat. Her dark skin contrasted pleasingly with her light blue Pan Am uniform. She sat there unconcerned, manicuring the fingernails of one hand with those of her other. Her shapely legs were crossed scissor-like, and her top leg swung gently back and forth. Boy—she looked lovely.

Palau is another three hours or so west of Yap by slow propeller-driven aircraft such as the DC-4s. We arrived in late afternoon and found the landing strip, although unpaved, much longer than Yap's. But it did have a noticeable angular dip near midlength, an aberration which no doubt would cause problems with faster aircraft. Located on the southern end of the big island of Babeldaob in the municipality of Airai, a small thatch shack stood as the terminal. After landing, the luggage was off-loaded from the plane, put onto a flatbed truck, and hauled a half mile to the baggage claim area, an old heavily built building of cement which had served as a Japanese communications center before and during World War II. The sides of the building bore holes caused by guns and rockets of American aircraft during the war. We collected our gear and piled into several pickup trucks, one of them a 1966 blue Chevrolet with "Peace Corps" painted on its doors, for the trip into Koror, five miles to the south.

The island of Koror, the district center and capital of Palau, is separated from Airai by a deep channel. An M-boat hauled two cars at a time back and forth across the channel, each leg taking about fifteen minutes. We parked in back of the line of cars waiting their turn to make the crossing. Nearby, some industrious Palauans sold beer and soft drinks out of the back of a pickup. Like Yap, Palau baked under the intense tropical sun. We had driven down from the airport through the damp coolness of dense tropical forest. Now we sat on the coral causeway without benefit of forest shade, sweating in the moisture-laden atmosphere, waiting our turn to cross on the ferry. No air moved; doldrums. To the northwest, beyond the reef, cumulonimbus clouds reached toward the heavens. Off to the southwest, small islands loomed delicately on the horizon. The lagoon's surface moved ever so slightly, lazily, like Jell-O. Bright solar flashes mirrored off the water into our eyes. Out toward the barrier reef, splendid hues of blue-green and turquoise, vivid colors uncommon in temperate zones, described varying water depths. The lagoon—clear, pristine, irresistible—teased me to jump in; to break the surface, bust through that intriguing mass of turquoise water. I shall always remember that first scenic view of the Palauan lagoon. I had arrived, and I was infatuated.

We crossed the channel and drove along the causeway, up over a hill called "topside" and down into town. Old rusty Quonset huts, leftovers from the postwar navy occupation, their tin roofs broiling in the sun, built up internal heat to infernal levels during the day, then took all night to cool off. Built to last a year or two, they remained functional, serving as house, store, office, or warehouse. Tin roofs, wonderful heat conductors, had long ago replaced much of the traditional thatch which kept temperatures bearable but lasted only a year or so. Convenience and durability took preference over tradition and comfort. Some Japanese architecture still remained. The old Japanese headquarters building, a two-story cement monstrosity built as if to resist atomic explosions, stood on the main road at the intersection to M-Dock and now served as the courthouse. A similar structure, located farther downtown, acted as the Palau Communications Center.

The Royal Palauan Hotel, built by the navy after the war, sat off the main road on a grassy knoll at the intersection to MacDonald Hospital. It had two main wings adjoining a central lobby and incorporated a tinge of island character. The lobby was spacious and high ceilinged. A bar adorned one wall, and the rest of the room was open except for several rattan chairs and a couch for relaxing. The ceiling had several fans which forever turned, forever slowly. Outside the front entrance, a thatch-covered open air veranda with tables and chairs was a favorite spot for evening cocktails.

Palau's single main road ran from the Airai Airport across the channel, through Koror and out across a bridge to Malakal Island. In the center of Koror town, a road went off perpendicular to the main road or "upper road" as it was sometimes called, down to a causeway and dock known as T-Dock. Near T-Dock, several bars sat precariously out over the lagoon on pilings. Back up T-Dock road toward the upper road sat Rudimch's Store, the premier general store of Palau. Here, a road known as "lower road" ran off westward paralleling the upper road for a quarter mile, finally joining it near Rudimch's competition, a store known as Western Caroline Trading Company (WCTC). Small tributary roads led into the various villages composing Koror. None of the roads were paved except for a single portion of the lower road which the navy bulldozers had spared. Previous to World War II, Koror had been a beautiful town, the paved upper road lined on each side with coconut trees, shops, temples, and spacious lawns. After the war, the Americans moved in with heavy equipment and razed it, destroying the roads, buildings, power plant, water works, and landscaping. Koror town reminded me of a Mexican village one might run across in lower Baja, California.

Most of the vehicles in Palau were Japanese made: Datsuns, Toyotas, and Mitsubishis. Because of the wretched roads and the additional effects of salt, moisture, and ultraviolet, the average automobile lasted about a year and a half. When Koror was dry, the dust from passing cars was like fog. Coral dust from the roads caused considerable health problems for the Palauans, respiratory ailments constituting the number one sickness at MacDonald Hospital. The situation with the roads was deplorable, and I always felt that the attitude of the people could be improved 110 percent just by paving the main road.

Our dormitory was located next to the boatyard over on Malakal, a small island just south of Koror and connected to it by a one-lane bridge crossing a deepwater channel. The dormitory had been built by the boatyard with Peace Corps funds, the agreement being the dorm would revert to the boatyard at the completion of our training.

Situated on the corner of a seawall, the dorm sat raised on cement pilings out over the water. Peter Wilson's personal boat was moored beneath it, along with the Marine Resources conservation boat. The plywood building was a single room about fifty feet by twenty feet with screens on the upper half serving as windows. Just beneath the screens, a chest-high counter ran around the perimeter of the wall. Each of us was issued a woven pandanas mat, a sheet, and a pillow stuffed with organic material, the origin of which I was always curious but never did discover. The married couples were given tents which they set up in front of the dorm. Bourne was breaking us in cold turkey. A pandanas mat on a hard plywood floor offers little comfort to a soft-fleshed American accustomed to a thick mattress.

Bathroom facilities consisted of two water seal toilets situated as outhouses or *benjos* in the adjacent jungle. You flush the *benjo* by pouring in a bucket of salt water. An old spring-fed Japanese well, located across the road and out in the jungle about fifty yards, served as our bathing facility. The boatyard had built two plywood shower stalls, but only the women used them. At the well, you soaped down, then rinsed with water dipped out with a rope and bucket.

Out in the jungle or boonies, fifty yards west of the dorm, sat three open air thatch roofed huts built for language training. Each hut had two parallel benches which straddled a central space for the instructor to stand in. A meandering trail led out to each one from the dorm.

Palau possessed two species of snakes. One was a small boa constrictor, a calm, gentle, relaxed snake not easily alarmed. It liked to hang out in trees and on vines. The other was a racer—a nervous, swift-moving snake which reached several feet in length and possessed a mean temperament. The Palauans had a myth about the racer. If a person took a chewed-up, depleted betel nut husk and threw it at the snake, the reptile would rear up like a cobra, extrude its scales, and charge the person, wrapping itself around his legs and slicing them with its sharp projected scales. The story intrigued me; however, I never opted to test the myth. As a kid I had little fear of snakes, but with adulthood came an escalating terror of them. But the constrictor was gentle and if I came across one, I would catch it and handle it. Sometimes the relative placidity of the jungle would be broken by a scream of terror as someone came across a snake. It was a fact of life at our training camp. Snakes dwelled in those woods.

But other snakes as well lived in Palau—sea snakes. I had read up on these after watching one slither onto someone's surfboard in the movie *Endless Summer*. Palau's banded sea snake, *mengerenger*, is deadly poisonous. Its toxin is far more potent than a king cobra's and no antidote exists. The toxin attacks the skeletal musculature, causing sweating, vomiting, blurred vision, spasms, convulsions, and death by respiratory failure. But the *mengerenger's* temperament is docile, so say the Palauans.

Snakes were easy. What I had a hard time dealing with were flies, mosquitoes, and cockroaches. From dawn to dusk flies landed on our food, crawled up our noses, and harassed our wounds. About 4:00 p.m. each day, mosquitoes turned aggressive and nasty. Four o'clock was a good time to stay clear of the jungle, go swimming, or something. And big brown, ugly cockroaches stormed the dorm at night. I had seen small ones in my friend's cupboards in San Francisco, but the Palauan roaches were three inches long and they flew. Like birds of prey, these were *insects* of prey, with six long legs and abdomens full of gonads, guts, and rot. Able to take flight in a split second, they flew with reckless abandon, landing on face or back. I loathed them, and they brought out my killer instinct. The Trust Territory entomologist, Bob Owen, told us that the big, hairy, long-legged, fast-moving spiders that lived in our dorm predated on roaches, but I never witnessed a kill.

Out back, behind and to the side of the dorm, was the boatyard, part of Peter Wilson's dynasty. It was a big yard, with a broad covered section, large enough to handle vessels in the seventy—to eighty-foot range. Built with government funds but slated for eventual public ownership, Wilson's idea was that it would build boats for the other districts of Micronesia and provide dry dock services, such as for the Van Camp fleet. Van Camp operated a freezing plant on Malakal and ran a fleet of sixteen Okinawan live bait boats which fished exclusively for tuna. By late summer of 1967, the boatyard was thriving with orders from throughout the Trust Territory. It was building small outboard runabouts as well as larger sampans in the thirty-six–to forty-foot range. In charge of construction was Matsumoto, an elder Japanese boat builder whom Wilson had recruited from Hawaii. Matsumoto built excellent, functional wooden boats in the Japanese sampan tradition. Just prior to our arrival in Palau, Matsumoto had completed construction of a seventy-eight-foot Hawaiian-style sampan, the *Emeraech*.

The *Emeraech* (pronounced emer-i-ah and meaning "morning star" in Palauan) was a live bait pole-and-line tuna boat which Wilson had built as part of his government program to get Micronesians into live bait tuna fishing. He wanted to prove that Hawaiian-style tuna fishing was more suitable for the islands than the Okinawan method. He recruited young Micronesians from the districts and sent them to Hawaii where they apprenticed on the Hawaiian bait boats. Then he brought them to Palau and put them to work on the *Emeraech* as journeymen. He hired Richard Kinney, an experienced tuna boat captain from Hawaii, as the captain/fishing master to run the *Emeraech* and provide training. Wilson visualized an expanded fleet as more islanders were trained and entered into the fishery. He felt that if the program was extended to the other districts, freezing plants and perhaps canneries would follow.

Tuna represented a major resource for the islands, and he saw the *Emeraech* as an avenue for the islanders to participate in the exploitation of their own resources. Why did Van Camp bring in Okinawans to harvest Palauan tuna resources? Because trained Palauan tuna fishermen were unavailable. Why the lack of trained Palauans? Palauans were skilled in inshore fishing, not in offshore fishing. They had little need to go to sea. Plenty of fish could be harvested on the reefs or close to shore. Solution: *Emeraech*. Train Palauans and other Micronesians the art of catching offshore tunas with live bait. Big payloads, tonnage; big money. But it wasn't working quite the way Wilson had thought. Micronesian trainees made so much money working on the boats in Hawaii that, rather than go to work on the *Emeraech* when they returned, they spent their money on new cars to use as taxis. Taxis were status in Micronesia in 1967. Micronesians disliked staying at sea for extended periods. They preferred to go fishing, then come home to the family. Consequently, many Micronesians who apprenticed in Hawaii never reentered the fishery after returning. Most of the fishermen on the *Emeraech* were outer islanders from Nukuoro and Kapingamarangi in Ponape district. Only one or two Palauans worked on the boat. But Wilson's idea had merit and the *Emeraech* was his "morning star."

Back down the road from the boatyard a half mile or so was the government fisheries complex. Located along a seawall, it was composed of a long open air building, with heavy cyclone screened walls and a tin roof. The building was divided into smaller areas which included the government subsidized Palau Fisherman's Cooperative (PFC), ice plant, and storerooms. Across the dirt driveway was the Division of Marine Resources, a small cement cube about twelve by twenty feet which housed the chief (Peter Wilson), two secretaries, an assistant (Toshiro Paulis), the president of the boatyard (Alphonso), and a Peace Corps volunteer, Paul Callaghan. The office was heavily air conditioned, and the inside resembled an ant's nest. I always felt intimidated as I squeezed through the cramped alleyways between desks and stacks of files, books, and papers. But Peter had a new office building under construction on the seawall about fifty yards north of the PFC. Next door to Wilson's office was the government freezer where the co-op stores its fish. To the south, several hundred yards across the bay, the Van Camp freezing facility and dock was located. Around the corner from Van Camp was the commercial dock and warehouse. The whole area was known as "fisheries."

Chapter 3

In Palau

That first evening, famished after the trip from Guam, we lined up for chow underneath the dormitory next to the two mooring slips. A table had been set up at one end, and two Palauan girls helped serve. I saw two giant pots of rice, a tray full of purple yammy-looking things, and two trays full of weird-looking fried fish. Scott Smouse, in front of me, asked one of the girls, whose name was Carol-ungil, what kind of fish it was.

"*Klesebuul,*" she said giggling, her mouth full of red teeth.

Don Bourne, standing nearby, yelled out, "It's rabbit fish," then went on to explain that the fish was well liked in Palau. "Sweet flesh," he assured us.

"Yeah, I'll bet," I thought, taking note that Bourne wasn't eating—anything. I stepped up and took a closer look at one. The laterally compressed, deep-bodied fish had a snout resembling a rabbit's. I took a bit of rice and asked Carol-ungil about the other food that resembled spoiled potatoes.

"Taro," she pointed giggling, "tapioca," she pointed at some whitish-yellow stuff, still giggling.

"I thought tapioca came as pudding," I offered jokingly.

Carol-ungil looked at me as if I was crazy, then giggled a few words in Palauan at her friend who joined her in the giggles. I took a slice of taro and a piece of tapioca, then fingered a rabbit fish onto my plastic plate.

"Fork?" I asked with a pleasant smile.

Bourne, standing nearby to make sure we didn't get out of hand or something, popped up again: "Fingers, Palauan style."

"Okay," I said. "What about drink?" I asked Carol-ungil.

"Ice coffee," she giggled, pointing to a large steel pitcher, where, next to it sat the spices, soy sauce, and ketchup. I doused my rice with soyu, poured some coffee into a paper cup, then found a seat next to Norman and Scott Smouse on one of the two picnic benches set up under the dorm.

"Fish ain't bad," commented Scott with shiny lips.

"A bit greasy," said Norm, holding up oily fingers.

My appetite was quickly diminishing. I took a bite of tapioca—a little stringy and mushy, and very bland—picked up the taro and bit. Bland as well. Then I gulped down some iced coffee, little more than cool now, and sweet beyond recognition. After fingering my rice and soyu, I stood up, disgusted, looking for something decent like water.

Later that night, I lay under my sheet on my new freshly woven pandanas mat, the hard plywood floor unyielding under my hip bones. I tossed and turned, tossed and turned. Everyone tossed and turned. After a while, to add to our discomfort, a flotilla of mosquitoes arrived. My pillow, full of something organic, probably derived from the jungle, crinkled with each movement of my head. Maybe this wasn't such a good idea, I thought. I could be home in a soft bed with a stomach full of a Bob's Big Boy hamburger instead of this. Moans of discomfort, bones thumping the floor, sheets being tossed, slapping flurries, and the buzzing of mosquitoes—these sounds reverberated through the plywood dormitory. Outside, crickets, geckos, and other creatures of the night clamored away in unabashed disharmony.

Early in the morning my hips finally numbed and I fell asleep—only to be awakened by *Ding ding ding . . . Ding ding ding*. Downstairs, Carol-ungil banged on her bell, giving us the get-up call. Breakfast was ready. Moans and groans filled the dorm. With my stomach lingering in a knot of deprivation, I sat up and rubbed my eyes. My clammy body told me that already the humidity was up around 99.9 percent, and I sensed the sweat on my forehead. I slipped on my shorts, hobbled down the stairs, and stepped in line at the *benjo*. Then I looked around and concluded that the jungle offered better facilities. As I started through the trees I met Norman coming out.

"Watch out for snakes," he said in passing. Snakes? Nah.

With an empty bladder, and stomach as well, I hurried over to eat breakfast under the dorm. Carol-ungil and her friend were serving again, or at least on standby, probably until we got used to using our fingers. I counted on at least some tropical fruit, hot coffee, maybe some toast and butter. Wrong. There, on the table in the same place as last night, sat the same ol' stuff, only less of it. Cold greasy fried fish, cold rice, and coffee. I headed for the coffeepot—one of those big urns with a spigot you find in cafeterias—and filled my paper cup. Lukewarm. It hit my lips just like the night before, so sweet even a kid would snub it. But I was hungry, and again I ate rice covered with soyu. Then I walked up to Carol-ungil.

"Why can't you give us plain coffee without the sugar?" I asked as politely as I could through bloodshot eyes. She looked at me and pointed at the coffeepot, obviously confused. I turned and walked away, pondering my fate in Palau. Starvation, of course. I would waste away and die. I was sure of it. My stomach would never lie.

On the other hand, after having gulped quarts of Safeway's own Brown Derby beer all summer, I was packing about fifteen extra pounds, and I could afford to starve a bit. Besides, like in the movies, I had planned to feast on tropical fruit out in the jungle. But where was it? The fruit, I meant.

Our food was catered by Alphonso, a rotund Palauan with a bulging stomach who always wore a smile and gazed above the horizon, as if looking for the North Star. Alphonso was the general manager and president of the boatyard. And because the boatyard was a government-sponsored project, he worked out of Peter Wilson's office. Alphonso kissed up to Peter because Alphonso had a magnificent gig going. Not only did Peter have PCV Paul Callaghan keeping the boatyard books, but Peter devoted the majority of Marine Resources' time, energy, and manpower to boatyard affairs. Alphonso also owned a bar downtown just off T-Dock road which he affectionately called Pete's Place. Alphonso had turned back flips when Peter asked him if he would cater meals for the Peace Corps training program.

After breakfast that first morning at the dormitory, Don Bourne hauled us all down to the Peace Corps office which was located downtown on the main road. Bourne introduced us to Peace Corps Director Jim Taylor and to the Peace Corps doctor, who then proceeded to inject each of us with vaccines. Woody, the woodsman, fainted just before the doctor stuck him. Woody abhorred needles.

With our butts full of gamma globulin, Dick Doughty and I decided to scout around. We walked up the main road, turned left down T-Dock road, then went left at Rudimch's Store on lower road. Nestled against the hillside, its walls painted dark green, was a bar called the Evergreen Café. Out front sat a prominent Australian pine, the bar's namesake. We walked up the dirt path to the screen door, hesitated, then walked in to have a look.

The place was empty except for two girls working in the kitchen who smiled at us as we looked around. A Japanese ballad played on the jukebox and several overhead fans rotated slowly to move the air, which was stifling hot because of the tin roof. We sat down in the extra-small metal fold-up chairs at a wooden table. One of the girls, her head held high, shuffled slowly over, dragging her Blue Dias zorries across the plywood floor. Her long black hair, curled and piled, rode atop her head pitch forked in place with a turtle shell comb. A thin line of sweat glistened above her upper lip, and an essence of mild body odor sent me back in my chair. She gave a slight sigh, as if she had better things to do, scratched her scalp, and remodeled her hairdo.

"*Ngar a somiu* (What would you like)?" she asked.

Huh? Doughty and I looked at each other sheepishly. She was playing with us, but we already knew the Palauan word for beer.

"*Biang* (pronounced be-young)," we blurted out in unison as Doughty pantomimed the "bottoms up" sign.

She laughed, her teeth only faintly red. "What kind?" she said in English.

"Do you have Kirin?" I asked. She looked down at me and raised her eyebrows once, the Palauan affirmative. We ordered two Kirins at twenty-five cents each; expensive.

The girls spoke a little English and as they prepared food in the kitchen we talked back and forth over the Japanese music playing on the jukebox, which one of the girls kept playing by manipulating a magic switch on the back. They asked about the new Peace Corps trainees and where we were from. Doughty and I kept ordering more Kirins, the cool fluid going down easily in the heat. The place seemed tailor made for a relaxed afternoon of serious beer drinking, and soon we began acting stupid. The two ladies had begun to look exceptionally good to us, and we tried to get fixed up with dates but without success. The girls thought us pretty amusing.

Later in the afternoon, Woody, Norman, John Rupp, and John Ives came in and told us that Bourne was in a tizzy because we'd ran off. He wanted all of us back at the dorm for supper and an early evening lecture of some sort, they said, leaving us to our destiny. Doughty and I guzzled another beer, then staggered out, yelling our goodbyes to the girls. At the Peace Corps office, we discovered the others had already left in the truck for the three-mile trip back to the dorm at Malakal. We flagged down a taxi and rode back to the dorm for twenty-five cents. Bourne, standing downstairs, glared at us as we exited the taxi.

"Finally made it, eh," he smirked.

My first demerit. Colleague Dan Leary snickered as I stepped in line for dinner, fish and rice. It had been a fun afternoon, though, giving me good feelings about Palau.

Bourne commissioned people to give us nighttime lectures in the dorm. Dirk Ballendorf, program director for Peace Corps Micronesia, talked on the American war strategy for Palau and Truk during World War II, and about the beachfront landings by the army and marines on Peleliu in Southern Palau, and on Saipan in the Marianas.

Elizabeth Rudimch, daughter of the high clan Rudimch family which owned Rudimch's Store, told us about the origins and meaning of Palauan money, its traditional value, and the uses of the money within the system today. Trinkets of ceramic or stone harbor special meaning and are worn by women tied snugly around their necks. One legend tells of a giant rat which gnawed caves in the southern islands of Palau, then traveled around defecating stonelike feces called *beblok* which later were used as money by the Palauans. This story, even though the parent stone of *beblok*, is not found in Palau.

Volunteers Jack and Sheila Hardy, both marine biologists, lectured us on poisonous and dangerous marine organisms. Palau has many. Some fish, for example, have dangerous spines. Rabbit fish (*meas* and *klesebuul*), favorite food fishes in Palau, possess poisonous spines that cause intense pain. The dorsal spines of stonefish may cause death. Surgeonfish have caudal appendages sharp as razor blades. The crown-of-thorns starfish (*ruusch*) is armed with sharp spines which can incapacitate a man. Poisonous jellyfishes, poisonous cone shells, spiny sea urchins, sting rays, moray eels, sharks, sea snakes, crocodiles; be careful, they warned, putting the fear in us.

We learned of the traditional Palauan political system, of the Palauan clan system, and of the Palauan matriarchal hierarchy. We learned how Palauan women could be loud and boisterous in a group, jealous and calculating as lovers. We learned that women dressed modestly, and that they shunned bathing suits. We heard about women's roles as agrarians, food gatherers, homemakers, and mothers; the role of men as fishermen and decision makers. We were told how young people were giving up the old ways in search of the new. We learned of the influx of people from the outer villages to the district center (Koror) in search of excitement and jobs, how Koror's population was approaching five thousand, how alcoholism and crime were on the increase, how public services were inadequate, the infrastructure fragmented, the government ineffective. We learned also, however, that food was plentiful. That no one starved. That because of the "extended family," poverty did not exist. That overall, things were pretty good in Palau.

Learning the language was a major part of Peace Corps training. Our training had two language programs, one for Truk, the other for Palau. The Palau group had two local instructors, Sabo Uchledong and Henry Sablan. The Truk instructor was Tatiechi Weir. Norman Vas, John Rupp, John Ives, Woody, and the Fuchs decided early on to go to Truk. The rest of us would stay in Palau. Later, Bourne decided to send Dick Doughty to Ponape.

Language was taught this way: the instructor would say a word or phrase in Palauan and we would repeat it as a group, even though we didn't know the meaning. In theory, after many repetitions, the meaning of the word or phrase would come to us. A language manual which contained the written language with English translations was given to each of us, and we were expected to study this at night—homework.

From the beginning, language baffled me. The instructor seemed to talk a hundred miles an hour. Words began with *ng* and ended with *ch*, the *ch* an "ah" sound and almost silent. I couldn't roll my r's, and reading the language proved impossible. Some people soon began to catch on, but I remained stymied. I was, and felt like, the dummy of the group.

Because the Palau group was large and required two instructors, language coordinator Red Unger divided us into two groups and rotated us between teachers. But Sabo became everyone's favorite. He was bright, conscientious, and serious about getting the language across. He nurtured a great sense of humor, and Scott and I joked with him constantly. Sometimes we got him going, the three of us laughing uncontrollably, disrupting the class. Then Sabo would get frustrated and plead with us to behave. After several weeks, I learned the phrase, *ngar ngee a chull*, which meant, "is there rain?" When Sabo would ask me something in Palauan that I didn't understand, I'd point to the sky and say, "*ngar ngee a chull?*" and that would crack him up. Later, I only needed point upward for the reaction. Conscientious Sabo finally threatened to quit unless we tried harder. Bourne got wind of it and lectured Scott and me, but it did little good. Sabo's good nature left him too vulnerable to our silliness. I wanted to learn Palauan, but I just didn't get it. Leary squawked to Bourne about Scott and me screwing off in language classes. Bourne gave me bad looks.

I habitually slept through breakfast, considering fish and rice unworthy of getting up for, and usually I arrived late to class. The situation was aggravated because I'd brought my rod and reel out with me and instead of studying language at night, I often went fishing off the seawall instead. Norman, armed with his rod and reel, often joined me at night for fishing and talking story, himself as disinterested in language homework as I. Big creatures would consistently grab our lines and take off, sending our adrenaline running and keeping us up to all hours.

Bourne issued each of us a pair of fins, a mask, and a snorkel to practice our underwater skills. He had four Hawaiian slings with spring steel spears, and I grabbed one immediately. A large school of *terekrik* (big-eye scad) resided in front of the seawall. In the evenings, just before dusk, the school would surface and migrate slowly out into the lagoon, to return again at dawn. After morning language class, I often dove on the school, spearing fish for use as bait in the evenings. Small black-tip sharks always cruised the school's perimeter and on the surface, large needlefish patrolled the fringes. When hooked, the elongated needlefish, with their long, bony snouts and needlelike teeth, would jump, tail walk, and thrash around like miniature marlin. Between classes I fished them using ultralight line, always releasing them after I caught them, to the chagrin of the Palauans who could not understand why anyone would release a fish. To a Palauan—catch them, then eat them. Sabo hounded me to save them for him, but I felt empathetic with the fish and always released them. They were hard to catch, and I loved playing games with them.

Because needlefish are surface feeders, they can be dangerous. Cruising along in a high speed boat at twenty-five knots with a flashlight pointed ahead will often attract speeding needlefish jumping flat-out toward the light. Nighttime collisions with needlefish have been well documented in Oceania, and Palauans have been pierced by them, sometimes killed. Boats have been sunk.

The excellent fishing in Northern California had drawn me to Humboldt State College. But Northern California could never match Palau. Tropical regions produce more speciation than temperate zones, and predator-prey relationships are more complex. The warm waters stimulate activity levels and large predators continuously hunt, looking for opportunities. Groupers, snappers, eels, jacks, barracudas, Spanish mackerel, wahoo, tunas, dolphins, billfish, sharks, and many more; all will grab a bait and run; strip reels, break poles, break line, straighten hooks, throw gaffs, bend spears, pull, thrash, jerk, jump, flip, flop, poke, bust up, cut up. As a fisherman, you burn calories; lose bait, gear, skin, fingers. And collect good stories.

—

Peter's office (Marine Resources) owned a small Mako air compressor, ten tanks, and seven regulators. Bourne had recruited Jack and Sheila Hardy to teach us how to dive and use SCUBA. As certified SCUBA instructors, they possessed considerable diving experience in the tropics. The Hardys put us through a comprehensive diving program, beginning with basic swimming and lifesaving. They even tried to teach Woody, Chet, and Bud how to swim.

After our first week in Palau, Bourne took us out on the *Milotk*, the thirty-six-foot Marine Resources boat, to the rock islands. Southern Palau is dotted with these unique islands. Some are extruded limestone formations, deeply undercut at the waterline from erosion and the rasping action of hungry chitons. The rock islands, their crowns covered with dense native vegetation, appear as giant green mushrooms growing from the water. Others are laced with beautiful white sand beaches, as close to tropical paradises as imaginable. Most of the rock islands were uninhabited, and one could pick and choose for a picnic or an extended vacation.

This particular island had a beautiful patch reef just off the beach. I had seen underwater photographs of coral reefs, but the actual experience of diving on one defied my imagination: the vivid colors and shapes of the coral, the sheer numbers of associated fishes, the clarity of the eighty-five-degree water, the absolute intrigue of this new environment—had me pumped with excitement. With my Hawaiian sling, I speared a surgeonfish and took it ashore. The Palauan captain had built a fire and he took the fish and threw it on, guts and all. I tried it, and it tasted good. I was catching on.

—

About two weeks into the training program, Peter Wilson showed up. Bourne had told us that Wilson was back and one night we waited in awe at the dorm for him to speak to us. Peter T. Wilson, mystery man; legend; our leader to be.

He walked into the dorm—shoulders back, chin up—everything I had imagined and perhaps more. Arrogant, I thought. He wore tan Levi's, a short-sleeved aloha shirt, and suede pull-on boots. Standing five foot eleven inches tall, he muscled in at about 185, had full brown hair and good looks. A few years previous, he might have passed as a third-string guard for the Los Angeles Rams. Speaking in a reverberating deep voice, he introduced himself as Peter Wilson, chief of Marine Resources, then walked over to a stool at the end of the room and sat down, chest out, shoulders back, hands lying across his thighs, good posture. On the floor, we sat on our butts like little elves, peering up at him on his stool.

"This program," he began, "is unique. And everyone in this room is unique."

I glanced over at Norman wondering if he was taking this seriously. He was. Peter continued speaking, talking about the exciting things that awaited us as fisheries volunteers, the diving, fishing, and research.

"Micronesia needs you," he said. As he spoke, I felt excitement fill the air. "There's an incredible amount to be done; a lot of opportunity; a lot of challenge out there," he went on. "But it won't be easy. Nothing is easy in the islands. Every bit of progress you make will be offset by frustrations. You'll be working under duress and hardship. Oftentimes you won't have the proper tools; you'll have to improvise, do what you can with what little you have. And that isn't always easy. If something needs to get done, I mean really is important, don't ask someone to do it. Do it yourself. That's the only way you know it gets done. It's never easy in the islands. But it's rewarding work, and you can see progress, most of the time anyway." He paused.

"Sounds like a lot, huh? Maybe even a little frightening? Maybe you're having second thoughts? Well, if you think you can't handle it, now is the time to throw in the towel because it'll be a whole lot tougher to do it later. But . . ." he raised his hand, "if you stick it out, the rewards will be tremendous. I guarantee it."

And that registered good enough for me. And for all the other elves.

Bourne had talked vaguely about Wilson off and on, mostly in a negative fashion. Wilson was an idea man, but practical. He viewed Peace Corps as a way to obtain manpower. Bourne felt that Wilson lacked the resources to support the additional manpower. Which is what Wilson was telling us, "you'll have to improvise." But Peter was a real salesman. He'd sold all of us that evening.

Peter, the salesman. While on vacation in California, Peter had been sitting in a bar and had inadvertently overheard some Hollywood filmmakers discussing a cinema project which would star Lee Marvin and Toshiro Mifune, a World War II movie depicting two stranded pilots on a deserted tropical island. The Hollywood people were mulling over where in Hawaii to film the movie. Wilson walked over to their table and introduced himself. Then he convinced them to consider a site where it might actually have happened: in Palau.

—

One day, Don Bourne showed up at the dorm with soft steeled butcher knives and sharpening stones which he issued to each of us. He lectured us on how to sharpen our knives.

Showing off his own well-honed knife, he exclaimed: "I worked for two hours on this knife last night. It takes a lot of patience to get a knife sharp."

Two hours seemed a long time to work on a knife, I thought.

After Bourne left the dorm, Norman took a file from his tackle box and ran it across his knife blade twice on each side. Then he ran the blade across the stone a couple of times. The knife cut hair better than a razor. I followed suit with mine, getting it sharp in a minute or two. Bourne figured we'd worked for hours getting those knives that sharp.

Don Bourne came up with another project to keep us busy between language classes and deprive me of spin fishing off the seawall for needlefish. He divided us into groups and assigned each group to design and build a smokehouse. The exercise, he felt, would sharpen our skills as smokehouse experts so we could show the natives how to smoke fish. Apparently, Don Bourne was unaware that at the produce market downtown, Babeldaob villagers sold smoked fish in all shapes and form—whole fish, filleted fish, halved fish, strips of fish. They sold it wrapped in banana leaves, in taro leaves, in plate lunches, and every which way. In the villages, Palauans grew up smoking fish right along with copra. The Palau Fishermen's Co-op had built a smoker out of an old ship's boiler system. Every three months or so, they smoked a half ton of filleted tuna, selling it in half-pound packages. And they produced *katsuobushi*, a high valued Japanese smoked fish product used in soups. The Palauans knew a little about smoking fish.

Bourne wanted us to use local materials as much as possible, wood from the jungle, that sort of thing; keep the technology low. He gave us a week to build the smokehouses; "then we'll have a *smoke-off* contest," he hyped.

My group included Woody the woodsman, Scott Smouse, John Ives, and Norman Vas. Norman, taking up the challenge, decided we should build a cold smoker, constructing it part underground and part above.

"Guaranteed to produce a fine, fine product," Norman asserted.

Sounded good to me. We dispatched Woody and Scott into the jungle with machetes to fetch lumber for the smoker, while the rest of us dug the ditch with sharpened sticks. A short time later we heard a horrid scream come from the boonies. As we looked in that direction, Scott, white as a sheet, sprinted out of the jungle. His arm was outstretched, and his eyes bulged wide behind his thick glasses. He talked gibberish, mumbling "machete, Woody, foot." In his hand he held half of Woody's big toe.

Woody spent the night in MacDonald Hospital, and the following day he told us a story more frightening than Scott's recount of the machete mishap. He'd awakened during the night, Woody explained, and found a rat nibbling on his bandaged toe, or what was left of it.

"Screw this," said Woody.

We lost him. Peace Corps decided that Woody was a liability. Unable to swim, now he was gimpy as well. Woody confided to me that he really wanted to go home. Without a toe the army wouldn't bother him, and he felt unsuited for the tropics. So we said our farewells to Woody and never heard from him again. Our smoker failed us, and our product flunked. But the project made us experts on smokehouses, I guess.

—

Don Bourne brought over a volunteer from Truk named Jay Klinck to teach us about outboard engines and give us lessons in seamanship. Norman had little good to say about Jay, but that was because Norman knew more about engines, as well as seamanship, than Jay would ever know.

I kept asking Jay what he thought of Truk because at that point I considered going to Truk with Norman and the others. Norman was my closest friend, and I wanted to know how Truk measured up to Palau. But Jay avoided me, never giving me a straight answer. Then someone told me that Jay considered me a jerk. So I quit asking Jay anything and decided I would stay in Palau. Little did I know that Jay hated Truk. After training, when Jay and I became good friends, he told me he never wanted to go back to Truk. So he figured out a way to stay in Palau for the rest of his term.

One Sunday morning, after Jay had given us outboard mechanic lessons for a week, we boarded the *Milotk* for a trek out to the rock islands and some fishing and diving. Marine Resources had a net skiff powered by a forty-horsepower mercury that we had been using for seamanship practice under Jay Klinck's oversight. It was tied up bow first off the seawall, an anchor holding off the stern. The skiff was the closest thing in Palau to a Boston Whaler (Bourne's favorite), and Bourne was enthusiastic. He and Jay would take it out.

On board the *Milotk* moored alongside the seawall, the rest of us trainees watched as Dan and Jay jumped into the skiff and Jay cranked the engine. Then Jay stepped up forward while Bourne, standing, took up the tiller.

"See you out there," Bourne yelled to us as he gunned the engine.

The boat lurched forward, then stopped dead when the prop wrapped up the anchor rope, freezing the engine. Bourne swan dived into the bilge and Jay, his legs bicycling in midair, flew off the bow into the lagoon. The nautical exhibition generated considerable excitement and guffaws from those of us on the *Milotk*. So much for the seamanship training.

But it wasn't all fun and games. Midway through training, my language skills remained pathetic and I worried. Sabo had even tutored me after classes but the language eluded me. Red Unger gave us a midterm examination which included an oral and written portion, and I failed miserably. But I kept trying. None of us liked Henry Sablan, the other Palauan instructor, and I told Unger that I wouldn't go to his classes anymore. Unger sympathized and scheduled me for Frank's classes after that. Henry, half-Palauan, half-Chamorro, was arrogant and impatient. He seemed bored by teaching.

Over in the Trukese language hut, training moved along slowly. We often heard the Truk trainees laughing during class, and their language skills were little improved. Tatiechi, the Trukese instructor, kept them howling. He didn't mean to be funny, but he came across that way. Tatiechi was a big guy, physically prominent, with an elongate, sloping forehead and exaggerated cheekbones. His mouth sparkled with gold fillings, gold teeth being highly desirable by Trukese. Like most Trukese, he wore his hair combed straight back, greased down by plenty of stinky pomade.

One day while Tatiechi talked story, the subject got around to food. When the trainees learned that Trukese ate dog, Norman asked Tatiechi: "How can you possibly eat your pet?"

"Oh," answered Tatiechi, "you just call dog over and hit head with stick. Then you eat."

Tatiechi had two Palauan girl friends who paled together and always hung around the dorm waiting for him. He entertained them between classes and after hours, dragging in each morning for breakfast looking as if he'd been on a binge. Poor fellow. We teased him constantly and he loved it; so did his companions, who continually smiled and giggled. *Klalo*, the Palauan word meaning "things," sometimes is used slang to refer to a person's sexual organs. Rumor had Tatiechi possessing the biggest *klalo* in Palau.

—

The food got worse. Alphonso was skimping on the old family recipe. We were sick and tired of fried fish and rice, boiled fish and rice, and fish soup and rice. Monotonous, boring, bad. What was unconsumed at breakfast showed up not cleverly disguised as lunch. And lunch leftovers appeared as dinner; or showed up in the next day's breakfast. It was poor, and my stomach growled for food; anything but fish and rice. Some of us had lost weight. We complained to Bourne. When Bourne registered our complaints with Alphonso, Alphonso told him he had no idea we were dissatisfied with the cuisine. He promised Bourne he'd spice up our diet, throw us some Spam or something once in a while. Alphonso kept smiling, but he had little use for us. Bunch of whiners.

We decided to form a co-op. Each of us chipped in a couple of bucks, which is what Peace Corps gave us as trainees, a couple of bucks a week, and Bourne arranged a wholesale deal with Rudimch's Store to purchase our goods. Generous Alphonso even allowed us to use a space in his refrigerator, which was located in the utility room under the dorm. We set up shop in the utility room selling stale cookies (anything in a package was stale), canned junk food, candy, beer, and soft drinks. We took turns running the store and keeping the books. I loved the little store. We could charge, and it offered a ready source of *cold* beer, right at my doorstep. I started drinking a six-pack a night while I fished for those big ones sitting out on the seawall. This was quality fishing. I was beginning to feel civilized again.

Then I got into trouble with Alphonso. When I speared *terekrik* for bait, I'd stash them in Alphonso's refrigerator to keep them fresh. Alphonso, not endeared to us, especially to me because I moaned the loudest about his miserable cuisine, complained to Bourne. Bourne came down on me. Alphonso felt I was encroaching on his territory, taking advantage of his refrigerator. He kept smiling at me, gazing at that North Star, but I knew he was bitching to Bourne behind my back.

So one day I offered to give him some *terekrik*, a prized fish in Palau. His eyes lit up, and he thanked me graciously. I told him I fished for *terekrik* every day and that if he wanted them, he could have them.

"I'll save them for you in the refrigerator," I said.

He nodded his approval and raised his eyebrows. That ended the problem. I paid him off, kept enough for my bait, everyone was happy. Micronesian politics. *Micropolitics*.

One evening as Norman and I rummaged around in the co-op store buying beer and getting supplies together for a night's fishing, Dan Leary's wife came in and bought a package of Oreos. As she was leaving, her husband, Dan, walked in. He glanced briefly at the cookies she held, then looked up at her, his eyes burning holes through her eyes. Ignoring our presence, he spoke to her in a low controlled voice: "Barbara, what do you think you're doing?"

"I just wanted some cookies, Dan."

"You know we can't afford that stuff, Barbara. And we don't eat sweets, remember?"

"I know Dan, but I just felt like something sweet tonight. I won't do it again."

"Damn right you won't," he said, raising his voice and snatching the cookies from her hand. "Let these other people do what they want. We didn't join Peace Corps to eat crap like this."

Barbara looked down in tears. "Oh, Dan," she said.

"I don't want to hear anymore," he told her.

Norman and I, feeling quite weird, slipped out, closing the door behind us.

"What a prick," I said.

"Yeah," said Norman. "That prick ought to have his nuts cut off. I'd do it myself if I had a long piece of bamboo so's I could tie the knife on the end—don't wanna get too close to that asshole."

We sat on the seawall drinking our beer and fishing, neither of us saying much. Our thoughts dwelled on that scene and Leary, the jerk. Spoiled our whole night.

Jim Taylor was scheduled to leave in a month or so, and Terry Clancy would replace him as Peace Corps director of Palau. When I told Terry I often fished off the seawall at nights, he started coming down to fish with me. He thought I knew what I was doing. All I really knew was that big creatures lurked out there, and they were tearing up my gear. But I played expert, advising him on how to rig his gear, how much weight to use, hook size, that sort of thing. He loved fishing.

Terry had worked in management at Italian Swiss Colony (the wine company) before coming to Palau. Having tired of the suit-and-tie syndrome, he had taken a job as Peace Corps staff. Through our fishing together, I got the feeling he really wanted to empathize, not with me in particular, but with the fisheries trainees in general. He wanted to find out what made us tick. But I was adept to tell him because I didn't know. All I could talk about was how great the fishing and diving was. Terry never bothered me about studying for language. He figured if I was fishing, I must be all right. He was right, I guess.

Sometimes Terry would charter a local boat to take him out fishing, and he always asked me to come along. I loved it. My first trip out with Terry was on a small outboard he chartered from WCTC. We went out to the barrier reef west of an island called Ulong where Captain Wilson of the East India Company packet, the *Antelope*, had shipwrecked in 1783. Wilson and his crew had been the first white men since Sir Francis Drake's arrival in 1578 ever to have made contact with the Palauans, which is where the term for white man, *chad er a ngebard* (man of the west) originated since they had approached the island from the west. The headhunting

Palauans, however, were friendly and had built the white men a new ship to continue on their voyage. Captain Wilson took King Abbathule's son, Lee Boo, back to England where he was fondly known as the "Black Prince," before succumbing to smallpox.

It was a day or so after a tropical storm and huge swells rolled in, forming up a quarter mile off the reef, making it apparent how easily the *Antelope* might have grounded had it approached the reef in seas like this. Terry's son, a ten-year-old, sat cross-legged on the bow hanging on to a rope, which made me fearful the boy might go overboard, although Terry seemed unconcerned. I had my spinning outfit and Terry used one of the boat's hand lines. We hooked twenty and thirty-pound *keskas* (wahoo) one after the other, nonstop, all morning long. I had never caught such strong and vicious fish, being accustomed to salmon and steelhead, lightweights compared to these meanies. These low latitude fish were absolute killers; all muscle, gut, and teeth, the meanest sons a bitches in the ocean. Designer predators. What could possibly be better than this, I thought.

—

A couple of characters were hanging around our training camp, two volunteers who planned to spend their second year in the outer islands. Peter Black would be going to Tobi and Gene Davis to Sonsorol. Peace Corps had never placed volunteers on these islands, and Pete and Gene would be breaking new territory. Both would be teachers.

Sonsorol lies about 190 miles south of Koror and Tobi about 360 miles south. The small, isolated islands are raised limestone formations, each about a square mile in area, Sonsorol being made up of two islands. Extended families of no more than fifty people lived on each of the islands. Tobi and Sonsorol each spoke a distinct dialect, language differing from Palauan and similar to the languages found in the Central Caroline atolls. In the District Center, Tobian and Sonsorolese immigrants lived in a small isolated village on Arakabesan Island near Koror. Most local Palauans considered them second-class citizens.

One night Pete and Gene held a rap session with us in the dorm. Pete and I had gotten to be friends, and he wanted me to forgo fishing that night so I could attend. He and Davis were both nervous about going to the islands. But that was part of the Peace Corps mystique. The unknown factor. The great adventure. Or misadventure, perhaps.

Pete sat on a stool in the middle of the floor looking the prototypical PCV. He was tall and skinny, and his light brown, overgrown hair, having rarely experienced a comb, fell over his ears. His Peace Corps-issue glasses, with round lenses and gold wire frames, worked their way down his king-size nose, prompting him every now and then to push them back up with his index finger.

"What would you do if you were in my shoes, and the chief wanted you to live with him and his family?" he began. We sat cross-legged on the floor, silent. Then . . .

"Well, what's the problem?" Scott said. "I mean, there's only a few people, so the chief probably isn't much more than the guy next door anyway—why not live with the chief?"

Pete thought about that for a minute. "Wouldn't that be kind of self-serving?" he said.

"It might be in your best interest," John Rupp countered. "If Paul Callaghan can live with the *Ibedul* (high chief of Palau), you should be able to live with the chief of Tobi."

"Yeah, what a great deal, hee hee," chuckled Bud Fuchs.

"Take it. I would," said Gene Helfman.

"Seriously, you have to consider your job and how this might affect your performance. The other people may be offended by this. Living with the chief wouldn't be right. That's not what we're here for," said Dan Leary.

"What *are* we here for, Leary? Does Peace Corps policy say we can't live with the chief? Huh, does it?" egged Scott.

"You know what I'm saying, Smouse. We have to be careful in what we do, that's all," answered Leary.

"You mean, like wear rubbers?" Scott said.

"Smart ass," piped Leary.

We spoke in rapid succession: "Do what you want." "Maybe the chief has a good looking daughter." "Yeah, maybe he has a boat." "The chief may not want you to live with him." "Maybe they won't even let you on the island." "What then?" "Maybe you shouldn't even go." "Why risk the embarrassment?" "Cancel out now." "Yeah, stay in Koror, where the bars are."

Pete grinned; Leary steamed. The discussion disintegrated into jokes and laughter and I moseyed downstairs to go fishing. Later, Pete came down and sat next to me on the seawall. "There's only so much of that Peace Corps stuff you can take," I said. "After the first week or so the novelty will wear off, and the people will expect something out of you other than just the pleasure of looking at your white face and gold rimmed glasses. Doesn't matter who you live with. That's what I think, anyway." Pete offered me a Winston and we smoked.

"I just hope I don't run out of cigarettes," he said laughing.

"That settles it," I said. "Move in with a nonsmoker."

—

Several weeks into training, Bourne showed up with a PCV from Yap who wanted to join the fisheries program. His name was Mike Constein. Already a full-fledged PCV, he wasn't subject to the same routine and restrictions as we. And since he was a volunteer, he was allowed to drive. As trainees, we weren't.

Dick Doughty quickly became pals with Mike. Since Dick was destined for Ponape and Mike for Yap, neither had language classes; which meant they had lots of free time. They started cruising in the Peace Corps truck, running bogus errands into town, hitting the bars, lining up girls, and so on. Then each evening after fish and rice, the truck would disappear, and so would Doughty and Mike. Naturally, this began to grate on some of the trainees because sometimes people wanted to go into town at night. But the two kept sneaking out, meagerly sounding out, "trucks going to town." By the time people reached the door of the dorm, only a cloud of dust would be visible. Doughty and Constein thought they had a good thing going.

One night, Scott jumped on Doughty about sneaking off with Constein in the truck. Scott rode him, prompting Doughty to stomp out and slam the door. Scott, wired, continued yelling at Doughty: "Have a nice time in town tonight, Dicky boy." Mike and Doughty drove off in the truck.

The night after this incident, Norm and I went fishing on the seawall. As usual, Constein and Doughty planned to go into town and after Scott's scolding of the previous night, they had made the effort to take along some others.

As they drove off, Norman said, "Hope they make it. Tires on that truck don't look good."

"Oh yeah—I hadn't noticed," I said, disinterested.

Just down the road we heard the truck stop. Someone swore. I walked out to the road to have a look. Both back tires were flat, and so was the spare. Doughty cursed as he looked for the missing lug wrench. I trotted back to the seawall, the others walking dejectedly along behind me. Doughty mumbled something about sabotage. I flipped my line out and looked over at Norman. He had his hand over his mouth to muffle his giggles, and his eyes watered with laughter. Then I got the picture. You could only screw the troops so long.

A few evenings later, those of us up in the dorm heard a commotion downstairs in the store. We heard Doughty: "Screw you, Leary, what's it to you?" and Leary: "All you care about is Dick Doughty!" *Thud! Boom! Screech!*—the picnic bench skidded on the cement floor. By the time we got downstairs, Leary had left and Doughty stood outside dabbing a bloody nose. Peace Corps forbids fighting, and Bourne was quite displeased about the incident. He talked with each one in private, then brought them together and they shook hands. Leary and Doughty had been two of Bourne's favorite trainees. It appeared the incident would blow over.

Sabo helped me make a spear gun. He gave me a stock made of local wood, and I bought some surgical tubing, a spear, and a brass trigger from WCTC. Tosh Paulis, from Marine Resources, gave me a piece of stainless steel wire for the ends of the rubbers. Palauan guns are efficient fish catchers. They utilize a long wooden stock, similar to a rifle stock, with a groove running from the trigger forward to a short barrel. The spring steel spear, powered with surgical tubing, is fast and accurate.

I started fishing with Sabo and his brother on Saturdays, and after a few trips I got proficient with my gun. On one trip, we dove on an enormous coral head located in an area southwest of Koror known as the baiting grounds, a body of water protected by rock islands where the tuna boats caught their bait. While we dove, a *ngelengal* (Spanish mackerel), about twenty pounds, swam up to me and veered off. I speared it behind the gills, and it ripped the stock from my hands. The powerful fish, my spear gun in tow, charged away into the blue and disappeared. I swam back to the boat, despondent over the loss of my gun. Taking a quick look around before getting into the boat, I saw Sabo swimming toward me carrying my fish and my spear gun. The fish had swum by him towing my spear, and he had shot it and hauled it in. That taught me a lesson about the strength of those fish. From then on, I hung on tight when I speared a fish.

In the tropics, sharks are ubiquitous. If you're going to spear fish, you had better get comfortable having them around or switch your method of fishing. Sharks are opportunists, and they want their share. One time, Sabo's brother dropped Sabo and me off at the entrance to Malakal Channel, the main channel coming into Koror from the east. We drifted along the side with the flooding tide, going from channel marker to channel marker, watching an incessant procession of sharks move along the channel bottom. Most of the sharks were grays, perhaps the most threatening of the inshore sharks because they're abundant, they reach a respectable size, and when excited, they behave like a pack of crazed jackals. Every now and then, one or two would break off from the bottom and swim up to look us over. This was the first time I had seen so many sharks, and Sabo and I refrained from spearing fish. Like on a roadway, the sharks cruised along, pectoral fins out like short wings; sharks in one lane going out, those in the other coming in—the Malakal underwater freeway.

Sharks represented only one hazard for divers in Palauan waters. In early 1965, a Ngeremlengui fisherman caught a fourteen-foot-nine-inch crocodile in his gill net. Later that same year, a Palauan spear fisherman was attacked and eaten by a croc over twelve feet long. The man had been diving at night near the mangroves in Airai, his friend poling along in a bamboo raft behind him. Suddenly the diver's light had gyrated wildly and moved quickly away toward the mangroves. The man on the raft heard a loud splash, then all was dark and silent. Knowing instinctively the fate of his friend, he poled the raft toward home. The next day, searchers found the remains of the body in the mangroves. Since crocodiles always return to a kill, Bob Owen, chief conservationist for the Trust Territory, set a cage trap baited with a live dog, the traditional Palauan crocodile bait. That night, they caught the crocodile, tied it up, and took it to MacDonald Hospital where they x-rayed it. Doctors confirmed the presence of human remains in the stomach. Bob decided to put the twelve-foot, seven-inch, 428-pound croc on public display and charge viewing fees which would go to the victim's family. They hauled the animal off in a pickup truck to be put in a cage at the Entomology Laboratory. Firmly bound up, the crocodile expired in transit, a victim of strangulation from its wraps. Don Bourne chuckled when he showed us Bob Owen's photographs of the dissection and the body parts. Bourne considered the incident amusing.

In an earlier 1966 incident, a crocodile had grabbed a spear fisherman across the chest and dragged him to the bottom. However, the fisherman was able to jam his thumbs into the croc's eyes which caused the animal to release its grip. The man's back and chest bore permanent scars of crocodile teeth.

Bob Owen kept a fifteen-foot croc at Entomology. The workers at the lab liked to feed it cats. Once inside the cage, a nimble cat got one jump; half a jump, maybe.

The Palauans caught crocodiles by tying up a dog near the mangroves and letting it howl during the night. When the howling stopped, it was time to kill the croc, which would be lying around digesting its meal. I wondered how anyone, in full knowledge of the dog's impending fate—death by jaws—could sit around listening to the pitiful, helpless thing howl. Perhaps it was part of the same instinct which prompted most Palauans to wing a stone at any dog that came within range.

While we were in training, a fisherman near Airai caught a twelve-foot crocodile in his gillnet and brought it in to the co-op. Bourne took us over to see it. Palauans eat the tail portion of smaller crocs, and we watched Alphonso buy this one. The next night, in lieu of fish and rice, he served us croc and rice, probably in spite. It was excellent, the meat solid and white like chicken. Best meal Alphonso ever gave us.

Chapter 4

More Training

After the smokehouse exercise and for the duration of the training program, Bourne wanted us to go out with various Palauan fishermen as observers. I volunteered immediately for the first trip. The fisherman, a young man named Rebluud, specialized in night-spearing for large parrot fish known locally as *kemedukl*. These fish get to be seventy or eighty pounds. At night, they secrete cocoons of mucous around themselves and sleep in schools near channels.

Rebluud was the premier *kemedukl* fisherman in Palau. He was lean and strong from the rigors of night diving. His skin glistened coal black, and his eyes were big and white. When he smiled, his bright white teeth were shown admirably against the dark background of his face. Rebluud's diving buddy was a well muscled little man named Jon.

Rebluud's boat was a Palauan built twenty-five-foot wooden skiff powered by a two-cylinder Yamaha diesel. Just aft of amidships was a small wheelhouse and behind that a larger boxlike plywood cabin. A fish box sat forward of the wheelhouse. The boat was steered by a bamboo pole connected to the rudder linkage, the pole running forward along the starboard side to the wheelhouse. Known locally as a *pong pong*, the boat was in derelict condition, serving as home to thousands of cockroaches. Fully loaded, it could clip along at about six knots.

Three of us went out with them one afternoon. Bourne, afraid of an accident, had forbidden us to dive with them, so we took no diving gear along. We left the dock in front of the Palau Fishermen's Co-op at around 3:00 p.m. Neither Rebluud nor Jon spoke English so it was up to us to converse in Palauan. We went under the causeway and into some rock islands across from the boatyard. Rebluud carried a .22 rifle and as we chugged along the rock islands, he shot several pigeons, making sure they fell from the trees into the water. We traveled west through the placid waters of the baiting grounds, then south along the long arm of Urukthapel Island, past the secluded cove where, before the war, Kokichi Mikimoto had raised his *akoya* oysters, teasing them with calcified irritants and tricking them into producing silver and black pearls.

Around 5:00 p.m. we reached the fishing grounds, anchoring in a channel near the island of Omekong. As it got dark, Rebluud and Jon replaced the batteries in their flashlights. They used long Eveready six-cell flashlights housed in bicycle inner tubes which were vulcanized on one end. They sanded and cleaned the contacts, their lights obviously having flooded before. Sealing the lights was not easy. They had to tease the open end of the tube up along the bulb end, apply grease, and then seize it securely.

Rebluud and Jon used traditional Palauan goggles, the frames fashioned from carved wood with crudely fitted glass lenses. Their old-model Voit fins, the kind used by California body surfers in the 1950s, were held together here and there by stainless steel wire. Their spear guns were large, about seven feet in length, and they used barbless spears. Each man had tethered to his waist a line running to a six-inch diameter section of bamboo which floated on the surface. The procedure was to dive down and brain shoot a fish, bring it to the surface, thread the stringer line either through the eyes or through the mouth and gill plate, then fasten the line onto the bamboo floater, letting the fish hang beneath. The fish sleep at about thirty feet in depth, so it was a hard way to make a living.

After they had fixed up their lights and fiddled with their spear guns, they pulled out some food and beckoned us to eat. We had brought Spam, which we referred to as "Micronesian steak," and ship biscuits. They brought out fish, rice, taro, tapioca, and pigeon soup that they heated on a kerosene stove. In the bowels of the aft section of the *pong pong*, we sat around the central pile of food, and along with the cockroaches, ate what we wanted, island style. The tough pigeons tasted good, a welcome respite from fish.

At around 8:00 p.m. Rebluud and Jon entered the water. It was a dark night and from the boat we were unable to see much, but now and then we heard shouting and splashing as a fish thrashed on the surface. When they had three fish on their stringers, they would bring them to the boat where we hauled them aboard. About 10:00 they took a break, reloading their flashlights with new batteries. They made two other dives during the night and the forty—and fifty-pound fish kept coming aboard. As the night wore on, the boat rode lower and lower in the water.

Around daylight we pulled anchor and moved over to the island of Omekang which had a nice sandy beach. Here they scaled, gutted, and beheaded the fish, leaving the offal for the black-tip sharks which had accumulated in numbers just off the beach. We packed the fish in ice and left for home, the overloaded boat rolling unsteadily in the lagoon chop. Their catch weighed in at over one thousand pounds dressed weight. The co-op paid them four cents a pound for their fish.

Peter Wilson had a conservation officer named Melisebes. In his midforties, Melisebes looked the classic Palauan—prominent cheeks, dark, handsome, and muscular. His height was average, about five foot six inches, and he had a full head of black and gray hair. Melisebes had been raised and schooled under the Japanese and was consequently strict and solemn, rarely speaking to Peace Corps people. Peter entrusted Melisebes with a twenty-two-foot government boat built by Matsumoto. The boat had a small cabin, was powered by a six-cylinder Mercruiser inboard engine with a Mercruiser outdrive, and was outfitted with a marine band radio. This fast boat was the most sophisticated in Palau. And Melisebes was extremely proud of it.

Working under Melisebes was a handsome twenty-one-year-old Palauan named Harson. At six foot one, Harson was one of the tallest Palauans, lean and well-proportioned. He was not overly built, but he had long, flowing musculature, as is apparent in track-and-field athletes. In high school, he had excelled in sports and in scholastics as well. His good looks and athletic ability had given him a reputation. But Harson was shy and modest, and even though girls swooned over him, he did not embrace conceit. Harson was often around the training camp during the day, because the conservation boat was berthed beneath the dorm next to Peter's boat. Melisebes kept Harson busy working on the boat, polishing the engine, checking the oil, scrubbing the bottom. Sometimes Harson would dive with me when I speared fish off the seawall between language classes. We became good friends.

One of Marine Resources' projects, which Melisebes was charged with, was rearing hawksbill turtles, the object being to increase the survival rates of the hatchlings. Melisebes and Harson would locate turtle nests in the rock islands, determine when the eggs were laid, and mark the nests. From their records, they would return the day of the hatch, incubation time being about two months, and bring back the young turtles. They placed the fledgling turtles into floating cages at an old Japanese dry dock and quarry down the road from the boatyard. Van Camp donated old freezer-burned tuna for food, and Harson would fillet the fish and feed the turtles each day. The Trust Territory had no regulations governing the taking of turtles or eggs and people continually robbed nests, the eggs being considered a delicacy by Palauans. An area to the southwest of Koror known as Ngerukuid, or Seventy Islands, had been set aside by the government the previous year as a conservation area. Off limits to the public, the area served as a major turtle nesting ground. It was Melisebes's responsibility to keep the area under surveillance and make sure no one trespassed.

Wilson wanted one of us to work with Melisebes in the conservation program after training. Adequate data was needed to justify conservation measures, and Melisebes lacked the education and knowledge to collect and analyze data. Gene Helfman expressed interest in the conservation program and informed Bourne and Wilson as much. Melisebes seemed responsive to the idea, and sometimes Gene would go out with him to patrol the Seventy Islands or to check on turtle nests. During training, none of us suspected that Melisebes disliked Peace Corps, or for that matter, Americans in general. Harson, in his exemplary English, often complained about Melisebes and once warned Gene about him. But Gene was comfortable with the arrangement and felt compelled to nurture his relationship with Melisebes.

Sitting on the seawall next to the dorm was a big Japanese built mast and boom apparatus which was perhaps thirty-five feet high. It had a large arm coming off the top of the mast at a right angle which was braced obliquely to the lower part of the mast. The boom was used for lifting heavy objects off the dock and loading them onto a boat or vice versa. One day after lunch, Scott took a notion to climb it. He walked out to the seawall where I was fishing and looking up, exclaimed: "I'm going to climb that thing." Wrapping his bare legs around the rusty brace, he slowly scrunched his way up. Entertained, I jabbered with him as he inched toward the top.

"How're you going to get down, Scott?" I asked.

"I've got to get up first," was his reply.

I decided Scott would probably break his head if he fell on the seawall, so I swung the boom out over the water. He kept climbing and was soon sitting on the end of the boom. It was a curious sight, Scott in shorts and T-shirt, clinging to the top of the mast on that bright sunshiny day. As the other trainees finished their fish and rice, they came over and stood around gawking at Scott, the pole climber, sitting up there about thirty-five feet, nowhere to go. About that time, Melisebes and Harson cruised into the bay in the conservation boat. Melisebes looked up at Scott on the boom and shook his head as he jabbered to Harson in Palauan. Scott sat up there for half an hour or so, and everyone was hanging around to see what would happen. It was a long drop to the water, and Scott appeared to be thinking hard about the situation. Finally Scott rolled over and released, falling, then hitting the water in a semi belly-flop, amid claps and cheers from the audience. Harson came over and joked that Melisebes's comment about all this was, "Look at those stupid Peace Corps; just like the monkeys in Angaur," Angaur being the monkey infested southernmost island of Palau proper. Melisebes had given us an indication of his *true* sentiments toward us.

One day after lunch I stood out on the seawall throwing rocks at a mooring buoy out in the bay but was incapable of throwing far enough to hit it. Sabo came over.

"What are you throwing at?" he asked.

"Just the buoy. See if you can hit it," I said.

Little five-foot five-inch Sabo picked up a rock and threw a line drive, bouncing the rock off the buoy. I stared at him, amazed, and he laughed. He picked up another stone and did it again.

"Palauans love to throw stones," he chuckled as he walked off, leaving me in a semitrance.

I called for Harson to come over and challenged him to hit the buoy. He threw once, twice, and hit it the third time. Then he started winging rocks way out beyond the buoy, twice as far as I could throw. Scott, Norman, and several others came out and started throwing. Harson easily outthrew them all.

I learned that Palauans are excellent throwers. Any dog over six months old knew it as well, for any dog making eye contact with a Palauan would put tail between legs and scamper for cover. The reason baseball is the national sport of Palau is because it's a throwing sport. One night in the Community Club I listened patiently as a Palauan friend related to me how good his baseball team was. "We could beat the Oakland As," he said in all seriousness. Another time, late at night as Harson and I walked to his sister's place, a well thrown rock hit me square in the arm just below the shoulder, breaking the skin and causing an ugly bruise. Lucky for me, I detected the throwing movement in my peripheral vision and flinched, otherwise it might have got me in the neck. Palauans were notorious for stoning houses and for hiding in the boonies and stoning people they disliked. It was not one of their more endearing traits.

—

The days passed along. Sabo drilled and drilled, but the language remained aloof to me. Scott and a few others struggled as well, but I lingered far behind everyone.

SCUBA lessons, however, progressed nicely as the Hardys put us through the paces. The course was more intense and rougher than a normal course would be, they told us. And I believed them. Our exercises included "war," where we all went to the bottom and then proceeded to attack each other, turning off air valves, ripping off masks, anything to make the other person drown.

Some people couldn't handle it. The underwater training was cake for me; it was the language that was drowning me.

About three-quarters through the training program we were asked to partake in a Peace Corps training exercise known as "peer ratings." Each of us was given a questionnaire which asked: "Which person in the training program would you least wish to live and/or work with, and why?" And then, "Which person would you next least wish to live with and/or work with, and why?" It was the most degrading, perverse, chicken shit thing we did during the entire training program; all of us sitting around the dorm denigrating one another on paper. Had I not been such a sheep, I should have refused to participate. No one refused.

The second part of the peer evaluation business was the interview with Don Bourne, where he enlightened us on how our co-trainees felt about us. I suppose this was supposed to scare us or something.

"Someone called you a 'zilch,' Bryan," Don informed me at the interview.

"Yeah, who?" I said, getting defensive. I knew who it was.

"You know I can't say," said Bourne, "but I can't think of much worse to say about a person."

That left me speechless. He criticized my poor performance in language, reprimanded me for my tardiness to class, denounced my attitude, and condemned me for my nighttime activities, fishing and drinking beer instead of studying the language.

"How do you expect to learn the language if you don't study?" he asked.

I bit my lip and told him I'd do better on the language final. Palau had captured my heart. I just couldn't flunk out now.

After peer ratings, Bourne kept riding me about the language. "How's Palauan coming along? Studying?" he'd ask, a twisted grin on his face. Or "Don't forget, Bryan, finals coming up soon. Better study." I was jumpy and nervous. The "ax" was coming to Palau in a few weeks to pass final judgment. Heads would role. Quotas.

Bourne had one more project for us. Perhaps he figured we didn't have enough to do, or that the more we did, the better it made him look. But this was much better than the smokehouse fiasco. He wanted us to survey fisheries in different villages; find out how many boats were fishing, the kinds of fishing taking place, how the fish were disposed of, and anything else related to fisheries or marine activities. I looked forward to it. It would break up the monotony of language classes and provide a reprieve from Alphonso's cuisine. I figured the more I saw and experienced of Palau, the better—because the ax was coming.

Bourne teamed me up with Dick Doughty, probably because Doughty sometimes fished with me off the seawall. We would go to Ngchesar, a village about halfway up the east coast of Babeldaob. Norman and the Truk group would journey to Kayangel, an atoll at the far northern end of Palau. The married couples would visit a village on the west coast of Babeldaob; Scott, Gene, and Chet, would go to a village in northern Babeldaob; and the others to Peleliu, in southern Palau. We would all return after three days.

The big island of Babeldaob, twenty-seven miles long by eight miles wide, was divided into municipalities, much like stateside counties. Each municipality had a magistrate and one elementary school to serve the constituent villages. At the village level, chiefs presided. Most of the villages were situated along the coasts, and in contrast to Koror villages, were kept clean and manicured, part of "village pride." Some municipalities operated small generators to power single-side band radios which were linked to a central communications center in Koror. Other than by boat travel, this was the only means of communicating with the capital.

Doughty and I were taken up to Ngchesar in the *Milotk* by an old *rubak* (elderly respected man) who worked for Marine Resources as a boat captain. He wore a fine woven sombrero which pressed down on his ears sending them outward. It was early afternoon as we approached Ngchesar, the *rubak* standing on the seat with his sombrero and shoulders sticking through the roof hatch, navigating a deep water channel through the lagoon. Most of the southern and central Babeldaob coast was mangrove swamp and no beach graced Ngchesar. Several houses, some with tin roofs, others with thatch, could be seen on the sloping hillside among the bright green savanna and coconut and betel nut palms. A large *bai* (pronounced "bye") stood just up from the dock. The dock, made of stacked coral, protruded about fifty yards out into the sea grass beds and formed a breakwater which sheltered boats moored along the lee side.

A young Palauan, clad in cutoffs and looking like a black Steve Reeves, grabbed the bow line as we pulled in. He talked earnestly with the *rubak* as he helped us unload our gear. Moments later, he walked back down the dock and disappeared into the jungle. In Palauan, the *rubak* told us he would be right back—I thought.

"*Cho choi* (Yes)," I replied, faking it.

A half hour later, the young man marched out on the dock carrying a large stalk of betel nut which he threw on the deck of the boat. The *rubak* bid us farewell and we cast him off, watching him make his way slowly out the channel, his sombrero sticking through the roof. We gathered our things and walked down the dock.

"That was my father," the Palauan said in English. "He told me to look out for you. My name is Josed. Just call me Joe." We introduced ourselves and told him what we were interested in. Joe worked for the government and was building a small medical dispensary for the village. On weekends he travelled back to Koror to be with his family.

We followed Joe up the trail to the *bai*.

"This is the men's house," he said. "You can stay here with me."

The *bai* was old and traditional, built on short wood pilings a couple of feet off the ground. The open floor was made of local hardwood (ironwood) planks, very heavy and beautifully fitted. Huge timbers and crossbeams, notched and seized with cordage, provided the framework for the thatch roof which rose steeply from the sides. At one end of the *bai*, up high on the wall, was a large storyboard, a plank of hardwood on which a folk story had been carved. In the old days, the village *bais* served as clubhouses for the village chiefs, who lounged around all day in idle, betel nut chewing bliss and were favored over by a following of sexually active young girls.

Annexed to the *bai* was a small shack which served as the temporary medical dispensary. It was manned by a young girl whom Joe introduced simply as Nurse and who couldn't speak a word of English. She was real cute, I thought.

After we placed our belongings in the *bai*, Joe took us up to the chief's house to introduce us, get permission to camp in the *bai*, and let him know what we were up to. The village courtesy call. The chief spoke no English but seemed pleased by our presence, dispatching a youngster to fetch some green coconuts for us which we drank thirstily. He beckoned us to come in, and we sat down cross-legged and watched him do his business. Only a few of his teeth remained and with a small steel hammer he busily pounded his *buuch* (betel nut; pronounced boo), which was held in a small metal mortar. This was how older men softened up betel nut to make it palatable. When he was satisfied it was chewable, he sprinkled *chaus* (coral ash, lime; pronounced "ouse") on it from an old beer can, wrapped the nut in *kebui* (pepper leaf), and gingerly popped it in his mouth. From a small purse-like *tet* of finely woven pandanus, he pulled out a tobacco twist, cut off a small hunk, and placed that in the hollow of his cheek. His mouth was a repugnant dark red, and his remaining teeth were black. Every now and then he leaned over the door entrance and spat red saliva on the ground. Joe, busy chewing and spitting his own fix, yakked away in Palauan with the chief. I was curious about this widespread betel nut addiction which all Palauans seemed to have.

    We left the chief and as we walked back toward the *bai*, I asked Joe if we might try a chew. I'd seen some of the volunteers chew it now and then, but I figured it was mostly showoff. Joe stopped at a house which had several betel nut trees behind it. He made small talk with the *rubak* of the house and borrowed a small towel. Tying the towel between his feet as one would hobble a horse, he quickly climbed a tree and cut some betel nut. A large *kebui* vine grew on a coconut tree nearby, and Joe picked some leaves and stems, stuffing them into his *tet*. Back at the *bai*, Joe showed us how to prepare the chew. He bit a large nut in half, dug out a portion of the very bitter soft inner seed with his thumbnail and discarded it, sprinkled the half nut with *chaus*, then wrapped the whole thing in *kebui* leaf. He warned us that the lime would burn the inside of our mouths if we overdid it. I prepared my fix, gingerly placed it inside my mouth, and chewed. It tasted peppery, slightly caustic. Soon saliva flowed, and I began spitting out thick red waste. Feeling weak, I grinned foolishly at Doughty. My head began to throb as if a balloon had inflated inside my skull. Intense heat spread throughout my body, and my face broke into a sweat. My hands and legs shook. I leaned back against the doorway, dizzy and reeling, unable to move, feeling close to fainting. Then it was over, the complex sensation dissipating. In short order, I could resume a normal conversation and walk without falling down. But I had scalded the inside of my mouth, ruining my taste buds for several days. Next time I would lighten up on the *chaus*.

Early the next morning, Doughty and I walked down to the dock, counted boats, and made sketches of a few. Then we went back to the *bai* and asked the nurse if she would join us for a breakfast of Spam and ship biscuits. She boiled up some water for coffee, put down some cold rice and soyu, and we sat on the floor eating with Palauan utensils—our fingers. She spoke no English, and I struggled with my limited Palauan to ask her how far away Melekeok village was.

After eating, we hiked the several miles north along a coastal trail to Melekeok, a pretty village with a central sand walkway, houses bordered with decorative plants, and a small beach lined with coconut palms. Clumps of sea grasses grew in the shallows off the beach and at one end a small dock ran out into the channel. For several hours we speared fish off the end of the dock, bringing back a stringer of fish which Nurse took and cleaned, happily, it seemed to me, and that night Joe cooked up that basic gruel loved by all Palauans, fish soup.

Joe tossed in everything, including the heads.

"The heads are *kote ungil* (the best)," he commented. "*Rubaks* love the heads."

Then, to my dismay, he threw in some sliced onions. After adding a touch of salt, he boiled the soup on the small kerosene stove in the medical dispensary, the odor giving me déjà vu of the lingcod head I once had to boil to collect the bones for my college ichthyology class. Nurse brought out three plastic Japanese rice bowls and Joe filled each one.

"She will eat later," he said. In Palau, women eat last, leftovers.

I picked and sucked at the bits of fish in my bowl, afraid I might choke to death on a bone if I drank the soup. Doughty plunged in with both hands. Joe slurped and sucked, then spit and blew roughage into the palm of his hand; dorsal spines, neural spines, proximals, radials, distals, postemporals, supracleithrums, basioccipitals, lachrymals, preopercles, opercles, scutes, and scales. He searched for the heads, then sucked the eyes from their orbits.

"Delicious," he exclaimed, between slurps, obviously pleased with himself. I cracked a smile.

That night, Doughty and I played a Japanese card game called *hana fuda* with Joe and Nurse. The dealer deals out the small, thick, rectangular cards, and the first person to slam a similar card down on the discard wins the cards. It was most important to slam the card down hard with a *Whap*, else you got dirty looks. After the game Joe went to a neighbor's house to sleep, and Doughty and I retired to our pandanus mats on the hardwood floor. As is customary, a kerosene lamp was left burning dimly and hanging near the doorway to the dispensary. Palauans possessed a guarded distrust of the dark. A few minutes later Nurse came over, spread out her mat in the space between us, and laid down. This was strange, I thought, but figured I'd better capitalize on the situation before Doughty did. I knew he was thinking the same thing. But what to do. Roll over on her? No, too noisy. Whisper "I love you?" She wouldn't understand. Reach out and grab her? Maybe. I reached over with my left hand toward what I thought was her stomach or somewhere in the proximity. Son of a bitch; Doughty's hand was already there and it wasn't on her stomach. Nurse, apparently unhappy with the situation, jumped up, grabbed her pandanus mat, and shuffled into the dispensary. "Tough luck," I said to Doughty and went to sleep.

The next morning, excitement gripped Ngchesar. A tropical storm was approaching Palau, Joe told us. Outside, the wind was already blowing out of the east at about forty knots, pushing in one rain squall after another. Typhoons often hit Palau without warning because of poor communications. Additionally, the National Weather Service seemed inept at both forecasting and tracking storms in the western Pacific. Forecasts often were made after the fact. "Palau is expected to be hit by tropical storm Whamo," would be the initial public bulletin, when, in fact, Palau had already been smacked by tropical storm Whamo.

But not this time. Having originated in the Marshalls, the storm had moved slowly west and Palau had been warned via radio that it would pass over us that night. Meanwhile, according to the radio, the storm's intensity had increased and we were now in "Condition 2," a condition I was unfamiliar with but which I later learned is somewhere between Condition 1 and Condition 3.

Between rain squalls, we helped Joe board up the window openings in the *bai* and rigged a door for the entrance. The *bai* was the biggest and strongest structure in the village, and Joe said many of the villagers would stay there that night. After securing the *bai*, we helped haul up two boats onto the beach; the other boats would be taken down the coast to take shelter deep in the mangroves, Joe said. Later on, we sat around playing *hana fuda* with Nurse, chewed betel nut, and waited for the onslaught.

Meanwhile, on Kayangel Atoll forty-five miles to the north, a white haired village wizard walked the shores of Kayangel Island. He carried a canoe paddle and chanted the secret verses which would curtail the menacing wind. No man was allowed on the beach as the wizard circled the island, for if he saw any man the typhoon would surely come. As the wizard acted out, Norman and the other trainees, having secured the Public Works thirty-six-foot boat off the beach, busily boarded up the village *bai*.

Kayangel's egg-shaped barrier reef enclosed a shallow lagoon three and a half miles long and one and a half miles wide. Four typical "low" islands composed of sand and coral rubble and topped by hardy, salt-resistant strand vegetation, sat along the windward barrier reef. Atoll islands have two horizontal dimensions: a lagoon side and an ocean side. The third dimension of an atoll is the coconut tree. Standing at sea level, a sharp-eyed sailor of average height can just spot the tops of coconut trees on an atoll from twelve miles distant. I once asked Neal Morris, the chief of Agriculture in Palau, what it was like living on an atoll, Neal having lived on Majuro in the Marshall Islands before coming to Palau. Without saying a word, he raised his arm straight out and away, palm down, and moved it slowly from left to right, right to left.

One Peace Corps volunteer lived in Kayangel. His name was Richard Howle, and he taught school. Rich was a giant by anyone's standards; six foot seven and an ex-champion collegiate shot-putter. He always stood straight up, shoulders back, and he chewed his fingernails constantly as he talked, in a monotone, his head oriented toward the distant horizon, only his eyes peering down at you. Rich owned a fine collection of shells which, unfortunately, he later sold for beer money.

Known as "bigfoot" by most volunteers because of his size sixteen feet, he was the only PCV in Palau who wore Keds sneakers in lieu of zorries, the Japanese zorrie manufacturers being unsympathetic to Rich's size. Rich had lived in Kayangel for a year, getting to Koror only once every four months or so. Living on an atoll can be lonely at times, and Rich was overjoyed with the company from Koror. He was also happy because he could hitch a ride back to Koror for some much needed R&R. People on Kayangel ate turtle, lots of it. Turtle steak, turtle soup, turtle sashimi, turtle every kind. Rich told the visitors he was sick of turtle. He couldn't wait to get to Koror so he could eat some Spam.

Kayangel was dry by local custom, but Rich wasn't. He knew that fermentation, if controlled, could create the stuff that made those atoll sunsets worth living for. So Rich made "tuba," the jungle juice of atolls. Cut the flower off the coconut tree, catch the drip, let it ferment, and drink it. He and Norman got so drunk on tuba one night down on the beach that they opted to sleep in the bushes rather than risk getting caught staggering back to the *bai*.

Despite the wizard's efforts, the storm hit Kayangel almost dead on that night. Most of the villagers avoided danger by waiting out the storm in the *bai* or in the school, which was built of cement blocks. The Public Works thirty-six footer, anchored as securely as possible, dragged anchor toward one end of the lagoon, then down toward the other end as the storm passed, magically missing all coral heads. The next day Norman and the others helped clean up the village, and the following morning they came back to Koror on the Public Works boat in the absolute calm left by the passed storm. Rich rode along, hoping to find some gourmet food in Koror.

After the storm, it took four more days for all of us to get back to Koror from the villages. Then we had to work up our reports. Bourne had brought down an old Underwood typewriter from the Peace Corps office which we took turns using between classes and at night. Each group gave an oral presentation and turned in written manuscripts to Bourne. Bourne was impressed with ours (so said his wife), which I had written, and he threw a party at his house for all of us in celebration of our efforts. Training was winding down, and language finals were coming up. Things were coming to a head.

With less than two weeks to go before the "ax" arrived to perform his deselection mission, Scott and I went out again with Rebluud, this time taking along our diving gear. Jack and Sheila planned to give us the first half of the final diving tests the following day. I would be tired after being up all night, but I didn't care. I knew I could handle it.

It rained most of the night and we kept moving around, searching for the elusive *kemedukl*. When we finally found the fish, I entered the water and watched Rebluud dive down out of sight, then come up with a big fish. I dove down to see what *kemedukl* looked like as they slept in their mucous cocoons. I never saw a fish.

The next day about noon we arrived at the co-op dock and unloaded about five hundred pounds of *kemedukl*. Norman and Jack showed up and Norman, having just taken the diving test, took me aside and warned me how tough it was. Jack took Scott and I in the skiff to an area with a sand bottom and constant depth over near the old Icebox on the west side of Malakal. We were to jump into the water without fins or mask, then dive down about fifteen feet to a tank and regulator held to the bottom by a couple of weight belts. The object was to get our weights belts on and "buddy breath," sharing the single tank of air as we walked along the bottom to a destination somewhere in the distance—a difficult task without a mask and requiring a cool head.

Buoyancy makes it laborious. The technique is to get situated sitting side by side with the weight belts across your laps, get the tank turned on, and start sharing air; take two breaths, pass the regulator to your buddy, and so forth, back and forth. Next, you have to strap the weight belts around your waists and then both stand up in unison. The best way to mobilize is for each person to wrap an arm around the tank, and, while one person controls passing the regulator back and forth, the other person clings to his buddie's waist. This keeps you together. Then, as you buddy breath and your eyes are burning like hell, you can both do a lateral jumping waltz across the bottom toward the destination. At fifteen feet, half an atmosphere of pressure is continuously forcing water up your nostrils and an ominous fear prevails, that at any second water will bust through your air locked nose and rush down into your lungs with all the force of Niagara Falls after a good rain.

Scott was doing fine until we stood up and started moving. Then he panicked and clawed to the surface to suck air. Jack, observing us as he floated along with the skiff, twice sent Scott back down, but Scott gave up. I continued moving on, the exercise suddenly easy without having to share the air, right past the finish line by about fifty feet. Jack finally brought the boat over to stop me, and feeling exuberant, I donned the lung on my back and swam around, showing off. When I got in the skiff, Scott, tired from the fishing trip and exhausted from this exercise, looked like a whipped dog. Jack asked Scott if he wanted to try it again but Scott declined. Scott was partially blind anyway, and in salt water without a mask, he was totally blind. Jack flunked him.

The second part of the test was the final dive, a simple dive down to ninety feet under Jack and Sheila's watchful eyes. The uneventful dive concluded our diving training. I was happy. I knew I would be diving a lot in the future, providing, that is, I avoided the "ax."

CHAPTER 5

The "Ax"

Suddenly it jelled. I could speak conversational Palauan. Since the trip to Ngchesar, my mind had assimilated the language. Phrases previously sounding like garbled police calls now had meaning. I understood Palauan, and I spoke it relatively clearly and accurately. Sabo was amazed. I was amazed. The week in Ngchesar, the absence of the language drilling and the constant worry had allowed my mind to put it together as a language, something I had been unable to do under the duress of training.

One night about this time, Terry Clancy came by the dorm to give us a pep talk and advise us on what to expect when the "ax" arrived from Washington. Ironically, the "ax's" name was Exener, and he was the Peace Corps equivalent of an executioner. Exener would decide, based on our dossiers and the recommendations of Bourne and the rest of the training staff, who stayed and who disappeared. He would fly in, chop, and fly out. Terry's talk filled me with apprehension. After having invested all this time in training, having gone through all the Peace Corps crap, the language frustrations, the peer ratings, the intimidation by Bourne, the anxieties—it would be unbearable to be sent home now.

After the "ax" business, Terry related some stories about his tenure with the California wineries. At one point he had been a high-ranking executive with Italian Swiss Colony, the colossal winery whose products loomed ever-present in stores throughout the world. Most of us were well acquainted with a brand called Red Mountain, a jug wine of questionable quality but with a good price. According to Clancy, Red Mountain was produced by Italian to tap college dollars. College kids demanded a meaningful price/quantity ratio. The wine, said Terry, "is the same Italian Swiss Colony red as that bottled under Italian's more exclusive labels and sold at a much higher price. It all comes out of the same vat." Having drunk my share of Red Mountain, I found this interesting, although it held little value in wine less Palau.

After Terry's talk, I got into a conversation with Norman and John Rupp about Scott's failure to get through the difficult diving test. Dan Leary idled over and listened in as we speculated on whether Scott would get axed or not.

"It would be criminal to ax a guy like Scott," Norman said.

"Yeah. Scott's the kind Peace Corps needs out here," said Rupp.

"There has to be total commitment to make it as a Peace Corps volunteer," Leary said. "Scott isn't performing in language, and I don't think he's serious enough about the job."

Norman rolled back his eyes. "Are you fully committed Leary?" he asked.

"I know what it takes. I'm an ex-marine lieutenant." Leary smiled as he talked, his long curved mouth contorting this way and that.

Norman and John walked off, leaving me alone with Leary. Uncomfortable, I said, "Well, see you later."

"Yeah, if you're still here," said Leary grinning. I walked away, full of rage. Had I been a violent person, Leary would have been DOA at MacDonald Hospital. But I wondered: Did Leary know something I didn't? He constantly gabbed with Bourne. At times it seemed he acted as Bourne's advisor. Maybe Bourne had said something to him. But was Bourne that unprofessional? Perhaps. Anyway, I would know my fate soon enough. Final language exams in two days, then Exener would arrive that afternoon, review our files, hold meetings with the training staff. By the following morning, it would be no secret who stayed and who took a hike. I speculated on my future verses that of Leary's and prayed I might somehow have the last laugh.

Two days later, we took our written and oral language finals. I felt good about my written test and even better taking the oral.

Red was flabbergasted at my competency. He told me I spoke and understood Palauan as well, perhaps better, than anyone in training. Feeling like a new man, I wondered how Leary was holding up.

With little to do but wait, Norman, Scott, and I speared some bait, bought some beer at the co-op, and settled down for an afternoon of fishing and drinking on the seawall. Exener had arrived from Truk where he had already wielded his ax on the other Group VI trainees in Moen. Now he sat in the Peace Corps office reviewing our files and conferring with staff to determine our fates. No reason to languish. Training was over. What had been done *was done*. Better to relax and enjoy the afternoon, hook some fish, drink beer, loosen up.

Then something happened. Late in the afternoon, a PCV came driving up in the Peace Corps truck and asked for Norman. Norman walked over and spoke with him, went up into the dorm and a few minutes later, without saying a word, drove off with the PCV. Shocked, I said to Scott: "Oh boy, there goes Norman. First victim of the 'ax.'" My best friend was gone.

That evening, our last night as trainees, most of us went into town to eat. For some of us, this would be our last supper. When we returned to the dorm later that night, Chet informed us that Norman had silently packed up and left with someone. No more *the Vas*. I felt remorse.

The next morning I cleaned up around my sleeping area, while we nervously waited for Bourne and Exener to arrive. Scott, trying to break the tension, cracked jokes, but no one laughed. Down below, the married couples talked quietly, laughing nervously now and then. Then we heard the Peace Corps truck banging its way down the road, in and out of the potholes; saw it turn in by the boatyard, a bleached-out, rusted blue wreck of General Motors sheet metal. How unfitting for an executioner to ride in such a thing. A shiny black Lincoln, roaring up in a cloud of dust, would have been more appropriate. But I was disappointed. Exener was hardly the evil looking "ax" my mind had fabricated. He was tall and mustached, and looked fortyish. Wearing long khaki pants and a silky flowered aloha shirt, he appeared relaxed and informal, yet had an air of business about him. One hand held a briefcase, probably containing important papers such as marching orders. We peered down at him through the screen, pondering our fate.

Bourne climbed the stairs and walked into the dorm. With a slight smile on his face, he called out several names and said, "Follow me." Scott, Chet, and two others followed him downstairs where Leary joined them. Bourne quickly shuffled them into the storeroom. Were they being sworn in downstairs? We heard Exener talking, but his words were too soft to understand. Minutes passed. We stared at each other and puttered around, frightened.

Abruptly, the "ax" came upstairs. Politely he knocked, then entered and introduced himself. He asked if any of us had second thoughts about becoming a volunteer or if anyone, for any reason, wanted to go home. "There is no shame in this. Step forward if you do." No one budged. "Then raise your right hands and repeat after me."

You bet! We took the oath. He gave us his congratulations, shook our hands, and that was that. Trainees no more, PCVs at last. Seniors. Big boys, and girls. Big money too. Our new status included a lofty pay raise, from twenty dollars a month as trainees to ninety a month as volunteers. Ninety dollars could buy a lot of Spam in Palau.

This was the end of frustrating language classes; of Jay Klinck's mechanical workshops; of Don Bourne's seamanship seminars; of underwater survival exercises; of lectures; of peer ratings; of fear and loathing; of the ptomaine cafeteria—now Alphonso could take his fish and rice and stuff it. I felt good about Peace Corps, about Leary getting axed; but the fate of Norman and Scott, two of my best friends, bothered me. Neither had deserved deselection.

Later that day I happened to pass by Leary. I gave him a nice big smile and winked. Had he been packing his M-14, I feel certain he would have cut me down.

To my delight, Norman showed up the next day. He hadn't been axed after all. Word had come in that his father had passed away, and Peace Corps had quickly whizzed him out of Palau to return home. However, in Guam he learned he was on standby to Hawaii, and from Hawaii on standby to California. Realizing he would probably miss the funeral anyway, he hopped on a special flight returning to Palau the next day.

When John Rupp and I asked Bourne about the logic behind Scott's deselection, Bourne responded: "The decision is strictly confidential in every form of the word. Once the deselect decision has been made, that's it. There's never a reversal; that's just the way it is. Peace Corps policy."

But Bourne commended Scott, saying he believed Scott would have made a good volunteer. We'd never see Scott again once he left Palau. He and the other axed trainees would go where they all go after deselection, wherever that is. No one knows where that is, however.[4]

Out of our original sixteen, two had attritioned, five had been axed, and nine of us had endured. Norman Vas, John Rupp, John Ives, and Bud Fuchs would go to Truk; Dick Doughty to Ponape; Jean Helfman, Dave Hodges, Dave Imes, and myself would remain in Palau.

I managed to get my licks in one last time before Leary left for good. The following evening, after deselection, Norman and I went to the well for a shower and found Leary soaping down in one of the bathing stalls. The well was about twelve feet deep and was encased in cement, part of the top portion covered with a cement slab overgrown with foliage from the adjacent jungle. The opening was about four feet square and had a cement lip around it. The spring fed well, always full of pristine, clear water, looked inviting. Wanting to perform the ultimate rude act to exacerbate Leary, I stripped and jumped into the well. Norman howled and jumped in after me. Leary came out of the stall and saw us cooling off in the well, our elbows hanging over the edge as if we were relaxing in a swimming pool.

You "fucking bastards," he said, grabbing his towel and walking down the path.

"What's wrong, Leary?" I yelled after him. "We'll be out in a few minutes and then you can have it."

Leary turned and flashed the erect middle finger, causing us to convulse. He was on his way back to the land of hot showers and Bob's Bigboy Hamburgers, lucky stiff.

Peace Corps threw a "get acquainted" party for us and the other Palau PCVs out in the rock islands. Leary and the axed

---

[4] What happens to those who are deselected or "axed" from Peace Corps? Your guess is as good as mine. I am unaware of the subsequent histories of any deselected individuals, and I have never met a person who has previously been deselected. Never.

trainees had already "disappeared" except for Scott, who wanted to stay for the party and make a last dive. Peace Corps policy was to get those deselected out of country with haste, but Bourne had agreed to let Scott stay for the party. That Sunday, a flotilla of boats converged on an island called Ngaiangas.

Ngaiangas is centrally located within the rock islands. It lays long axis oriented north and south and has nice long white sandy beaches on both eastern and western sides. Known also as Neco's island, it was leased by a prominent local businessman who had built two small huts on the western beach. Most of the rock islands were owned collectively by the people of Palau, but the government leased a few, like Ngaiangas, to private individuals.

The rock islands flourished with wildlife. Tropic birds, shearwater petrels, terns, and native pigeons nested there. Introduced species of parrots and cockatoos lived high up the rocky slopes among the palms and shrubs, causing major damage to the native palms. Cryptic native mega pods, about the size of a small chicken, built huge nests, as large as six feet in height, along the beach strand by piling up twigs and other organic material. The nests made easy targets for egg-robbing Palauans.

Sea turtles, mostly hawksbills, nested on many of the beaches. Coconut crabs, a fine delicacy, could be collected at night after setting a trail of staked down half-coconuts. Small baseball-sized land crabs, also good to eat, lived in burrows along the strand. Some beaches contained a thumbnail size white clam which made excellent soup. A larger clam, handball size, lived in the mangroves along with a delicious oyster. Large mangrove crabs, with huge powerful claws capable of snapping fingers like toothpicks, lived in holes in the mangrove mud. The Palauans would reach blindly down into their holes, about arm size in diameter, and pull the crabs out. Crocodiles, believed to have emigrated from Indonesia, lived throughout the rock islands, sometimes running off the beach into the water as people approached. Some islands had monitor lizards which reached six feet in length, but these were not eaten. One rock island west of Koror contained a population of goats.

Fruit bats, with wingspans up to five feet, nested communally in the trees. Like their little brothers, they hang upside down, flying off in the evenings to feed on the fruit of various trees. Palauans rarely hunted them, although some Palauans ate them.[5]

Gentle dugongs, algae, and sea grass feeders whose vertebrae were valued by older Palauans as ceremonial bracelets, were fast disappearing and rarely seen. The advent of fast outboard boats had rendered the slow sea cows vulnerable to hunting.

But the paradisiacal rock islands held a few irritants. One plant gave you skin lesions if touched, or even if water dripped from the plant onto your skin. And certain beaches had tiny chiggerlike insects known as "no see ums" which burrowed into your skin causing welts and itching terribly for several days. The antidote, after a day of frolicking on the beach, was to mix a quart of vinegar in with your bath, if you had one; then soak.

As I stood on the beach of Ngaiangas, Peter Wilson, his wife Ann, and their three boys arrived in Peter's speedboat—the beautiful people in paradise. Big, strong, Peter; Size D Ann, tall, tanned, and very pretty; the three kids, blond toe heads, the oldest about eight, the youngest a toddler. What a way to live, I thought. Nice wife, nice kids, nice boat, living and working in Palau, a very nice place.

---

[5] In the Marianas, particularly in Guam, overhunting has so decimated fruit bats that they are on the Federal Endangered Species List. So desired are they for cuisine by the Chamorros (people of Marianas descent) that a black market exists. While working in Saipan in the mid-1980s, I once accompanied a scientific expedition composed of Northern Marianas government personnel from the Division of Fish and Wildlife to the northern island of Sarigan. When we went ashore, the chief of the agency, Rufo Lujan, a Guamanian by birth, immediately dispatched one of his conservation officers to shoot several fruit bats so that he might eat bat soup, a delicacy no longer available in his own island of Guam. The Chamorros make bat soup by throwing the complete, uncleaned animal into the pot. Fur, guts, bones, teeth, flesh—every trace is devoured. I asked Lujan if the bats tasted special, since they may have been the last two specimens in the Marianas. He grumbled defensively that as a Chamorro, he had a right to eat fruit bat because it was custom, a perquisite of the native people of the Marianas. I went on to prompt him to be sure and describe the experience to his children since they probably would never be able to partake of the ritual. When we returned to Saipan, Lujan fired me.

Later, Peter took us out on the *Milotk* for a dive. A deep channel ran through the islands to the southwest, and we followed its meandering course skirting patch reefs along the way. It was a good idea to wear polarized sunglasses when navigating within the lagoon. You could easily sink a boat in Palau from grounding on any of the innumerable coral heads and patch reefs. The same benthic formations which made Palau an underwater wonderland were also dangerous navigational hazards to unknowing skippers.

The current flowed with us, boosting our speed. The edges of the channel dropped vertically from the flats bordering the islands. A dark gray school of sardines broke the continuum of green water along one of the white beaches. Occasionally a fish jumped, in pursuit of another. Small mushroom-like islands sat as if glued to the water. The limestone surface beneath the foliage of the rock islands is so pocked and laden with sharp vestibules that climbing on them is hazardous and difficult. A pair of zorries might last two steps. Many of these rock islands had probably never been trespassed by man. We passed a limestone bridge, a giant arch, entrance to a lake of sorts within a volcano-like limestone formation. Just behind it we anchored off a patch reef bordering the channel. Scott and I teamed up for the dive.

In 1967, diving was relatively hassle-free. In Palau, the water was eighty-four to eighty-five degrees so a wet suit was unnecessary. You wore a short vest equipped with an emergency CO_2 cartridge and a manual blow-up valve; double-hosed U.S. Divers regulator; and U.S. Divers standard pack and steel tank with J-valve. Depending on how much adipose tissue you packed, you may have worn a weight belt. You donned the vest, threw on the tank, grabbed a fin, two if both were convenient, spit in your mask, and jumped in.[6]

---

[6]   · Today diving is a chore. Getting suited up in modern SCUBA gear requires patience and dexterity. The typical diver has so much extraneous stuff hanging off him he's bound to have trouble. Whatever happened to the old "ditch it" technique? Won't work nowadays. You're so tied up, bundled up, and strapped up in your gear you'd never get out. With this modern high-tech gear, it may be safer diving in a swimming pool but not under field conditions. Consider the new single hose regulators called an "octopus." Long hoses shoot out from the first stage behind the neck; two of them lead

The most dangerous elements of diving in the tropics are not toothy critters, but currents. Depending on moon phase, Palau can have five, six, sometimes seven-foot diurnal tides, which means water is either flowing into, or out of, the lagoon, with only twenty to thirty minutes slack time between tides. In the channels, water movement is river-like, reversing direction every six hours.

The *Milotk* tailed off into the channel, and as we descended the current drove us out away from the patch reef. At sixty feet, Scott and I reached the bottom and struggled hard to reach the base of the reef. The others had already worked their way around to the lee side of the patch reef. Within a minute I had lost Scott. I swam over to the others, but saw he was not among them. Circumventing the coral head, I swam back to Norman, signaled I had lost Scott, and gave him the thumbs-up sign. The whole group followed me up along the anchor rope and busting surface, I yelled to Teruo, the boat captain, that Scott was missing. As we hauled aboard one by one, Teruo heard a faint yelling in the distance and spotted Scott bobbing along in the channel about a quarter mile down current. We pulled anchor and picked him up, Peter in a state of discomposure and our diving finished for the day. We spared Scott our effrontery; he would be gone the next day.

---

into second-stage mouthpieces. The others terminate in pressure gauges, depth gauges, nitrogen gauges, and alarm clocks. As if alive, all those gauges and hoses seek out places to hang up in coral or rocks. And consider also the huge vest-backpack combinations with all the valves, bells, and whistles. Better read the directions. Pull the wrong cord or push the wrong button and you may go down instead of up. Or worse, go up, too fast.

Perhaps the worst anomaly in the diving industry was the introduction of aluminum tanks in the early 1970s. Larger than steel tanks, they hold more air; and they weigh considerably less, which only forces the diver to wear extra weight. In SCUBA diving, wearing extra weight is a necessary evil, dangerous; a practice to avoid if possible.

Having followed the development of diving equipment over the years, I feel that much of the new gear is junk. The diving companies, like automobile manufacturers, have, at the expense of quality, littered their stuff with chrome, push buttons, and microprocessors; all of which have an aversion to salt water.

—

The fisheries group disbanded. The Truk group departed for Truk where they would work under Ron Powell, a fisheries expert from the Cook Islands who had been newly hired by Peter Wilson. Dick Doughty flew off to Ponape, a lone PCV without direction and with no understanding of the language or customs, to get something going. Mike Constein had already left for Yap. Those of us staying in Palau needed to make living arrangements, find families, get settled in. Gene Helfman would help Melisebes with the marine conservation program and had already moved in with Melisebes and family. Dave and Jan Imes would live in Chol on the northeast coast of Babeldaob where she would teach school, and Dave would spark up fisheries projects, perhaps. Dave Hodges, having little aptitude for the marine environment, would act as fisheries correspondent between the different islands, writing newsletters, exchanging ideas and information, that sort of thing. And I would be working with the Palau Fishermen's Co-op.

Meanwhile, the Group VI Palau bunch, mostly teachers, who had survived training in Truk, arrived to begin their terms as Palau volunteers. The new volunteers needed places to stay, inoculations, money. Peace Corps was already planning its next phase, Group VII, training to be held in Peleliu summer next. Peace Corps was flooding Micronesia with PCVs. The more, the betta, ya know? Peace Corps knew.

Peter took me over to get acquainted with Kailang, the manager of the Palau Fishermen's Co-op. As we walked along the dock, Peter mentioned that Kailang might be going to Japan for training in the business end of fisheries. "Oh," I said, not thinking much about it.

Kailang was about thirty-seven, half-Japanese, and like many Palauans born before the war, spoke fluent Japanese. Bourne had talked about Kailang, saying he drank heavily and could turn wild under the influence. His slight body did little to suggest meanness, however. Now, as we talked, he seemed pleasant and nice, and was enthusiastic about me helping out. Walking with Peter back to Peter's office, Peter mentioned that Kailang was doing an excellent job but needed some help with the books.

"Me, help with the books?" I gulped. I knew as little about bookkeeping as Dave Hodges knew about fish.

"You can learn," Peter piped, "and you'll never regret you did."

Later, Paul Callaghan, PCV bookkeeper for the boatyard, told me he would help me if I needed it. Paul was an economics major and knew about keeping books, and he'd been in Palau for a year.

Gene Helfman, Dave Hodges, and I set up a makeshift office in the room next to the co-op. It was a partially open storeroom with heavy rusty cyclone wire for sides and a tin roof overhead which sent afternoon temperatures into the high 90s. A long wooden table occupied the center of the room, and we scrounged some rusty folding chairs from Peter's office. Dave would sit in there all day long writing newsletters to send to the other guys in Yap, Truk, and Ponape. Gene contentedly worked with Melisebes, and I struggled with the co-op books. Kailang wanted me to live with his family and relatives in Yebukl, a village in northern Koror. Hodges and I still stayed in the dorm, but the boatyard was pressuring Peace Corps to get us out. Hodges was in a dilemma, no place to go.

One evening I went with Kailang up to Yebukl just below Mindszenty High School and met his family. The head of the household was an elderly *mechas* (older respected woman; pronounced ma-ahs) named Asuma, whose husband, Techur, resided in the village of Ngkeklau in northern Babeldaob. Asuma and Techur were in their early seventies. Mechas (I called Asuma, Mechas) was raising her granddaughter, Melanna, a lovely young girl about nine who was the daughter of the Kintaro's living a few houses away up near the road; and a teenage grandson named Vini. This familial adoption system, "the extended family," allowed larger families to better support themselves by giving certain of their offspring to grandparents, aunts, or uncles, who still wished to raise children. In return, the children provided the older adopters with needed help. The system was well suited to the Palauan way of life.

Mechas's house, built on pilings about two feet off the ground, consisted of a main room about fifteen by fifteen feet. The floor and walls were plywood and the roof corrugated tin. In the back wall, a small recess held several pots and pans and a one-burner

Japanese kerosene stove. A smaller room with a cardboard ceiling and a fuse box stuffed with pennies was annexed at one end. A separate tin roofed, plywood shack about fifteen by eight feet sat at right angles to Mechas's house and served as Vini's room. Vini's cousin, Obi, often slept there as well. In the back of Vini's room was a small partitioned cube where I would sleep. A closet space with a small shelf was attached where I could store what few possessions I had. A bare lightbulb hung in each room, turned on or off by screwing the bulb into or out of the socket. Termite droppings had to be swept out of the rooms each day, and mosquitoes ran rampant at night. In the ensuing months, I often burned mosquito coils in my room to ward off those little bastards while I slept. I sometimes wonder how many years my life was shortened from breathing those noxious fumes night after night.

In front of the two houses was an old cement slab which had been the foundation for a sake brewery during Japanese times. Several betel nut trees, each wrapped with *kebui* vines, grew through holes in the cement. Off to the side, a large mango tree shaded Mechas's house during the heat of the morning. The *benjo* was located in the rear, downwind of the residence but not distant enough to be unnoticeable. Two fifty-five gallon drums caught water off the roof of Mechas's house. When these were dry, water had to be fetched from a communal spring down the trail. Showers were taken next to a drum by the dip-and-pour method.

The next house down the path was Kailang's, who lived with his wife and two kids. Kailang's niece Terresa, who taught grade school at Maris Stella across the main road from Yebukl, stayed there as well. Terresa was tall, had long, straight, thick black hair, and nice white teeth, one of the front ones being slightly crooked. There were one or two brothers of Kailang from Ngkeklau who stayed either at Mechas's or at Kailang's from time to time. I was forever confused by the familial relationships of all these people, and I eventually gave up trying to figure it out. I was part of the Asuma-Techur clan and that was really all I needed to know.

The household spoke Palauan. Mechas spoke no English. Vini, who was bashful, spoke a tiny bit of English but preferred to converse in Palauan. Melanna was too young, but knew a few fundamental English words. And I spoke only rudimentary

Palauan. I would soon learn the language, however. It was a Palauan household, and I was a minority.

The first night I moved in, I sat around chewing betel nut with Mechas and Melanna. Mechas had been pretty in her youth. Old and wrinkled now, she kept her waist long hair up in a bun. The sides of her legs were tattooed in blue from the ankles up, and one of her earlobes had a dime size hole in it from wearing heavy earrings through her ears. She retained strength enough to work in the taro fields, dig clams, gather food, and she could still carry a ten-pound basket of taro on her head. Unlike most people her age, she enjoyed excellent teeth and could chew betel nut without first pounding it.

Mechas sat now cross-legged in the corner, combing and braiding Melanna's long black hair. Melanna already possessed the red gum lines of a betel nut chewer. She was light skinned and had a slight hint of oriental in her pretty face. Small gold rings hung from her pierced ears. Melanna talked and laughed constantly, always ending a phrase spoken in English with, "Wheee." Mature for her age, she never needed scolding and I rarely saw her cry.

Melanna served me the stock meal, fish soup and rice, which I picked over but ate little of. The soup kettle was a perennial item in any Palauan kitchen. The soup was always there; sometimes it had been there too long. There was no dining together family style. When you were hungry, you ate.

Terresa came to the door, slipped out of her zorries, stepped up, and sat cross-legged on the floor being careful to cover her long dark legs with her dress. Her hair was braided into a single braid which fell across her shoulder and down over the curvature of her bust. She gave me a betel nut, and we chewed and talked in English. She spoke English well, but she was the only one from either household who did, other than Kailang. She interpreted for Mechas and they shot questions at me. Was I all right? Did I need anything? How did I like Palau? What state was I from? Were my parents still living? What did my father do? Mechas and Melanna listened intently as Terresa answered for me in Palauan. Later, Terresa explained to me that I was the oldest son, Vini was my brother, and Melanna my sister. Mechas was overjoyed to have me, she told me.

I was unhappy with the shower situation at Mechas's house. Dipping water out of a drum with a tin can was inconvenient, awkward (everyone watched), and after two or three days without rain, there was no water. Why bother, I thought.

After training, Peace Corps had given us a "settling-in allowance," a special stipend to help us buy what we needed to get settled after training. Just as I had previously imagined, I would indeed build a water distribution system. But not of bamboo. Kailang had already run water to his house, and he helped me plan out what I would need; then I spent hours looking around town for the PVC parts. Kailang showed me where to tap discreetly into the city water pipe, a remnant of the prewar Japanese water system which ran along the village road above. I ran pipe and a spigot into the kitchen; then I tee-ed out through the back into an overhead faucet which would serve as a shower. I borrowed the Peace Corps truck and with Vini and Obi's help, stole the shower stall, which had been built by the boatyard, from the well at our training camp and installed it around the overhead faucet. Kailang gave me some old shipping pallets to use as a floor. Now we had a shower and wash room complete with running water, as well as a faucet in the kitchen. That may have been my paramount contribution as a Peace Corps volunteer. Certainly it was the most tangible. Mechas was happy. So was Melanna and Vini. I was ecstatic. And Alphonso never did figure out who ran off with the boatyard shower room.

Dave Hodges, meanwhile, was still having problems finding a place to live. Gene Helfman was staying with Melisebes and family but was having second thoughts. Melisebes lived in a village called Meyungs on the island of Arakabesan, which was connected to Koror by a long causeway. One night after carousing in the bars, Gene came home around midnight and Melisebes jumped all over him. Melisebes, a strict *Modekngei* (the local religion, *Modekngei* meaning "we people together") abhorred the use of alcohol. Gene, full of beer, made the mistake of bickering; after all, he was old enough, he reasoned to Melisebes, and went to bed. But Melisebes held the grudge, ignoring Gene and entering into a passive-aggressive mode. Helfman, perplexed and stewing, went to Wilson for help. Peter promised to talk to Melisebes about it.

Chapter 6

Life in Koror

Each PCV had a mailbox in the Peace Corps office, and one day I found a notice in my box. It said that twenty bicycles were available to volunteers who could justify the need for one. I justified my need immediately and picked up my bike, a "made in China" product designed for dwarfs. Even with handle bars and seat at maximum height, it was so small I had to splay my knees to avoid banging the handle bars on the upstroke. I rode it all over Koror and Malakal, bouncing in and out of the potholes and ruts. I bent the frame, bent the handle bars, sent the wheels out of kilter, and broke the chain. Peter's carpenters somehow always managed to fix it for me. When a tire went flat, a sympathetic gas station attendant patched it up. But a blow out did me in; no replacement tires available on island. By this time, I was the only PCV still pedaling around, the others having given up long ago. So I put the bike in storage down at fisheries while I figured out how to get a tire, and that was the end of it. Dead, it just rusted away, disintegrated, decomposed, as everything does in Palau.

One time when a Catholic priest named Father Hoar stopped by to see Peter at his office, I hitched a ride into town with him in his new Datsun pickup. It was raining heavily, and the enormous holes in the road were full of water. He accelerated going across the causeway, always the roughest stretch. "If you get it going at just the right speed you can hydroplane across the potholes," he explained, justifying his lead foot. Sure enough, we cruised along without a glitch, as smoothly as a '57 Chevy at three in the morning on the Hollywood Freeway. Hydroplaning—the closest sensation to a ride on pavement Palau could offer.

Palauan roads, full of ruts and holes, made driving an automobile anything but pleasant. Automobiles had no resale value; they turned into so much junk after a year on Palau's roads. Cars would bounce cartoonlike down the road, the impacts shaking the headlights out of their sockets, leaving them hanging by their wires from vacant cavities. The government's pile of ramshackled vehicles grew larger each year. Palau's government could have paved the road several times had it used the money for that purpose rather than to buy new replacement vehicles each year. A paved road would have negated the constant need for new vehicles. Public Works' standard excuse for the condition of the road was "inadequate funds." I doubt Public Works ever requested funds to pave the road. I saw little logic in its operation.

Koror's roads were either wet and muddy or dry and dusty, often both, like the tides, several times in a day. Many people walked in Palau, particularly on the main road. The coral dust kicked up by passing cars was annoying and unhealthy. The hospital was inundated with patients suffering respiratory disorders. When it rained, passing cars splashed mud on walkers. Cars, dodging mud holes, often swerved recklessly to avoid pedestrians who, themselves, also dodged mud holes. During the Japanese Mandate Koror boasted paved roads, sidewalks, and landscaping. Palauans living in those days might have questioned the logic that drove the Americans to destroy all that after they had won the war. Perhaps the Americans might rebuild what they had destroyed. Sorry. Here was Koror twenty-three years later, almost as the Americans had left it: razed. No wonder many older Palauans harbored suppressed, but deep-seated resentment toward Americans. Even after thirty years of Japanese colonial rule, at the end of the war the Palauans had composed this song in their honor:

> *We won't forget you good people*
> *who were our teachers for thirty years,*
> *My favorite sakura.*
> *Our relationship with you has ended.*
> *We don't know which direction to go next.*

Now, older Palauans displayed the Japanese influence through their language, mannerisms, the music they listened to, the food they ate, their attitudes. Perhaps many of them missed those days.

How was the government set up in the Trust Territory? At headquarters, located in Saipan in the Northern Mariana Islands, a presidential appointed high commissioner (Hicom) reported to the Department of the Interior. The Hicom and his cabinet of department heads presided over the six districts of the Trust Territory. At the district level, a district administrator (Distad) and deputy Distad supervised the various District Division Chiefs.

And how did the government operate? In fire drill mode. Word would come down from headquarters that a high "mucky muck" was coming to town for this reason or that. One always knew something was up because suddenly the government would turn to. Division chiefs would shave and cut their hair. Government workers would clean their offices and clear their desks of papers. In spite of the perpetual water shortage, government trucks would be washed. The most manifest piece of housecleaning came from Public Works whose workers would jump-start their road graders and bulldozers and grade the road from the airport to the Distad's Office—and any other route the officials might take while visiting. The locals questioned these maneuvers: "Why not let them see what it's really like?" Perhaps then Interior would *demand* the road be paved.

When a United Nations evaluation team came through the Trust Territory in 1968, the administration made monumental effort to paint a rosy picture. The road, of course, was smoothed over wonderfully for their visit. At a public hearing on the issues, many PCVs complained about the deplorable condition of the road, but to no avail. After the team's departure, Public Works parked its heavy equipment and it was back to normal: dust, mud, and potholes.

The Trust Territory applied a double standard pay scale: one for Americans and one for Micronesians. American contract employees were paid Civil Service wages while Micronesians worked for substantially less. In a few cases, local workers possessed education, experience, and skills equivalent to expatriate workers, yet they earned far less money for equal work. This pay scale dichotomy chafed at indigenous government employees. Peace Corps aggravated the situation because volunteers lived and worked with the locals yet earned far less than anyone. Volunteers eagerly voiced their opinions, often to the chagrin of American contract workers, many of whom distrusted Peace Corps volunteers. Contract workers felt intimidated by our presence. We were young, smart, adventurous, idealistic; most of us were college graduates. And we had absolutely nothing to lose.

Some people considered Peace Corps as just a vehicle for avoiding the draft. This was untrue. Peace Corps was not exempt from the draft and, in fact, volunteers continued to be drafted during the Viet Nam years. None too proud of America at the time, most volunteers were unbothered by the insinuating comments of some Americans on the island. We traded insult for insult. But we had to use tact with the Palauans. There were those who failed to grasp why volunteers would choose working peacefully in Palau over going to Viet Nam and killing people over something unintelligible. They viewed the military in awe and were unable to empathize with our antiwar, antimilitary attitudes. To them, wearing a military uniform brought the ultimate prestige; anyone could wear shorts and zorries, they reasoned, because that's what they wore. This, however, was the inverse of my line of thinking. Early on I learned to circumvent conflicts of opinion over the Viet Nam war by avoiding the issue, especially in bars. Trying to reason with a Palauan over drink was out of the question. Drunken talk was just that.

In the bars, the best way to avoid trouble was to employ the "great disappearing act," as Norman Vas later coined the maneuver. Drunken conversations regarding venerated issues (such as Viet Nam) or concepts were meaningless. The minute you heard the "no answer" question put forth by your Palauan friend, it was time to take a hike, to head for the *banjo*, to disappear. Things would only disintegrate if you stuck around and played the game.

It would be wrong to infer that all Palauans supported the Viet Nam war. Certain college students and graduates who had returned to Palau held anti-Viet Nam war sentiments. Valentine Suguino, a graduate of UC Berkeley with a degree in literature, was one. Another was Kathy Kesolei. And Sabo Uchledong hated the Viet Nam War. University of Hawaii student Cisco Uludong was the complete radical; anti-Viet Nam, anti-American, anti-capitalism, anti-TT, anti-everything. Uludong was the editor-publisher of a government sponsored news tabloid called *Didl a Chais* (Bridge of News), later renamed *Tia Belau* (This is Palau). He adeptly used the news format to roast Americans over selected topics each week, and he pulled a journalistic scoop when he published a highly classified document known as National Security Action Memorandum No. 145 (NSAM-145), a policy document issued in 1962 which aimed at influencing a Micronesian plebiscite toward a permanent relationship with the United States. Valentine was a part-time reporter for the tabloid, and he often wrote poetry for it as well. Kathy worked for the Community Development Office. Pro-Viet Nam War they were not.

—

Peter moved out of the old office across from the co-op and into the new office down at the end of the dock. It was a brick building, fully air conditioned, large and spacious, and contained a private room for Peter, a large central office area, and a library-conference room. Out front, a large lawn extended to the seawall at the water's edge. Kailang moved into Peter's old office and that freed up a lot of space in the co-op store area.

I was learning the books of the co-op operation as well as recording weights of fish species brought in by fishermen. In November, Kailang would be leaving for Japan for four months of training, and Peter wanted me to manage the co-op during that period. Fearful of the job, I argued with Peter but he was resolute I should do it. "There *is* no one else," he said when I suggested he get someone else. So I determined to learn the bookkeeping part before Kailang left, and the word "balance" took on new meaning for me.

The co-op owned a red Mitsubishi pickup truck which travelled the road into town and back five or six times daily. Its suspension had long ago disintegrated, and the only semblance of cushioning came from the tires. The driver's seat had deteriorated into a gaping hole, the driver now sitting on a piece of plywood and pillow to see over the steering wheel. Rust had opened a large hole through the floor boards near the brake pedal and the cabin filled with dust on the go. The frame was fractured and bent between the cab and the bed, the bed sitting slightly askew, loosely attached to the frame by bailing wire. The bed had broken into sections, each section bouncing independently with each bump. Parts of rusted metal dangled off the fenders, and the headlights bounced around loosely in their sockets, dead. The muffler had long ago fallen off, making the roar of the four-cylinder engine almost unbearable. The engine—leaked oil; clutch—shot; brakes—variable; emergency brake—broke. The odometer had frozen up at four thousand miles and the truck was, after all, a year old. But it ran.

Kailang was up and on the road each morning at 6:30 a.m. He made the rounds, picking up the employees along the way. But that was too early for me. Unprogrammed for early starts, I chose instead to sleep an extra hour and catch a ride to fisheries with Wilson as he came down from his house farther up the hill around 7:30 a.m. If I missed him, I'd start walking and someone heading toward Malakal would pick me up. Few people could afford an automobile and government vehicles were commonly used for transporting employees to and from work.

Paul Callaghan lived with *Ibedul*, high chief of southern Palau and the most powerful Palauan leader. His house was located near the center of town, at the upper side of the intersection of T-Dock Road and Upper Road. Peter considered Paul the model Peace Corps volunteer. Like Peter, Paul was rarely late to work (but he never worked longer than 4:30 p.m. either). More mature than the rest of us, Paul spent less time carousing and in the bars, choosing instead to run with the more subdued volunteers. Peter picked him up for work each morning, and Paul sometimes took a government truck home. But Paul was friendly, never flaunting his good fortune.

Toshiro Paulis, Peter's assistant, lived in a Quonset hut down in southern Koror near a village called Medalaii. His family included his Palauan wife and their two children. Tosh was from Kapingamarangi, a small atoll in southern Ponape. Folks from Kapingamarangi and Nukuoro, an atoll just north of Kapingamarangi, were of Polynesian descent. They were big, stoutly built people, many over six feet in height, although Tosh was only about five foot eight.

Peter had hired Tosh off one of the old Trust Territory vessels when Peter began his job in Palau in the late 1950s, and Peter regarded him as his right-hand man. Tosh was a skilled seaman, fisherman, and diver; and he liked his liquor. After work, Tosh loved to stop by the Community Club located across the street from his house and close the place down. Often he arrived late for work or was absent. But Tosh was dedicated to Wilson, and Peter seldom reprimanded him. Peter would just huff and snort around the office until Tosh showed up, usually around 9:30 a.m.

Tosh loved to joke and socialize, and he held an excellent command of English. He also spoke some Japanese, Trukese, Ponapean, and of course, he spoke Kapingamarangan. His face was large and round with a flat nose, and his course frizzy hair was receding at the temples. Over the years, Tosh had stacked on pounds, mostly from a diet rich in fat and alcohol, and the gout had slowed him down from a few years before. Despite this, however, on weekends Tosh and I often went fishing or diving.

—

Harson stopped by our room next to the co-op to chat with Gene and I. Melisebes, he said, had been bad-mouthing Gene all week, saying things like "Gene's a liar, Gene drinks all the time, Gene did this, Gene did that." Harson said to Gene: "Why don't you just tell Melisebes, "*techel a delam*," which means your mother's vagina is open, a very bad thing to say to anyone, particularly a *rubak*. Harson disliked Melisebes and had threatened to quit a number of times, although Peter had always talked him out of it. I failed to understand Peter's high regard for Melisebes. He spent a good portion of his time hanging around the boatyard yakking in Japanese with Matsumoto and Alphonso. Illiterate in English, he could not write reports, and he never, ever, apprehended poachers. Harson did all the dirty work, such as feeding the turtles, writing reports, and maintaining the boat.

When Peter had talked to Melisebes about Gene, Melisebes had persecuted Gene. So Gene told Melisebes he wasn't going to work with him anymore. He moved out of Melisebes's house and went to live with Bliok, a *rubak* who worked at the co-op. Then Gene quit fisheries altogether, moving up to Bob Owen's entomology laboratory to work in the conservation program there. This displeased Wilson, but he said little about it.

A bit of friction existed between the two chiefs, Peter and Bob Owen. Bob, as chief of Conservation for the Trust Territory, had jurisdiction over conservation, which meant that Melisebes was not officially a bona fide conservation officer, even though Wilson called him one. Bob and Peter's disputes were inveterate and they argued constantly, usually about conservation practices and jurisdiction, development projects, and government policy. Peter was a go-getter, a gung ho type. Bob was low keyed, cautious, and adept in the island way. Both were burdened with the frustrations of having worked in Palau over the years. More than once rumors flew that one or the other was getting booted out of Palau. That never happened.

Bob Owen had been in Palau since 1951—sixteen years. During World War II, he had been a B-25 bomber pilot, crashed landed and lived to tell about it. After the war he earned his degree in entomology, then came to Palau to wage war on the giant rhinoceros beetles which were destroying Palau's coconut palms and ruining the copra trade. Bob was an outstanding naturalist and intellectually adept, but his position as Chief of Conservation was unenviable. Conservation was an unpopular concept in Palau. Palauans resented being restricted from taking anything they pleased. Once, while Bob stood in his living room, a spear whizzed by his chest and stuck decisively in the wall beyond. Merely a warning, Bob speculated: "Otherwise I'd have been dead." Bob's wife, Hera, a meticulous, intellectual, empathic woman, had started a small but significant museum in Koror. She made considerable effort toward preserving Palau's history and culture, although the government lacked interest and gave little support to her endeavors. They had two children, but only one, Ramona—a freckled, rambunctious blond of nineteen—lived with them. Ramona spoke fluid Palauan.

Bob was of average height, had receding brown hair, and thick, bushy eyebrows, reminding me always of a thin Humphrey Bogart. He talked in a low monotone, and his dry humor was often hard to follow. Bob often stopped by the Community Club after work and sometimes got rip roaring drunk. At such times, he would periodically let out a loud roar, similar to something a sick and miserable cow might bellow out. The years of drinking had emaciated Bob. Teetotaler Hera continually chastised Bob about his drinking, and she may have been the only reason Bob's liver still held out.

Up at the entomology laboratory, Bob kept several crocodiles in fenced cages. Palau had a feral dog problem, and people often brought unwanted puppies and kittens up to the lab for disposal. Bob would put them away and feed them to the crocs. Many people thought him cruel and inhumane for this, but it was really an efficient way to get rid of unwanted animals which otherwise would suffer. Bob, I guess, enjoyed the crocodiles.

Palau's chief of Agriculture was Neal Morris. Of course, Palau had little agriculture; some taro, tapioca, and coconuts; a few pigs, chickens, and one or two water buffalo on Babeldaob. But Neal put in his time at the Ag station and also helped support the Community Club by showing up without fail every single working day at 4:35 p.m. Neal had his own stool at the end of the bar and no one, unless they weren't from around there, ever sat on that stool but Neal. It was tradition. Neal was the pillar of the club.

Everyone liked Neal, including me. He was a small man, thin from booze. His sandy blond hair was combed straight back, pomade style. Neal moved with slow deliberate motions, as if he might pitch forward at any given moment. He always leaned slumped over the bar, elbows on, nursing his scotch and water, which is what all the hard core drank at the club. His Winstons were always on the bar nearby, along with his silver Zippo. Quiet and reserved, Neal's face always held a slight smile, as if he knew something you should know, but didn't. Dry, sarcastic, and funny, Neal looked and talked like George Gobel, dragging out his words in a low voice. "Hiii, Peeaace Coorrps," he'd say to me, probably trying to offend me, although he never did. He courted a nice Palauan lady with oriental looks. She drank straight tonic and made sure that everything was okay with Neal, Neal having a habit of slipping off his stool. Mild-mannered Neal never drank on the job, but he was permanently pickled from his consumption at the club.

Sometimes, when I was in the club with Tosh or Peter after work, a man named John Sakie from the Department of Education would come in for a drink. He was tall, athletic, had short blond hair, and looked thirty-eightish. His weathered face was pocked from teenage acne. A loner, he rarely spoke conversationally to anyone except Peter and it seemed that everyone respected him, perhaps suspiciously. Sakie frequently travelled to destinations off island and rumor had him as CIA. But that was only rumor, and rumors were easy in Palau.

Peter's good friend, Father Hoar, lived at the parish across the road from my village of Yebukl. Father Hoar never visited the Community Club, preferring instead to drink his scotch at the rectory. He was a ham operator and often sent patches for people needing to communicate with folks on the mainland. Peter made good use of his friend in this regard. Father Hoar had been in Palau for many years and spoke fluent Palauan. Father Hoar's light complexion found Palau's sun intolerable and he dressed accordingly, usually wearing a locally weaved sombrero to shield his face from ultraviolet. Skeptical of Peace Corps, he thought us naïve, which we were.

The Community Club was housed in one of the old Quonsets thrown up by the navy just after the war as temporary shelter to last a year or two. It was a social club, a drinking club, really, a place where government workers, local and expatriate, went after work for drinks, to talk over the day's happenings, to gossip, tell stories, get ripped. On Saturday and Sunday the club never closed, and some folks would spend the whole weekend there. Every other Friday night was steak night, and I often made it a point to hang around Wilson's office at quitting time those Fridays so I might get invited. Peter had a whole freezer full of red meat and I craved it. I was giving him free labor; he could at least feed me now and then.

—

Peter applied for the dealership for Taperflex water skis, and the company sent him two slalom skis, a set of doubles, and new tow ropes. Peter loved to ski as did I. We started skiing in the evenings after work in front of fisheries. Most Palauans had never seen such a thing, and they'd line up on the dock and watch us. I'd jump-start off the seawall, and they'd all go wild. We'd ski across the bay, up through a narrow canal built by the Japanese and into the channel which ran up through rock islands into Iwayama Bay. The sheltered water provided by the rock islands made for superb skiing. You could lean and swing out and, looking down into the clear, coral-rich water, watch the fish scatter, like fireworks on a dark night.

One evening after work, Peter, Dave Hodges, Gene Helfman, and I went skiing over on the boatyard side in the bay. When we finished, Peter drove the boat into the slip beneath the dorm just as his wife Ann drove up.

"Dave, tie up my boat will you." he said to Hodges. "Pat, take my truck and pick me up in the morning."

"Okay," I said as Peter got in the car with Ann. Hodges still lived in the dorm so Gene and I took the skis and headed home, leaving Dave to secure the boat. Dave knew as much about tying up a boat as I did about playing a guitar. He tied it up pretty good, however, never considering the five—to six-foot tides Palau was pulsed with.

That night, as the tide ebbed, the boat hung itself, the half-inch nylon rope strong enough to pull the cleats out of the gunwales and deck.

The next morning Matsumoto threw the cleats and deck parts of Peter's boat in the back of his truck and drove over to fisheries to show Peter. Minutes later, Peter stormed over to the co-op looking for Dave, who was holed up in the room next door to the co-op office where I sat staring at the ledger.

"Where's Hodges?" he shouted.

"I think he's next door," I replied, looking up from my spreadsheet. What's with him, I wondered, as I recorded another debit.

Kailang, sitting nearby, gave me the "cutthroat" sign and I confirmed it by nodding, realizing that Peter's mad might possibly be related to his boat, of which he was very proud. We heard high frequency profanity, Peter dressing down Hodges as if he were a piece of meat or fish. It took only a few seconds. Peter, his chin in the air, stomped back down the dock to his office. Skiing was out that evening.

The next day, Dave, still visibly shaken and upset, came into the co-op office.

"I've had it, Pat," he said. "I don't know anything about boats. I don't know what a fish is. I'm not a water person, and I'm really not that interested in finding out." And so, that ended Hodges. No one ever saw him again.

Gene was doing well living with Bliok's family in Meyungs. Bliok, in his midfifties, had a wandering eye which liked to observe some distant event in the heavens while the other focused on the subject. A friendly fellow, he loved to joke, often using Palauan profanity to express himself. His mode of greeting was usually to tell us something about our mother's *klalo* (genitals). Being addressed in profanity by this aberrant old man with a wandering eye was a bit unnerving. Initially, his filthy ribbing had offended me, but eventually I got used to it. As my profane Palauan vocabulary improved, I began to trade insults with him. He loved it, laughing when I'd inform him that I'd been out with his mother the previous night and that she was *kot techel* (wide open). Bliok, uneducated, was one of the best workers at the co-op. He was honest, had scruples, and was always available when I needed him.

I learned the books at the co-op and Kailang began relying on me to run the place, preening me for the dreaded acting manager position I would assume in his absence. One day when Kailang was gone, an older man drove up on a motorcycle and side car. He dislodged his helmet and, with a hairless head as shiny as a chrome pool ball, introduced himself as Mr. White. He was the government's small business comptroller, he said, whose job it was to help private businesses with their bookkeeping. He explained that Kailang kept good books, but that he had to get rid of the credit books he kept on each of the members, a widespread Palauan business practice. Each retail store had a notebook identified for each customer that charged. Someone might buy a can of Spam, fish hooks, and something else on credit. Each item would be listed in his book along with the price. When the person made a payment, it would be subtracted from the balance.

"Get rid of those books," Mr. White told me, in no uncertain terms. I said I'd talk to Kailang about it.

"Never mind Kailang," he harked. "Just get rid of those things."

When Kailang returned, I told him what Mr. White had said.

"He's a stubborn old *rubak*," Kailang said. "Every time he comes in, he tells me that. Just tell him 'okay,' but never mind him while I'm gone." I said okay.

I tried to implement a few things I felt would improve the co-op operation. I wanted to set up a fuel tank on the dock for selling gasoline and diesel. The existing operation consisted of siphoning fuel out of fifty-five-gallon drums in front of the co-op. Every other day we had to load up the drums in the truck, then drive over to Mobile Oil for more fuel. It was time-consuming, inefficient, and environmentally unsound, although the environment was of little concern in those days. Peter had great contacts with the military, always getting parts for the *Emeraech* flown in from Guam or Honolulu on military transports. I hounded him to use his sway to procure a couple of surplus tanks from the navy in Guam. Finally, after several months of my harping at Peter, the Coast Guard flew in a five-hundred-gallon tank for diesel fuel. Peter had his carpenters build a tower for it out on the dock. But the gasoline situation remained unchanged.

Freshwater at the co-op was obtained from catchment off the roof. Water was held in a cement reservoir, then pumped up to an elevated holding tank for distribution by gravity. When the power failed, which was often, the pump would short out and the water would siphon back down into the holding tank. Even when the elevated tank was full, pressure remained inadequate to efficiently wash down the dock and weigh-in areas where the boys handled fish. The co-op was bacteria rich, fly heaven, unsanitary and smelly—dead fish smelly.

Out on a table near the weigh-in station sat an electronic fly catcher, a box holding a dead fish as bait and covered with an electrically armed grill. Each time a fly landed the grill bars would arc, roasting the fly. As long as the co-op had electricity, the noise was endless: *zaaap, zaaap, zaaap*. Along with the fish stink mingled the unique smell of fried flies, an obnoxious stink which repulsed the nose, disgusted the stomach, and repelled most American customers. The trap held thousands of flies and had to be emptied three or four times each day.

I figured seawater could be used to wash down the co-op dock. I found an old pump in the warehouse across the way and spent several days scrounging hose and fittings to get it hooked up. It worked, but lacked enough power to lift water up over the seawall without priming. Since Kailang showed no interest in this area of improvement, I finally gave up. Just another Peace Corps failure.

Peter had me set up a diving shop in the room next to the co-op. Public works wired the room for 220 volts and installed a big air compressor which Wilson had acquired through the military. The compressor would fill a seventy-two cubic inch tank in about two minutes, a far cry from the thirty-minute routine of the old Mako compressor. The boatyard carpenters built lockers for gear storage and racks to accommodate the tanks. It was a first-class shop.

I started doing a lot of diving; almost every day I'd go out. Sometimes Paul Callaghan would go out with me. Other times Jack Hardy would go. If no one was around, I'd load up the skiff and go by myself. I was macho, and stupid, diving alone.

Doug Faulkner was making diving trips to Palau during this time. Doug, a professional underwater photographer working on a book about Palau's underwater world, needed air, lots of it, and Marine Resources had the only compressor in town. We became good friends. Doug often dove alone, but I started diving with him when he wanted to dive in sharky places or explore new areas. I carried my spear gun to poke at sharks while he focused his Rollei Marine camera. Each photograph yielded an expended bulb which would float to the surface. I asked why he didn't catch the burned out bulbs, the irony being that each pristine photograph he took yielded a piece of "junk" into the environment, a contribution to a polluted environment his work could never tolerate. He shrugged and said "good idea." From then on I carried a bag and caught the bulbs as he ejected them. I wanted to change bulbs for him as well, but he balked at that. He didn't want me touching his camera.

"I can do it easier and faster myself," he told me.

Pollution often started innocently enough, even with those who admonished it. But few Palauans grasped the concept of littering; it just wasn't there. On the water Spam cans went overboard. On the road beer cans flew out the window or out the back of the truck. Anything disposable was chucked anywhere, except in one's own house. The out-of-sight, out-of-mind attitude prevailed in Koror. Babeldaob, on the other hand, was different;

the villages were kept clean and groomed. Babeldaob possessed a pride that Koror, the capital, conspicuously lacked.

—

Kailang flew off for Japan, leaving me to manage the co-op and the five employees for six months, rather than four months I had been previously told. Unhappy about the changed time frame, I voiced my displeasure to Peter. He assured me that the six months would pass swiftly and that I would gain considerable business knowledge from the experience. Keeping the books and running the operation bothered me little, but handling and accounting for the money worried me. And as it turned out, my apprehension was justified.

Most of the guys who worked at the co-op, excepting Bliok, were young. All were afraid of Kailang. Whatever Kailang told them, they did. Mekreos had worked there the longest and was the most intelligent of the group. He spoke good English and could tally up the receipts at the end of the day. When I was gone, he was in charge. After Mekreos, Albert was senior. Then came Mitsuo and Bliok, two year veterans. Only Masahiro was new. Almost a dwarf, Masahiro possessed a slightly hunched back and limped horribly from one shortened leg, a product of infantile poliomyelitis. Early in his life his right eye had been negated by a well-thrown rock. Straight from the school of hardest knocks, his upper body was stronger than an ox, and he took licks from few people now. His vocabulary contained only several words in English, but he did whatever I asked and worked harder than anyone else. Because he was from my village, he felt protective of me. But I got along well with all of them.

Before Kailang left for Japan the co-op membership threw a bon voyage party for him on a rock island known as Morei's Island, named after a judge, Judge Morei, who was also president of the co-op. It was going to be an all-night party progressing about 5:00 p.m. and lasting until the following morning. No women were present, only co-op members, twenty or so crusty fishermen. Judge Morei, being of high clan, was absent. The moon that night was full, a Palauan party signal.

They built a big fire on the beach and roasted fish and lobster. We sat in a circle around the fire, ate and drank beer; Asahi, Kirin, and Schlitz. The older Palauans preferred their beer warm, ambient temperature, and they favored warm Schlitz, the most popular American beer in Micronesia. Along with their beer, some of the fishermen drank a local brew called *Apollo*, a distilled liquor of guarded origin brewed by one man in Koror and bottled in a variety of containers. At the *Apollo* brewery, quality control was said to be lax.

I sat in the sand close to Kailang watching the men sing songs and dance around the fire. Kailang sat crossed-legged, yakking in Palauan, emphasizing his words with his index finger as his listeners nodded in agreement and muttered an "*cho choi*" (yes) every now and then. About 1:00 a.m., with the moon full overhead, Kailang, having switched from beer to *Apollo*, pulled out a large fillet knife and jumped up. A fisherman named Mogami scrambled toward the water, Kailang in hot pursuit and screaming that he would cut Mogami's heart out. Mogami swam to his boat, cranked the diesel, pulled anchor, and chugged off in the moonlight toward Koror as Kailang paced the shore screaming insults. Mekreos and Albert attempted to talk Kailang down but Kailang was in the throes of alcoholic madness, out of control. He turned on another fisherman, his repressed animosities suddenly apparent. Better play the great disappearing act, I thought, lest Kailang turn his blade on me for whatever reason. Maybe I'd screwed up the books or something; good chance of that, actually. Overloaded on beer, I staggered off into the jungle searching for a place to hide and sleep. I slipped under a deep undercut beneath the limestone cliff adjoining the beach and fell asleep in the soft sand. No one found me that night except the sand fleas.

At first light, I was awakened by the unmistakable sounds of *pong pongs* starting up. I stumbled out of my enclave and found Kailang and several others lying asleep in the sand, the fire still smoldering. I saw no blood, no wounded, no dead bodies as I had envisaged. Kailang looked anything but formidable now, his face partially encrusted with the fine, white rock island sand. Two fishermen hefted Kailang over to a boat and within minutes everyone but myself and Mekreos had gone, leaving the beach in a state describable only as "trashed." I walked around throwing empty beer cans and bottles into a pile while I asked Mekreos if we shouldn't clean up a bit.

"*Bedrai* (Never mind)," he said. "We just throw in a pile."

We meandered over the beach, throwing the obvious trash into the pile, Mekreos reflecting on the past night's events.

"Ah that Kailang," he said, "no good when he drinks. He went after everyone, *ollei* (friend), just showing off his blade. *Kmal chad er a oles* (man of the knife). I run away too, *ollei*."

We finished quickly, then sped off in Mekreos's *ert* (speedboat) toward Koror five miles to the northeast. That was my first experience with a Palauan party of drunken fishermen in the rock islands. Kailang never mentioned a word about it again.

The next morning was Sunday. I was on my way down to Harson's place when Jim Taylor, the Peace Corps director, stopped me on the road. After we had departed Morei's Island the previous day, Jim had passed by in his boat and was dismayed to see the mess on the beach. Knowing of the co-op party, he knew I had been along. I explained my situation, telling him I stood willing to go out and clean the place up. We bought some beer, went back out to Morei's, and cleaned up the island. Jim was getting ready to leave Palau and when we came back later that afternoon I asked him what he wanted for his boat, knowing full well volunteers were disallowed such luxuries. He said he'd give it to me for a good price. It was a Matsumoto built *ert* with a small cabin, remote steering and controls, and powered by a forty-horsepower mercury. I disliked mercurys, but the boatyard dealt in them so I figured parts would at least be available. I wired home for some money I had saved from selling my Volkswagen and paid him the following week, strictly against Peace Corps rules. But I wasn't the only PCV who owned a boat—Paul Callaghan owned a small *ert* as well. Peter chuckled when I told him I'd bought a boat from the Peace Corps director.

I kept the boat for two months, long enough to do a lot of water skiing, thoroughly explore the rock islands, and make several trips to Babeldaob with Harson. But it soon became apparent that I didn't need a boat. Working for Marine Resources, I had plenty of boats and Peter was liberal when it came to using fisheries equipment as long as the use was fisheries related. I decided to sell the boat while it was still in good shape. Matsumoto's *erts* were light boats, constructed of marine plywood, and lasted but several years. Mekreos had previously told me his brother wanted to buy it, so I let it go for what I paid for it and Mekreos's brother had himself a boat.

Several days later Mekreos's brother came by the co-op to get ice for a fishing trip. The co-op ice machine was broken, as usual, so he motored across the bay and tied up at the Van Camp dock, forgetting to put the plugs in the transom before he jumped out to get the ice. Mekreos and I stood on the co-op dock watching the boat sink stern first. We yelled and screamed at his brother who talked unknowingly with one of the dock hands. Mekreos sprinted to the truck and sped over to Van Camp, arriving in time to alarm the others and get a rope on the bow cleat just before the boat sank from sight. A forklift hoisted it up onto the dock where they flushed the engine with fresh water. The following day the *ert* was back in business. Mekreos and his brother were very proud of that boat.

—

As acting manager of the PFC, I was charged with more responsibility than I deserved at the Peace Corps rate of ninety dollars a month. The workers often spent considerable time fooling around, and there was always work to be done. At lunch everyone would sneak off somewhere to take a siesta, always alternating spots so I couldn't track them. Naturally, this would be the exact time it would get real busy, people wanting to buy fish, fishermen landing their catches, or errands needed doing. It was frustrating.

About once a month the co-op exported fish to Guam on various Trust Territory steamers. After we packed the frozen fish in boxes and strapped them, I'd book the fish and they'd usually tell us to bring them over around midnight. At midnight, we'd load up the truck and take the fish over and invariably they wouldn't be ready. So we'd return to the co-op, unload the fish back into the reefer, and wait. Sometimes the whole crew would be standing by all night to load fish when the ship gave us the ready; then no one would be in shape to work the following day.

Shortly after Kailang left, Jerry Facey and Harry Brown from the Social Security Office in Saipan came down to see me. They were charged with implementing the Federal Social Security system throughout the Trust Territory and the co-op was on their list. I had glimpsed the Social Security brochure, a menial explanation of the program, and Kailang had mentioned it to me before he left, saying the Palauans disliked the program. So I argued with them.

"The employees don't understand it," I said. "To them it's just another rip-off, someone taking money out of their paychecks every two weeks. You need a thorough public education program, not just this little explanatory pamphlet you put out in English which no one can understand anyway."

They agreed to voice my sentiments to the higher echelons, and my complaints later helped initiate public education meetings on the Social Security program in all the districts.

That night I walked up the road to meet Harson in a bar called the Boom Boom Room. He must have been on Palauan time for he never showed up. Before I left, Jerry Facey came in with a pretty Palauan girl. She wore a long, tight-fitting blue dress which enhanced her figure. Jerry played a slow song on the jukebox and danced close to the girl. She stood a bit taller than he, and the matchup seemed a little odd because of it, but she swayed ominously to the music. And Jerry seemed euphoric.

Two weeks after Kailang left for Japan, I began coming up short of cash at the end of the day. It worried me. I consulted Paul Callaghan to determine if I was in error. No, he told me, my work looked okay. Perhaps, then, someone might be dipping into the till?

One evening the Public Works mechanic, who worked in the reefer shop across from the co-op, confided in me that he had seen Mitsuo open the cash register. For the next several days, I kept my eyes open but saw nothing. Then one night as I stood at the open air counter of Kintaro's store on the corner of my village and the upper road talking with Terresa, I saw Mitsuo drive by in the co-op truck, breaking the cardinal rule; the man on overnight watch must never leave the co-op. I hailed a taxi down to the co-op and waited for him to return.

When Mitsuo drove in an hour later I fired him on the spot. He threw some things around, said some bad things about my mother, then left, walking up the road toward town. Uncertain of the consequences of my actions, first thing in the morning I went over and told Peter what I'd done and why. That afternoon, Judge Morei came down to have a talk with me. He insisted I let Mitsuo go back to work, almost commanded me. But I refused. That night my books balanced and things returned to co-op normal. A week later, Mitsuo came down to the co-op and apologized to me. He had gone to work for a local business establishment helping his wife run a bar on lower road.

"Bring Harson and come to the Texas Saloon and we'll play," he told me in Palauan as we shook hands.

The Texas Saloon was situated next door to a shanty movie house called Ichie's Theater, both part of the same establishment. Just inside the Texas Saloon's door, a long pink plywood bar curved to the left around a kitchen of sorts. Old decrepit wooden stools, some with crippled legs, sat here and there along the bar. To the right, on a green plywood floor, were several round wooden tables painted various colors and complimented with junior-size rusty folding chairs, perhaps once painted yellow. The interior walls glowed in fashionable pink and blue, and bright Christmas tree decorations hung from the iron wood rafters throughout the year. The jukebox was heavily weighted with country western and Japanese songs, but also held several vintage popular tunes. Every bar in Palau had its theme song, and the Texas Saloon's was the Beatles' "Revolution."

Sometimes the bar girls served complimentary popcorn as chasers, leftovers from the previous night's movie next door. Smart patrons kept their eyes on the floor around their feet because *sumo* rats ran around foraging on dropped popcorn, or whatever. Living back somewhere behind the bar was a very obese mangy rat with a bald back. It would run out from under the counter every few minutes, pause to look over the clientele, then scoot through a big hole in the wall. We always tossed popcorn to it. It loved popcorn, and we called him Scab.

Sometimes we'd go to Ichie's to watch a movie before going to the Texas Saloon. Moviegoers at Ichie's sat on long, uncomfortable, termite-infested, wooden benches. The building itself was disintegrating. A divergent spark would have sent Ichie's up in smoke; and everyone smoked in Ichie's. But somehow it never happened. The movie's soundtrack was unsynchronized with the visual track, actor's lips moving before or after the words, and the volume was permanently stuck at maximum output, causing considerable distortion. Deafness was a real danger for Ichie's customers. At the movies, I was always troubled by an "inverse reaction" response by the locals, especially the youngsters. They would laugh and scream delightedly during dismal, pathetic, sad scenes, then sit mysteriously silent through funny scenes.

Midway through the film, a ten-minute break accompanied the reel change. When the power went off, which was often, you had to quickly get your feet up off the floor and out of the way of grazing rats. Even during the movie I liked to keep my feet up on the bench in front of me to keep them from getting run over by wayward rats. Rat harassment was part of the show at Ichie's, something you paid for at the door when you bought your ticket.

About twice a year, the Department of Health would spray for mosquitoes. The practice distressed me for it was a futile exercise, unhealthy and dangerous. They would drive along in a truck spraying bug mist from nozzles mounted behind a tank. Local youngsters would run along behind the truck, playing in the bug fog, breathing it, oblivious to the dangers of inhaling DDT (or whatever it was) into their fragile lungs and absorbing it through their skin. They sprayed indiscriminately, starting at one end of the road and ending at the other end. Then they repeated the process down the other side. One time while I was in Ichie's watching a movie, the whole place filled up with bug spray. I think I was the only person who charged out for fresh air. If some strange tropical disease didn't get you, insect poison would.

—

Harson lived with his sister, Sabed, her husband Mike, and their small son in Medalaii. The typical open air house, with wood shutters and tin roof, was located down a path from the main road in a secluded spot next to the mangroves. They had a PCV named Sandy Fluharty living with them. Harson's other sister, Erica, a tall, attractive girl, sometimes stayed with them as well. Mike worked for the government in the Economic Development Office, and Sandy worked as a nurse at the hospital. Sabed sometimes taught elementary school. They were a good family, and I enjoyed being around them. The four of us, Sandy, Erica, Harson, and I often went out at night together dancing or fooling around. We usually ended up back at their house late at night where the girls would cook huge amounts of *saimen* to satiate our hunger. On these occasions I usually spent the night there.

One night the four of us walked back from the Peleliu Club about a half mile away. Before reaching home, a rain squall engulfed us. Giddy from drink, we negotiated our way down the steep path to the house, slipping and sliding, tearing the thongs out of our zorries, and rolling in the mud while laughing our heads off. When we reached the house, we looked like mud-wrestling tag teams.

After showering, I took the trail out to the *benjo* which stood on stilts out over the water from a coral seawall in the mangroves. While I was inside, I heard some splashing, and when I came back to the house Erica and Sandy were on their way out with a flashlight.

"Watch out for that crocodile out by the *benjo*," I joked.

A minute or so later Harson and I heard a yelp from Sandy. Then Erica screamed. We ran out, almost bumping into the girls running back from the *benjo*.

"*Ius* (crocodile)! *Ius!*" Erica yelped.

With the girls behind us, Harson and I picked up some stones and walked down to the *benjo*. Harson shined the flashlight out behind the *benjo* in the channel coming in through the mangroves. In the beam of light, two red eyes glared out at us. While I held the light, Harson chucked a stone at it and it quickly disappeared beneath the surface.

"*Kekerei* (small one)," declared Harson, "maybe six feet." But we had to stand guard with the flashlight as Erica and Sandy relieved themselves in the *benjo*.

Infections were giving me a hard time. Every little ding or scratch turned red and septic. Still incompetent at wearing zorries, I continually stubbed my toes, knocking skin off. Walking around with wounded feet in the fish slime co-op environment only enhanced infections. A cut on one foot or the other would manifest in a red streak running up my leg into my groin. The Micronesian germs thrived on the new Peace Corps blood, and my body was taking a beating. In California, you stuck a Band-aid over a cut and forgot about it. When it came off, you were as good as new. If you tried that in Palau you'd come down with gangrene or something comparable. Only antibiotics would cure my infections, and Sandy was my source.

After training, Peace Corps had issued each of us a medical kit. Peace Corps medical kits were famous for having a nice pair of stainless steel scissors and little else of value except the case. Standard procedure was to immediately snatch the scissors before they disappeared, since they had legs, and stash them someplace or give them to your family. The humid environment rendered Band-aids useless. The tape was old and gooey, the gauze in short supply, and the other stuff was specialized—snake bite kit, that sort of thing; useful, perhaps, in New Mexico, but not in Palau.

We learned in training, after the rat chewed on Woody's toe, to avoid MacDonald Hospital at all costs. The hospital was staffed with medical officers trained in Fiji, and the Peace Corps doctor was rarely available since he travelled to all the districts. Being a biologist, I knew a little about what was happening to my body, usually enough to diagnose my symptoms and come up with a solution easily resolved through the PCV nurse pool. I'd ask Sandy for Kaopectate or antibiotics or aspirin. She would always come up with the drugs. It was part of the PCV pact.

Two PCV nurses, JoAnn and Ann, lived several houses down from me in Yebukl; and they supplied me with anything my family needed. Mechas continuously traumatized her fragile old teeth chewing betel nut. She'd ask me for pills, and I'd go down the path to JoAnn and Ann's place and get the drugs. If they didn't have them, they'd get them for me. They always kept a good supply of medical items on hand for village emergencies.

On payday when we'd get our ninety dollars; I'd buy a can of Spam and other canned delicacies like corned beef and have Melanna cook it up. JoAnn, Ann, Sandy, and sometimes Harson and Erica would bring other high priced goods over, and we'd feast on buggy bread from the local bakery, fried Spam and mustard, corned beef, fresh coconut, canned kimchi, and canned whale meat which tasted like pot roast in a sweet gravy. Melanna would sit and watch me gobble the gorp down, perhaps wondering why

I neglected to consume the standard bowl of fish and rice with the same gusto.

Filled up on canned food, we'd walk up the path and on up the main road several hundred yards to the Boom Boom Room to dance off the calories. The Boom Boom Room was built out over the edge of a cliff, similar in some respects to those tenuous looking houses built on the slopes of Hollywood Hills, with long timbers and cross braces for support. It had a wraparound bar and a step-down dance floor with a bench around the perimeter. Screen ran up and outward from the bench providing a view of the boonies down below and the roof hung far out, protecting the dance floor from rain. The jukebox sat to the side near some tables and chairs which sat in dimly lit cubicles. Like all the bars in Palau, the Boom Boom Room was decorated for Christmas all year round. The soft lighting and sparkle from flashing Christmas tree lights gave it a warm and cozy atmosphere, and it was the most popular hangout for Peace Corps volunteers and young Palauans.

A girl named Rose worked behind the bar with her sister, Pauline. They continually played songs by Hank Williams on the jukebox by manipulating the magic switch on the back. But the real theme song of the Boom Boom Room was "Hey Jude." Rose was eighteen, beautiful, and Palauan hard-bodied with perfect proportions. I spent a lot of time in the Boom Boom Room ogling over Rose, a sweet tease, and never got further than a New Year's kiss and a couple of *ma nine's* (meet you at nine), which never happened.

I was happy with my family situation. Mechas would scold me from time to time for neglecting things or doing things I shouldn't, and she worried about my skimpy eating habits. She and Melanna would tease me for being so thin. In Palau, rotundness signaled prosperity, and I failed the profile. I had lost weight, but now I was beginning to eat better. Several times each week I brought home fresh fish from the co-op, and Vini would clean them and make soup. Mechas favored *ruul* (stingray), and I bought it each time someone brought it in to the co-op.

Melanna swept my room out each day with the Palauan broom, bending over the long bundle of coconut leaf midribs, swishing it from side to side, one arm tucking her long loose dress between her legs. Every Saturday she would wash my clothes, pounding them to death in the shower room with a block of wood. When the sun burned me she would rub my back with coconut oil, scolding me in Palauan as she did so. "Oh, Patriiick. Wheee, hee hee. You have to wear a shirt," she'd say, then go on and on about how hot the sun was and how red my skin looked. She always wore a smile and I was very fond of her, the perfect little sister. Vini studied hard but his English remained appalling. Terresa was always around, chewing betel nut with Mechas, sometimes making fun of me, but most often ignoring me, although I often caught her glancing at me. She infatuated me, even as I watched her expertly spit betel nut juice six feet or more. When she worked at Kintaro's store in the evenings, I always hung around talking with her, chewing betel nut, drinking a beer or two.

Terresa's girlfriend, Kilad, lived within rock-throwing distance just across the path from my room. She was an attractive twenty-year-old with a small child, and she loved to toss stones at any dog she saw. Constantly giggling, she spoke poor English but somehow always got her meaning across speaking half and half. She was part of Mechas's clan and she knew I longed for Terresa, the forbidden fruit. "Never let Kailang catch you with her," she warned me once. Kilad was my confidante.

One of the things that Kailang and Mechas wanted me to do was to teach English to the kids at night. "Just a half hour every other night," Kailang pleaded. So finally I figured I'd give it a try. Not being an educator, I had little idea how I would teach English to a bunch of kids ranging in age from about six to fifteen years old. I decided to use the same methods and dialogues as we were taught in training, simply reversing languages. Using the Peace Corps language training manual, I would recite the word or phrase in English, they would repeat it in English. The meaning would come later.

"Hello."
"Hello, come in."
"Is Drottio here?"
"No, he's not here."
"Where did he go?"
"He went to the store."
"What store."
"Neco's store."
"Oh, thank you. I'm going now."

"Goodbye."

It worked great, and the kids loved it. They would shout out the words, eager to overpower the others, and the old shack would shake. After the first week, every kid in the neighborhood joined in, filling the room to capacity. Then the adults started coming around. They would sit next door with Mechas, Terresa, and Kilad, chewing and talking, watching their children reciting English, observing this new village event.

The kids progressed steadily and eventually got through the whole book. My Palauan improved as well. I'd ask them questions in Palauan, and they'd answer in English. But some of the kids were troublemakers. If a kid acted up, I might ask him where he lived. Then when he answered, I'd ask him if he wanted to go home, which would cause laughter among the other kids, shaming the kid into silence. Sometimes, when the kids got too rowdy I'd call off the class. Later, Melanna would come to me and apologize for everyone, making sure I'd be there for the next session. But the kids' improvements were rewarding to me, and I felt good about it. After word got around that I was teaching the kids in my village English at night, Gene started doing the same out in Meyungs and a couple of the other volunteers started similar endeavors in their villages.

Sometimes, on Friday nights, I'd bring home the Marine Resources movie projector and show one of the government films that Wilson kept stored in the office library. Something like a conservation documentary—anything at all, the kids didn't care what it was. I'd buy some beer, set the projector up in the spare room using my sheet as a screen, and every kid in the village would show up for Friday night at the movies. When the movie was finished, I'd show it backward and the kids would laugh through the whole thing. Didn't matter to the kids, backward or forward, same same. When Melisebes complained to Wilson about me taking home the projector and using it for "personal," Peter fielded his complaints by asking me to be discreet enough so Melisebes wouldn't see me taking the projector home. I obliged.

One night after showing movies I covered the projector and left it sitting in the room, still plugged in to an extension cord running from a light socket. Then I hustled up to Kintaro's store to drink a beer and serenade Terresa. Suddenly Kilad came running up the trail, yelling, "Patrriiick! The house is burning!" I bolted down the path and saw the room with the projector ablaze. Mechas and Melanna were out in front, Mechas pacing around shouting orders to Vini who was dipping water from the two fifty-five-gallon drums and throwing it on the flames. I grabbed a tin can and did the same, but it was an electrical fire and getting worse. Ignorant about the house's wiring system except that it was dangerously inadequate, I remembered a main switch in the back of the house. As I scurried around the house, I kicked the sharp edge of an open can, slicing my toe to the bone. I threw the switch, shutting off the power; now all was dark except the flaming room. A host of neighbors showed up and together we tossed enough water to put out the fire. As we stood watching the smoke, a neighbor punched the pennies out of the fuse box and talked briskly with Mechas about it. Mechas, understanding little about electrics, closed the door; and no one ever went in there again. Luckily, the projector had been in its case and suffered minimal damage. As the adrenaline wore off I discovered my foot was bleeding badly. Melanna cleaned my wound, and Mechas sternly ordered me to the hospital. I limped over to Ann's place, and she fixed me up.

My obsession over Terresa grew and grew. Sometimes she was nice and would come over and talk to me, tease me a little. Other times she would sit around talking and chewing with Mechas, completely ignoring me. Her dichotomous behavior perplexed me. When I emulated her style by ignoring her, attempting to get at her like she was getting at me, she seemed unmoved. Nothing worked. I was frustrated, pissed off.

One Saturday night, Harson came over with some beer. Across the way, Terresa and Kilad sat on Kilad's porch chewing and gossiping, and we could see them from my doorway. Later, after Mechas and Melanna had shut their window boards and gone to sleep, they came over; and we sat around in Vini's room and played *hana fuda*. Kilad asked for a beer; and Terresa, incredibly, took one as well. We gave Kilad some money, and she dispatched a young village kid to buy more at Kintaro's store. He came back with a four-dollar case of warm Kirin; and we sat around drinking, laughing, teasing, and telling jokes. More than once Mechas yelled out to us to shut up, go far, or both. Finally Kilad and Harson left.

I led a tipsy Terresa into my sleeping room and unscrewed the lightbulb, and we lay down on my mat. On my back, with the girl of my dreams finally at my side, I struggled through several seconds of hyperventilation. Sitting up, I pulled off my T-shirt and rolled over on my elbow, at the same time placing my arm across her chest just under those wonderful mammaries. She grabbed my arm, threw it back, and was up and out the back window before I could stutter, "Wait!" *It was*, as the Palauans say.

About a week later, I brought home a girl who was short and skinny. She worked at George's theater on the upper road in the concession window, and I thought she was cute. After the movie *Sanjuro*, starring Toshiro Mifune, she went with me first to the Boom Boom Room and then to my house. We went in to my sleeping room through the back window. I'd usually go in this way if I came home late rather than have to stumble over Vini and his friends sleeping in the main room.

The next morning we went out through the main room which exited in front of Mechas's house, Mechas speaking briefly to the girl as we left. When I got home from work that night Mechas started harping at me.

"Patriick, where is the tiny girl?" she said in Palauan. I smiled, accepting her ribbing, but later Kilad yelled across to me from her house, "Patriick! Where's the tiny girl?" Still later, Melanna came up to me and inquired, "Eh, Patriick. Where's tiny girl? Wheee, tee hee."

Hey, this is serious, I thought. I walked over and talked to Kilad about it. Kilad scolded me.

"You're too big and strong for that tiny girl," she said. "Mechas is disappointed in you for choosing such a tiny girl." I guessed the "tiny girl" stigma would haunt me for a while.

After the "tiny girl" episode, Terresa ignored me for two weeks. Feeling torn inside, I asked Kilad what I could do to make up with Terresa. A bit irritated, she said she didn't know but that I'd better not bring home any more "tiny girls." Later, I approached Harson about what I should do. He advised me to say to her in Palauan: "Terresa, I want you but you always ignore me. What am I to do?" I practiced this script all week, rehearsing what I would say in several possible scenarios. Harson had told me to wait until she went to bed, then knock on her window shutter and ask to talk.

One dark night, I got my courage up and sneaked over. I knocked lightly on Terresa's shutter, being quite lest I should wake up Kailang's wife and effect a scandal.

"Terresa, I want to talk to you," I squeaked in Palauan.

"Who?"

"It's me, Patrick."

"What do you want?"

"I want to talk to you."

"Where's your tiny girl? Go talk to your tiny girl." Then, in a loud whisper, she said: "Go home." But I knew what to say to that.

"*Ngak a tang* (by myself)?" I answered in Palauan. Silence. Maybe that got her. I started in with the script.

"Terresa, I want you, but you always ignore me. What am I to do?" I heard her giggle. What the hell was so funny? Embarrassed, I shut up. I was near the breaking point. Just below my inhibition threshold a very strong urge tempted me to tear off the window shutter, jump in, and embrace her, press my lips to hers, show her who I was, make her see the light. Didn't she know what she was doing to me? Of course she did. I tiptoed back down the path to my room and hit the mat, *ngak a tang*; how pathetic.

But Terresa began to speak to me again after that. My obsession with her continued on a higher level. She was a different girl than most; she rarely drank, avoided bars, and had no children. And what a specimen. But a volunteer who taught at her school also yearned for her. He sometimes came to the village on weekends to see her, and now and then he'd show up at Kintaro's store after work to talk to her, infringing on my territory. I played ho hum, as if indifferent. But it bothered me, more than I wanted to admit. I spent many, many, nights talking with Terresa, speculating on her. Now I felt she was moving closer to me.

One night, after Kailang had returned from Japan, I walked home from the store with Terresa. It was late, about 10:00 p.m., Kailang was still out somewhere, and everyone was asleep in the family complex. As we walked down the dark path, she took my hand and whispered, "Come to my room, Patriick." Her words nearly knocked me over. This was it.

She went in through the front door, quietly let me in through her bedroom shutter, and laid out her mat. I stripped quickly to my underwear and sat on the mat, watching in the darkness as she undressed. At that moment I heard the unmistakable squeaking and banging of the co-op truck as it bounced down the half-trail, half-road. It was Kailang. Echoes of Kilad's warning flooded my mind: "Don't let Kailang catch you with Terresa." He'll cut my gonads off if he does, I thought. Inside, I felt a major adrenaline spill. I jumped up and threw on my shorts, my heart pounding wildly. Sometimes when he'd been drinking he'd come home and have Terresa prepare food for him. That night was no exception. He banged on her door telling her to fix some food. I stood there in the dark, afraid to breath. Terresa whispered to me, "*Bo mo cheroid* (go far)." Carefully I pushed open the window shutter, eased myself out, and slipped quietly home. That close call scared me to death. But worse, it had undone the event I had been working so long for. Destiny, it seemed, had ruled out a score with Terresa.

CHAPTER 7

The *Emeraech*

Before the end of the year, 1967, Lee Marvin came to town. He wanted to evaluate Palau, see if it really was a suitable location for shooting the film Peter had talked to the producers about earlier that summer. His pal, Michelle, accompanied him. They stayed at the Royal Palauan Hotel.

Lee loved to fish for marlin and other large fish, and he fished in tournaments all over the world. One of Peter's selling points to Lee had been that Palau offered excellent fishing for billfish and other big game species. Strictly virgin territory, unknown to the rest of the world, he'd boasted to Marvin while in California.

Lee came prepared to go fishing, bringing along a substantial amount of gear, the best equipment money could buy. His fishing rods were custom-made Fenwicks with Fenor gold series reels. He set up shop in the smokehouse room across from the co-op and began making lures and tying up leaders. I liked to go over and help him work on his gear.

Meanwhile, Michelle hung around with Peter's wife, Ann. Together, they personified the two beautiful girls about town. Michelle, dark and attractive, cherished bikinis and suntans, so Peter would send her and Ann and the kids out to the rock islands in the afternoons accompanied by one of his employees, either Melisebes or Teruo, the captain of the *Milotk*.

Since people in Palau fished mainly with hand lines, the fisheries boats lacked rod holders, essential gear for trolling with rods and reels. Peter sent Lee out on the *Emeraech* for his first fishing trip, and the crew had to seize the rods in place by lashing them to the gunwales. Lee complained to Peter about it. Peter wanted to keep Lee happy to ensure that the Hollywood deal materialized, so he had several holders flown in from Guam on the next flight and got them mounted on the *Milotk*, a far better vessel for trolling than the seventy-eight-foot *Emeraech*. I fished with Lee whenever I could, but we never found any marlin. The catches of *mahi mahi*, yellowfin, and wahoo, however, impressed Lee. Both he and Michelle fell in love with Palau, and at the end of the week Lee mentioned to Peter that he might want Matsumoto to build a fishing boat for him at the boatyard. Peter promised to have plans drafted up when Lee returned in a few weeks to begin filming.

A couple of Peter Wilson-inspired projects were developing at Marine Resources. One project was for a baitfish survey in Truk to determine the feasibility of starting a live bait pole-and-line tuna fishery in the Eastern Carolines. The *Emeraech* would voyage to Truk and be used as a working platform to conduct the survey. The skipper, Richard Kinney, whom Peter had hired from Hawaii, had tried without success to train one of the crew members as an engineer; the islanders wanted to fish, not play mechanic. Richard was resolute about finding a competent engineer for the trip, and he told Peter as much.

The *Emeraech* was controlled in the wheelhouse by use of a buzzer system. The skipper would activate a buzzer which sounded in the engine room for various functions, such that one buzz meant more throttle, three buzzes meant reverse, and so on. The system obviated the need for remote controls in the wheelhouse. A couple of weeks before leaving for Truk, on a day Richard Kinney had stayed home, the *Emeraech* had come in from fishing late in the evening. As the boat approached the Van Camp dock to unload, the man in the engine room inexplicably got his signals crossed, shifting into forward (instead of reverse), and giving throttle (instead of throttling back). Jack Adams, a jack-of-all-trades who often helped out Peter by troubleshooting the *Emeraech's* big Caterpillar diesel, happened to be standing on the dock. Realizing the boat had increased speed and would crash head-on into the wharf, he grabbed a wooden pallet and threw it in front of the bow an instant before the boat made contact with the dock. The impact disintegrated the pallet, knocked Jack to the cement, and lodged a foot-long splinter deep in his shoulder. Aboard the *Emeraech*, Amaram, at the helm, flew forward into the five-foot diameter wheel, knocking out several teeth and breaking his nose. The crewman standing by on the bow grabbed the Samson post just before impact, saving himself from flying overboard onto the dock. Several crew members standing on the stern flew forward and tumbled onto the deck, while another crewman flew into a bait well. The boat suffered moderate damage in the stem above the waterline, and the engine jarred out of alignment, all of which laid the *Emeraech* up for a week.

Peter wanted Jack Adams to attend the *Emeraech* to Truk as engineer, but Jack had an aversion toward salt water. "I'd really like to go," he said, when Peter asked, "but I can't stomach the bloody ocean." I suggested to Peter that he bring Norman over from Truk to crew as engineer. Norman, the wizard, knew all about diesels and boats and seamanship. "He can do it, no problem," I told Pete.

The following week, Norman arrived to begin his new duties. Happy to be out of Truk, he explained: "Truk is the anal orifice of Micronesia." He looked thin, having lost weight since training. Norman had two brothers, both of whom had dark hair and dark complexions. Norman, with his light skin and blue eyes, was, like me, unsuited for the tropics. But like me, he preferred to run around wearing only shorts or a loincloth. Except for protection from the sun, clothes were unnecessary in the tropics, the weather being oppressively hot and humid. In those days few sunscreens were available, and suntan lotions offered little protection from ultraviolet. Too young and heedless to care about skin cancer, we lived with sunburn. Today, I'm paying for that careless naïveté; skin cancer is as real as baldness.

After the boatyard repaired the *Emeraech*, it began fishing again. Norman worked as engineer and I often went out as crew. It was on the *Emeraech* that I learned to eat sashimi Kapingamarangan style. From the first school of the day, crewman

Steven always took several skipjack, gutted them, and hung them up by their tails from the cabin overhang, usually until late afternoon; long enough for bacteria to partially break down the flesh. The fish were not rotten, but rotting. I grew to like sashimi prepared this way—rotting, but not rotten.

From a nutritional standpoint, the diet on the *Emeraech* was superb. About once a month, Tosh bought fresh vegetables for the boat. The crew utilized these in fish soup, but they lasted only two or three days. The boat had a stainless steel barbecue built into the gunwale lockers for cooking. Breakfast consisted of hot fish soup and hot rice. Cold rice, cold fish soup, and fresh sashimi constituted lunch. And dinner—a hot pot of new fish soup, hot rice, and fresh sashimi or sashimi Kapinga style. Soy sauce provided flavoring, and the boat never left the dock without it.

For snacks, the *Emeraech* crew ate fish hearts. Thomas, a Kapingamarangan, shocked me the first time I watched him cradle a just caught still-fluttering skipjack under one arm, jam his fingers through the connective tissue of the gills, and pull out the heart. The heart pumped on as he popped it into his mouth like a bing cherry. I relished sashimi heart, but ripping hearts out of live fish bothered me. I tore my hearts out of dead fish.

At the co-op one evening as I sat sweating over the day's receipts attempting to find some missing cash, I looked up and saw the *Emeraech* ease around the corner and slide up to Van Camp across the bay. I'd been crunching numbers for two hours, and the beautiful lines of the sleek fishing boat emphasized by the brightness of the dock lights stole my attention. "Screw it," I said to no one in particular and closed the ledger. Masahiro, standing on the dock trying to hook some cruising jacks with a hand line, looked over at me.

"What, *ollei*?" he inquired.

"Tell Kailang I can't find the error and that I've gone fishing. See ya."

Masahiro, leaning on his short leg as if he might topple into the water, shook his head in mock disgust and jerked his line as he got a hit. I walked out to the road and over to Van Camp just as the crew off-loaded the last ton of tuna. It had been a good day, ten tons, including some big yellowfin. I jumped aboard and talked story with Steven while the others washed up in the open air shower stall down at the end of the wharf. Soon Deisen eased the *Emeraech* off the dock, slowly fished-tailed around and headed her toward Malakal Channel. At the black marker he turned northwest around the sea wall and headed through the west pass, turning hard west around a rock island and on to the sheltered baiting grounds deep within the confines of the rock islands several miles away.

The journey took thirty minutes and when we tied up to the mooring buoy it was 9:30 p.m. Off the port side the crew hurriedly pushed out a long bamboo pole with a super powerful lightbulb affixed to the end to attract small anchovies. Norman shut down the big Caterpillar, leaving only the low droning of the generator to disturb the stillness of the cool night air. The water lay placid, and after only several minutes the telltale flashing of anchovies could be seen around the submerged bait light.

Several hundred meters to the south a Van Camp boat lay moored, its bait light casting an eerie greenish glow beneath the surface. Steven and Thomas, clad in red *thus*, sat on the starboard gunwale dropping hand lines baited with cut tuna. They tugged in snappers one after the other. This would be breakfast, snapper and hot rice. I yawned twice, then hit an empty bunk down above the engine room stairs. Norman, in a *thu* of his own design, worked on the big Caterpillar down in the heat of the engine room. I felt glad I didn't have to do that as I fell into a sleep.

Around midnight, Norman shook me awake.

"Get up Pat, we have to pull net."

I dreaded this, too much like work, but jumped up and rubbed my eyes. Out on deck, the crew was already busy pulling the huge bait net down from the platform behind the bridge and stacking it into the skiff tied alongside the port side. Norm and I stepped out on deck and looked overboard at the gigantic school of anchovies circling the light several meters under the water.

Deisen, watching from up on the bridge, yelled down to Norman, "Okay, dim light and pull in little bit."

Norman ran into the engine room and turned the rheostat to the halfway mark while I untied the bamboo and helped slide the pole across the deck, bringing the light several meters closer to the *Emeraech*'s port side. From the stern of the *Emeraech*, three crewmen rowed the skiff out, slipping the net overboard in a vast arc around the light and bringing the skiff up alongside the forward port side of the *Emeraech*. From the stern came loud grunts as pulling began. I jumped up to the bow and with several other crewmen began pulling the 3/4-inch nylon rope which would bring the heavily weighted bottom of the net under the school and up to the gunwale. Wisps of salt water flew into my face and chest and tiny medusae stung my arms as my hands slipped up the heavy rope after each tug. Heave, slip; Heave, slip. "Uhh, slirrp; uhh, slirrp." It took forever, and I was almost ready to collapse when the lead line finally clunked into the port side. Now the light was pulled in close and Deisen and Tengadink, the bait man, carefully pulled the netting up over the gunwale, forming a nice deep pocket alongside. From the bridge, bright deck lights suddenly illuminated the fishy business taking place on the spacious back deck. Tengadink grabbed a long handled dip net and dipped out several large jacks before they could damage the bait. The jacks thumped on the deck as they flopped around. They would later be sold to the co-op along with the excess bottom fish caught during the night. Someone handed Deisen a large stainless steel bucket and he began dipping out anchovies, the buckets of bait passed along by a line of crewmen and carefully poured into the four bait wells. The baitfish represented the most important asset to these fishermen, for without live bait there would be no catch. The haul produced ninety buckets.

"We go again in two hours," Deisen said. We pulled the net aboard, then stacked it into the skiff, ready for the next set. Tengadink swooned over the bait wells, dipping out dead baitfish and tossing them overboard. Norman cranked up the light, and the crew set it back out off the port side again to attract more anchovies. Then the deck lights perished, leaving only the glow of the bait light far out in the water. Soon the crew disappeared into dark cubicles for two hours of shuteye. The generator purred on in the dark, producing its own sort of quietness.

We pulled net three times that night, producing full bait wells. We had just finished the last set and dawn was breaking as Norman fired up the Cat. I looked overboard and saw fish breaking on the dead anchovies flowing out the bait well overflows. Scampering to the side of the cabin, I grabbed my pole just as the *Emeraech* began moving slow ahead on its journey out to sea. Quickly I whipped the lure into the water and jerked out a nice *kawakawa* (inshore tuna), leaving it fluttering on deck. Norman, standing on the engine room ladder and looking out the back of the cabin, yelled out, "*kawakawa!*" which sent Thomas and Tengadink scurrying to get their poles. Now the boat was idling along and we could see the mooring buoy and skiff fading into the grayness off the stern. The three of us poled *kawakawa* as fast as we could, landing about 150 fish. These would also be sold to the co-op as Van Camp would not take this species. Thomas took two nice ten pounders, gutted them, and hung them by their tails under the cabin overhang for afternoon sashimi. Then Deisen signaled Norman to throttle up so we could escape the confines of the lagoon and get out to sea, to the real action, the early morning schools of skipjack.

I hiked up the ladder to the bridge and walked into the wheelhouse where Deisen stood, his muscled arms outstretched to the huge wheel.

"We go west side, out Uchlong. Tide high and good for *kine* passage," he said. Then chuckling, he commented, "Peter not like us go this way, but high tide okay. Only watch out for coral heads"—he laughed—"*bom-by* no more *Emeraech*."

"Yeah," I said, "big hole in bottom, *bom-by*, ha ha."

Uchlong referred to the island off our starboard quarter and there was no passage, only a great expanse of sand, coral heads, and blue water stretching out to the west barrier reef. I watched the big corals slip by our bow as Deisen cranked the wheel back and forth. Occasionally a big fish or shark would dash away from the bow's entrance while smaller, blue, green, red, black, and white coral-associated fish would streak inward to the shelter of the corals. We entered a narrow natural pass through the reef on the north side of a small sand spit which sported one small coconut sprout some three feet high. As we reached the ocean side, the big boat sliced into the incoming swell, sinking deeply, then rising over the next swell, in a sweet loftiness indicative of the excitement of things to come, of fishing on the high seas.

About a mile out we swung southwest and headed in the direction of a floating log off of Peleliu which had yielded the great catches of the past few days. The crew had been able to find it over a series of days and if we could locate it again, we would load up because tons of tuna were associated with it, tunas being attracted to floating objects. Thomas, Steven, and Moko came up and stood on the platform in front of the wheelhouse, their elbows resting on the railing while they squinted into the horizon searching for seabirds; the seabirds picking baitfish off the surface as the tuna worked the bait from underneath. Thomas searched intently through a huge pair of ten power binoculars which Peter had conned from the U.S. Coast Guard. The islanders, with their marvelous eyes, could spot birds from miles away. Moko, a short, stocky Palauan with shining white teeth, was missing a large portion of one ear.

"Hey Moko," I said while leaning my chest onto the railing, "why your ear like that?"

Moko had interned in Hawaii for several years, fishing on one of the boats out of Kewalo Basin in Honolulu. He proceeded to tell me the story of how he had lost his ear to rookies fishing next to him in Hawaii, their lures hooking his ear and ripping part of it off. Thomas, on the other side of him, howled.

"No good," Thomas joked. "You see the *kine*? It's bite."

The outline of Moko's ear did appear strangely bitelike.

"Big *waihinee* bite it for lunch once when Moko make french style, ha ha, hee ha," Thomas chided, bringing Steven into the grinning mode.

Moko looked at me and laughed sheepishly, the bright sun above his head making his face look super black and his teeth look super white.

"She not like this," he said sticking his tongue out and moving it side to side. "Honolulu *waihinee* very tough. No can take joke. Bite off ear. Hurt good."

He laughed gleefully as did all of us, causing Deisen to wrap his knuckle on the wheelhouse window in a gesture for us to get back to the important business of spotting birds. When it came to fishing, Deisen was very serious.

The seas picked up and the *Emeraech* plowed on, her fine bow slicing into each swell, rising over, then dropping into the trough, rock and roll. The sun glared down from the east and the brisk fifteen knot morning wind whisked up white water, dispersing it over the bow in fine spray. Keeping my legs apart and my hand on the rail to keep from being thrown overboard from the violent lurches, I waddled over to the ladder, then eased down to the gunwale and slid out my bamboo pole from the rack alongside the cabin. The squid lure, a short piece of chromed lead engulfing a barbless hook much like a bent nail and skirted with white and red feathers, was old and rusty having not been used since my last trip. I garnered a new one from the lure box in the cabin, tied it on to the monofilament leader, then put the pole back into the rack and slipped out a shorter one that would be used for bigger tunas, like yellowfin. The squid looked fine so I slid the pole back in. Just then the buzzer went off, a loud noise that told those down on deck and in the bunk room that a school had been sighted and to prepare for fishing. Norman stuck his big spectacled head up from the engine room.

"Got fish?" he asked.

The buzzer sounded again, two short raps which meant throttle up, sending Norman hurrying down to goose the big Cat. Sleepy-eyed crew members appeared from the cabin donning their pads, the pad a square piece of thick rubber which hung in front of the groin from a heavily weaved cloth belt, protection against the butt of the bamboo pole when fishing. Tengadink, the bait man, stood alongside the port forward bait well, his dip net in one hand, his other hand steadying himself by holding on to the long handle of another dip net lodged between the deck and the gunwale. He stared forward into the assaulting spray, his gray hair streaked back, waiting for Deisen's signal to begin throwing bait. The crew took their places on the platform off the stern of the vessel, Thomas and Steven, as seniors, taking the corners where the action was always hottest. Taking advantage of the islander's good-naturedness, I squeezed in next to Steven where I knew fishing would be good, rather than in the middle position where by rights I belonged since I was a rookie. I wore wraparound sunglasses which immediately blotched from the spray. However I kept them on, afraid of getting hit in the eye by the whipping lures. In contrast to the Okinawans who wore full protective clothing, much like judo outfits, and jungle helmets to protect themselves, those of us on the *Emeraech* wore only shorts or *thus*.

The boat slowed to half speed and Deisen appeared on the net deck behind the cabin. He threw out his arm, signaling

Tengadink to throw bait. Tengadink scooped out bait with his net and threw handfuls over the port gunwale, setting up a trail of anchovies behind the boat. In the distance skipjack began jumping, following the line of live anchovies. Norman threw the switch starting the spray system which shot streams of water out from tiny nozzles stationed on a pipe beneath the platform, the streams splashing onto the surface several meters out from the stern. The spray enticed the fish to bite, or shielded us from view, or whatever. Only a fish would know what that spray did. But in the tropics, spray was necessary for successful live bait pole-and-line fishing.

Now we could see the blue streaks of skipjack under the water as they darted here and there, feasting on the anchovies. We whipped our squids into the water and jerked them back and forth. To my right, I saw Steven's pole bend down. His legs bent slightly as he pulled a twelve-pound skipjack up through the surface, cocked the bamboo as the fish sailed by his head, then whipped the lure back into the water, leaving the lonely skipjack pounding on the deck in a desperate attempt to swim. Soon more landed, increasing the pounding, the thumping, the cadence of fish death. A fish grabbed my squid, bending my pole toward the water. It hit with such force I nearly went overboard. I bent my legs and lifted my pole. The bamboo bent radically, then slowly lifted the tuna from the water. It flew to my left side and I eased up, allowing the fish to slip off the hook and land on the deck. Then I whipped the lure back into the water where another fish immediately hit it.

Now the tuna bit "wide open" and fish were flying everywhere. Few words were spoken and in my peripheral vision I could see fishermen swaying back and forth, dodging hooks and fish. It hurt to get pinged by a lead squid, impaled by a hook, whacked by a pole, smacked by a twelve-pound skipjack. In a matter of minutes two tons of tuna lay fluttering on deck, their muscles generating intense heat from the high-frequency contractions. Tunas are the only fish in the sea which operate at higher temperatures than the surrounding sea water and when they die struggling, they quickly heat up. I pulled up on my pole, letting the lure dangle above the surface to rest my aching back while the others smacked the water with their squids, trying to entice the fish to bite again. The boat drifted downwind, the big swells rolling in under our platform, sending us high into the air. We bent our legs as we settled into the trough. The next swell broke over the platform, flooding us in knee deep water.

"No more," Steven said about the fish.

"They go somewhere else," Thomas said.

From behind the bridge, Deisen yelled down: "Pack! Pack!"

We laid our poles along the gunwales and began throwing fish into the empty bait well where the circulating sea water would keep the fish cool. Norman came up from the engine room and knocked out the big scupper plugs, sending streams of fish blood into the ocean.

"Don't wash the deck," he said, "log up ahead."

He attached a block to eyes in both gunwales and threaded 5/8-inch manila rope through them. Then he opened up the rudder house on the deck, fitted a long handle over the stud, and attached the rope to the blocks on the handle. Now Deisen would be able to steer the *Emeraech* from the stern. Norman ran up to the engine room, as Deisen took his place and gathered up the rope. The vessel eased slowly ahead, and Tengadink began throwing bait as we eased by the log. Off to starboard, two Van Camp boats steamed toward us.

On the platform again, I could see huge brown fish streaking here and there. Then a school of rainbow runner darted out from the log, and we poled them. Next, *mahi mahi* hit our lures, whipping back and forth in wild gyrations as they flew through the air. Suddenly my pole jerked down into the water nearly sending me in head first. "Holy mother!" was all I could say. I heard Moko yell for a gaff. My line broke and so did Steven's.

"Big fish, need short pole," he yelled.

Everyone hustled to get heavy gear. Moko ran around with the gaff. As soon as someone would pull a fish's head up he would gaff it and haul it aboard. Soon the deck was covered with fifty—and sixty-pound yellowfin among all the other smaller fish. Now and then a shark would grab a lure, usually cutting through the leader, sending someone swearing to the lure box for another squid. The action was so incredibly swift that fish would hit instantaneously when the squid hit the water. You might bring up a twelve-pound skipjack, get hung up with a hundred-pound yellowfin, or get ripped off by a rogue shark. It was hard, furious work, and incredibly fun.

We'd been poling for about thirty minutes around the log when the Van Camp boats showed up. They eased by the log throwing bait, and suddenly our fish disappeared. Moko yelled some Palauan obscenities at them and gestured with his middle finger.

"Okay, pack now. We get later," Deisen said.

The deck held so many fish that every now and then a good roll in the rough seas would send one sliding overboard. Tengadink busied himself with transferring the remaining bait into the other wells as we loaded the fish into the empty bait well. Again Norman ran out and knocked out the plugs, turning the ocean a dark green around the boat. This time he turned on the pump and washed down the slimy deck with a four-inch stream of sea water so Deisen could have better footing.

We had drifted away from the log and about one hundred meters off our stern the Okinawans were poling tuna onto the sampans. The Van Camp boats fished differently than the *Emeraech*. The seventy-foot sampans had high bows and crew fished both off the stern and bow, those on the bow a good eight feet above the water. We watched them pole, swearing at them for taking our fish. Van Camp had just rotated crews, and these men were new, having just come out from Okinawa. They were unprepared for yellowfin. Moko pointed as a big fish pulled a man off the bow of one boat and then, almost immediately, another man flew off the other vessel. Standing on the platform of the *Emeraech*, we laughed at the spectacle. The first fisherman swam hurriedly to the stern, and the crew pulled him aboard.

The other man, however, thrashed around wildly; he appeared unable to grab a rope his crewmen had thrown to him. Then we saw telltale brown fins break the surface near the man. *Sharks.* Seconds before we had enjoyed a comedy; now the show had turned tragic. Deisen ran to the bridge and yelled at us to stand by. Then he began backing the *Emeraech* down toward the other boat, trying to close in so we could grab the distressed Okinawan. The stern plowed into the seas, almost washing us from the platform. Realizing he could not back down safely, Deisen swung the boat around bow first and pulled in downwind of the Van Camp boats near the panicked Okinawan. As we coasted by,

Thomas heaved a rope and life ring which landed close to the man. He struggled over, grabbed it, and we pulled him to our stern. Thomas reached down, grasped the back of his garment, and hauled him aboard while sharks zoomed in and out through the blood-green water.

The man lay white with shock, his shredded foot and ankle bleeding profusely onto the deck. He would soon bleed to death. I had taken all those Red Cross first aid and life-saving courses—now I could recall only a few things. Bleeding and shock: stop the blood flow, keep him warm; apply pressure, maybe a tourniquet. Watch his breathing, keep his mouth clear. From the wheelhouse, someone brought down the Peace Corps medical kit I'd donated to the *Emeraech* months previous. I shuffled through the already cockroached container finding little of use for this injury. We placed the Okinawan in a bunk, wrapped his wounds tightly with a shredded towel, elevated his feet to retard bleeding, and covered him with a blanket. Then we called Koror Communications on marine band and steamed home. He lived.

—

Peter's other project concerned crocodiles. In many Babeldaob villages, each day kids walked several miles to and from school through mangrove swamps; and the children increasingly sighted crocodiles. In response to the growing fear by Babeldaob villagers that sooner or later a child would be attacked by a crocodile, Wilson contacted a group of professional Australian crocodile hunters who sold the skins for profit. The Aussies expressed interest in coming to Palau to harvest the animals and train Palauans in their methods if a survey indicated commercial quantities. Thus, Peter planned a two-night survey covering Babeldaob and Koror, as well as the rock islands and Peleliu to the south. He called on village resident Peace Corps volunteers to organize the surveys and conduct the counts in each village. One survey would be conducted during dark moon, the other during full moon. As incentive, Peter gave participants a four-cell flashlight which they were allowed to keep after the surveys. When a light is shown on a crocodile, the eyes show up like two glowing bright-red coals on the surface of the water.

Peter charged fisheries volunteer Dave Imes, who lived with his wife in Chol on the northeast coast of Babeldaob, with coordinating the Babeldaob surveys. I organized the surveys for the Koror and Airai areas. Teruo took care of the rock islands, and the Peleliu PCV took care of the Peleliu area. Excellent weather helped the dark moon surveys produce good results.

Later in the month, however, the full moon count proved more difficult when a tropical depression produced high winds and rain. On the north side of Koror, Harson and I, in the thirty-foot fisheries boat, *Ngermeyaus*, grounded on a patch reef for four hours during low tide but saw a number of crocodiles.

When morning came, up on the west coast of Babeldaob, Dave had lost a PCV along with his Palauan partner from the village of Ngatpang. They had taken a boat up the Gabatouru River and had not returned. Wilson dispatched Melisebes to search for them, but before he got up there the pair had already walked back to the village. During the night, in a driving rain, they had hit a submerged log which sunk their boat. They counted numerous crocodiles in the river, several as they walked out.

The surveys verified that crocodiles were indeed abundant. The dark-moon survey yielded a count of over 200 crocs and the full moon survey counted 160. Several months later, the Australians arrived and began their assault on the animals. Peter recruited a Palauan guide to work with them and learn the trade. They camped in the villages, at night moving in a boat along the mangroves shining a bright spotlight. When they sighted a croc, they shot it between the eyes with a .30-06, rushing over to recover the animal before it sank. At dawn, they skinned the reptiles, salted the pelts, then packed them in boxes for shipment to the orient. They found interesting items in the guts—watches, beer cans, clothing, fish hooks, lead, line, and bottles; and turtles, birds, crabs, and baby crocs. During those first months, the hunters averaged five crocs a night, some of the animals reaching thirteen feet in length. The Aussies hunted in Palau for a year, harvesting over five hundred crocodiles.

Lots of small crocodiles lived in the strand vegetation on the secluded beaches of the rock islands. Out fishing one time in the fisheries runabout with my friend Becky Madraisau who worked at Marine Resources, and Bob Moncrief from the Bureau of Commercial Fisheries, we happened upon a small croc about four feet long sunning itself on a beach. Startled, it scrambled off the beach into the water and sank to the bottom. In the boat, we ran circles around it until it swam up for air. Just as its eyes broke the surface, Becky whacked it hard over the head with a paddle causing it to roll over as if dead. Moncrief, a big strong fellow, grabbed the croc by the tail and flipped it into the boat. The beast hit the bilge with a decisive *thud*, then snarled to life, forcing us to jump up on the foredeck to escape. Standing up on all fours, its stomach off the floor, the croc hissed and snapped at us. Now it owned the boat, and it seemed content to wait us out. Our options—either repossess our ship or swim. Finally, Becky took the bowline and coaxed a rope around its neck. With the help of the paddle, we wrapped the hissing reptile up and tied its jaws shut. We took it back with us and it became the fisheries pet, living in a cage next to Peter's office. Perpetually pissed off, it continually hissed at any human. We fed it fish, mostly.

—

I ate my heart out watching the crew load up the *Emeraech* in preparation for the trip to Truk. I wanted to go, but with Kailang away in Japan, I had to stay back and run the co-op ship. The day before leaving, as the crew loaded ice at Van Camp, skipper Richard Kinney spotted an old Briggs & Stratton gasoline-powered pump sitting on the dock. He needled Peter to borrow the pump from Van Camp for the voyage.

"We just might need something like that," Richard told Peter.

The pump came aboard. Kinney, an old time bait-boat captain from Hawaii, could navigate by dead reckoning but not by sun or stars. So Peter asked an Air Micronesia copilot named Rudi Nemi to go along as navigator. Rudi, an avid sailor as well as pilot, agreed. This put Richard Kinney at the helm, Rudi on the sextant, and Norman in the engine room. At the last minute, Peter decided to accompany the boat as far as Yap.

The night before the *Emeraech* departed, Norman, Deisen, Amaram, Thomas, and I went barhopping. We started at T-Dock and walked from one bar to another. A beer shortage plagued the island and only a few bars had beer, the inflated price prompting

Norman and I to drink rum. Palau (and other Micronesian islands as well) consistently lingered in some shortage crisis, either rice, beer, or cigarettes. I always suspected shortages as being conspired by devious island merchants, for once the price of the shortaged article increased, it never returned to what it had been before, even after the ship came in.

During the sojourn that night, Thomas and I separated from the others, ending up in a lower road bar called the Smiling Café. The bar sat perched on the edge of a hill, the hill sloping down into the mangroves where several residences and businesses, including the Smiling Café, had tossed their garbage over the years. Thomas and I sat down at a table to the rear. After the waitress brought us our drinks, a rock flew through the door and beaned Thomas on the head. Then several more stones sizzled in. We hit the deck under the table and peeked out. I saw several Palauans standing outside the door pitching stones, apparently intimidated by big Thomas. The waitress yelled at us to flee out the back door. Thomas jumped up and kicked the door with his oversized foot, knocking it off its hinges. As rocks thudded into the wall, we ran out and sprinted over the edge, tumbling and rolling down the slope into the garbage dump. Clambering across the slope, we lost our zorries to the soft muddy hillside, and our feet got butchered by cans, glass, and garbage. We hastened up to the lower road behind Ichie's Theater, made our way up to Yebukl, and slept on the floor in Vini's room.

In the morning, the plywood floor was stained red with dried blood from our cut feet. Thomas had a large gash over one ear from the rock. Melanna cleaned our wounds and washed our feet, scolding me as she did: *"Mekngit* Pateriiick! Wheeee." Vini gaped at Thomas, the giant.

We drank coffee, then hurried up to the road and grabbed a taxi to fisheries, Thomas jumping on the *Emeraech* just before it got underway. As Kinney eased the boat away from the dock, Peter stood on the afterdeck shouting orders to me.

"You clowns just made it didn't you! How 'bout doing some work while I'm gone!"

Norman's white hair popped up from the engine room entrance. He grinned and indicated by sign language that Peter was full of flatulence. I looked down at my bare feet and kicked the flies off. More infections. Need zorries.

They were halfway to Yap when the generator overheated. Impossible to run it more than twenty minutes at a time, the situation put the *Emeraech* at considerable risk without lights and electronics. Norman diagnosed the problem as a blown head gasket; however, they made Yap without much difficulty. But repair work in Yap set the trip back about four days, and Rudi had to report to work, which would leave the *Emeraech* without a navigator. So Rudi put Norman through a three-hour crash course in navigation, including celestial recognition and sextant sighting. With this, Norman became engineer-navigator, and Rudi flew off to Guam. Peter, as usual in a hurry, flew off to Truk.

Between Yap and Truk are the Central Carolines, an immense area of ocean dotted with atolls. Richard's plan called for island hopping from atoll to atoll, traveling at night, making about one hundred miles each night and hitting designated atolls at first light. In this way, if they missed an atoll, they would have the entire day to find it.

Shortly after leaving Yap, the *Emeraech* developed fuel trouble, causing them to lie to for a full day while Norman worked on the problem. That evening, before they got underway again, Norm took a sextant sighting and got a loran-A fix. Later that night, as they motored along, Norman and Deisen lay sleeping on the bait net out behind the wheelhouse on the upper deck. The moon was dark, and Tengadink, the old Palauan bait man, stood watch on the wheel. Norman woke up to check the engine room, peered out toward the bow and saw a squall line, dead ahead.

He yelled to Deisen: "Deisen, wake up. Rain coming."

Deisen sat up and peered ahead. "Rain? That's an island!"

He charged into the house, grabbed the wheel from Tengadink, and cranked it hard to starboard. Heavy rain fell, but as the boat came about, they saw the tops of coconut trees lining the beach. When Norman got another loran fix, they were more than twenty miles off course. They had nearly put the *Emeraech* on the reef of some obscure Central Caroline atoll.

They spent the day on West Fayu with the *Emeraech* sitting bow first on a beach of a small island, her bow line tied to a coconut tree. Norman dove and photographed a Japanese Zero lying in thirty feet of water directly beneath the stern of the boat.

That evening, as they motored slowly out of West Fayu lagoon, the *Emeraech* hit bottom, slightly bumping off a patch reef hidden in the sun's glare. The hit produced a noticeable jar, but Norman found no apparent damage.

On the last leg into Truk, about midnight while plowing through heavy seas, Norman went down to check on the engine and discovered the bilge filling with water. He turned on the two bilge pumps but by two in the morning, the engine room floorboards were floating. Norman roused the crew and had them form a bucket brigade from the deck down into the engine room and commence bailing. Then he went to work on the old Briggs & Stratton Peter had borrowed from Van Camp, but it refused to fire up. After two hours, he gave up. The crew, dead tired now, was almost keeping up with it. Norman started up the generator, and Richard radioed Truk of their predicament.

On Truk, Peter got the news early that morning. With the help of some Public Works employees, he loaded a P-250 pump on the Public Works' thirty-six footer and headed out to meet the *Emeraech*. At sunup, several miles outside the pass in heavy seas, the thirty-six footer came alongside the *Emeraech*; the *Emeraech* riding bow down in the water, lurching and pounding through the twelve-foot seas. The water was too rough to transfer the pump over, but somehow Peter managed to jump aboard. On the *Emeraech*, drenched by salt spray, Peter assessed the scene—the crew bailing furiously, the Briggs & Stratton sitting on the deck, dead; water coming through the scuppers, the deck awash. He scrambled up the ladder to the bridge as the lurching boat pounded through the seas, sending water and spray over the wheelhouse.

"What's wrong with the pump?" he asked Richard.

"They couldn't get it going," he answered.

"Are they keeping up with it?"

"I don't think so. She's getting more sluggish every minute."

"Shit!" Peter barked, taking the wheel from Richard. Feeling his pride and joy sinking, he yelled out in desperation, "Richard, go down and try that pump again."

The boat lurched and bucked like a crazed stallion, the movement amplified up on the bridge. Richard carefully backpedaled down the ladder to the pump on the deck. Between lurches, he pulled again and again on the starter cord. Nothing.

"Son of a bitch!" he yelled.

Frustrated, he kicked the old engine, knocking the air cleaner off the carburetor; then, as an afterthought, he gave it one last feeble yank. *Putt, putt, puttputtputt* . . . The engine sputtered to life. The old Briggs & Stratton pumped two hundred gallons of bilge water each minute and saved the *Emeraech* from sinking.

When they finally reached the dock at Moen, Norman dove under the hull and found a hollowed shaft alley. When they had hit bottom on West Fayu, the shaft had shifted and the oakum under the shaft alley had worked out, allowing water to flow in. Diving with SCUBA, Norman quickly fixed the problem.

Near the end of the baitfish survey, bad weather encroached on Truk. Typhoons usually originate east of the Carolines, in the Marshall Islands. The storms generally move westward, building strength, then either continue on their westward course into the Carolines or veer northward up through the Marianas chain. This one continued to the west and bludgeoned Truk.

It was Friday night, and the *Emeraech* lay tied alongside the Moen dock. A mild wind blew, but its velocity was increasing. The wind shifted from off the starboard stern to off the port bow, causing waves to pound the boat against the dock. Richard sat up at the Truk Club having a few drinks, unaware of the hostile weather building up outside. By the time the crew fetched him, the boat had already torn off the weather stripping along the starboard side. The fierce wind gave Richard problems maneuvering the boat away from the dock and when he finally got her away, the ship had pounded a hole in the hull above the waterline in the forward starboard section.

Richard took the boat around Moen and down the lagoon behind Udot where he anchored in the lee of a small island for two days while the storm passed. After the crew patched up the *Emeraech*, they journeyed back to Palau without incident.

—

Kailang returned from Japan full of stories about carousing, Pachinko, and Japanese ladies. I felt relief at having Kailang back—it meant I could phase out of the co-op. The six months I had been manager while Kailang was away had exhausted me. I was sick and tired of the co-op and all its problems.

I'd bought a new Toyota pickup for the co-op after the bed on the Mitsubishi had disengaged from the frame. Kailang liked that; it saved *him* from having to request a new one from the Board of Directors. Kailang quickly rehired Mitsuo. I started spending less time with the co-op and more time in the dive shop and out fishing and diving where I wanted to be.

After the Truk survey, Norman stayed on in Palau to train an engineer to replace him. Meanwhile, Richard Kinney's contract expired and Peter threw a weekend going-away party for him out in the rock islands on a beach called Ngeril. Norman and I and the rest of the *Emeraech* crew took out the *Milotk* with the bait skiff in tow. Peter, Ann, Tosh, and Richard came out in Peter's boat. Peter brought along a large gill net to catch lobster. That evening, from a beach across from our island, we stretched the net out and down into the channel and left it to soak overnight.

The next morning, we took the *Milotk* across the way to pull the net. Current had fouled the net on several large coral heads down deep in the channel, so Norman and I threw on tanks and dove down to have a look. We could hardly believe our eyes. The net stretched down into the channel about fifty feet deep and was full of gilled sharks, some of them seven and eight footers and many still alive and struggling. As we worked the net free from coral heads, several sharks rolled themselves free, then swam around weirdly from anoxia (sharks must continuously swim to oxygenate their gills). Their freeloading groupies, the remoras, abandoned their dead and dying hosts, looking for new homes. Remoras, having evolved the dorsal fin into an efficient sucker disk on the top of their heads, hitch free rides on sharks, turtles, big fish, and mammals. As we worked, the remoras swam around aggressively like mosquitoes, attempting to attach to our legs, stomachs, backs, or faces. I found few things more unnerving than having a fat remora suck onto my body. I poked at them with my spear gun, then speared them in self-defense. Norman worked on the net, unconcerned. After we got back into the boat, Deisen pulled three remoras off Norman's back and one off my tank. Then Norman stomped around the deck showing off a six-inch remora hanging off his stomach, just above his belly button.

We pulled the net and took it back to our island where we cleared it of sharks and fish. The net had snagged twenty-five sharks and two huge, half-eaten barracudas, but zero lobster. Richard loved lobster but had never eaten it since coming to Palau. Peter had counted on having a net full of lobsters so Richard could gorge himself into a euphoric bliss.

After dumping the ton of sharks into the channel, Deisen, Amaram, Steven, Norman, and I took the skiff out through a passage to Kasao Reef several miles away. We speared fish and collected six lobsters, returning to the skiff with our catch in late afternoon. In the boat all set to go, Steven yanked on the mercury's starter rope. He yanked it again, and again. We took turns yanking the rope. Norman checked for fuel, then checked for spark, finding none. Dead engine.

We waited, passing the time in the water bringing up tridacnid clams to crunch on. We kept searching the corners of the reef but saw no one. The sun started its descent, falling from the sky as it does only in the tropics. We finally heard the faint sounds of a boat far off in the distance, but the white water on the reef prevented us from seeing it. Norman tied a shirt on top of a spear gun, stood up, and waved it back and forth. The light was fading fast and just before dark, Tosh and Peter came chugging around the reef point in the *Milotk*. On the way in, Peter harped at us for neglecting to file a float plan. But Richard feasted on lobster, and we felt lucky as we relaxed on the beach and drank beer.

Sunday afternoon we went back to Koror. After unloading the *Milotk*, Norman and I bought a case of Kirin at the Van Camp store for five bucks, then went over to the *Emeraech* to sip warm beer and talk story. About 7:00 p.m., a car drove up to the dock and four Palauans got out. They'd been drinking. The *Emeraech*, tied up stern first to the dock, had a 2 x 12 timber as a gangplank. At low tide, the plank oriented steeply to the deck below, making boarding a perilous task, even if one was sober. Low tide now, the Palauans wanted to come aboard. As they hunched over and eased their way down the plank, one of them slipped and fell in. Several crewmen fished him out, but soon after he accused the crew of causing his fall. The unrelenting accusations prompted Deisen to tell them to leave. When they refused, Deisen threw one man overboard and the rest of them scrambled up the plank. Before driving off, they threw rocks and bottles, breaking a cabin window. The *Emeraech* served as home to the Kapingamarangan and Nukuoroan crewmen whose islands lay some 1,300 miles to the east of Palau. They had no family in Palau, and no relatives other than Tosh Paulis. Some Palauans considered the *Emeraech* as open house, an unfortunate situation for the crew.

—

Peter owned an old 1944 jeep which Richard used to get around in. The old World War II jeeps were the best vehicles on the island. This one had some problems, but Norman kept it running for Richard. When Richard left Palau, Norman and I inherited the jeep, more or less with Peter's blessing.

He told Norman: "Fix it up and you guys can use it for a while."

"Sure," Norman said.

Peace Corps forbade volunteers to own automobiles, but we had only borrowed the jeep. We acted like two kids with a new toy. But the new toy proved troublesome. The gearshift extension kept slipping out of the transmission and was difficult to fit it back in. Reverse was gone, so we had to keep that deficiency constantly in mind. The suspension was shot and if we drove over 10 mph the front wheels shimmied, jerking the steering wheel back and forth. A short in the headlight circuitry made night driving particularly hazardous. Of course, nighttime use was most important to us.

One Saturday afternoon down at fisheries, while Norman and I worked on the jeep attempting to get it running on all four cylinders, the Australian, Jack Adams drove up in his late-model 1952 jeep. Tall and lanky, Jack always wore a greasy railroad cap, white undershirt, long khaki pants, and combat boots. He walked over to our jeep, spat a shot of tobacco on the cement, and peered under the hood.

"Where's the problem?" he asked.

"Aw the s-o-b is only firing on three cylinders," Norman answered.

"Well piss," said Jack, "what's wrong with 'at? It's got four 'a the bloody things, more 'n ya need. Three's pleny; two's fifty percent and that's really all ya need. If I's runin on three, ya still got 'n extra. Why worry 'bout the bloody fourth?"

"You're absolutely right, Jack," said Norman, and he lowered the hood. The jeep ran on three cylinders for the rest of its life.

Jack was married to Yvette Etscheit, a Belgian who was the only Caucasian to hold Trust Territory citizenship. The Etscheit family owned substantial real estate in several of the islands and operated import-export businesses out of Ponape. But Jack worked for the Trust Territory as a fix-it man. He could fix anything that the Trust Territory broke, which was everything. Before coming to Palau, he had helped install the prodigious loran-A tower on Yap. Jack always had a pug of tobacco tucked under his tongue or in his cheek, and he could spit as far and as accurately as any betel nut chewer in Palau.

After the war, Jack had been a scrap dealer in the Trust Territory. One of the things he collected was old oxygen bottles. The shipping company refused to ship oxygen cylinders unless Jack could prove they were empty. So Jack would line them up on the dock and point them out to sea. Then he'd knock the valves off each one with a sledgehammer. If a bottle contained oxygen, it would zoom off into the water. The bottom off Malakal Dock was littered with valveless oxygen bottles. One night over a beer, Jack told Norman and I a story:

"One time Public Works brought down a bunch of bottles in the weapons carrier and dumped 'em on the dock. I started line'n 'em up so's they was point'n toward the lagoon, then I'd knock the bloody valves off with my big sledgehammer. One of the stevedores, seeing what I was doin', takes a sledgehammer and starts knock'n 'em off too. Only he don' catch on I had 'em point'n into the lagoon. Well, 'e hits this one, an *vroom*, the bloody thing takes off across the dock and slams into the warehouse; pokes a hole right through the bloody wall and smashes into a ton of beer stacked up in there. Beer was spew'n everywhere, bloody Schlitz, I think t'was. This Palauan boy was bust'n 'is gut at that. They fired 'im. No bloody sense."

After Peter repossessed his jeep, which only ran on three cylinders, Norman and I borrowed it one time to do some running around. We had taken Peter home for lunch, then gone downtown. Peter, a stickler for promptness, always arrived back at the office at 12:30 sharp and we made sure we got back to pick him up at 12:25. "I'll drive," he said, as he left the house. Norman sat in back, and I moved over to the passenger side on the wooden seat. Just as he eased out the clutch and we started to move, the front tire blew out with a plangent *bang*! We jumped out and searched for the jack; gone. Peter punched the spare; flat.

"Son of a bitch. You guys take my jeep and go screw around. Now I'm going to be late for work. Shit!" He kicked the flat tire hard. Norman and I staggered around guffawing like idiots, driving Peter to fumes. "You jerks get it fixed!" He stomped off down the road, looking to hitch a ride.

Norm and I always had the proclivity for getting into trouble, especially where Peter was concerned. Peter cringed when he saw us together, knowing that something bad might happen. Sometimes things did happen.

After work one Friday, Peter, Paul Callaghan, Norman, and I went skiing in Peter's boat out in front of fisheries. Peter and Paul left early, and Norman and I continued skiing. Just before dark, we headed for the boatyard to secure the boat under the dorm. The high tide had filled the lagoon to the brim, and I decided to take a shortcut through an underpass beneath the causeway. We stood in the boat looking over the windshield, the boat cruising along at about twenty-five knots, planning across the smooth water as a butter knife glides across icing. Coming through the small bay around the corner from fisheries, I lined up the underpass. The opening grew closer and closer, looked smaller and smaller.

"Oh no!" I yelled.

I jerked back the throttle lever while both of us ducked, just in time. The boat flew through the opening—*Crunch!*—the top of the underpass ripping off the windshield. When we poked out the other side, I stood up shakily and turned the boat around to pick up the pieces. Matsumoto happened to be standing on the road fishing for squid as he always did in the evenings, a witness to the whole fiasco. Peter's boat was Matsumoto's prideful piece of work. Now we'd customized it. He glared down at us as we nonchalantly picked up the pieces floating in the water. Luckily, the Plexiglas portions, unbroken, had flown into the back of the boat. Norman looked over the mess.

"I might be able to fix it," he said.

We continued on to the boatyard, tied up and scrounged some glue from the boatyard night watchman. Norman went to work gluing the windshield back on Peter's boat. Two hours later we left, the windshield looking good as new in the reduced light. We stopped by Peter's house to tell him the story ("the throttle stuck, Pete") but he and Ann had gone out, much to my relief.

The next morning, Norman, Bob Moncrief, and I left fisheries in the bait skiff to go diving. As we turned out of Malakal harbor and entered the Ice Box passage, Peter and Ann came out of the boatyard bay in his boat, about a half mile away. Seeing us, Peter turned and headed our direction.

"Oh shit," I cried.

Peter roared up in front of us and slowed. He wielded part of the windshield frame in his hand like a sword, waving it in contempt.

"You idiots!" he boomed. "You sons a bitches!"

Ann's bulging bikini top rested securely on the unbroken part of the windshield. The giant smile on her tan face caused me to grin back like the idiot Peter had just called me.

"Shit!" Peter said, disgusted at my what-me-worry smile. He jammed the throttle down and they sped off toward the rock islands, Peter still waving his sword. Norman and Bob laughed and laughed. It *was* funny, but I dreaded the thought that Monday morning I would have to face Peter. I visualized Matsumoto telling Peter about it. "Dumb *haoles* (Hawaiian for 'white man')," he'd say, waving his short arms. "Under causeway. Full speed. High tide. Stupid, dumb, *haoles*!"

Monday morning came. Norman and I bided our time at the co-op, delaying the inevitable. We could see Jack Adams's jeep parked over at Peter's office and knew he was inside talking with Peter. A few minutes later, Jack came walking over. Jack, with his good sense of humor, always joked. But not now. He'd come to fetch us.

"Boys," he said. "You'd best be get'n over to the office. Peter's so worked up he can't bloody sit down. He's pace'n back and forth, piss'n in there. The secretaries 're all hid'n in the bloody conference room wait'n for 'im to settle down."

"Okay, Jack, we're going." We started down the dock toward Peter's office, taking small steps. My mouth felt parched, my pulse raced.

"Good luck, boys," Jack called.

Peter's office window offered a view of the dock over to the co-op, and he must have watched us walk over. When we walked in, the secretaries grinned red teeth. Tosh and Paul sat at their desks, neither of them looking up. I walked into Peter's room first, ahead of Norman. Peter, pretending to be hard at work, looked up from behind his desk.

"Sorry, Peter," I said.

"Is that all you have to say?" his snarl making me twitch. "Well, I don't really know what else to say. I'm sorry. I screwed up."

"You're damn right you screwed up, you son of a bitch. You ruined my boat. Don't you care about that?" He pounded the desk with his fist, his tongue working the inside of his cheek, his face flushed. Glaring at us, he continued: "Both you guys, always trouble. Why? You're just irresponsible, no good, probably never will be any good."

My dad told me that once, maybe twice, I thought.

He continued: "What's with you guys? Don't you have any respect for anything? Did you think you could get away with this? The damn windshield broke apart in my hands. How dumb do you think I am, anyway? Matsumoto thinks I should get rid of both of you."

Uh oh. Now we were fired.

"We weren't trying to hide it, Peter," I said. "We just thought we could fix it. I mean, we broke it, so why not fix it?"

And then I broke into that uncontrollable, foolish grin of mine. I glanced at Norm and he bowed his head as if in prayer, a conspicuous smile enveloping his face. Peter looked at me, gritted his teeth, and looked down at his desk so I wouldn't see his cheeks recede. But I saw.

"Why can't you be more responsible? You act like little kids. And it's not just my boat. You could have been killed doing that. You're lucky you still have your heads."

"I know, Peter," I answered. It won't happen again, I promise."

"You're damn right it won't," he said, getting hostile again. "I'll give you the bill when it's finished."

"Of course, I'll pay for it; I'll just rob the bank," I said.

"You're damn right you will!"

"A little each month? Or how about we fix it, good this time."

"You stay away from my boat. I saw how you fixed it," he said, his tongue poking out the side of his mouth.

"We'll do a good job this time, eh Norm?"

"Get the hell out of here," he barked.[7]

---

[7] One February evening in 1991, some twenty-three years later, Norman and I reminisced about this incident over on Lana, Hawaii. We harked over why the windshield had fallen apart after he'd repaired it that night. "It was

Peter's mad quickly dissipated. The next week he had to fly off to a meeting in Saipan. The Community Club was having an overnight party at Ngaiangas over the weekend, and he asked me if I would take Ann and the kids out in his boat. Sure, I told him.

"And Pat—no shortcuts, please," he said.

Friday after work we went out to the party. Ann's part-time babysitter, Dumae, came along with us. Dumae was nineteen and lived in the village down the hill from Wilson's house. She was a strong girl, stocky and cute. Long ago, a miscued machete had scarred her cheek. We liked each other.

Tosh brought his family out in his boat. With his Kapingamarangan skills, he cut coconut fronds and fabricated a huge mat across the beach for people to sleep on. Others built a big fire and laid out all the food on a table. About dark, boatloads of people showed up. Dr. Swei, from the hospital, brought along several nurses. I recognized one of them as the girl I'd seen dancing with Jerry Facey that night at the Boom Boom Room. She wore a bathing suit, something most Palauan women never did. My eyes followed her.

Dumae and I built a bed up on a platform which served as a roof over a lean-to at the beach's edge. We lay around chewing betel nut, watching the activities on the beach below us. The parents bedded down the kids at one end of the sleeping area, then the adults gathered around the fire, drinking and joking. I kept watching the nurse. The reflection from the fire accentuated her exotic face. She was tall for a Palauan and had a slender figure. I asked Dumae who she was.

"That is Teo, a nurse at the hospital. She is mean when she drinks," she warned.

"What do you mean, mean?" I asked.

"She will beat you up. *Cho choi*, it is true Patrick. She is *kebelung*, crazy."

Much later, when people had bedded down, Dumae woke me.

"Look down there—look at that *rubak*." She giggled in delight.

I rolled over, just in time to see the district administrator sneak over to Ann's closest friend, Lynn, whose husband slept next to her. Lynn took the Distad's hand and carefully stood up. In the moonlight, they stole off—down the beach.

---

my mistake," Norman explained. "I used salt water to mix the glue. It was Weldwood, an aliphatic glue. If I'd used fresh water, it never would have broken again."

Chapter 8

Helen Reef

Peter sold things. He was always getting dealerships for this or that, knives, diving watches, water skis. The water ski thing was a good one. The company supplied him with demos, which is what we skied with.

He sold Victorinox Swiss Army pocket knives of stainless steel and aluminum with red plastic handles marked with the Swiss Army shield and cross insignia. The basic model had two blades, a corkscrew, bottle and can opener, and toothpick and tweezers inset in the handles. He charged $4.50, and most of us bought knives from him during training. John Rupp coined them "Super Pete" knives, and the name stuck. They lasted a year or so, until salt water corroded away the aluminum frame and they fell apart.

Girls adored them. The first time Sandy saw mine, she asked to see it. She caressed and fondled it, then refused to give it back. The following evening, JoAnn and Ann sauntered down the path to my shack. They wanted me to get them each one of those cute red pocketknives like Sandy had. Within several days, every female PCV on the island had asked me for one of those charming little red Swiss Army knives. Then the boys followed suit. Within a two-week period I gave Peter orders for over twenty knives. I told Peter he should give me a cut of the profits. Without a pause he answered, "There are no profits," and thanked me for my help.

Tom Glover, a four-hundred-pound moose of a man in charge of a large construction firm doing contract work in Palau, obtained his Super Pete the hard way. One night he and several friends sat drinking in the Royal Palauan Hotel. When friend Peter walked in to have dinner, giddy Tom challenged him to a finger-wrestling contest. After Peter beat his right hand, Tom challenged him to the left. They locked middle fingers and went at it—*Pop*! Tom's finger lay at a grotesque right angle across his others.

"Oweeee!" he yelled. Peter eyed the broken finger then took out his Super Pete and flipped the blade open. "Here," he said, "let me fix that useless appendage for you."

Tom, feeling little pain, downed his scotch with his right hand, then looked at the little red knife Peter held like a scalpel.

"Hey, Pete. You broke my fucking finger, let me have that knife," he said.

So Peter gave him the knife in exchange for snapping his finger. Later, whenever the two passed on the road, Tom would wave his left hand, middle finger enclosed in a fat white cast, sticking straight up.[8]

---

[8] One of the best demonstrations of Super Pete knives came about after I had returned to Palau under contract in 1974. Two contract workers, as everyone knew, were secretly diving on a sunken ship in the west passage several hundred yards northwest of the Mariculture seawall on Malakal where I worked. They had spent months prepping a safe they had located in the captain's cabin, getting it ready to salvage.

One Saturday down at Mariculture, Peter showed up from Saipan for a visit. Earlier, I had seen the two divers in their boat towing out a fifty-five-gallon drum. Later, they towed the drum (which supported the safe) over to the Mariculture dock where I helped them hoist the safe up onto the seawall with the boat winch. As it sat dripping on the dock, a crowd gathered around, speculating on the contents—gold, jewels, yen, *sake*? One of the guys gave some orders: "Get a hammer. Get a crowbar." About that time, Peter sauntered over in his imposing manner. "What do you have here, a safe? Let me see." The crowd split. He stepped up and pulled out his Super Pete. The hammer and crowbar man came running over with his tools, shouting, "Here's the crowbar and hammer!" Peter stuck the blade of his Super Pete in the door crack and gently pried, first in the middle, then at the bottom, then at the top. Everyone stopped breathing. Peter stepped back, and the door top slowly fell out and away from the safe: *whap*! The door hit

Peter also dealt in Swiss-made Blancpain diving watches. These he sold for twenty-five bucks, but they weren't worth it. In those days, Rolex made the only watches that wouldn't flood at depth, but Rolexes were far too expensive for PCVs. Peter's watches looked great, with rotating bezels and glow-in-the-dark radioactive faces, but under pressure they died, slowly or otherwise. You'd surface from a dive and notice fog inside the crystal. Later, the fog would disappear, recurring after the next dive. Then it was just a matter of time before it quit. Forever. If the watch survived for several months, the bezel would fall off, leaving it looking like a Timex or a kid's watch. After Peter graciously replaced my first leaker, I learned to leave the new one on the boat when I dove. But later I got careless again. Norman had been too smart to buy one, recognizing the radium threat of the face as well as the probability of flooding. John Rupp always took his off before diving. Peter, of course, wore the deluxe model. Twice the size as the leakers he sold us, his had a giant orange face with generous globules of green radium marking each number. The bezel's edge was deeply serrated, and it clicked like a ratchet when rotated. The band, almost as wide as the watch, was a heavy stainless steel Rolex imitation.

After observing the troubles we had with the cheaper models, Peter began taking his watch off when he dove. One time out diving, I asked him if he feared his watch might leak if he left it on. He thrust his tongue into his cheek and gave me a broad grin, never answering. But he was bothered. He should have severed his relationship with Blancpain. The watches just weren't up to snuff in our environment. As with the knives, we called the watches Super Pete watches, but they were undeserving of the name. Later, I dubbed them "blankouts."

—

In June of 1968, Peter sent me to the southwest islands several hundred miles distant. I went down on the Trust Territory field trip ship, *Yap Islander*, a 120-foot tramp steamer which made

---

the cement. Peter gently wiped the blade of his knife on his pant leg, closed it, and stuffed it back in his pocket. The safe was only full of mud.

the trip every three or four months. Built in the late 1940s, it had only several sleeping quarters so most of the passengers slept on deck. Don, a PCV nurse's aide, and her husband Kerry Fitzgibbons, were along; and we camped out on the bow among all the other unfortunates. Bodies lay in every conceivable nook and cranny, and the smell of retch permeated the air. Rain turned the decks into mud and vomit compost. Salt spray kept us damp and miserable. The cramped little galley served bowls of greasy gruel and rice to three or four passengers at a time. The *benjos* were backed up and overflowing, adding to the dismal atmosphere of a hopeless situation. People had warned me about these trips, but I had never imagined anything this bad.

We stopped first at Sonsorol, one of two raised limestone islands with fringing reefs, off-loading supplies and people and taking aboard others wanting to journey back to Koror. I watched from the deck as the landing party hit the beach. A black cloud of mosquitoes engulfed them, and they slapped and flailed their arms in wild self-defense. Gene Davis, on his way back to Koror, smiled gleefully as he came aboard with his single duffel. It had been a year of misery and frustration, he told us. The several families inhabiting Sonsorol were inbred and fought often. "The atmosphere was usually pretty tense," he said.[9]

We left Sonsorol later that morning and headed toward Pulo Anna in calm seas, arriving at the tiny island late that afternoon. Four people stood on the beach waving as we drifted off the reef. When the skiff went in a fierce swarm of hungry mosquitoes forced the landing party to submerge themselves in the water while the four island folks unloaded the skiff.

Tobi, farther south, was a similar island in size and appearance to Sonsorol, but having about fifty occupants. Pete Black had also finished his tour and was returning with us, but he was reluctant to leave and opted to stay on the island until our return from Helen Reef, an uninhabited atoll about forty miles to the southeast of Tobi and marking the southernmost border of Palau.

---

[9] Later that summer the *Emeraech* was dispatched to Sonsorol to evacuate two local teachers who had guzzled duplicating fluid. One person died en route to Koror; the other became permanently blind.

The ship would travel south to Helen Reef and return to Tobi the following day.[10]

Helen Reef lies three degrees north of the equator. It is a picture-book atoll, having a classic oblong barrier reef enclosing a lagoon and patch reefs. At the northern end lies a very small sand island, about the size of two football fields, which contains beach strand vegetation and coconut palms. Seemingly in the middle of nowhere, Helen Reef acts as refuge and breeding area for seabirds, turtles, fishes, and invertebrates. The lagoon was loaded with valuable giant tridacnid clams. Helen's isolation made it an easy target for Asian fishing vessels looking for giant clams, turtles, and anything else of value.

The *Yap Islander* arrived at Helen Reef in late afternoon, the captain able to squeak her through the meandering deep water channel through the west barrier reef and anchor inside the lagoon just south of the island. On my return to Koror, I described the events that happened next in a memorandum to Peter Wilson. The following is the original memo:

June 19, 1968

To : Peter T. Wilson, Chief, Marine Resources
From : Patrick Bryan, PC Fisheries Volunteer
Subject: The Rape of Helen Reef

Recently I had the opportunity to experience as an eyewitness the total rape and destruction of a beautiful Pacific island and breeding ground hardly larger than the area of a football field. The reference is to Helen Reef, an atoll southwest of Tobi in the district of Palau. The voyage took place during the week of June 7 through June 14, 1968, and was an official government field trip to the southwest islands on the TT ship, *Yap Islander*.

It seems that the *Yap Islander* in most cases tries to go to Helen Reef almost every field trip, which is every

---

[10] After Peace Corps, Peter Black did his PhD dissertation on the sociological aspects of Tobi, earning a degree in anthropology from the University of California at San Diego.

three months. On this particular occasion we went in (to the island) at night under a nearly full moon. Among the occupants of the ship were officials of the Palau Legislature, at least two doctors, two policemen, Peace Corps volunteers, a Catholic priest, and passengers from Palau, Tobi, Pulo Anna, and Sonsorol. The ship itself anchored on the reef, and the dories provided transportation to the island for the passengers. Almost everyone went to the island. Fires immediately sprang up on the beach, and small duckling "Quell" (a large cormorant-type bird) were slaughtered and roasted—many were simply left dead or dying, there simply being more than the demand. Many of these baby birds were captured to take back to Palau. The number of eggs on the beaches was fantastic, and similarly there were hundreds of tiny baby birds. The eggs were collected in large numbers as people trampled over the island. Later the eggs were shaken to determine how well developed they were, the ones most recently laid being thrown aside rendering them inviable. A member of the Palau Legislature brought a gun ashore and proceeded to shoot birds at random—leaving the dead and dying on the beaches. Still others went out in the dories and ran down green turtles which had come to the shallow areas to lay their eggs. There was also an abundance of beer brought ashore to accompany the feasts. The whole scene could very possibly have come out of the movie, *Mondo Cane*.

The rape went on all night long, and the next morning we went to shore to have a look. What we saw was truly an ugly spectacle for such a beautiful sunshiny day. Hundreds and hundreds of crushed eggs and dead and dying baby birds littered the beach. Parent birds, unable to locate their siblings, flew around helplessly while their trampled young lay dying near crushed eggs. Flies were having a field day. Crippled birds shot by the gunman the previous night sat in stunned grievance. And to add to the glory of the expedition, beer bottles were left strewn around the beaches near the still live smoldering fires.

We toured the whole island in a state of disbelief, and we particularly were even more appalled by the fact that we could find not one live baby *quell* on the whole island—one of the most valuable birds in the Pacific.

Returning to the ship, we found that they had captured ten or eleven turtles, some being very small, and the rest ranging from medium to large. Another turtle was taken during a stop off Merir. The stop was made exactly for that purpose, to catch some turtles, since we sighted many on their way in to lay their eggs. Another thing I found distressing was the fact that guns were allowed on board and that people were allowed to shoot off the ship. I myself recall seeing two .22 caliber rifles and one M-1 carbine. At one point, the member of the legislature who murdered the birds on Helen Reef proceeded to shoot at coconuts in the water from the stern of the ship toward the bow. Some large birds were also shot from the ship along the way.

As you can well understand, this truly was a ship of fools. Why this type of action was allowed I don't know. Similarly, I question the better judgment of the field trip officer to allow it.

In light of what happened this last trip and what perhaps happens on most of the trips to these islands, I would like to raise the following questions:

1. Is it the policy of the Trust Territory government to allow the above fiascoes to take place on a government-sponsored field trip even with two policemen, government officials, doctors, Peace Corps volunteers, and a Roman Catholic priest aboard?
2. Besides the fact that the captain of the *Yap Islander* receives $5.00 for each turtle he brings back, is there not sufficient conservation legislation to protect these animals which have historically been exploited to extinction from most of Palau—protection especially during their breeding season?
3. Is there not something which can be done in the future to protect Helen Reef from the devastating effects of human rampage and slaughter—does not the fact that it is the major

bird breeding ground in this area of the Pacific for many different kinds of sea and shore birds merit it worthy of protection and sanction especially in light of its minute size?

I should hope that this account might have some kind of constructive kick back in the initiation of an inquiry and perhaps some disciplinary action. I should also hope that this might start some minds clicking and some spontaneous action toward conservation legislation aimed at proclaiming Helen Reef as a game preserve, with further conservation measures to protect the remaining bird and green turtle populations in the Palau district.

Patrick Bryan

cc: District Administrator, Palau
    Conservation Officer, Palau
    Donald Bourne
    Terry Clancy
    Robert Owen

Peter had suggested I write the memo after I had told him about the trip. The memo was naïve and emotional, but it rang true, made big news, and stepped on more than a few toes. Word soon got around that I was worth very little, that my time in Palau was short.

Peter forwarded his comments along with my memo to District Administrator Boyd Mackenzie who quickly responded with a stiff memo of his own:

"A standing order is being prepared to regulate the field trips to the uninhabited Southwest islands, including Helen Reef, in respect to fish, birds, and animal conservation policy, a copy of which will be distributed to all concerned."

"In the future, Southwest field trips will include the Conservation Officer or his representative from your department to ensure that the laws, regulations, and policies regarding wildlife and fish conservation are observed and to take corrective measures where warranted."

In my memorandum, I made two serious errors which worsened my already delicate status as a living organism in Palau. The Catholic priest I referred to was Father Hoar—but he had not accompanied the vessel to Helen Reef as I proclaimed, having instead disembarked on Tobi. He was very angry with me, and Peter persuaded me to write an official apology to him in recognition of the error, which I did. My other goof was stating that members of the Palau Legislature were aboard, when, in fact, none were aboard. Someone had given me false information regarding that, and I should have made confirmation before I wrote the memo. The Field Trip officer was a good friend of Peter's and of a lot of other folks as well. He was a Palauan named Don Pedro, the government's Security and Safety Officer. Despite all the secondhand threats, his vengeance constituted the only requital I experienced over the whole Helen Reef incident. No one killed me and no one ran me out of town. For some reason they let me live. But Don got me.

A short time after the trip while I was driving downtown in the government Marine Resources truck, Don pulled me over. He flashed his badge and demanded to see my government driver's license. Of course I didn't have one, no one did. It was pure harassment.

"Follow me down to Public Works," he ordered. I did. "Surrender the keys to your vehicle," he ordered. I did. "The next time I catch you driving a government vehicle without a proper license, I'm going to arrest you," he bellowed in front of the director of Public Works. Laughing like hell I'm sure, he roared off in a cloud of dust leaving me to hike back to fisheries about two miles away. In truth, I thought it was pretty funny. Back at the office, Peter frowned when I told him his truck had been confiscated. Then he laughed. "Get your license like you're supposed to," he barked.

The following week I went down to the police station to get my license. Having never issued one, the cute Palauan secretary at the police station looked at me in confusion, then expertly spat a glob of red juice into a Schlitz beer can. "You mean there is two kinds of license?" she asked. "I never heard of *government* license before."

"Where can I get an application for one?" I asked. Already this was turning into a *Catch 22*.

"Maybe Public Works has. Let me call them." The phone didn't work, or perhaps no one home at Public Works.

"Why don't you call Don Pedro and ask him who has the application forms for a government license. He should know—he's the one who's making me get one," I said with some contempt. She dialed the three digits, probably D-O-N. Don was out—out chasing delinquent drivers perhaps.

Several days later I tracked down Pedro and asked him for an application for a license.

"Never mind an application," he said. "You have to take the driver's test." He was serious, really out to get me.

Kailang let me borrow the PFC truck to take the driver's test in since I couldn't legally drive a government truck. He thought it was real funny. So did Peter. So did I, for that matter. Undoubtedly I was the first person ever to take a driver's test in Palau.

Don had me drive around town while he sat in the back of the truck. Every now and then he'd tell me to turn left or right, park, backup, or do this or that. Now it was my turn. I drove right at the speed limit, much too fast for the condition of the roads, keeping Don bouncing around uncomfortably in the back.

"Slow down!" he kept yelling.

"What was that?" I'd ask, aiming for another bump.

After several minutes of that, he ordered me down to Public Works where he lectured me on several mistakes I'd made during the driving test. Perhaps he figured he'd hassled me enough to exonerate me for the Helen Reef memo. Don sat down behind an old Underwood and hunt-and-pecked my license, a regular license with the word "Government" typed across the top. Squaring his shoulders, he firmly shook my hand.

"Congratulations," he said with a grin.

Peter, meanwhile, fielded the brunt of the wrath from those I had embarrassed. Getting word that I might be in danger, he suggested I go off-island for a while until things blew over. Norman had returned to Truk to take delivery of a new Matsumoto built thirty-six footer for the Truk Marine Resources Office so I made reservations to fly to Truk and go fishing and wreck diving with Norman and the boys.

I arrived in Moen, the district center of Truk, on a Friday afternoon. Norman and his brother Willie, who was out from California for a visit, picked me up and we went directly to the Marine Resources Office. The thirty-six footer had suffered transmission problems and was up on the ways for repair. That meant that fishing and diving were out, which left me in a quandary.

Peter had hired Ron Powell, a Kiwi from the Cook Islands, to run the show. When Ron had first arrived to begin his new assignment as chief of Marine Resources for Truk, Norman, Rupp, and Ives took him around in the fisheries jeep to have a look at Moen, the district center. Ron spoke few words that morning, but when they arrived back at the dock site where the new office was to be built, Ron spoke up. Having spent considerable years in the South Pacific, twenty to be exact, he said: "I've been to a lot of places in the Pacific region, some of them good, some of them bad, and some of them disgusting. But this place," he went on, "this place is definitely the armpit of the Pacific."

Ron drew the plans up for the new Truk Marine Resources office on a paper bag and Ron and the fisheries PCVs built it accordingly. Ron was a soft-spoken, very knowledgeable person, who worked slowly and methodically. A perfectionist, he was uncomfortable doing things almost right, temporary, or half-assed. Norman and the rest of the boys admired and respected him, and he taught them much about the ocean, fishing, and island ways. Ron knew how to absorb what was good, gracefully reject what was of little value, and make light of the everyday inconveniences that island living presented. His sense of humor obviated the stress and ulcer syndrome so many Americans were prone to.

I had heard many stories about Truk from Norman and Jay Klinck, and neither had spoken well of it. Truk was no paradise, no tropical notion, no place for a vacation. The people seemed unfriendly, uninterested, and uncaring. Truk harbored hordes of flies, a result of the rotting breadfruit which lay everywhere. In the evenings, mosquitoes swarmed in black clouds. Moen was dusty (worse than Koror), dirty, and undignified. And Moen held its own fragrance, a sweet stink derived from fermenting bread fruit and peach pomade.

Norman limped noticeably as we walked around town. His malaise, he explained, had resulted from a "clever-no-remember" trick. Since the new thirty-six-foot boat was Norman's charge, when it had arrived from Palau, Norman, a man of few possessions, had decided to live on it. He moored the boat alongside the dock in front of the Marine Resources office and kept his clothes hung on hangers from the roof over the deck, stashing his other valuables down in the engine room. In the evenings he often walked to a local restaurant and ate dinner, then walked back to the boat and slept on the deck. Several nights while he was away, people had gone onto the boat and stolen whatever they could find; "didn't matter what," as Norm explained it. The boat had a large open deck space aft of the cabin which comprised several storage lockers and four bait wells, all covered by hatch covers to make the deck flush. Norman decided to catch the assholes who were stealing from him. One dark night before he left the boat for town, he carefully removed all the hatch covers and stowed them forward in the engine room. Then he turned off the light in front of the office, leaving the boat in total darkness. The trap was set. Let the bastards come on board tonight, he thought.

Norman came back to the boat late that night, a bit tipsy after having downed a few beers, stepped aboard the boat and crashed into a bait well. His body never quite recovered.

Down below the house in Moen where Norman, Rupp, and Jim Maloney lived, the main road continued on to another village and dead ended. One time while they stood watching from the house, a bunch of bandits in an old Datsun sedan whizzed down the road toward the dead end leaving a rooster tail of dust.

"Where do they think they're going, through the dead end?" commented Maloney.

Moments later, one of Truk's two police cars, red light flashing, siren screaming, and horn blasting, roared by shedding its own rooster tail and pounding its suspension to death. The little blue and white Datsun police car looked toy-like with five oversized policemen seemingly stuffed in through the windows but left half-hanging out. Thirty minutes later, the police car rumbled back down the road, empty handed. The robbers had escaped.

In Truk, the cops played cops and robbers, but the cops avoided the catch. By blood or marriage, everyone was related. How embarrassing to nab your cousin (a thief), or your mother's cousin (a mischief maker), or your friend's cousin (your brother and a run-amucker). Socially unacceptable; not right.

One time, five policemen hanging out the windows of a Datsun police car came flying through downtown Moen in hot pursuit of a Datsun pickup that had sped through moments before. At the far end of town, the road forked and encircled a small hill, forming a continuous loop. Part of the loop was a blind corner, the only blind corner in Truk. At the fork, the pickup veered right. When the cops reached the fork, they slid to a stop and broke into an argument. Seconds later, the police car peeled out left. A minute later, a loud crash occurred. At the blind corner, the cops had unwittingly captured their men—by head-on collision.

Because Micronesians operated under the "extended family" system, anyone working for the government was obligated to share his hard-earned dollars with his relatives. This fact, probably more than anything else, contributed to the rampant use of alcohol on payday weekends. It was imperative to cash that check with haste because soon the greedy hands of the relatives would whisk that money away. Consequently, every two weeks, by 4:30 p.m. on payday Fridays, many government workers would already be intoxicated and would soon be on the road.

In Truk, Friday afternoon drunks loved to drive around with little purpose other than to scare the other guys. Trukese rarely drove off the road; they drove into other cars. Then they jumped out with machetes, hoping the other party would flee. Usually, both parties would turn tail. *Real* confrontations were against the rules in Truk.

Paydays in Palau were similar, but events differed. Usually little happened until late at night when barhopping brought on causeway speeding. Collisions were rare but it was almost a sport to drive one's car into the lagoon, the lagoon apparently magnetized, sucking the Datsuns and Toyotas into its watery field. Mishaps involving the lagoon caused no drownings and rarely did anyone get hurt. As in Truk, usually the party would run away and make up a story. "Someone stole my car while I was drunk at the Peleliu Club," they'd report. The proud owner of a Datsun on Friday night would show up for work Monday morning on foot as if he had never owned a car. Once a car was in the drink, the lagoon owned it, until, a few days later, the Public Works crane would pluck it from its watery grave and a flat bed would deposit it down at the M-Dock dump to rust away. Routine. One of the hazards of possessing a car. If you felt unwilling to risk driving into the lagoon after downing a quart of Apollo on Friday or Saturday night, then you had little business owning a car. Not in Palau, anyway.

Government trucks were no exception. Many higher level officials drove government vehicles to and from work, to and from the store, and to and from the bars. Marine Resources possessed two vehicles. One was an older Datsun, No. 50, that Tosh drove; the other was a newer Datsun, No. 23, that Peter drove. Tosh usually stopped off at the Community Club for several drinks after work and always on payday Fridays. Sometimes he would park himself on a barstool and spend the night. One night, after a particularly heavy session of scotch and soda, he attempted to drive to his home across the street. Possessed, perhaps, by the lagoon's allure, he instead made a left, drove a mile down to the causeway, and launched no. 50 into the lagoon.

The following Monday, Peter picked me up and as we drove to work I commented that over in the lagoon, the truck that we had just passed looked like No. 50. Peter slammed on the brakes, reversed the truck, and jumped out to view the Datsun submarine.

"Shit," he barked. "That damn Tosh." He mumbled unintelligibly under his breath and gnawed away at his lip as we continued down to the office.

When Tosh arrived later that morning, Peter resumed business as usual, saying not a word to Tosh about the truck. Peter rewarded Tosh with No. 23 and ordered a new Chevy pickup for himself. Several months later, after Tosh drove No. 23 into the drink, Peter again ordered himself a new truck, giving Tosh the Chevy. The island chain of command syndrome.

—

Hukaluk (a navigational star) was the prescribed name of the Truk Marine Resources thirty-six footer. For reasons known only to them, Norman and John Rupp decided to change the name to *Wogut,* the Ut Indian (a Utah tribe) name for vagina.

One time Norman, Jim Maloney, and John Rupp took out a reporter from the *Los Angeles Times* named Charles Hillanger who was doing a human interest story on the Japanese shipwrecks in Truk Lagoon. They did some diving on one of the wrecks and as they motored back to port on the *Hukaluk,* the reporter asked

Norman what the name of the boat might be since a name had yet to be painted on the boat.

"*Wogut,*" said Norman with a chuckle.

Suspicious, Charles asked, "And what does it mean? This may make the *Times*, so tell me straight. I don't want to print anything that might prove offensive." Already deep into the lie, Norman and the others explained to Charles that *Wogut* was Trukese for a navigational star.

About a month later, Charles sent them a copy of the *Los Angeles Times* which contained Charles's story on the wreck dive in Truk accompanied by a photograph of Norman and the Marine Resources vessel, aptly captioned the *Wogut*, as it lay too off the mast of the wreck.

Down on the dock on a day the *Truk Islander*, a Trust Territory interisland ship (sister of the *Yap Islander*), arrived in Moen, John Rupp did a double take of the ship's insignia. On the side of the wheelhouse, the TT insignia heralded the words "Trust Territory of the Pacific" encircling six stars representing the six districts; but the "T" had been obscured by rust, making the emblem read, appropriately, "rust Territory of the Pacific." Rupp clicked off several photographs of the *Truk Islander*, a rust Territory vessel.

—

Since the *Wogut* was laid up and we were unable to go fishing or diving in Truk, I decided I'd rather be back in Palau where I could do both. The next morning I went down to the Continental Air Micronesia Office and booked a flight to Guam for that afternoon. Continental had recently won the contract over Pan Am for Micronesia and now flew DC-6s, pure luxury after flying Pan Am's DC-4s. The Truk group was sympathetic to my desire to leave. Without a boat, Truk had little to offer. It had nothing to do with the company; the local flavor disagreed with me, I explained. They understood that perfectly as I boarded the DC-6 and flew off to Guam.

In Guam, I walked to the Continental counter to book on the next flight to Palau. Standing in line, I saw Dale Jackson, a PCV from Saipan whom I had met once before in Palau. Dale worked in communications and was a good friend of Jack Adams, having helped Adams construct the loran-A tower on Yap before going to Saipan. When I told him why I was in Guam, he popped up: "Let's go to Saipan." Why not, I thought. Probably should stay away from Palau awhile anyway.

Kailang had given me the name and address of his brother in Guam. We walked down to the new four-lane highway known as Marine Drive to hitch a ride toward Dededo where Kailang's brother lived. After being in Palau for a year, Guam seemed like a metropolis. We went into the J&G supermarket and bought a quart of milk. I'd forgotten how much I missed milk, even if it was recombined.

Dale and I stashed our things at Kailang's brother's house, borrowed his car, and that night drove into Agana and watched *2001: A Space Odyssey*. The huge wraparound screen and stereophonic sound mesmerized me. I'd forgotten what watching a good movie in a good theater was like, and I wondered what else I might be missing by living in Palau.

The following morning we left for Saipan, about 150 miles north of Guam. After landing at Isley Field, Dale hitched us a ride with a friend to the Royal Taga Hotel where we ate french toast. And I'd forgotten how good french toast was. Wiping syrup from my mouth, I peered out the plate glass window overlooking the lagoon. A few hundred yards off the beach which bordered the hotel, two American tanks sat dead in the lagoon, casualties of the beachfront landing during World War II. The Royal Taga Hotel had first opened in December 1967. It was Micronesia's first luxury hotel, boasting three stories, fifty-three rooms, a decent restaurant, and a swimming pool. It fitted nicely within the lagoon-side environment.[11]

We rented a car, and Dale took me up to Trust Territory Headquarters on Capitol Hill. Saipan had served as a Central Intelligence Agency training base in the late forties, fifties, and early sixties, the Americans training Chinese nationalists in commando warfare for assaults on Mainland China; later they trained South Vietnamese advisers and agents. Now the Trust

---

[11] Twenty years later, the Royal Taga succumbed to a three-hundred-room high-rise monstrosity called the Diamond Hotel. Completely at odds with its beachfront environment, it appeared as if it had been plucked from downtown Tokyo and dropped on a Saipan beach.

Territory Administration occupied the old CIA Headquarters building. Fabricated entirely of cement, its fortresslike construction rivaled any bomb resistant building built by the Japanese prior to the war. Typhoon-proof cement houses, originally built as living quarters for CIA personnel and their families, dotted the spacious lawn covered grounds surrounding the headquarters building and now served as living quarters for Trust Territory Administrative personnel. Overlooking the villages of Garapan and Tanapag, the houses sat divergent to the wood and tin shacks of the villagers down below.

We drove out to Marpi at the northern end of Saipan where Japanese soldiers and civilians had jumped from the cliffs after the American invasion of Saipan in World War II. Secondary growth of *tangan tangan*, seeded by the Americans after the war, covered much of the terrain. Wartime ordinance could still be found in abundance in the boonies. We walked up to some limestone cliffs and entered a cave. Just inside the entrance we found bones, an old rusty helmet, and ammunition clips. The cave was dark and quiet, creepy.

Then we drove down to Agingan Point at the southern end of the island and stood on the cliffs looking south, across rough and turbulent waters. Two miles across the channel was the low outline of southern Tinian where the B-29 bomber *Enola Gay*, laden with "little boy," an atomic bomb, lifted off August 6, 1945, and headed for Hiroshima, Japan. The USS *Indianapolis*, after delivering her atomic cargo to the *Enola Gay* on July 26, had been torpedoed and sunk by a Japanese submarine west of Tinian. Nine hundred persons perished, the majority eaten by sharks.

We stayed at Jerry Facey's house on the beach just up the road from the Royal Taga Hotel, spending the weekend in the bars and whooping it up. Dale was relocating to Palau to assist Jack Adams with a job at the communications center. When we left Saipan Monday morning, Jerry seemed relieved to see us go.[12]

---

[12] During the 1980s, Saipan developed into a Japanese tourist Mecca. By 1990, ten luxury resort hotels, several others planned, lined the western coast of Saipan. Propelled by Japanese and Asian capital, the once sleepy, relaxed, tropical island cosmos metamorphosed into a greed-driven, hustling,

At the Guam Airport we ran into Dick Doughty, also on his way to Palau. He had contacted Wilson, he said, and had asked to transfer to Palau since little was happening with Ponape's fisheries. Wilson had told him to come on over. Peter would later regret that decision.

---

bustling, multinational community based on resort hotels, real-estate deals, gambling, prostitution, and garment factories.

Chapter 9

A Bird, a Bomb, and Camping Out

When I returned from Helen Reef, someone on the ship gave me a homeless baby booby. The infant brown booby, a coconut-sized ball of white fuzz with a great aberrant bluish-gray beak capable of drawing blood, needed a mother, nourishment, and care. I named him *Quell* (the Palauan name for boobies), took him over to the co-op, and set him high atop a wooden box underneath the roof overhang so he could look out over the bay. The co-op was his new home.

At the time, few small fish were coming into the co-op. I offered Quell small fillets of fish which he ignored. When I dangled squid in front of that formidable beak, he would turn his head in disgust. I wrestled with him, forcing food down his throat, but he was too strong and regurgitated anything I got down. The bird had not eaten on the ship, and after another three days of this I was getting worried. Six days without food. How much longer could Quell last?

Desperate, I went into the reefer looking for sardines or anything small. Deep down in the frost I found some scraps of a small goatfish which included a head and partial fillet. I thawed it, then walked up to Quell holding the fish's skeleton by the tail, its head hanging down. Quell looked at my offering and went bird nuts, almost gobbling my hand. The fish's eye had triggered the feeding response. From that time on, Quell ate like a pig.

Sometimes I would feed Quell four or five fish one after the other until, unable to get the last fish down, it would hang out from his beak. Stuffed, Quell would turn his head back between his wings, tail of fish sticking up from his beak, and fall asleep. As digestion worked on Quell's meal, the fish would slowly disappear, sliding down into that flask of hydrochloric acid that was Quell's stomach.

Quell grew fast. We overfed him and spoiled him. I suppose he was fat, although fat seabirds are difficult to recognize. When he was hungry, he could be ornery and vicious and my hands shown cuts and scabs from that beak. But he could be gentle as well and in a good mood he would nibble your hands, arms, or scalp gently with his beak. When he got older, he would jump down from his box, waddle down the dock into the office, and perch on the cross brace beneath the desk. Pecking at my feet, he would ask: "Hey, Pat! Where's the fish?" He always wanted food, and if he saw it and didn't get it his temper would flare, and he'd squawk, and peck, and draw blood.

One time an old *rubak* brought in a load of bottom fish and sat cleaning them on the dockside steps. Quell stood on his box sleeping in his twisted-neck position, beak between his wings. He hadn't been fed that day and was hungry. Suddenly Quell woke, swung his head around, and stared down the dock at the *rubak* busy cleaning his fish. He jumped from his roost and hopped down the dock to the *rubak*: "Squaaawk, squaaawk, squaaawk"—give me fish, he squawked. The old man, clad only in his loincloth, squatted on his haunches, knife hacking fish flesh; Quell charged him. The *rubak* chuckled and in jest, swung his knife at Quell. I watched Quell, wings outspread, charge again, and smack at the fish in the *rubak's* hands. The old man shooed him off with his arm. Quell drilled him with that fearsome beak, drawing blood. Uh oh. *Rubaks* don't take that from a *bird*. The old man stood up, knife in hand, and glared down the dock at me; better call your bird off, he beckoned. I rushed toward Quell.

"*Kebelung a quell*" (The bird is crazy), the *rubak* said as I grabbed the bird up, taking a few raps on my hands and arm as I did. Going back to his fish, the *rubak* grumbled something scurrilous about Quell's mother. I fed Quell a couple of goatfish. He slept.

Bob Owen gave me a red band that I put around Quell's leg when he began flapping his wings. Bob told me that the mother had to encourage the young ones to fly, that they wouldn't just take off one day by themselves. So I gave Quell flying lessons. For his first lesson, I took him up on the roof of the co-op and threw him off. Alarmed, he squawked and spread his wings, flapping frantically while losing altitude, then crashed into the water. As he thrashed around trying to lift off, he put his head under the water as if looking for something—perhaps sharks? Quell lacked the sense to swim over to the steps and get out, so I swam out and rescued him. I repeated this routine over several days, but Quell always ditched at sea. I wondered if Quell might be developing neuroses, for he seemed frightened of the water. But Quell was not a pheasant or a pigeon; he was, after all, a seabird, complete with webbed feet. And seabirds foraged in the ocean. Why then, I wondered, was he acting like such a wimp?

One bright day I took Quell up on the roof, and he took off. He lost altitude and skimmed the surface, his wing tips just brushing the water as he leveled out and started up into the sky. The co-op crew standing along the dockside pointed and cheered. Quell made a great oblong circle to the south out across the bay and lined up for a landing on the dock. He came down backpedaling his wings, hit the cement, rolled over, and hoped up squawking. I proudly sat Quell on his roost, where, unabashed, he pruned his feathers apparently satisfied with his performance. His approach needed work. But he could fly.

In his maturity, Quell had taken on the size and markings of his species. His back was dark brown and black, his belly white. His light blue beak was hooked at the end, and his yellow and black eyes always looked quizzical. With his five-foot wingspan, he glided gracefully and dove magnificently, tucking his wings back, extending his neck and head, and entering the water like an Olympic diver. Sometimes he chased fish underwater, surfacing in another place, fish in mouth.

With his new dimension of flight, Quell became a free spirit. He would fly off for a day or two and return hungry, squawking, demanding food. After a feed and a nap, he'd fly off again. Sometimes I'd take him out on the *Emeraech*. Quell would sit on the edge of one of the bait wells and eat and sleep while we pulled net all night, stocking the wells with bait, those delicious little anchovies that both tuna and seabirds love so well. About sunup, after we had got under way, he would take off, circle the boat several times, and be gone. His bright red band on his left leg made him easy to recognize, especially through the eyes of a Kapingamarangan or Nukuoroan. Sometimes Quell would show up sixty miles offshore and follow the boat, working schools in among the other birds as we fished. Later, as we approached the island, he'd land on the boat and squawk for anchovies. Sometimes Quell would voyage with the boat for a week or so, then disappear for several days, finally returning to the co-op for a handout.

Quell enjoyed the attention and pampering he received by everyone down at fisheries. But as with all wild things, the call of the wild was strong. Over the months the frequencies and lengths of his absences increased until finally he rarely came around anymore. The *Emeraech* crew would report now and then that they'd seen the old bird with the red band out hustling schools. He would buzz the boat, they said, and sometimes he would hitch a ride for some anchovies. I often wondered what went through Quell's mind when he watched us pole tuna aboard the *Emeraech* out on the high seas. Perhaps something like, "if I could only swallow one of those."

—

Peter listened intently when I told him about the problems in Truk regarding the new thirty-six footer. He was critical of Ron Powell for his slowness. Peter pushed to get things done and always had a million things to get done. As a consequence, very little got done *right*. Peter's life was full of half-finished business. He had a shotgun approach to fisheries development. Ron focused on each project or problem and plugged away, taking delays and setbacks in island stride, which drove Peter crazy. Peter wanted quantity. Ron gave him quality instead. Consequently, the two butted heads; which is why Ron quit soon after Norman and the others left Truk.

Peter inspired another problem in Truk which constantly grated Ron. Dildo Aten was a big dynamite king from Tol, an island in Western Truk. Aten was a six foot, 210-pound hulk, a bragger whose exploits as a dynamiter were well known throughout Truk. Peter, with his sometimes perverse logic, figured the best way to stop dynamiting in Truk was to hire an "ex-dynamiter" as a conservation officer. "Who else would know more about it," he reasoned. So Peter hired Dildo and swore him in. Then he gave him a badge, a gun, and a nice Matsumoto inboard-outboard boat to patrol in. Dildo had it made. He cruised around the lagoon in his fancy speedboat blowing up the reefs. Then he strutted around town flashing his gun, selling his catch. That told folks how dumb the government was and how smart Dildo was. Ron's complaints to Peter about Dildo's activities went unheeded, until one day Dildo lit a fast fuse and blew himself up.

Kailang often complained to me about Peter. Peter always charged gas for his boat at the co-op. Kailang let him charge, then he'd complain that Peter never paid his bills. "Always charge, charge, charge. Just because he's the chief, he thinks he doesn't have to pay," he'd rave. Kailang's frustration grew out of Peter's primary attention to the boatyard rather than to the co-op.

One time, after I'd listened to Kailang bitch excessively about Peter's delinquency in the co-op credit department, I walked over to Peter's office and, feeling haughty, sat down in front of his desk. He looked up from his papers. "Yes, Pat?" he said.

"Hey Pete, you're not paying your co-op bills. Kailang is very upset." Peter sat up. "Well, he never gives me a *bill*," he said with a straight face. How can I pay if he doesn't bill me?"

Peter was playing the American way; he would gladly pay, but he needed to be reminded, to be billed, just as they did back in Hawaii, or in California, or New York—but not in Palau. The Palauan way was you charged, and you paid a little back now and then. It was *your* obligation to pay, no billing necessary. They *billed* people in developed countries, not on small obscure Pacific islands where things operated on a personal level. So I billed him, charging interest. He threw a fit.

Peter lacked empathy. He refused to understand that Palauans will tell you what you want to hear, then do what they want to do anyway. He liked to walk over to the co-op and make suggestions to Kailang about what needed to be done to improve this or that. Kailang would nod in agreement, as if to say, "Good idea, Peter, I'll take care of it." And that would be the end of it.

And Peter operated on American time, a frequency far removed from island time. The American concept of time was continually being forced on the islanders, but to little utility. Palauan culture had never embraced the concept of *on time*. To Peter, work started at 7:30 a.m. and ended at 4:30 p.m. To a Palauan, work started when you got there. "Micronesian time" was a characteristic of all the islands, not just Palau, and it drove some expatriates crazy, like Peter; gave some people ulcers also, like Peter. "Palauan time" simply meant that if you made a date for 8:00, for example, you might show up at 9:00 or 10:00 or 12:00. Or not at all. It just did not matter. Which is one reason no government office had a time clock. Tosh was consistently late, arriving at 8:30 or 9:00 or 9:30. It irritated Peter, gave him toothaches from grinding his teeth. Bob Owen accepted Palauan time, lived by it. So did Neal Morris. So did I.

But despite Peter's quirks, he operated above board. Although gung ho, often loud and imperious, he was also honest, sincere, and usually, reasonable. He believed in what he did.

Peter's devotion to fisheries and his adventurous spirit allowed me a great deal of freedom. I used the boats and diving gear when I wanted. I went out on the *Emeraech* whenever I fancied. I went fishing whenever I wanted. Nearly everything I did was fisheries related because coral reefs, fish, and the ocean had me captivated.

Tosh and I did a lot of fishing and diving together. He taught me seamanship and marlinespike, invaluable knowledge which continues to be useful to me. He taught me how to handle the *Milotk*, how to snuggle up to the dock in tight quarters, how to ease away from the dock stern first. He taught me how to pull an anchor, using a buoy to do the work. Tosh taught me a lot of things.

Tosh was a good diver, but he was overweight and exhausted quickly. Once we had Teruo drop us off at the Malakal channel entrance, where, using SCUBA, we drifted the channel on the incoming tide. We speared fish on the way, sometimes fighting the current to get to a fish. About halfway down, Tosh ran out of air and signaled to go up. I followed him to the surface where, confused and exhausted, he struggled to get his weight belt off. I yanked at the buckle, but the hitch was jammed from the pressure of his fat belly.

"Ditch the tank!" I sputtered.

He did, and I yanked his CO2 trigger, inflating his vest. Then he floated on to the boat. I bucked current, went back down, and recovered the tank. Back on the surface, I inflated my vest and drifted back to the boat, exhausted. At night, several months later, we took the bait skiff out looking for lobster and anchored on the slope of the same channel. We planned to swim toward the channel entrance on the end of the ebb tide then, after the tidal change, drift with the flood current back down to the boat. We swam up-channel several hundred yards, picking up four lobsters. Then the tide relaxed, and the current changed as the tide began to flood. Tosh crossed over to the other side of the channel, the opposite side from the boat, and waved his light for me to follow. But I felt wary and decided to stay on the same side. The current began to rip, sucking us along like leaves in a strong wind. I looked down toward Tosh as he tried to cross the channel, but the now-tremendous current swept him past the boat. Struggling to make headway against the incoming tide, he soon disappeared from view, he and his light carried out into the deep water of the lagoon.

At the boat, I grabbed the anchor rope and held on tight, the current stringing my body out downstream like a flag. Then I let go, grabbed the gunwale with one hand, and slid down behind the transom in the eddy. I threw my spear gun and lobsters into the boat then struggled aboard from the stern, the current rushing around the sides of the boat like a river. Tosh yelled out of the blackness, somewhere out in the lagoon, but I couldn't see his light. I yanked on the starting rope, firing up the outboard, then struggled with the unyielding anchor line. I tied the rope off and ran up-current trying to free the anchor. The engine stopped suddenly and the boat swung around, tailing down-current from the anchor line now wrapped up around the propeller. Tosh's cries sounded fainter now as he drifted further away. But I was stuck. Looking inside my *tet*, I located my Super Pete knife and hacked my way through the half-inch nylon rope. The boat drifted swiftly down-channel as I unwrapped the rope from the prop. The current had taken Tosh a good distance into the lagoon, and I yelled out to him to keep shouting so I could get a fix on his location, my light too dim now to be useful. Homing in on his panicky shouts from out of the darkness, I finally found him, his head bobbing along like a black cork. With Tosh back in the boat, I started out toward the dock. Tosh, the fear still with him, hung his head overboard and lost his dinner.

—

I was good friends with Bob Moncrief and his wife Trudy, and they often had me over on weekends to eat lobster or fish curry. Bob, who worked for the Bureau of Commercial Fisheries, collected data on the catches brought in to Van Camp and Trudy taught at a protestant elementary school. Bob owned a Matsumoto-built runabout with a thirty-three-horsepower Johnson on it, and we regularly went diving and spear fishing on the weekends.

Hungry for lobster, one Sunday afternoon Bob and I decided to take Bob's boat out to Uchelbeluu, the barrier reef several miles east of Airai channel. When we left Bob's house in his white truck with Bureau of Commercial Fisheries stenciled across the doors, Bob had yelled to Trudy: "We're just going to run out to Uchelbeluu for lobster. Get the curry ready." Trudy had smiled at that.

We approached the reef from the inside, choosing a shallow area just inside the break for anchorage. It was one of those fluky, windless days, and out to the west of Babeldaob dark thunderheads puffed up high in the sky. I jumped in and set the anchor firmly in the coral, and we began swimming our way northward on the reef. Many large limestone boulders sat near the surf zone, and *mengerenger* occupied every crack and nook in those rocks. Many were swimming, and every now and then I would raise my head and find one staring into my face mask. Bob plowed ahead, apparently unbothered by the banded reptiles, and his courage forced me to continue. Even though I had never heard of anyone being bitten by a *mengerenger* in Palau, I felt uneasy. Perhaps they were birthing, although I saw no young. Sometimes in Ngaraard they came into the beaches in great numbers; but for what, no one seemed to know.

We fished for about an hour when the sky turned prematurely dark, and heavy rain began to fall. Looking up, I saw a squall rolling through, the northwest wind turning the seas rough and sloppy. Peering above the water, I was unable to see the boat in the turbulence, so I began swimming back along the reef toward

Bob about fifty yards away. The squall passed in fifteen minutes and when I looked up again, I saw the boat in the distance but on the *outside* of the reef, blowing out to sea. It had broken anchor. I swam to Bob and grabbed his leg. He wrenched around, saw it was me, and raised his head from the water.

"Hey, Bob! The boat's gone over the reef," I yelled.

He stood on a coral head and looked out over the waves.

"I'm going for it," he yelled back. Then he threw me his spear gun and stringer.

"Don't do it," I said, but he was gone. Bob, big, strong, and powerful, may have had a chance—but the boat moved swiftly in the wind, sailing away to the south.

Fear engulfed me. At that moment I reasoned I might never see Bob again. I was alone on that reef. Only me and *mengerenger*. And really, it was their reef, their ocean. They had the upper hand. Only they were not devious, and I had the brains. Not many, but more than a damn snake.

Now what? I thought. Attempting to swim across blue water, traverse the channel, and fight current to reach land several miles distant would be foolish. Trying to hold onto the boulders wouldn't work. The only logical alternative was to swim for the coral spit at the end of the reef. Assuming I would need all my strength to reach the end of the reef, I ditched the spear guns and stringers, an act I later regretted.

Full of adrenaline, I swam along the reef, stopping every few minutes to peer out in search of Bob. But I could see little through the rough seas. Finally I reached the coral spit and as I sat resting, despondently watching a *mengerenger* slither into my fin beside me, I failed to notice Bob swimming up from the other side, a few feet behind. "I couldn't catch it," he gasped, out of breath. Thinking I'd heard a ghost, I flew into the air and spun around. Bob lay on the sand panting. My heart pounded from fright, but I felt elated for I thought I would never see him again.

The next order of business was to clear the spit of snakes. I picked up my fin and shook out a *mengerenger* which landed with a faint thud in the coarse sand. We flipped snakes back into the water with our fins, then began digging down into the coral rubble, making a depression to lay in. Large drops of rain dropped; the black sky signaled storm.

In her upstairs apartment back in Koror, Trudy finished making up the curry sauce. Lobster curry, tonight's menu. Only the lobster, and the prime consumers, had yet to arrive. She looked out the window at the black sky and watched the rain fall in ever increasing sheets. It made her shudder. They'd better hurry up, she thought. It's getting dark.

—

As we dug away at our nests with raw fingers, the impending darkness was hastened by black squall lines and fierce winds. At high tide, sea level would be a mere six inches below the peak of the spit. Though the tide was not yet high, we hit water several inches down. We would have to lie in a pond of water—either that or lay completely exposed to the wind and rain on top of the spit. We kept digging, looking for better shelter.

Each new squall brought whipping thirty—to forty-knot winds. We lay in our troughs shivering, our masks on, our fins wedged against our sides as shields against *mengerenger* which kept slipping into our holes.

—

Trudy's psych had evolved from calm concern to nervous wreck. It was long after dark, going on 8:00 p.m., and raining. Unsettled, she wrapped up the baby, grabbed an umbrella, and hurried downstairs to hail a taxi. In Palau, anyone fortunate enough to own a car immediately painted "Taxi" on the door and operated as such when he chose. But tonight, even as Trudy stood in the rain by the side of the road with her infant, no one would stop. She began to sob. "Taxi!" she screamed at a little red Datsun dodging potholes. It pulled over, and she jumped into the back seat.

At fisheries, she found Bob's truck parked near the dock next to the co-op. Trudy asked the cabbie to wait, then got out and walked into the co-op where Masahiro sat at the counter under a single lightbulb hanging from the rafter. He turned and saw her.

"Hey, Trudy. They not back," he said. "I like call but phone broke already."

Trudy held back tears, then asked, "Are you sure they're not back?"

"*Cho choi* Trudy. The boat *ngdebus*," he said, pointing to the end of the dock. "I wait for them. Me all night watch. Cannot leave."

On the dock, in the heavy rain, Masahiro, leaning on his one short leg, watched the taxi drive away, its lights beaming back and forth as it meandered here and there to miss the gut—wrenching holes. Now it was past 9:00 p.m. and Trudy felt panicky, unable to decide what to do. Up the road, she asked the taxi driver to turn right at the Royal Palauan Hotel and take her up the hill to Bob Owen's house.

—

Sometime that night, when the rain eased off a bit, I stood up and looked out at the ocean. In the deep water a few steps off our coral spit, I saw two gigantic bioluminescent or phosphorescent silhouettes pushing through the black, like super blips on a mammoth radar screen.

"Hey Bob, look at this," I yelled through my chattering teeth.

Bob jumped up as if expecting to see a boat and walked the two steps to the edge.

"Big buggers," he said as we watched the huge green blurbs swim in, then swerve and swim out into the blackness.

"Whatdya think? Tigers?" I asked, now quite thankful that I was standing on this tiny spit rather than treading water.

"I don't know," he chuckled. "But they look hungry."

We picked our way carefully back to our little depressions and laid back down, drawing our legs up, fetal-like, our fins laying against us. The wind made little whistling sounds as it raced over us, invading our fins. The rain kept us wet and shivering.

—

Trudy stood on the doorsteps of Bob and Hera Owen's Quonset as the taxi drove off in the rain. Hera beckoned her inside and took the baby, while Trudy sat weeping and told the story of the two missing men.

"And where did they say they were going?" queried Bob.

"I think it was Peleliu," she answered. She felt better now, here with friends. They would help her.

Bob picked up the phone and dialed Peter's house. He got an ear full of cacophonic static and slammed it down.

"Shit," he grumbled. "Useless." He collected the keys to his government truck and, leaving the others, drove up to Peter's house.

—

As the tide reached maximum high, small waves broke into our nests, forcing us to stand up. We stepped around carefully, avoiding *mengerenger*, our arms crossed over our chests. Sometimes, in the distance, we spotted the lights of Van Camp boats returning to the harbor from fishing. We wondered when the word would go out that we were overdue. Only Trudy and Masahiro knew we'd gone fishing. But Masahiro, stuck at the co-op all night, would be unable to sound the alarm, unless the phone worked, and it never worked. It would have to be Trudy, we speculated. "I think Trudy will be upset—but she probably won't report us missing till early morning," Bob thought out loud. I figured by then I'd be dead from hypothermia.

—

Up on the hill, Peter, sat in his favorite oversized rattan chair while Bob explained what he knew of the dilemma.

"And where did they go?" Peter asked.

"Trudy indicated Peleliu," Bob answered.

It was now almost 11:00 p.m. Peter stood and walked to the phone, picking up the receiver. He looked over at Bob, sitting on a stool at the kitchen counter, and stuck his tongue into his cheek.

"Shit!" he roared, slamming down the receiver.

"Only in Palau," Bob mumbled, raising his bushy eyebrows.

—

On the spit, I shivered uncontrollably. I can't possibly last the night, I thought. The cold is too much. My speech had become fragmented, and my teeth chattered like a bowl of vibrating marbles. I took a fin and swept the coral gravel to scatter snakes away, then I performed jumping jacks. But I possessed little energy, and the exercise seemed futile. Bob seemed better off. He had more meat on his bones, more brute strength to fight off the cold.

—

Peter was in an uproar. "Son of a bitch. What the hell would they be going to Peleliu for that late in the evening. And to catch lobster? Son of a bitch!" He paced around the kitchen looking in cupboards. Pouring himself and Bob a shot of Black Label he said: "Well, I've got to go wake up Ed Townsley and organize the Van Camp boats. I guess we'll send the tuna boats south toward Peleliu to search open ocean. I'll have Tosh organize our boats to search the rock islands. I'll either be at Ed's house or here. Why don't you notify the police to keep an eye on Bob's truck in case they show up. If anything comes up, come and get me. It'll probably take the rest of the night to get the search organized. We'll try and get mobile by sunrise." "Yeah," Bob said taking a drag from his Winston. He raised his eyebrows, "Hope they're okay."

—

On the reef, another big blob of bioluminescence glowed in the blackness about fifty feet out. It moved slowly, disappeared, then reappeared, a succession of events which kept us marveled, relieving us somewhat from the misery of the cold. "What is it?" I wondered out loud.

"Could be a school of fish," said Bob.

"Or maybe a whale," I countered, "or the monster of Uchelbeluu come to get us?"

"Maybe it's a big ball of snakes, a gigantic snake orgy out here on Uchelbeluu," said Bob.

"Kind of looks like snakes, huh?" I said, my imagination running wild. "If it is snakes, every damn *mengerenger* in Palau must be here tonight. Look at the size of that thing,"

"Every frigging snake in the Pacific is here for tonight's celebration," noted Bob. The big ball of bioluminescence seemed to pulsate, to glow bright and then fizzle repeatedly.

"Well, I hope to God they don't decide to come to our spit to rest after their orgy," I said.

"I'm swimming for Babeldaob if they do," said Bob. And then the ball of light faded completely.

We could see nothing but blackness and hear only the persistent breaking of the small waves on the spit. Whatever had caused the light show had gone, or dispersed, or—suddenly, *mengerenger* were everywhere on the spit, slithering up from the ocean. The orgy, apparently, was over, and my worst fear had been realized. With their black and white bands, it was difficult to make them out on the spit. We tiptoed back to our depressions, and each of us grabbed a fin. Then we started house cleaning, flipping snakes back into the water where they only swam back to our island. They slithered around our feet, seeking shelter beneath our insteps and we kept flipping them away. And then they seemed to leave on their own, as if the ocean had called them back. Just as quickly as they had appeared, they disappeared. We sat down in the sand, relieved.

—

On Malakal, Peter and Van Camp manager Ed Townsley sat in Ed's kitchen planning out the search effort.

—

The night of shivering and snake hassles had sapped our strength. At dawn, it seemed the weather, still blowing and raining, might worsen. But soon after sunup the rain ceased, and the wind died. We stopped shivering, warming up as we flicked off several rogue snakes.

"Trudy should be calling Pete anytime now," Bob said. It was about 6:30 a.m.

On the ocean side of the spit a long branch from a tree laid partially buried in the coral rubble. We dug it out and stuck it into a coral head near the spit so that it stuck up about twelve feet in the air. We kept watching the old white lighthouse which marked the Malakal Channel entrance about four miles distant, looking for boats to appear.

Eight o'clock a.m., no sign of a boat.

"Maybe Trudy figures she won't notify anyone until tonight if you still don't show up," I joked, with concern.

"Ha! That'd be just like her," he answered. Son of a bitch—I wanted off that coral spit; all those snakes, black and white bands, black forked tongues, fangs.

Nine o'clock a.m. It's hot. The sun is beating down on our little spit of like a blow torch. We stand knee deep in water, keeping our feet cool. My lips are parched, so are Bob's, and we are both very thirsty. Four coconuts are on this spit, but we have no way to get at the juice because I'd been stupid enough to ditch our spear guns. If we had them we could poke holes in the nuts and drink. I smack my lips. Bob must think I'm an idiot, I think. Then I wonder if I can last a full day under this relentless sun without drink.

Ten o'clock a.m. We spot a Van Camp boat as it passes the lighthouse, then turns south, toward Peleliu. Behind it is another boat and behind that another, all travelling south.

"What kind of rescue operation is this?" I ask. "Everyone thinks we're in Peleliu."

Then we see the unmistakable *Emeraech*—but it too turns south. Screaming and yelling, we jump up and down, waving our arms in desperation. Four miles distant, they could never hear us. The *Emeraech* continues south in apparent pursuit of the Van Camp vessels. I begin to realize we might have to spend another night out here with our serpentine friends. The thought depresses me.

On the *Emeraech's* bridge, Thomas, with his incredible eyes and peering through binoculars, spots the branch sticking up.

"Tosh," he says, "something over there."

Tosh takes the binoculars and peers north, toward Uchelbeluu. On the coral spit he sees something sticking into the air; next to it are two minute figures jumping around like crazed monkeys.

"Look!" Bob yells.

Two flares, one after the other, shoot up from the *Emeraech*. The boat rotates to the north, puffs black smoke, and bears down on us. I pivot and kick sand at an encroaching *mengerenger*.

Meanwhile a Van Camp boat, fishing several miles off the reef, has moved close, apparently having spotted us jumping around and waving. Bob and I, both anxious to abandon our island, swim out to the boat and the crew pulls us aboard. Bob hops up to the bridge and gives sign language to the Okinawan captain to wait for the *Emeraech*, now steaming fast in our direction.

Twenty minutes later the *Emeraech*, having traversed the mileage to our sand spit, pulls up next to the Van Camp boat. From the bridge, Tosh yells out, "Jump! Swim over here!" Without hesitation, Bob, fins and mask in hand, jumps in and swims for the *Emeraech*. Feeling guilty about abandoning the Okinawans who had just rescued us, but not that guilty, I jump in and swim for the stern of the *Emeraech*, which by that time is drifting dangerously close to the sand spit. Thomas and the crew help us aboard over the stern-fishing platform. Tosh waves off the Van Camp boat, and it heads off in search of tuna. We are rescued.

Island gossip travels fast. By 6:00 a.m., everyone in Koror had heard of our drama. Word of our rescue had spread just as quickly and when the *Emeraech* pulled into the dock at fisheries, Trudy and Peter, government workers, the ambulance, and about half the island were there to greet us. The hospital medical team headed by Dr. Swey clambered aboard wanting to take us away in the ambulance.

"How about a shot of Apollo," offered Swey. "Then we can go to the hospital."

"No thanks," I said.

"I'll pass," said Bob.

Fully recovered after gulping ice water and stuffing ourselves with hot fish and rice the crew had cooked up for us on the way in, I was ready for sleep.

But we had business. After the landing party broke up, Bob went down and bought several cases of beer to give away. I borrowed some money from Kailang to help defray the cost. We took beer over for the Van Camp boats, then went back to the *Emeraech* and drank with the crew in celebration. About 11:00 a.m., we stopped by the Peleliu Club for more beer and a bowl of *udong*. By midafternoon we had made our way up to the Royal Palauan Hotel for more beer. When Lee Marvin and Michelle came in, they bought us several beers over some snake stories. As they were leaving, Lee remarked: "Gee, I figured you guys would go straight home, eat some chicken soup, and go to bed." That's what we should have done; but we got snockered instead.

The next day, I went down to work just as I always did. First Peter called me in, wanting to know all the details. I told him what had happened, that I had anchored the boat by hand, that the anchor line must have broken. "The anchor had about four feet of good chain on it," I said. Peter gave me a dubious look, so later that morning I took the skiff out, found the anchor, and brought it back in. When the boat had swung around in the wind change preceding the squall, the 3/8-inch nylon rope had fouled on the coral and frayed through; unfortunate, but one of the risks of diving.

The day after that, Terry Clancy called me down to the Peace Corps Office. He didn't think I should be going out diving with only one boat.

"For safety, there should always be two boats," he said.

True, but that was just unrealistic Peace Corps logic. I assured Terry I'd be very careful from now on. Clancy knew as much about the water as I did about wine. Besides, these were exciting times for me, and I wasn't about to be intimidated by Clancy. If Peace Corps wanted to send me home because of my adventures, that was their problem. I could never slow down in Palau, not with all that stimulation.

About a week later, Teruo returned from a trip to Peleliu with information that a *rubak* had found the remains of Bob's boat on a small beach down near Peleliu. The boat had blown southward across an expanse of ocean, then gone over the reef, breaking up before hitting the beach. There had been gear in the boat, some spear guns, and my rod and reel. Teruo told us the man lived on Ngerchong and that he had recovered our gear and the engine.

We went down to Ngerchong with Teruo on the *Milotk* to talk to the *rubak* and see about getting our things back. Teruo acted as our go-between as we negotiated. The *rubak* wanted money in exchange for our gear, and he wanted plenty. He held my best spear gun and rod and reel, items which I would miss dearly, but I was unable to give him money for them, since I had none. Bob, likewise disgusted with the man's show of greed, elected to forget it, and we left the *rubak* with his booty. The engine probably never ran again after having been underwater. The boat lay in several pieces partially buried in the sand, unsalvageable. It represented a significant monetary loss to Bob.

—

Public Works decided to renovate the top of Malakal Bridge. The bridge, built by the Japanese before the war, had seen little maintenance. When Peter noticed rebar reinforcing rod laying on the bridge one day, he called up Otoichi Wong, the Public Works engineer in charge of the project.

"Otoichi! Peter here. What's with the bridge?"

"We're going to fix up the road tracks—lay a cement roadway across," he answered.

"Holy shit! Are you nuts? It'll collapse. Those beams are rotten down there. I know, I've seen them!"

"Listen, Pete. The beams are okay near the top, which is where corrosion would happen, at the water's surface. They should be fine down below where there's no oxygen."

"Well, they're sure as hell not. Let me make a dive, and I'll take some photos. That bridge will topple over if you lay cement on it. Guaranteed!"

"But . . ."

"Hold up on it for two days, Otoichi. I'll prove it to you."

Late the next morning at slack tide, Peter, Tosh, and I slipped into the water below the bridge. With only twenty-five to thirty minutes in the forty-foot deep channel before the current became overpowering, we had to work fast. Peter had an underwater Nikonos camera and took photographs of the pilings as we worked our way across the channel inspecting each one. The badly deteriorated pilings contained many large holes from corrosion, greatly reducing the strength of the bridge. After reaching the far side of the channel, we turned around and began our inspection of the opposite pilings. As the current began to stream, we had to swim hard between pilings, grab, and hang on.

The bottom lay sprinkled with old World War II munitions and near midchannel I spotted a two-hundred-pound bomb laying a short distance up-current of the bridge. I signaled Tosh, clinging to a piling, and pointed out the bomb. Tosh swam hard up-current past the bomb and grabbed on to an outcropping of junk metal above it. His fins, dangerously close to the bomb, kicked up silt and sediment, blocking the bomb from vision. Suddenly the bomb appeared out of the silt, rolling with the current directly toward Peter and I on the downside of the pilings. I grabbed Peter's arm and pointed at the bomb rolling our way. As if in a race, we released our holds on the piling and swam hard down current. Meanwhile, the bomb lodged itself in some junk metal directly under the bridge. Peter and I surfaced about one hundred yards down current from the bridge, swam to the edge of the channel, and walked across the reef flat to the road. At the truck, Tosh waited for us, full of apologies. Had the bomb exploded, it would have solved the problem of the bridge and all of our problems as well. Now, however, the bridge was armed and dangerous.

There was an ordinance demolition expert in Palau at the time, a navy chief on loan to the Trust Territory to clean the districts of derelict munitions left from the war. He and his wife stayed at the Royal Palauan Hotel, where she spent her days at the bar sipping gin. Their four-year-old boy, who everyone called "pig pen," ran around the hotel all day with soiled clothes and a dirty face, a swarm of flies buzzing around his head.

The chief's name was Steve Aetkin, or Chief Aetkin, and he was expert at detonating ordinance. But that two-hundred-pound bomb sitting under the Malakal Bridge was problematic. After we showed Public Works the photographs of the pilings and made reference to the bomb, Chief Aetkin was called in. He couldn't work on it alone where it rested, and we couldn't realistically retrieve it without considerable risk. We made one more dive to photograph the bomb and record its position and condition. Several days later, the navy flew in a demolition team from Hawaii to help Chief Aetkin take care of it.

When we met with Aetkin and the demolition team, we showed the photographs, described the bomb's location, and drew diagrams. Too dangerous to defuse, detonating it where it lay would take out the bridge. Then we told them about all the other stuff lying around down there—like mortars, fifty-caliber machine gun bullets, and artillery shells. Unconcerned about the small stuff, they decided to move the bomb down the channel about fifty yards then blow it. The following day, as we watched from the road, the navy divers successfully moved the bomb down channel and blew it up. The explosion sent a column of water 150 feet in the air and killed considerable numbers of fish, eels, and other marine organisms.

In the 1960s, all the districts had problems with local people using explosives for fishing. Widely available World War II ordinance provided the powder source to anyone willing to make a bomb. The typical homemade bomb was fashioned by stuffing a Kirin bottle with powder and sticking a fuse in the end (Kirin bottles were preferred because of their thick glass). The fishing with explosives was very common in Truk, and many people had been maimed, lost limbs, or killed from the practice, Dildo Aten included.

Palau had its share of dynamiters, some easily recognizable by the conspicuous absence of fingers, hands, or arms. There were laws on the books prohibiting the use of explosives for fishing. Every now and then someone would lose a few body parts while dynamiting, and one notorious Palauan continued to fish actively with explosives, even after having lost his arm at the elbow to an explosive. The classic story is of two men in a boat tracking a school of mullet. One man worked the engine in the stern, and the other stood in the bow holding the bomb. As he lit the fuse, the man running the engine yelled "*hal!*" (wait). The man with the bomb turned around to question why, and the bomb blew his arm off.

The dynamited portion of a reef is recognizable as a white circular area of dead coral rubble having a radius of eight feet or more, depending on the strength of the explosive. A selfish, wasteful, meaningless method of fishing, dynamiting kills indiscriminately. But those who practiced it seemed addicted, even after the loss of hand or limb. It must have been something in their blood; the same narcotic that drives people to gamble.

While dynamiting remained an illegal way to harvest resources, other technological advancements were working to facilitate fishing. In the late 1950s, the introduction of superefficient monofilament nets greatly increased the exploitation of reef fish. Monofilament gill nets work nonselectively, entangling anything large enough to make contact; fish, turtles, dugong, crocodiles, divers.

In the early 1960s high-speed outboards suitable for marine use became available, making the exploitation of marine resources easier and more efficient. Not only could islanders venture farther away to harvest fish and shellfish, they could carry larger payloads as well. Mobile fishermen in high-speed outboards fished wherever they chose, ignoring traditional village fishing rights. And dynamiters could "get in" and "get out" quickly.

Some Palauans were learning to use SCUBA and HOOKA for spear fishing. The freewheeling cash economy, introduced by the Americans, made ocean resources commercially valuable and no longer just subsistence. The Palau Fishermen's Co-op was deriving substantial income from exporting fish, clams, turtles, and fruit bats to Guam. Giant clams, previously abundant, now were diminishing from the reefs around Koror. On land, rifles had replaced blowguns, and native Micronesian pigeons were in danger of overexploitation.

In the late 1960s, conservation measures went largely unheeded, and were even laughed at. "What right did *chad er a ngebard* (men of the west) have dictating laws governing our (Palau's) natural resources"—was an often heard theme among Palauans. Palau was so rich in marine and terrestrial resources that the concept of "conservation" was almost incomprehensible. As was the future. For the most part, Palauans lived day by day.

—

The head mechanic over at Van Camp was a short Italian fellow named Marcello. Marcello's lips always looked as if they'd been smeared with olive oil, like he'd just finished a greasy pasta dinner, and I always expected to see a fragment of spaghetti stuck to his chin. Unable to swim, Marcello, nevertheless, enjoyed fishing so long as it was close to shore. He lived in a big company mobile home on the Van Camp grounds, made lots of money, and spent very little.

Bob Moncrief and I twice did Marcello favors by diving off the Van Camp dock and retrieving heavy steel carts which the tuna boats loaded their fish into for weighing. It wasn't fun diving; the water was oily and filthy, and the bottom was littered with rotting tuna as well as with every other thing imaginable, toxic or otherwise. We missed meeting any large sharks, such as tigers, although we saw many small gray, blacktip, and whitetip sharks.

When we concluded those dives, we scrubbed ourselves and our gear thoroughly with detergent to rid the grease and grime. For our efforts, which made Marcello look good by saving Van Camp substantial expense, Marcello invited Bob, Trudy, and myself over for a spaghetti dinner one night. My mother is not Italian, but she makes excellent spaghetti—much better than Marcello's.

One night Marcello wanted to go fishing. He owned a Matsumoto runabout with a 33-hp Johnson on it, similar to Bob's boat, the one we lost. Marcello explained to us that his workers had caught a lot of fish near the entrance to Ngell Channel on the northern side of the harbor. "We go try, eh?" he chirped.

The three of us, Marcello, Bob, and I, went out with our handlines. We caught a few fish, but nothing big. That night a full moon brought on spring tides and about midnight, at extreme low tide, we pulled anchor and started back.

Many lagoon patch reefs lay exposed and as we idled slowly along, I sat on the bow with a flashlight to spot coral heads. The flashlight was too dim to see more than a few feet in front of the boat. Suddenly there was a *crunch*! The boat suddenly stopped, almost throwing me overboard.

"Oh shit," cried Marcello.

Bob and I slipped into the water and pushed the boat off the coral head. When we climbed back inside, water gushed in freely through the hole. Marcello pulled the plugs in the transom, and we sped off toward Van Camp hoping to avoid the other coral heads in that low tide labyrinth.

When we reached the Van Camp dock, the boat was quickly filling with water. One of the workers drove a mobile dock crane over, and we strapped up the boat and hauled it out. We stood on the dock watching the boat hang from the straps, water draining from a gaping hole underneath the bow.

"What happened, Marcello?" one of the Palauan workers asked.

Marcello shrugged, then threw his arms up: "I don-a-know. Pat on bow, Bob behind, I in back. I don know. I just don-a-know."

—

Bob Moncrief's assistant was a *rubak* named Sumong. Sumong was a stocky man, and starchy food had packed on the pounds over the years. Sumong had a couple of attractive daughters of whom he was very protective, and sometimes he brought one along when he helped Bob weigh fish at Van Camp. Marcello liked to hang around and joke with Bob and Sumong and make eyes at the young girl. Marcello was in love.

Sumong enjoyed fishing. Sometimes Bob would bring him along when we went spear fishing. If Sumong stepped to port, the boat would lean precariously to port. If he leaned to starboard, the boat would sit on its starboard ear. Bob once had Sumong step on the fish scale at Van Camp. Sumong weighed in at just over three hundred pounds.

One time the three of us went out to the barrier reef outside of Ulong. Sumong always wore a loincloth, which left the cheeks of his butt exposed and looking like large balls of brown cottage cheese. He could roll from the boat into the water by himself, but he required help getting back into the boat. On this particular trip, I noticed an unusual number of sharks as we were diving. After about an hour, we came together and swam to the boat. Each of us had a stringer of fish, and Bob climbed into the boat. I handed Bob the three stringers of fish, then climbed in while Sumong hung onto the stern next to the engine. I moved up forward to keep the boat balanced, while Bob pulled Sumong aboard. It was tricky getting the big heavy *rubak* back inside. Bob grabbed the belt portion of Sumong's loincloth with one hand, his arm with the other, and pulled Sumong partially over the stern. As he did, a large shark broke water just behind Sumong, in the very spot where Sumong's rear end had just exited the water.

"Wow," I said, startled.

"Holy shit," Bob said, having seen it as well.

Quickly I put on a mask, leaned over the gunwale, and stuck my head in the water. I saw nothing. I raised up and pulled off my mask.

"*Ke mla omes*? (Did you see it?)" I asked Sumong.

"No. What you see?" he asked.

"That looked like a big boil to me," Bob said.

"It was big—real big," I answered.

Bob donned his mask and stuck his head in, and I leaned over the opposite side. Off in deeper water we saw a twelve-foot tiger

shark cruising along the reef. I rose up and stared at Bob, already sitting up, his mouth agape.
"Holy shit!" he said.
"I don't believe it!" I answered.
Sumong, oblivious, fixed a chew: "What?" he said.

PART II

Only in Palau

CHAPTER 10

Hollywood Comes to Palau

I got hooked on betel nut. Mechas wove me a *tet*, a small purse-like basket made from pandanus leaves which the Palauans use to carry their betel nut fixings; *buuch* (betel nut), *chaus* (lime), and *kebui* (pepper leaf). It had a long strap which I draped over my right shoulder, allowing me to pack the *tet* on my left hip and rump. The *tet* carried my *buuch*, sunglasses, cigarettes, checkbook, pen, change, Super Pete, and whatever else would fit. Several mornings each week while I slept, Melanna would come to my room and stuff my *tet* full of *buuch* and *kebui*. I had learned to smoke, chew, talk, and spit all at the same time, as well as any respectable Palauan. And like any respectable *rubak*, my teeth shown red, especially down around the gums—the unmistakable trademark of a veteran PCV. Even *Smoca*, the ultra-abrasive Japanese tooth powder with the twenty-five cent PCV price, failed to abolish the red.

After several months of teaching English, the kids turned rowdy. Kailang's kids kept acting up. Never sitting still, they continually disturbed the other kids. Perhaps I had run out of things to teach. For whatever reason, they had lost their concentration and I found myself impatient and irritable. I cut back to two classes per week—then to one a week. Finally I told Mechas I would quit teaching in June. When Melanna heard about it she begged me to continue teaching through the summer, but the little Palauan outlaws had burned me out.

"Maybe when school starts again," I hedged.

Mechas's husband, Techur, lived in Ngkeklau, a village in northern Babeldaob. He came down from Ngkeklau to Koror once every four months or so to visit. A fine old man of seventy plus years, he was thin and nice looking and had short-cropped white hair. He had few teeth, and he pounded his *buuch* before he chewed it. He did this by placing the *buuch*, *kebui*, and *chaus* in a small metal receptacle similar to a shot glass, then pounding it carefully with a little homemade hammer fashioned particularly for that purpose. After about five minutes, he would carefully place the macerated vegetable matter in his mouth and gingerly chew it. In the traditional way, when he sat back away from the door he spat into an empty beer can or bottle. He spoke no English, and he always addressed me as Rubak. Likewise, I called him Rubak. Sometimes I would travel up to Ngkeklau and stay a day or two with him. Ngkeklau, the southernmost hamlet of Ngaraard, was a tidy village of only a few houses and a *bai* set behind the mangroves. Entrance to the hamlet was by a tiny beach nestled among the mangroves lining the shore. Only about ten families and one PCV lived in the hamlet.

The Easter of 1968, Terresa informed me she would be going up to Ngkeklau to spend her vacation time. Unhappy about that, I tried in vain to convince her to stick around Koror for the holidays, explaining that there would be lots to do. She told me there would be lots to do in Ngkeklau. Feeling miserable, I asked if I might escort her up there.

"No," she said.

—

Lee Marvin and his girlfriend Michelle came out to Palau several weeks in advance of the movie ship. Also accompanying Lee was his fishing friend, Ray Accord, who planned to oversee the construction of Marvin's boat. Ray fished in billfish tournaments the world over and held several world records with the International Game Fish Association. Pushing sixty, Ray was short and skinny and always combed his slightly thinning grayish hair straight back. He smoked heavily, drank plenty, and ate like a bird. A mechanical engineer, he held the patent for Bumblebee fuel engines used to power model airplanes. Ray practiced perfection, rigging his gear carefully and knowingly, as if his life depended on it. Like Lee, Ray thrived on fishing; knew it inside and out.

Peter gave Ray a small room at the southern end of the dock to use as office and equipment space. The program would utilize Lee's boat to run charters and survey Palau for marlin and other big game species while Ray trained a Palauan captain and fishing master. The effort would be the initial impetus for the development of a sports fishing industry in Palau. Lee would come to Palau at his convenience for fishing trips. The operation would pay the government a nominal rental fee for the small shack and dock space for the boat.

Matsumoto wasted little time lofting the boat. It would be forty-six feet in length and have the sampan lines of Matsumoto—low in the stern, rising high in the bow. Matsumoto estimated three to four months to completion.

One day, Lee dropped by the boatyard to check progress on his boat. Ray was there, talking intently with Matsumoto about the just completed flying bridge on the cabin roof. Lee walked completely around the boat watching it intently as he did. He climbed up on the stern deck and pretended to fight a marlin in the chair, pumping an invisible rod to tire the fish. Looking up, he saw that the rod tip would hit the end of the roof, which was built out over the back deck to provide shade. Lee grabbed a handsaw, climbed the ladder to topside, and began sawing off the back part of the roof. Matsumoto's face turned white, like chalk.

"Hey! What do?" he yelled, pointing at Lee.

"No good like this," proclaimed Lee, sawing away, sending sawdust to the deck below.

Matsumoto spidered up the ladder. "Okay okay, we make short. You stop now," he cried to Lee. Matsumoto shortened the top.

—

Lee and Michelle stayed at the Royal Palauan Hotel. Lee had a healthy aptitude for alcohol and in the evenings, Lee and some of his Palauan friends would meet out on the hotel veranda for five o'clock cocktails and to talk story. Sometimes it would get noisy out there. Out on the veranda about 10:00 one night, Lee acted out a scene he once did in his old TV series, *M Squad*. Several high clan Palauans sat around laughing at his antics. The bar wanted to close, but Lee kept ordering last rounds for everyone. About 11:00 p.m., one of the Palauans began arguing with Lee about the CIA, claiming that Lee was actually a CIA agent sent to Palau by the U.S. government to spy on Palauan activities. Lee played along. Taking up the theme, he emulated a CIA agent involved in covert intelligence gathering activities. Moments later a scuffle broke out between Lee and the agitator. When the man tore Lee's shirt off his back, Lee put him on the deck. Hearing the commotion, Michelle ran out of their room and found six crazed men shouting and screaming at each other. One of the waitresses called the police and just as the authorities pulled up Michelle waded into the melee, yelling orders and breaking up the riot.

"Go home and go to bed, right now!" she barked, sending the stunned Palauans off into the darkness. The policemen stood paralyzed by Michelle's show of power. In Palau, women didn't do such things. Michelle grabbed Lee, still rambling on about the CIA, and hauled him off to bed.

—

The Liberian registered *Oriental Hero*, the Hollywood ship, came into port. The skillful captain had navigated the 655-foot vessel with its twenty-six-foot draft through that narrow convoluted channel and into the harbor without a hitch. The largest ship ever to visit the Port of Palau, the *Oriental Hero* demanded the entire wharf. Her decks were loaded with boats, jeeps, and movie props. On the helipad extension over the fantail sat a helicopter, a piece of machinery many Palauans had never seen before.

On the dock, a big reception staged as the captain maneuvered the great vessel alongside. Red-cheeked Palauan girls in grass skirts danced provocatively and young men, dressed in breechcloths and brandishing spears, marched and stomped their feet to a background of rhythmic clapping. Smiling Chinese crewmen lined the upper deck to view the festivities. The Distad (district administrator) and his entourage stood on the dock next to their official Mitsubishi jeeps, sweating in the hot sun, ready to place leis on the ship's dignitaries. This was the biggest thing to hit the island since World War II. Hollywood had come to Palau.

Over the next several days, the American and Japanese film crews flew in on Continental Air Micronesia. Toshiro Mifune, the Japanese film star, flew in by private jet, demonstrating that a jet could indeed land in Airai. The Selmur Productions movie was to be a joint venture between Hollywood and Tokyo, and the film crews of both nationalities were to lodge on the ship.

The American film crew was comprised almost entirely of young men. Medical support was provided by a fifty-five-year-old American doctor, known as "Doc" of course, who had bright white hair and a weathered face. Doc consumed enough alcohol each day to tranquilize several elephants, and he gulped reds, blues, and greens to counter the alcohol jitters and keep him up and running. Like Doc, most of the crew partied excessively and openly, and there were enough drugs and marijuana on that boat to stone all of Palau and Truk as well.

On the other hand, the Japanese remained aloof and obscure. They avoided Palauan women. On the ship and on the set, they occupied their own niche, eating together, socializing together, and working together. Most of them spoke little English, which made communication between the two groups difficult. A Palauan translator helped moderate, but his command of English was marginally sufficient. High-strung Toshiro Mifune, at the apex of his career and one of Japan's most respected actors, was all business. He spoke no English at all.

The production managers wanted a beach and jungle setting on which to film most of the scenes. The theme concerned the confrontation of two World War II fighter pilots, one American (Lee Marvin), the other Japanese (Toshiro Mifune), both shot down and taking refuge on the same small uninhabited island somewhere in the Pacific. They eventually strike a mutual respect for one another, construct a raft, and sail off, only to land on another island where they find an abandoned hospital. The ravages of war remind each that the other is the enemy, and they go their separate ways to rejoin their own confederates. Such was one ending to the film. In the alternate ending, both were killed. The filmmakers initially named the movie *The Cowards* but later changed it.

English Director John Boorman worried over finding the right filming location. When he explained to Peter the kind of setting they needed, Peter already had a location in mind.

"No sweat, John. Its right out front of my office, right around the corner," Peter told him.

But John remained skeptical.

Peter took Boorman and head cameraman Connie Hall out to an island known as Ngerengchol, only ten minutes away from Fisheries. It had a beautiful white sand beach and lush greenery as background. When they landed, John and Connie ran around excitedly taking trial shots here and there. Beautiful limestone forest covered the slopes of the island behind the beach. Tropic birds floated around high over the forest, and exquisite bird calls echoed from within. When Peter said: "Okay, why don't we get moving? I've got some other spots I want to show you," John looked at him as if he were crazy.

"Peter," he said. "I'm not interested in other spots. This *is* the spot."

Off the beach of Ngerengchol, a fringing coral reef made access difficult at low tide. To counter this problem, M-boats were used to transport equipment and crews to and from the film site each day, their shallow drafts proving adept at crossing the shallow reefs. The filmmakers had also brought along a jet boat powered by a Chevrolet V8 engine and a smaller inboard/outboard runabout which was perfect for water skiing. Ronald Sakuma, local salvage man, supplied war remnants such as machine guns, antiaircraft guns, LCVPs, ducks, landing craft, and other items useful as background props.

An interesting aura accompanied the making of the film. Lee Marvin and Toshiro Mifune had both fought in the Pacific in World War II. At age twenty, Marvin had landed on Saipan in the Marianas and fought his way up to the Aslito airfield. On his fourth day of battle he was wounded, and he spent the next thirteen months recovering in a hospital. Each man possessed deep-rooted feelings stemming from the war and before the filming began they travelled together to Peleliu, the site of one of World War II's bloodiest battles, to pay tribute to the thousands who had died there. The cement monument commemorating the battle still stood, but the inscribed metal plaque had long before been stripped off, perhaps sold as scrap for a few cents a pound.

Each morning from the dock in front of the co-op, the movie crew would load into the M-boat. I made friends with the crew, and they let me use their rental cars anytime I wanted. Sometimes they asked me to run an errand for them in town while they were out on site.

After several weeks, the film crews tired of their lunches, which were provided by a local business. They asked me if the co-op could provide them with fish fillets for barbecuing at the site two or three times each week. Good business for us, we started filleting fish and delivering to the island about 11:00 a.m. on Mondays, Wednesdays, and Fridays. I liked to take the fish out so I could watch the filming; then I'd hang around and eat lunch with them.

One time Masahiro went out with me and as we walked up to the set, I noticed everyone watching director Boorman and his Japanese equivalent argue over a technical detail. The Palauan translator sweated as he attempted to accommodate each faction. I glanced at Tony Wade standing by a camera, and he gave me the thumbs-down sign. Lee, in shabby khakis and shirtless, sat in the sand building a castle. Nearby, a stern Mifune spoke softly with his compatriots in Japanese. Uncomfortable, Masahiro and I left the fish on the table and shuffled down the beach toward the boat. Lee looked up from his work.

"Hey, Pat. Can I catch a ride in with you? This sucks," he said.

"Sure," I said, continuing on to the boat.

Lee turned and shouted to Boorman and the Japanese. "When you guys get it figured out, let me know. I'm going fishing."

Boorman ran down the beach, intercepting us at the boat.

"You can't go, Lee," he said. "We have work to do. We'll get it straightened out."

Boorman had directed Lee in *Point Blank*, and he understood Lee's quirks. Boorman, in brown shorts and T-shirt, stood hands on hips, beads of sweat on his forehead.

Unmoved, Lee said: "What the fuck you want me to do, sit around all day while you argue with the Japs? You go ahead and argue. I'll go fishing. That's all I want to do, go fishing."

Boorman put his arm around Lee and slowly led him back up to the set. What a cut, I thought. And those last words, "that's all

I want to do, go fishing," constituted one of the most meaningful expressions I had ever heard.

But now Mifune, dressed in his own movie rags, seethed. He pointed at Lee and in Japanese, threatened to quit if Lee continued his shenanigans.

Lee threw up his arms and grumbled to Boorman: "What the fuck! I hurt his feelings. *I quit.*" And we left.

And so it went. These incidents were common on the set, the filmmakers told me. The Americans, irritated with the regimentation and stuffiness of the Japanese; the Japanese, bothered by the loose, brash behavior of the Americans. On the set, little interaction developed between the two groups, and none occurred after hours. The Americans spent their time downtown in the bars; the Japanese holed up together on the *Oriental Hero*.

The movie people usually filmed on Saturdays, but on Sundays I often accompanied the film crew to the rock islands where we water-skied, dove, and picnicked. One time late in the evening, as a bunch of us, including Michelle and Ray Accord's wife, Dorothy, cut through the glassy waters of the baiting grounds in the jet boat, the engine coughed and died. It was a perfect night to be lost at sea—full moon, clear sky, and no wind. Well inside the waters of the surrounding islands, we took turns paddling toward Koror several miles to the north while taking sips from a bottle of scotch someone passed around. A few jokes floated around for a while, until, about midnight, some of the movie people began to get fearful over the situation. But there was little to fear; the worst scenario would be having to spend the entire night in the boat.

About 2:00 a.m., as if out of a James Bond movie, the helicopter suddenly appeared over the black rock island silhouettes. It flew low and fast, blazing a spotlight down upon the water. I scrambled to light a torch we had previously fashioned but, fumbling, failed to ignite it before the pilot circled us twice, and then flew off toward Koror. Our members speculated: "Did they see us?" "I don't know." "Oh God, I hope so." Soon we could no longer hear the chopper, and we stared out at the moon's reflection on the placid water. A half hour later Peter, Lee, and Melisebes showed up in the *Milotk* and towed us in. On the dock, the rest of the Hollywood bunch greeted us with champagne, acting as if we'd been rescued from a three-week drift in a life raft. Another Hollywood production.

When Dick Doughty got to Palau, he had little to do. Peter wanted to involve him in the crown-of-thorns starfish program, but that project had yet to materialize. So that first week, Doughty hung around the co-op talking with me and watching the fish landings. In the evenings, he would go up to the Royal Palauan and have drinks with Lee and Michelle. Before long, Doughty had become good friends with the Hollywood couple.

Michelle, meanwhile, was bored with the filming routine. She needed other diversions, and in Palau the real diversion was the rock islands. Peter would have Teruo or Melisebes take her out to the islands so she could stay happy and tan. Sometimes Ann would go along, the two of them clad in skimpy bikinis, like rock island nymphs. But Teruo and Melisebes were uncomfortable in their escort roles with the two babes. Melisebes especially, complained to Peter about the way Michelle dressed. Palauan women shunned bathing suits; would never consider wearing bikinis. They swam in old dresses or cutoff shorts with blouses or T-shirts. In Palau, a fashion statement was a new pair of Blue Dias zorries, only sixty-nine cents at Rudimch's Store.

One day Peter had the answer. He asked Doughty to take Michelle out to the rock islands in the bait skiff for an afternoon. Dick could conduct research on starfish while she sunbathed, Peter theorized. Dick agreed to the inconvenience, and the two went out in the bait skiff. The following day Dick took Michelle out again. And again the next day. Every day Dick and Michelle journeyed to the rock islands, Dick to conduct starfish research, Michelle just tagging along to sunbath. They always carried along a picnic lunch and a cooler with beer and wine. Michelle ceased complaining about her boredom.

They left in the bait skiff from the co-op dock each morning after the movie crew had gone, while Mekreos and the other workers, standing on the dock, peered down Michelle's bikini top and giving Bliok an opportunity to comment on Michelle's *klalo* (things). One blistering and humid morning as the two left the dock in the skiff, Michelle's breasts pushing daringly at her bikini straps, Mekreos put his hand on my shoulder.

"*Ollei!*" he said. "Give me one cup cold water."

Doughty had few friends in Palau, and he considered me his buddy. One day as I filled SCUBA tanks in the dive shop Doughty came in and let me in on what he and Michelle did every day out in the rock islands. He spoke proudly, a grin on his face. I wondered how he could ever look Lee in the eye.

Talking to Peter a few days later, I asked him if he didn't think it a bit odd that Dick took Michelle out to the rock islands each day.

"I mean, he's under your supervision. Don't you think this will cause you trouble?"

Peter, his tongue poking out his lower lip, gave me a curious look and mumbled that it was important to keep Michelle occupied and off Lee's back. Then he asked: "Why, what do you know about it?"

I shrugged and raised my eyebrows, which made him smile. Everyone in Palau knew about the rock island picnics. Peter seemed content to let it ride.

After several weeks the island buzzed with gossip about PCV Dick and sun bunny Michelle and their rock island excursions. The two were items, the talk of the town. Lee had to know that Dick and Michelle were interested in more than just starfish and the sun, but if he did, he declined to let on. Lee and Doughty appeared to be great pals, and Michelle played the "mother" role. When the three of them were together, it was Lee and Michelle—and adopted son, Dick.

When the *Ngerengchol* was launched, Lee staged a big party. All of the Hollywood crowd, some of the Japanese, and many local dignitaries gathered at the boatyard to eat and drink. Matsumoto, with his wonderful sense of "lines," had produced a spectacular vessel and *she* looked extraordinary sitting on the ways in preparation for her christening.

Peter gave a speech, and Father Hoar blessed the boat with a short prayer. Then Michelle stepped up on a small platform in front of the bow to christen the boat.

"I do christen thee," she said, as she swung a bottle of champagne at the bow stem.

The bottle hit solidly with a decisive "thud," unbroken. Again and again she whacked the bow, but the bottle refused to break.

"Hit it hard," Lee yelled.

She regrasped the bottle by its neck and drew back just as Alphonso stepped up behind her to help out, the bottle smacking him square in the forehead, christening him. Alphonso's knees buckled and he fell down, his head bleeding like a stuck pig. For several seconds Michelle stood motionless, uncomprehending. Then, "Oh my God," she yelled, dropping to her knees to tend to poor Alphonso. They stood up together, blood streaming down Alphonso's face from above his eye. Michelle dabbed at him with a hanky and someone took him off to the hospital. Later Alphonso returned, all smiles, his forehead riddled with stitches. I think he was prideful over being decked by Michelle.

Michelle was finally able to christen the boat with a "prefractured" bottle of champagne provided by the boatyard crew. Then a worker groaned as he struggled to release the brake on the ways cable. The gears ratcheted back, *clickety, clickety, clickety* . . . faster and faster. The *Ngerengchol* creaked on her cradle, slid backward down the ways in a roar and entered the water with a *swoosh*, the crowd cheering. Matsumoto raised his hand and sang out, "*Sayonara.*"

Peter recommended Ray hire a *rubak* named Oerbelau as skipper and another younger Palauan-Japanese by the name of Sinichi Wong as fishing master. Known in Palau for his uncanny piloting abilities, Oerbelau knew Palau waters better than most men knew their own house. Sinichi owned a small boony store and had previously worked on a sports fishing boat in Guam. But like Ray, Sinichi was stubborn and the two fought from the start.

Ray liked me and always called me Lloyd (for Lloyd Bridges of *Sea Hunt*). When he asked me to help set up a mooring system for the Ngerengchol, I used SCUBA to lay out the chain and set the anchors to hold the boat off the dock, earning myself instant respect from Oerbelau and Sinichi. I started going out with them in search of billfish. Peter jumped on me about it.

"All you do is go out fishing and diving. Is that what you came over here for? You've got to start channeling your energies," he told me.

"Yeah, okay. I'll do that," I said. "But I'm getting out of the co-op. Remember, that's the deal. I want to do the starfish thing."

Peter had already agreed that I would run the starfish control program when he got funding. Meanwhile, Ray could teach me lots about big game fishing.

Shortly after the boatyard launched Lee's new boat, Peter and I went out in the *Milotk* to take at-sea photographs of the *Ngerengchol* fishing. As the *Ngerengchol* cruised along about two miles out, Lee, Ray, and several other people were down below, talking, drinking beer, and watching the rods. Up on the flying bridge, Doughty sat on the bench as skipper behind the wheel, bikini-clad Michelle sitting next to him, her hand on his thigh. They looked over at us and flashed grand smiles as we came alongside, Peter shooting with his Nikon F.

"Charming couple," I said.

Unable to repress his distaste for the affair any longer, Peter growled back, "The son-of-a-bitch." He knew things were out of hand. Earlier, Peter had said he was worried about the situation and how it might be affecting Lee. Terry Clancy had also talked to me about it, wanting to know if the rumors were true. I told him I didn't know. Lee and I were friends, and I considered telling him what I knew. I had asked Ray if he thought Lee knew what was going on.

"I don't know, Pat," he said, "but I don't like it."

But Lee *must* know, I thought. It was just *too* obvious, and the talk was rampant.

CHAPTER 11

Palau Graffiti

On the east coast of Babeldaob, up between the villages of Melekeok and Ngiwal, a large mangrove-bordered estuarine bay lay at the mouth of a river. The bay held no barrier reef, leaving the powerful ocean ground swells to sweep in unobstructed. About half a mile out from shore a submerged shoal, deep enough to be unobtrusive but shallow enough to act as a bar, gave rise to large waves which built up without warning. Boats travelling the coastline traversed this bay, usually between the bar and shore. Navigating this dangerous passage required finesse and caution.

Once, on a trip up north in the Marine Resources runabout, Harson and I made the passage just at dark. I steered by the tiller of the forty-horsepower Mercury, and Harson sat on the bow holding on to the bow rope and giving me directions. The sea was placid and black and the horizon barely visible in the coming darkness. Suddenly we heard the unmistakable sound of a breaking wave.

"*Alii* (danger)!" Harson yelled.

I turned the boat to starboard directly into a huge wave, white water forming at its crest, and gunned the engine. The boat climbed the face, sending Harson sliding backward, grasping for the rope, one leg going outboard. We flew over the crest and into the air, the boat's bow angling up at seventy degrees, the wave passing beneath us and crashing down. With Harson hanging on precariously with one hand and myself leaning hard forward into the bilge, we glided down in an eight-foot free fall. The engine rpm's wound to red, the pistons floating out of control, and I twisted back on the throttle arm. The boat touched down transom first, then the bow, spreading the water and sending Harson off into the water. He struggled alongside as another black wall loomed up in front of us.

"Get in, quick!" I yelled.

Harson porpoised into the boat. I throttled the engine, and we climbed up the face of that next black swell as it raced shoreward. The boat launched again, landing on the back side of the wave near the trough. This time Harson landed back near the transom with me. He jumped quickly forward, and we powered up and over the third wave. Staying on full throttle, we headed north toward Ngiwal, my heart pounding, my arms shaking. Out of danger, Harson yelled, "*hal* (stop)!" I throttled off and killed the engine. In the darkness I watched Harson nervously tilt a Clorox jug and drink water. Still breathing hard, I whispered, "Son-of-a-bitch, Hars." I resolved never to make that crossing again after dark.

Several people, including Harson, had told me that foundations of an ancient village lay fifteen to thirty feet deep on the bottom of that bay. On one of our trips to Ngaraard, Harson and I stopped to see if we could find the ruins. We anchored inside and to the south of the bar break, which was producing big waves due to the large swells rolling in from the northeast. A strong undertow kept pulling us out, the surge pushing us back in toward the mangroves. The overcast sky afforded little light, and the turbid water offered us only a few feet visibility. Always uncomfortable diving in murky water, I dove down fifteen feet to the bottom and peered through the dark green gloom. Shadowy forms of large surgeonfish and parrot fish picked at the algae growing on massive coral heads. I jammed my spear gun's stock into my groin and pulled back one arm of rubber tubing, hooking the stainless wire loop over the brazed nipple on the spear, then did the same with the other rubber. The fish moved slowly off, staying together. Slowly kicking my Otarie fins, I followed along with my body extended, spear gun out front, my right hand gripping the stock, index and middle fingers on the trigger while my left hand held the butt to keep the gun steady. Pick one fish, sight down the spear, aim just behind the gills above the pectoral fin, squeeze, just like a rifle.

After a half hour, with several fish on my stringer, I paused to check on the boat about fifty yards away. A log floated nearby, between myself and Harson. It moved. A log? It splashed water. My heart felt as if it had jammed into my throat. I lifted my head and screamed to Harson, "*Ius! Ius!*" Adrenaline flooded my body. Kicking with all my strength, I plowed over to the boat and catapulted over the gunwale.

Meanwhile, Harson, not having heard me yelling, continued diving. I yelled again: "Harson! Get out! Crocodile!" Harson dove down, his legs kicking up the surface. Very little sound can be heard when your head and ears are underwater. Standing up on the bow, I looked around for the croc, but saw only green-brown water. Harson appeared on the surface, and I cranked the engine, pulled the anchor, and sped over to him.

"Get in, quick," I said, taking his stringer of fish.

"What's wrong?" he asked while climbing in.

"I saw a *klo ius* right over there," I said, pointing.

Harson's eyes grew to Ping-Pong ball size.

"*Delam!* (Someone's mother's . . .) I didn't see it," he said. Harson jumped up and pointed behind me. "There!"

I turned and saw the crocodile, on the surface again, about sixty yards away. It looked about ten feet long, and it kept thrashing around as if in distress. I passed Harson his throwing spear.

"Get on the bow," I yelled, cranking the engine.

I eased the boat around and approached the crocodile. As we neared, we saw that it had a large green turtle in its mouth. But the croc's jaws had closed on only one of the turtle's hind flippers. The big turtle struggled, almost towing the croc.

On the bow, tall Harson stood poised, his dark legs scissored, left leg forward, toes spread for balance, right leg back; left arm out in front, right hand grasping the spear, arm cocked up and back. Idling slowly up behind the croc until only ten feet remained between it and us, Harson winged the spear, sticking it solidly in the croc's back near its head. The big reptile rolled and thrashed, throwing water in all directions, then disappeared beneath the surface, leaving concentric waves traveling outward on the calm water. I shut down the engine, and we stood in the boat looking for the croc while waves slammed down on the distant bar. Thirty yards out we saw the turtle, its head breaking the surface like a fat little periscope. Freed of its aggressor, it gulped air, then dove, leaving only a slight boil to mark the event. We waited patiently for the crocodile, but it never showed.

"*Klo ius,*" (big croc) Harson said.

"*Cho choi,*" I answered. "And it's a pissed-off croc now."

I never dove in that bay again.

Palauans threw their spears as adeptly as they threw rocks. They fashioned them out of cured bamboo, using copper electrical wire to fasten three or four sharpened steel prongs to the end. Some they made by fastening a single solid steel barbed spike, these usually used for spearing turtles. High-speed outboards made capturing turtles easy. Having located a turtle, usually near the inner barrier reef, they would speed after it across the clear flats, then run circles around it, confusing it, until it surfaced. Then they would spear it in the head or through the flipper and jump in to grab it. Speared through a front flipper, a turtle swims in circles, making its capture easy.

—

Ngaraard, where Harson's parents lived, was situated adjacent to a long sandy beach which ran north several miles to the end of Babeldaob. The village was known for its spear throwers. Kids could throw their spears fifty, sixty, seventy feet and bag their prey; mullet, milkfish, jacks, sharks. I loved to throw spear. My spear always flew sideways, and I never hit a thing.

About half a mile north of Ngaraard, layered formations of limestone projected up along the strand behind the beach. During certain times of the year, these rock formations served as sanctuaries for *mengerenger*, the snakes hiding in the cracks and depressions. Village kids liked to show off by hanging *mengerenger* around their necks like leis. Then, holding them by their flattened tails, twirl the snakes around like lassos, flinging them out into the water. Seemingly unaffected by these capers, the reptiles would patiently swim back to the beach in search of another resting place.

Betania School for Girls sat at the northern end of Ngaraard village. It was a pretty school, protestant, with spacious grounds and an adjacent beach. Every young male in the village schemed on the Betania girls. Harson's friend, Benhart, knew all the girls in the school. A recent high school graduate, he spent his days fishing and his nights serenading the young Betania maidens. When Harson and I visited the village, Benhart always lined us up. The missionaries, of course, held strict reins on the young ladies, and it took some planning to get close. With Benhart's help, we arranged to serenade two girls one Saturday night.

Harson and I met the girls on the beach just after dark, and the four of us walked down the beach to Harson's family house where Harson picked up a gallon of *tuba*. Then we strolled north up the beach, passing around the Clorox jug of fermented coconut sap. When we'd finished the jug and the girls were afflicted with giggle fits, we walked back to Harson's house and noisily snuck into the back room, the two girls giggling silly. "*Alii,*" Harson's father warned when he heard us come in. He knew what was going on and wanted Harson to know he knew. We laid out mats and sat down. My stomach began to ache, and I chewed betel nut hoping the lime might neutralize the acid from the tuba.

"How the hell are we going to get them back over to Betania without getting caught?" I whispered to Harson.

"Never mind," he said, "just go to sleep."

Too bothered by my stomach to care, I laid down beside my now snoring friend. A short time later, stomach cramps sent me stumbling outside for the *benjo*. Back and forth I went all night.

About 5:00 a.m., Harson woke me. The girls sat awake, rubbing their throbbing heads. We left the house, and I staggered down to the water and tossed up what remained in my stomach. Then we walked down the beach to Betania, the dawn showing its first faint light on the ocean horizon. In the Palau tradition, which is to escort the girl home in the early morning, we walked the girls up through the line of coconut trees along the beach and then across the grass to the entrance of the dormitory corridor. Harson whispered to them in Palauan, "See you tomorrow night." They glided down the walkway, and we turned to go.

"Hey you, Peace Corps!" a ladies voice rang out from across the way. Our feet spun out, and we sprinted across the lawn and down to the beach, never stopping until we reached the house.

"How did she know me?" I panted, sitting on a coconut log in the fresh dawn. Harson plopped himself on the *iasumba* (bamboo bench), out of breath.

"Ha ha. C'mon Pat. They know everything. This is the village, remember? Ha."

We boiled water on the one-burner kerosene stove and fixed instant Hills Bros coffee, Harson building the typical Palauan cup—hot water, one level tablespoon coffee, three heaping tablespoons sugar, and four ounces of Carnation evaporated milk. We watched the eastern sky brighten until the sun burnt through the ocean. In the foreground, waves pounded the reef, booming like distant artillery. Village cocks, in contest, crowed from all directions, and the astringent smell of last night's fire filled our noses.

The backyard of the house, composed of course beach sand, extended a hundred feet down to water's edge where over to one side, a mangrove stand grew. The mangrove trees, with their thick green leaves, grew on sets of vertical aerial roots, like the legs of giant spiders. From beneath the sand and mud, rhizomes shot up between the plants like curious worms. Uniquely adapted to this environment, black and white archer fish, with flat heads and mouths that caressed the surface, cruised among the mangrove roots, spitting globs of water at insects in the branches above, then gobbling them up when they tumbled in. At low tide, tiny orange and yellow crabs made loud snapping sounds, popping down minute holes in the sand when alarmed. And in the larger holes, giant mangrove crabs waited for darkness to venture out into the forestlike world.

Up near the house, an old Johnson thirty-three-horsepower outboard sat loosely clamped to a two-by-four nailed onto two coconut trees. Parts. Harson's father had just purchased a new engine for his Matsumoto runabout; a major investment. Down near the water, a large monofilament gillnet hung on a line stretched between two coconut trees. Harson's father, though crippled, was the best *kelat* (mullet) fisherman in Palau.

Next to the outdoor fireplace a sharp wooden copra stake projected firmly upward from the sand and was lashed at an angle to a coconut tree. Jamming a coconut down onto the stake, I sweated and tore at the husk. Harson chuckled, picked up a nut, and husked it in two seconds.

"What do you want, *ollei?*" he said, the nut resting in his hand.

"I want to eat it," I answered. He whacked the nut with the back edge of a machete, breaking the shell cleanly into two halves and spilling the water. With the blade, he neatly cut concentric rings of white meat, then handed me the full shell of rings. I chewed. Harson sat grinning at me.

"Why you laugh?" I said self-consciously. "Don't you want any?"

Harson cupped his hand lightly over his mouth and giggled: "We don't eat that. That's for the chickens."

He tossed the remaining meat on the sand and three scrawny hens, squawking and cackling, attacked it. Chicken food, eh. Harson laughed out loud now, prompting me to discard my coconut to the hungry birds.

Harson's father, Shiro, limped out and drank coffee with us. He stood tall and powerful, even with his diseased leg. Harson's mother, dark and pretty, brought out boiled fish and hot rice, and we slurped and fingered the food. My stomach welcomed the warm fish soup, and I felt better. Harson's parents wove baskets from split coconut fronds, then filled them with taro, yams, tapioca, and smoked fish. As was the custom, we would take these baskets, along with stalks of green coconuts and betel nut, to Harson's sister and family. On the incoming tide, loaded to the gunwales, we left for Koror, twenty miles down the coast.

—

Dave and Jan Imes decided to leave. Jan was pregnant, and Dave wanted to get into graduate school. That left only myself in Palau fisheries, unless I counted Dick Doughty from Ponape.

Peace Corps brought in a new group of trainees for training in Peleliu, south of Koror. The new training philosophy was "in-country training." If they were to work in Palau, they trained in Palau. Jay Klinck worked his way into a staff position, and he hired Harson as a language instructor. I saw little of Harson for the next three months while he stayed in Peleliu.

Terresa, back from a trip to Babeldaob, resumed teaching at Maris Stella and working at Kintaro's store at night. She continued to drive me crazy, sometimes acting friendly, other times ignoring me. Tiring of the game, I decided to try a new ruse. I stopped visiting her at the store at night, started going to the Boom Boom Room instead to see Rose.

Midway through the Peace Corps training program in Peleliu, all the trainees came up to Koror for a taste of the city. One evening

Harson brought two female trainees over to the house. I knew Mechas and Kilad would tell Terresa, and I was anxious to see the effect. After eating some Spam and ship biscuits, we took the girls to the Boom Boom Room, then over to Harson's sister's place.

Early the next morning I went up to Yebukl to get my *tet* for work. Terresa sat talking with Mechas and chewing betel nut as I walked up.

"*Ungil el tutau* (good morning)," I said.

"*Tutau*," Mechas answered and offered me coffee.

Terresa gave me a dirty look and abruptly left for school. She ignored me for a week.

When in Koror, Jay Klinck lived in a small one-room cabin below the Boom Boom Room. It sat in a stand of *tangan tangan*, the tin roof just visible from the roadside, and he had it fixed up; a real pad. The floor was covered by a used rug he'd cockroached from a contract worker, and he had pillows strewn about the room. A single lightbulb hung from the rafters and was shaded with a red plastic bag, giving the room a red hue. In one corner of the room, a small stereo and Dale Jackson's hijacked tape deck sat on a wooden box. On a table in another corner sat a little kerosene stove and a tiny refrigerator. Out back was a one-seat *benjo*.

While Jay coordinated training down in Peleliu, Dale Jackson cabin sat for him. Dale had worked for the Yap radio station, and when he had moved to Koror he had brought along a commercial-grade Akai sixteen-inch reel-to-reel tape deck. The big machine sometimes shifted into high-speed mode, and it had destroyed a good many of Radio Yap's tapes. Dale offered to fix it. He did. Then he recorded several reels with music and set it up in Jay's cabin. Radio Yap played its backup record player and waited for the return of its machine.

Dale and I started seeing two young Palauan girls, recent graduates from high school. We met them one night at the Boom Boom Room and afterward took them over to Jay's cabin. After that, the four of us often spent nights at the cabin, listening to music, dancing, and partying.

During this time, Terresa had resumed speaking to me again and one Friday night, after she closed the store at 9:00 p.m., I took her over to Jay's cabin. I'd spent a week talking her into it—"Have you ever heard Blood, Sweat and Tears? The band?

Or The Doors?"—finally convincing her we'd just listen to a little music, then leave. Dale always left the key hidden under the steps so I could use the cabin when I wanted to. He'd gone to the movies that night, the movies lasting until 11:00 p.m., so I had little reason to worry about him barging in on us.

We went inside, and I opened a Kirin for myself and gave Terresa a Coke. We sat on the rug, and I played Johnny Rivers. The room, full of hot air from the afternoon sun, was stifling. I stood up to open the door for circulation just as Dale walked in with our girlfriends.

"What's up?" he said. "Party time?"

"Uuh," I moaned. He had a six pack of beer and popped one open. I crossed my legs and sat next to a seething Terresa, and I could feel the heat. Beads of sweat rolled down my cheeks. My girlfriend glared at me, then at Terresa.

"I'm going," Terresa mumbled. She stood and shot out the door. I jumped up and scrambled after her, catching her on the road.

"Wait, Terresa," I pleaded.

"Shut up!" she said, stopping me in my tracks. I stood watching her long black hair fly from side to side as she ran down the road toward Yebukl. Not again, I thought.

—

Jay had a Peace Corps friend from Truk who came through Palau on vacation. Jay's friend loved Truk, and Jay had sometimes talked about him as being bizarre, perhaps even crazy.

In Truk, the local concoction was a cheap, dangerous, quick, and easy brew made from sugar and yeast. One night in Jay's cabin, Jay's friend made up a batch and several of us sat around and drank the yeasty brew. We turned up the big Akai tape deck, overwhelming the Boom Boom Room's jukebox just above us. When rocks rained down on the tin roof of Jay's shack, we turned the Akai up another decibel or two, drowning out the sound of the rocks ricocheting off the roof. Soon my vision doubled, the room spun, and I lay down.

At dawn I awoke, shaking and feverish. My eyes would barely open, and my throbbing head nearly exploded as I sat up. I looked at the other bodies lying around, probably in similar shape as I.

Jay's house stank of vomit, making me woozy. Get out of here, I thought. I stumbled the quarter mile home, went straight to the shower room, turned on the faucet, and guzzled water. We had been told in training, "Never drink water from the tap." Ha! I was dying of thirst, and I continued gulping water as I showered. My puffy eyes stung and teared; my tongue felt swollen; my mouth felt stuffed with wool; my stomach churned. I staggered to the *benjo* and puked through the hole, watched the big brown cockroaches scatter outward, then scamper in for breakfast. Cramps bent me over. Hurriedly I dropped my shorts and sat. The warm, humid, tropical air made me sweat, even after my cold shower.

In the background, I heard Mechas speak to Melanna. In a few minutes the *benjo* would be in demand, a popular place as family awoke. I grabbed the *Time* lying on the bench beside me. The cover showed army platoon leader Lieutenant William Calley Jr., accused of slaughtering 109 Vietnamese civilians in the village of My Lai. My bowels moved loosely. Calley's leader, Captain Medina, had given the order to "kill everything that moves." I visualized American soldiers in search of VC approaching Mechas's hooch, their M-16s at the ready. Mechas, sitting cross-legged in the corner of the room, gently fussing over Melanna's hair; too old now, anyway, to care about doctrine. Closing my puffy eyes, I could almost hear weapons firing: *Pow! Pow! Pow! . . . Pow! Pow! Pow!* I imagined Mechas pitching to the side; Melanna crumbling to the floor, like a discarded rag doll; the soldiers moving on to the next house.

The previous month, President Nixon had addressed America: "North Viet Nam cannot defeat or humiliate the United States. Only Americans can do that." Senator William Fulbright, chairman of the Senate Foreign Relations Committee, remarked about the My Lai scandal: "This incident can cause grave concern all over the world as to what kind of country we are."

Dropping the magazine, I felt ashamed to be an American. What did the Palauans think about all this? I wondered. They respected the military. Did they respect Calley after what he'd done? America called its problem with Viet Nam a "conflict." Surely the Palauans considered Americans *kebelung* (crazy).

I rested my head between my hands. The heavy stench inside the *benjo* turned my stomach, and I heaved bile between my thighs. My luck at having missed the military perked me up a bit, but just a bit.

I lay prone for two days. My head hurt so bad I could barely stand up. Cigarette smoke killed me. I suffered a fever, drank gallons of water, and threw up everything I ate. For a week, my eyes were intolerant of light. Jay's friend must certainly be brain damaged, I thought. He drank that evil brew night after night. I vowed never to drink a Trukese yeast drink again.

—

Because Palau was the end of the line, most people travelling there had business and many had marine interests, which meant that sooner or later I would meet them. Such a person was Harold, a photographer from a travel magazine called *Venture*, on assignment to shoot a pictorial essay on Micronesia. He showed up in Peter's office one day wanting an escort to the rock islands to do a photographic session. Peter sent him out with me on the *Ngermeyaus*, and I gave him the grand meandering tour through the rock islands while he shot photographs and chattered excitedly over the sheer beauty of Palau. Back at the dock, he asked me if I water skied.

"Sure," I said, "anytime."

Harold wanted to photograph me skiing through the rock islands, so the following day I accompanied Melisebes in the conservation boat out to the rock islands while Peter and Harold followed in Peter's boat. Peter wanted Melisebes to pull me behind the conservation boat while he and Harold took photographs from his. The day was perfect, with little wind and bright sunshine. Out near Ngaiangas we stopped near a mushroom-shaped island, and I gave instructions to Melisebes:

"When I nod my head, you hit it, right?"

Melisebes grinned: "*Cho choi*," he said. I needed full-on power to come out of deep water on a single ski.

I jumped in with the Taperflex, and Melisebes threw me the rope then idled off. When the rope tightened, I nodded at Melisebes, yelling, "Okay, hit it!" Melisebes eased down on the throttle giving it just enough to pull me bulldozing along through the water. I let go just before my arms gave out, and he circled around.

"Give it *full* power when I give you the signal," I yelled.

"*Cho choi,*" he nodded.

The rope tightened and I yelled: "Hit it!"

Melisebes gave it half throttle and again I bulldozed the lagoon.

"Why you not standing up?" he said when he came around again after I had finally released the rope.

"*Full* throttle, Melisebes. *Full* throttle."

"Full too much," he said.

"Full throttle," I yelled again as he idled away. This time Melisebes gave me three-quarters, almost enough, but not quite. Peter pulled alongside to prod Melisebes into giving it full throttle. Melisebes gave Harold a big smile. Melisebes liked cameras.

I climbed into the boat with the *rubak*.

"Melisebes," I said. "All the way, full on this time. Give it full throttle when I yell. I'll start from the beach over there."

We idled over, and I jumped to the beach, put the ski on, and coiled several loops of the ski rope. From the boat idling away from the beach, Melisebes looked back at me, grinning. Perhaps he envisioned my arms disengaging from my shoulders, hands still gripping the handles and towing along as he raced away, my armless body left standing on the beach. I dropped six coils of rope and yelled: "Hit it!"

Not holding back this time, he gunned the Mercruiser and I took off. Melisebes, probably disappointed my arms remained attached to my shoulders, was, nevertheless, ecstatic at being on camera, and Harold got his shots.

Several days later, I sat in a small restaurant on the lower road eating lunch with Norman Vas who had come over from Truk to help overhaul the engine on the *Emeraech*. Two days of steady rain had turned Koror muddy and sloppy. Looking out the window I saw Harold pull up in his U-drive.

"Look, there's Harold," I said.

In the downpour, Harold jumped from the car and dashed toward the restaurant door. Norm turned to look just as Harold disappeared beneath the window.

"What the hell? What happened to Harold?" I asked, looking at Norm for an explanation. He shrugged.

Confused, we walked to the door, opened it, and peeked out toward Harold's car. Harold's head stuck up from the water in an open hole about eight feet deep which had been left uncovered. He splashed around, unable to get a grip on the muddy sides to pull himself out.

"Help!" he yelled.

We rushed over and together yanked him up and over the edge on his belly, his long pants scooting part way down over white buttocks.

"Thanks," he said, crawling to his knees in the mud.

Soaked and filthy, his hair pasted against his forehead, he stood and jerked his pants up, then let his arms dangle out away from his body as if he were wet.

"Just a Palauan tourist trap," Norman said.

"Works good," said Harold. "Well, see you." He got back into his U-drive and drove off.

Two months later, a double-page photograph of me skiing with a mushroom-shaped rock island in the background appeared in *Venture*. The caption identified me as a Palau PCV and explained that Peace Corps volunteers were introducing new ideas in Micronesia. I liked it. Peace Corps Director Terry Clancy did not.

—

Peter Wilson and Bob Owen sponsored a Pacific Science Foundation Technical Meeting in Palau which attracted scientists from the Pacific region. On a field trip, I took several participants down to Peleliu on the *Milotk*. On return, we came back up the west side into Barnum Bay and over along the southernmost island of the Ngemelis group. There, the barrier reef wraps around from the west and borders the island. As we motored along, I looked down into the clear glassy water and saw a cliff which I never knew existed. Excited, I stopped the boat, letting it idle and drift as we free-dove along the ledge. The vertical wall made me feel as if I was suspended off a skyscraper. Yellow and red fan corals, whip corals, and multicolored soft corals protruded from the wall. Down deeper, a school of rainbow runner darted in, then out into blue water, a gray shark following. The sun's rays protruded down and faded off into the expansive, seemingly fathomless clear blue water.

The next day we went out again, this time with Peter at the helm of the *Milotk* and the bait skiff in tow. The night before, I had told Peter about the Ngemelis discovery, and we looked forward to diving the wall with SCUBA. Several renowned scientists and marine biologists accompanied us: Vernon Brock, Phil Helfridge, Jack Randall, to name a few. Stan Wayman, staff photographer for *Life* magazine, was along, as well as Ed Janz, a wealthy philanthropist who held high regard for the marine environment. Peter had been romancing Janz for a monetary endowment to build a marine laboratory in Palau.

Peter decided to dive first in a channel beyond the large island of Eil Malk. We dropped anchor in a small inlet in the reef, and Peter explained that the area held unique coral formations about sixty feet deep. Water streamed through the channel like a river, but I assumed these professionals knew of the danger of currents, particularly in a channel, and I didn't mention it as I helped them dress. They struggled and fussed with their gear: "I think my valve's leaking." "Hand me that fin there, will you." "Hey, my regulator's on backward." "Is my strap caught in the pack somewhere?" "Hell, my 'O' ring's missing." "Hey, this ain't my weight belt."

I maneuvered the bait skiff alongside the *Milotk* to allow divers egress off the stern. They entered the water loaded with cameras, collecting bags, knives, hammers, clipboards, and other gear. I suited up and rubbed spit in my mask. Teruo, the captain, pointed behind the stern and yelled, "*Alii!*" I looked out and saw Vernon Brock frantically waving his arm about one hundred yards down current. He was easily recognizable because he wore prescription lenses built into his face mask which made him look like an aviator. I watched the air bubbles of others move down the channel, the divers losing ground while struggling to buck the current. Discarding my tank, I hopped in the skiff, cranked the engine, and ran down to help Vernon Brock. With Vernon in the boat, I ran around picking up divers as they came up. One of them, out of air and exhausted, dropped his Nikonos at the boat.

"The current owns it now," I said, wishing I could jump in for it.

Peter and Stan had swum cross-current to the shallows and worked their way back by grabbing corals and pulling themselves along. Teruo helped them in from the stern of the *Milotk* as I pulled up in the skiff with my load of half-drowned professionals.

But Jack Randall, the ichthyologist, was missing. Teruo and I stood on the roof of the *Milotk* searching for him while the others sorted their gear. I had dove with Jack before and knew he was an excellent diver, absolutely competent, and almost fearless, prone to push the limits. We'd once done repetitive dives and had to decompress by hanging on to the anchor line. Later, Jack had laid in the bottom of the boat suffering a piercing headache. Now he was nowhere to be seen.

Thirty minutes later, with Peter nervously pacing the boat and all eyes searching, someone spotted a dark speck about a quarter mile outside of the reef. Then an arm stuck up and slowly motioned back and forth. I picked up Jack in the skiff and brought him back to the *Milotk*. He carried a bag full of fish specimens he had speared.

"Weren't you worried about the current, Jack?" Peter asked.

"What current?" he said with a smile. "I've got at least two, maybe three new species of fish here."

We never made it to Ngemelis. The confrontation with the Palau current had exhausted everyone, so Peter headed back to Koror. On the way in, Stan Wayman talked to Peter and I about doing an underwater photographic story on Palau, including Helen Reef, for *Life*. He would need a diving partner and wanted me to help him out. He'd be back in Palau in a few weeks to get started, he said.

I recalled seeing Stan's work on the Arctic wolves in *Life* some years before. I asked him how he got close enough to the wolves to get the incredible photographs which *Life* published. This is what he told me:

He and his assistant established a base camp at the end of a four-wheel drive road about ten miles from the wolf pack, which they had been monitoring from a light aircraft. To get to the wolves, Stan would hike in the ten miles, leaving his assistant behind to look after the camp. Each trip lasted ten days, and he made four trips. His weight budget was so tight that he limited himself to twelve cigarettes, one for each day, two spares. It took one day to hike in and after eight days with the wolves, he would hike out, arriving back at the base camp on the tenth day. Once, caught in a blizzard, he holed up in his tent for three days.

"The wolves knew I was there after the first day," he related. "At night they'd come around and growl. I made sure I never left any food out. I had a .22 pistol with two clips, but that probably wouldn't have done much good. The first trip was scary, but then I got used to it, and the wolves usually ignored me after that.

"They were recognizable after a while. One big male was all torn up. He was on his way out, you could tell. He'd gimp around snarling at the younger guys around the kill, but then give way. He scared me the most because I knew he was hungry and might try and get me at night.

"On another night, I was building a fire to try and warm up. I was having trouble getting it started when suddenly I heard a ripping noise. I turned around and shown my light and my damn tent was collapsed. This big ol' brown bear was standing there chewing on it. Now this really had me scared—I didn't know what to do. My gun was in the tent and that peashooter wouldn't have helped anyway. So I decided I'd better scream. And I screamed bloody murder. That old bear took off like a scared rabbit."

Later, Stan told Peter and I another story. He was filming great white sharks out of a shark cage hanging overboard from a research vessel. "This monster great white was swimming back and forth in front of the cage—a big male. Finally it came up and bumped the cage with its snout, rolled on its side, and rubbed its belly along the cage. I reached out and grabbed its claspers—and for one brief moment I had the meanest bastard in the world by the balls."

—

While Stan made ready in the states, Doug Faulkner came back for another session of underwater work, and I dove with him every day. With Doug it was down, shoot a roll with the Rollei, up to reload, then down again. Up, down, up, down. Twelve frames to a roll. I mentioned that Stan Wayman was coming to Palau to do an underwater story for *Life*. Doug looked at me and frowned. Later, when I related Stan's story about photographing the wolves, Doug only mumbled, "Yeah, he does good work, *on land.*"

I took Doug out to Ngemelis, and we dove for a week on the cliff. Diving on a cliff or wall leaves you vulnerable from beneath, and the sides and backside as you face the wall. In 1968, wraparound masks and low profile masks were nonexistent. The flat-plated, high-profile U.S. Divers Champion masks we wore gave us negligible peripheral vision. To see to the side, you had to turn your head or body, an impractical task while you concentrated on something of interest in front of you. Big sharks are found near walls; tigers, grays, and white-fringed sharks, to name several. Armed with a spear gun and carrying a bag full of flashbulbs, I always faced blue water to repel sharks while Doug faced the wall and shot with his Rollei Marine. As long as we stayed above about sixty feet in depth, sharks kept their distance, but when we went deeper, gray sharks, and an occasional white-fringed shark—a big coal colored shark with white-fringed pectoral and dorsal fins—intimidated us.

But sharks are but one hazard to wall diving. Diving on a wall is different than diving to a bottom. To a diver, a wall like Ngemelis has no bottom, so depth is unlimited. If you are a bit negative, which is the usual circumstance, you tend, without knowing, to go deeper and deeper. One minute you're at thirty feet, the next you're at one hundred feet. Then, all drugged up on nitrogen, two hundred feet is easy, and beyond that is never-never land, maybe a one-way trip. As with low profile masks, most diving manufacturers had yet to develop buoyancy compensators (BCs) and most divers wore regular inflatable vests. Stan Wayman wore one of the first BCs ever made, a French-made Buoy Fenzy which had its own miniature bottle of air.

Doug and I traveled up Western Babeldaob to Ngeremlengui Channel, or West Passage, a deep water entrance from open ocean which runs through the barrier reef, transects the lagoon, then intersects an inner channel running parallel with the shoreline. In some areas, the channel was ninety feet deep—shark territory. Doug must have wanted some excitement when he suggested we dive the channel.

We spent several days diving up there, always anchoring in a small indent near the entrance through the barrier reef. In the water, we would make our way down the sandy slope and into the channel about sixty feet deep, hiding behind a huge brain coral head the size of a Cadillac limousine. Keeping our backs to the coral, Doug would shoot while I tried to track the gray sharks which we always seemed to attract, and which, for some reason, were always excited, swimming swiftly and mercurially, perhaps sensing an easy lunch. I kept after them, punching them with my spear gun when they came close, and when I could no longer count them, I'd elbow Doug in the ribs and we would flee to the boat.

One time, when the action got slow and Doug wanted to photograph some sharks, I speared a big parrot fish. Bleeding profusely, the fish struggled to break free and before I could get it under control, several excited gray sharks had homed in on us. As I attempted to twist the spear out of the fish, I failed to notice a fat gray shark streak in at full speed. It rammed the back of my spear which stuck out away from my midsection, jamming the pointed end and fish into my thigh, gashing me. Now human blood mixed with fish blood. Embraced by fear but fueled by adrenaline, I grabbed the parrot fish by the gills, tore it from the spear, and dropped it out and away from me. Doug and I back-pedaled up-slope, our eyes sighting downward toward our pumping fins, in line with the frenzy. Six or more gray sharks pounced on the fish, creating a cloud of green blood. They zoomed in and out—a high speed composite of fins, white bellies, eyes, and teeth. The large scales of the parrot fish twirled about in the fin washes, then twinkled down like falling leaves. Nothing left, only a faint fading cloud of dissipating blood and a scale or two floating down-current. Milling around like hornets, the aroused sharks followed us up to the boat. Doug tied his camera off on the overboard rope and quickly pulled himself in. I followed on the other side. From inside the boat we watched the sharks circle us, dorsal fins cutting the surface, just as the cartoons depict them, only this was no cartoon. Blood flowed from the gouge in my thigh.

I looked at Doug who lay slumped in the bottom of the boat gasping: "Screw it, Doug! I ain't diving in this fucken channel no more. Period."

Doug looked up at me, his face ashen. "You're not the only one," he wheezed.

But I knew Doug was dissatisfied at being unable to get good action shots. We had been too caught up with getting our butts out of there for him to shoot, and I knew he'd want to go back. He was no slouch. Doug was in excellent shape, macho and strong.

But sometimes I disliked his antics, and I wasn't surprised by what he came up with next.

The following morning, Doug picked me up and we drove down to Fisheries. When we loaded the boat, he threw in a rice bag full of something heavy and big. Flies buzzed around. Oh shit, I thought.

I untied the blood soaked bag and peered in at a pig's head and a pile of entrails.

"What's this?" I said, knowing exactly what he had in mind before I asked.

"We've got to go back to the West Passage for one more dive, so I can get some shark shots. I couldn't get any yesterday," he said, a slight grin on his face.

No shit, I thought. We were lucky to have escaped alive yesterday, let alone get any photographs of our friends.

"Yeah, sure, Doug. You do that," I said. "I'll sit in the boat and tend anchor—make sure it doesn't drift away." I was pissed. This was crazy.

In the channel we anchored in the inlet, and Doug dropped the pig head and guts overboard.

"Maybe we won't even have to leave the boat," he remarked cheerfully, sticking his face mask in the water and peering down. The s-o-b knew what we were in for. He was getting rich and famous for this. All I was getting was a nice opportunity to lose my ass to our toothy friends.

In paranoiac response, as soon as we entered the water I immediately put my head down to survey the situation. I saw no sharks. We reached the big coral head and peered out into the channel. The pig head and offal lay on the sandy bottom looking quite out of place. A few small fish nibbled away on it. In the distance, one or two grays cruised by as if half-asleep. A big hawksbill turtle swam by the offal, took a look, and circled back around. It seemed interested and glided down for a closer look. As if enfeebled by the sight of the pig's head, it turned and paddled off, never glancing back.

We finished our first tanks, then went back down on our second. Still no sharks. As we watched, several Jacks circled the offal. I drifted down and speared one, quickly twisted out the spear, and let it loose as I swam back to the safety of the coral head. Wounded, the fish swam in confused circles and seconds later, two grays rushed in from the blue and jumped the struggling fish. Doug shot off a roll, and we fled to the boat in a hurry.

—

A few of the rock islands embrace unique limestone formations which house bodies of salt water, forming lakes or reservoirs. These are isolated biological communities, distinct from the lagoon environment. Some of the lakes are fed from the outside through underwater tunnels. Others simply rise and fall with the tides, lagging behind the lagoon. Several of the lakes are home to thousands of jellyfish. It took getting used to, diving among those gelatinous globs, but they caused no pain. Access to the lakes was difficult and often exhausting. To get to one lake, Doug and I, carrying our diving bags, cameras, and SCUBA tanks on our backs, hiked several hundred yards through dense foliage, straight up the limestone side of a rock island, then down into the jellyfish lake. The lake reminded me of scenes from an old Tarzan movie. We never saw crocodiles in the lakes, but the lakes struck me as excellent places for crocs to live.

—

One morning when I came to work, a research vessel sat at anchor in front of fisheries. The boat was about sixty-five feet long and owned by Dr. Walter Stark, underwater photographer, marine biologist, oceanographer, and engineer; inventor of the Beckman mixed gas re-breather, for deep dives to four hundred feet. Supported by research grants from various foundations and institutions, Stark travelled around the world on his vessel. Currently, he was developing recompression tables for mixed gas diving.

That morning, Walter came into Peter's office and introduced himself. He had been conducting research on shark behavior down in New Guinea, was on his way to Japan to dry dock the boat, and had stopped in Palau for provisioning, he explained. His wife and crewman accompanied him. Walter took us on a tour of his ship. On deck was a recompression chamber and a transfer capsule to bring up a diver under pressure, and up on the bow sat a small submersible. We walked downstairs and into the stateroom. Wall to wall carpet and a grand piano furnished the room. Stark's gorgeous blond wife walked in from the galley. Dressed in white shorts and T-shirt, her long tan legs drew stares from both Peter and me. Peter, riveted by Walter's wife as well as by the submarine, coerced Walter into a submarine dive the following day. When I asked to go along, Walter replied: "Sure. You don't mind hanging off the wing like a remora, do you?" I guess I did. The sub was a two-man job.

The sub had a cockpit and canopy which flooded. It was powered by batteries and had an enclosed propeller with a nozzle on the stern. Two small wings protruded from the body, which made it look similar to the old Air Force experimental Bell X-1 rocket. The divers sat in the cockpit with their tanks on their backs, one person behind the other, the forward person controlling the machine. Divers in the sub were restricted by depth and rate of ascent just as in SCUBA diving. The same dangers of narcosis and embolism applied.

Having decided to dive near the entrance of Malakal Channel, we took the boat outside the channel and laid to. Peter and Walter donned their diving gear, gathered up their camera equipment, and got situated in the cockpit. Walter slid the canopy shut and latched it from the inside. The crewman lowered the sub into the water with a boom and winch and released them. From the deck, we watched the little yellow submersible disappear into the blue.

About thirty minutes later, we saw the sub surface several yards away. I jumped into the water, got the hook on, and we winched the craft aboard. As the winch lowered the sub into its cradle, I noticed that the canopy was shattered, just like a spider web. Peter told us about the dive as they shed their gear.

They had flooded and cruised slowly down while maneuvering back and forth in front of the channel entrance. They saw several grays around but they seemed only curious, not excited. Then a big gray, with several smaller sharks tagging along, came up out of blue water and passed in front of them. The sharks circled once and then the big gray charged the sub from the side, smashing into the canopy, shattering it.

"I yelled through my regulator and threw my arm up in defense. Scared the shit out of me," Peter said.

"The whole sub shook," said Stark. "The shark just bounced off and took off. Then the other sharks turned aggressive and we came up."

We stood around looking at the sub, admiring the spider webbed canopy. Then Walter said: "Listen. I'm going to paint this thing black. Sharks are intimidated by yellow. Every time something yellow goes in the water I get bothered."

Some of our new U.S. Divers diving vests were yellow, and I remembered I had been wearing a yellow vest with Doug when the gray had hit my spear. After that, neither Peter nor I ever wore yellow diving vests again.

Chapter 12

Voyages

A Belgian doctor named Von Schute sailed the Carolines in a Hong Kong-style thirty-two-foot ketch named *Kate*. Von Schute provided medical aid to the outer islanders, setting up medical clinics, training midwives, pulling teeth, and giving vaccinations. Based in Truk, Von Schute received compensation from the Trust Territory Government for these services. He spoke Trukese, ate Trukese food, sometimes acted Trukese. The people loved him because of it, and also because of his medicinal efforts. Von Schute detested the Catholic Church, disliked priests, despised Protestants, abhorred the TT Government, and loathed Peace Corps. Trust Territory officials, the Catholic Church, the Protestant Church, and Peace Corps, hated Von Schute. Every six months or so, the young and handsome Von Schute would sail in to Palau to take on provisions. Stories of Von Schute's extracurricular exploits with the ladies shadowed him through the islands, and more than once he was said to have fled for his life from jealous husbands.

Despite Von Schute's disdain for men of the west, Von Schute inexplicably took a liking to PCV Paul Callaghan; and since one of Von Schute's stops in Palau coincided with Paul's termination from Peace Corps, Paul approached the doctor about crewing for him to Truk. Von Schute welcomed Paul aboard.

They left Palau in excellent weather, sailing well south of the Central Carolines to avoid the treacherous atolls. Midway through the journey they encountered the fringes of a typhoon which had originated in the Marshalls and was spinning west, northwest toward the Marianas. The boat suffered sail and mast damage and sprung several leaks, but they managed to limp into Truk lagoon some twenty-two days later. From there, Paul flew home.

While he waited for parts and his boat sat on dry dock, Von Schute travelled on the Trust Territory field trip vessel, *Truk Islander*, to the Namanuito Islands to provide medical assistance there. The *Truk Islander*, on its way to Japan for repairs, dropped him off, the captain agreeing to pick him up on the return voyage to Truk two weeks hence. But when the ship returned to Moen two weeks later, Von Schute was not on board. The captain, it seems, had forgotten about the doctor. Four months later, the ship returned to Namanuito and picked an outraged Von Schute.

Von Schute's last voyage began in Truk as he left for Japan. Von Schute had taken on two young Trukese youths as crew. At sunup, on the morning Von Schute sailed, Norman stood on the dock watching the crew hoist sail as the *Kate* pulled away. Von Schute, on the bow rigging the jib, yelled to one of his young crewmen: "Don't start the engine! Don't start the engine!" The young Trukese, apparently hearing only "engine," cranked it up. That signaled the first inkling of trouble; an omen, perhaps.

As the boat fell off the wind into a reach, Von Schute adjusted the furling on the mainsail. Suddenly, the sheet-line began to snake out through the block.

"Look at that! Look at that!" he yelled, meaning grab the sheet-line. While the boom swung out, the crew stared blankly at the sheet-line running through the block—just as they'd been ordered. Von Schute steamed.

"What you think? No think you? Grab the sheet, stupid!" he barked.

Then the jib fouled on the forestay. Von Schute pointed to the problem and yelled to the crewman nearest the bow: "Let it out!" The young Trukese grabbed the jib sheet and hauled in, fouling the jib even more. Von Schute looked to the heavens and mumbled something.

That is how Von Schute's last voyage began. Sometime during the trip the *Kate* fell prey to foul weather, and no trace of Von Schute, his crew, or the vessel was ever found.

After Peace Corps training in Peleliu, Harson decided to enter the University of Guam. His sponsor would be a well-to-do retired American couple who had previously adopted one of Harson's older relatives. The night before Harson was to leave for Guam, we took two Palauan girls up to the Boom Boom Room and found a place in a booth near the jukebox. Three Americans who worked for construction companies on the island sat at the bar. Other people sat on the bench around the perimeter of the dance floor. Harson went up to the bar to get some drinks just as someone shoved a glass into the face of Tom Glover, one of the three Americans at the bar, cutting him badly. I looked over and saw Harson in the middle of the dance floor having words with Tom's friend, Rusty White. Harson hit him across the face with an open palm, and Rusty went down. In the next instant, a Palauan sitting on the bench rushed in and kicked Rusty several times in the side of his temple. He wore black leather ankle boots with pointed toes, and he must have been from Guam since no Palauan living in Palau would be caught dead wearing pixie boots. I jumped up and grabbed Harson, and we rushed out with our girlfriends. We walked down to the Texas Saloon, had a beer, then went home, Harson still upset about some comments that Rusty had made to him.

The following morning, I drove the fisheries truck to Harson's place to take him to the airport. Sabed told me that the police had come and taken him to the police station on assault and battery charges stemming from the night before. I hustled down to the police station and filed a report as a witness. They had charged Harson with putting Rusty White's eye out. Harson wouldn't be going to Guam for a while, at least not until after the trial.

In Palau, court cases were decided by a judge based on testimonies by witnesses and the accused. I testified in court on Harson's behalf because he was innocent of injuring Rusty White. Harson had knocked Rusty down, but he had taken no part in kicking Rusty in the head. And Harson, I testified, as usual, had worn zorries that night. The American judge disbelieved my testimony, and at lunch recess the district attorney took me aside.

"The judge thinks you're lying—that you're protecting Harson," he said.

And I answered, "Why should I be lying? I'm not lying. Harson didn't do it. It was the other guy."

I just could not believe the judge thought I was lying.

After lunch the judge called me to the stand again, but his line of questioning led nowhere. Several other witnesses testified, and soon it became obvious that the other person was responsible for injuring Rusty. Harson got off but with a stiff warning about fighting.

That night we celebrated with Sandy at Mike and Sabed's house instead of the Boom Boom Room. Then Harson flew off to Guam to get educated. Harson and I had been like brothers, and his leaving saddened me. I knew that Sandy would also miss him, as well as a lot of other girls in Palau.

The new Group VII volunteers who had trained in Peleliu were a different breed. They seemed overly concerned with luxuries, and many of them rejected living with families. I put the three new fisheries volunteers through a SCUBA course modeled after Hardy's program. They grumbled and complained; lousy gear, too hard, too hot. They balked at loading gear, filling tanks, mooring the boats, anything like work. And they depressed me. I called them "bitch wimps." One married guy quit during training, telling Wilson before he left that his program "stunk." Peter told him that few people were tough enough to live and work in Palau, and he wasn't one of them anyway, so good thing he was leaving. I wondered where Peace Corps was getting these recruits. I had a few friends left from Group VI; only one or two from Group VII. I stayed away, avoiding the Peace Corps office and all the chitchat.

—

Stan Wayman returned to Palau to do his underwater photographic story. He chartered the *Ngerengchol*, and we traveled all over Palau diving and photographing, carrying a small Mako air compressor on board to refill our tanks. Each trip lasted three or four days, then we'd return to Koror, reprovision, and take off again.

Stan's routine called for shooting as many shots as possible per dive. He had two auto-wind Nikon Fs encased in bright yellow Giddings housings, and I often carried the spare camera down so he could shoot two rolls, seventy-two frames, before we had to surface. I would be stuffed with gear; bands of flashbulbs, nylon bag, camera, and spear gun. I carried bulbs everywhere I could stash them, tying strips of rubber inner tubing, which held the bulbs by their nipples in small slits, around my arms, waist, and above my knees. Stan's right hand was missing all but two fingers, and he had difficulty changing bulbs so I did it for him. After each flash, I'd pop out the expended bulb, which would float up into an open dive bag I held over the reflector, and stick a new one in. I got so good at this that Stan would shoot again instantaneously, never looking away from focusing. Stan always dove in an old pair of blue pajamas and wore a Buoy Fenzy vest which controlled his buoyancy. Sometimes he'd give me a Nikonos and tell me to snap off a roll. I knew little about photography but I'd shoot away. I asked Stan if he'd heard of Walter Stark—no—so I told him about the yellow submarine incident and Stark's theory about the color yellow aggravating sharks, as a bull is aggravated by red.

"Well, no problems yet," Stan chirped, eyeing one of his yellow camera housings.

While Stan was in Palau, a sixty-foot cruising sailboat from Australia called. The owner-captain of *Frigate* was an Australian named George Holland, a rich, arrogant, middle-aged man who thought little of Peace Corps and less of me. Having made his money on Australian real estate, he now cruised the Pacific. Unscheduled, he and his crewman were enchanted by Palau and tied up for an indefinite period, enjoying the local flavor, the Hollywood goings-on, and all the rest.

When Stan finished his work in Palau proper and concluded the charter of the *Ngerengchol*, Ray Accord hosted a party for him at his house. Many people came and when George Holland showed up Stan asked him about chartering his boat to take us to Helen Reef. Another guest, a visitor in Palau, was a young American girl named Bobbie, on university sabbatical to study sociological structures of Micronesia. Stan took to her like a fly on garbage and later that night they left the party together.

After hearing my stories, Stan was excited about going to Helen Reef, and he chartered the *Frigate* to take us. He asked Bob Owen to come along and brought his new friend Bobbie along as well. Peter had intended to go but backed out at the last minute.

We would be gone ten days, and Peter could little afford to leave the office for that long on a diving junket.

The sloop rigged motor-sailer *Frigate* was set up for cruising in exquisite style. On the cabin roof was a flying bridge, and just inside the cabin was another steering station. On the afterdeck, Australian beer and soft drinks were kept in refrigerated compartments beneath the seats of built-in benches along the aft cabin wall. Below the afterdeck was a walk-in freezer and behind that the captain's stateroom. In the cabin, up forward of the galley were three-quarters, each with two bunks, and a shower room with both salt and freshwater nozzles. The main engine was diesel as was the smaller one for the generator.

When we got underway, I agreed to help out by standing watches. George gave me lots of other chores to do as well, making sure I earned my keep. I worked hard, and drank lots of that Australian beer too.

Bobbie and Stan looked like father and daughter. She was short and freckled, and she spoke with a high-pitched voice while continually actuating her hands for emphasis. Stan, almost a foot taller than she, had white hair and a scruffy white beard. Stan's crooked front teeth seemed to go off at adverse angles and his long nose bent to one side, such that it pressed against his face mask while diving. She ogled over him and he over her, and they spent every moment together, always sleeping out on the afterdeck stateroom roof.

Atolls are oases in the oceanic vastness. Low and autonomous, they sit out in the middle of nowhere. We spotted Helen Reef in early morning, the tips of the tiny island's coconut trees lying on the horizon like some far-off ship, and late that morning, with the sun at our backs and water smooth as marble, we approached the west passage to enter the lagoon. Off to port, a big rusty Japanese freighter with guano-streaked sides, her bow aiming for the lagoon, sat high and dry on the reef—a victim of pilot error—now a mid-ocean ghostlike aberration. Disturbed by our presence, hundreds of seabirds gawked, squawked, jumped, glided, and flapped from the ship's superstructure. Curious boobies circled us like buzzards, then tried to land on the masthead, only to be thrown off with each roll.

The deep passage into Helen Lagoon concatenates through the reef and forks before entering the lagoon. George, on the midship steering station over the cabin, revved the diesel to buck the tidal flow from the lagoon as I stood on the bow with Polaroid sunglasses in search of coral heads. We cleared the channel easily and motored slowly north along the inner western barrier reef toward Helen Island several miles away, anchoring about noon in a deep sandy inlet about a quarter mile south of the island. The sky over the island was speckled with birds and photographic slides taken of the island later appeared dusty; dusty with birds. Up on the bridge, George stood surveying the island with his binoculars. Suddenly he yelled out, "Hey! We're not alone!"

We launched the dinghy hanging from starboard davits, attached the twenty-five-horsepower Johnson to the transom, and motored into the elongate sandy protrusion that is the southern end of the island. Six Taiwanese sailors dressed in dirty white judo pants and jackets greeted us with sheepish smiles. They offered us pieces of roasted turtle as we walked ashore, George with a loaded six-cylinder Smith & Wesson stainless steel .44 magnum strapped to his hip. They looked like teenagers and spoke no English. Bob knelt down on spindly legs in front of them and scratched the outline of a boat in the sand with a stick. He pointed at them and gave the palms-up sign which prompted them to point to the north, out to sea, their ship having apparently run off and left them on the island—stranded poachers—when we approached.

Bob Owen, chief of Conservation for the Trust Territory of the Pacific Islands, stood up.

"You are under arrest," he said, pulling his badge from his pocket and waving it in their faces.

Sensing trouble, the six orientals shook their heads, then began jabbering with each other in their language.

Bob looked at George and raised his bushy eyebrows.

"Shut up!" he barked.

The startled fishermen stared at Bob. Demonstrating the crossed wrist sign, Bob pointed at them, then patted the gun on George's hip. They seemed to get the point and watched carefully as Bob again knelt on the sand and drew figures of a turtle, a bird, an egg, and a rat, drawing an "X" through each figure except the rat. Drawing a circle around the rat, he nodded the okay while pointing to their mouths.

"Okay to eat rat," he said. They had already killed at least one turtle and probably some seabirds as well.

We had no way of knowing what went on before our arrival nor how long they had been there. We started a slow stroll to check the tiny island, being careful to avoid stepping on the bird eggs which lay like pepper on the white beach. Near the northern end, we found a coconut tree laying across the sand, apparently cut down by the orientals to get to the nuts. The Taiwanese stood behind us as we stared at this thoughtless act.

"Let's tie the bastards up so they can't do any more damage," I said to Bob.

He thought about it, seriously I think, but decided it would be inappropriate. We confiscated their saw near their fireplace, which lay in a sandpit with feathers and bones strewn about.

That evening George was able to contact Koror on the radio. A Trust Territory field trip ship happened to be in Tobi, and it would be diverted to Helen Reef the following day to pick up the stranded sailors. Later that night we saw lights off to the east, probably those of the Taiwanese ship.

The Trust Territory was plagued with foreign poaching, particularly from the Taiwanese. They dispatched small dilapidated fishing sampans specifically to poach, targeting small remote atolls and islands such as Helen Reef and taking turtles, birds, eggs, and giant clams. During my tour in Palau, several Taiwanese boats were apprehended, their holds full of tons of frozen giant clam muscle. Pathetically, they took only the muscle, leaving the rest of the animal, about 95 percent, as waste. The boats belonged to poor companies which cared little about the welfare of the boats and their juvenile crews. Nor would the Taiwan government acknowledge the problem. This left the Trust Territory with the expensive burden of sending the crews back to their homeland. Life was cheap in the east.[13]

---

[13] In April 1975, the Palau Office of Marine Resources sent myself and several other biologists to Helen Reef to conduct a resource assessment of marine organisms, in particular giant clams. The entire lagoon had been systematically harvested of giant clams. The largest species of giant clam

The next morning, Stan and I took the dinghy and made our way across the lagoon to the southwest outer slope of the barrier reef, a dramatic drop-off and wall. We anchored the dingy on the reef margin and let it tail out over the wall with the ebb tide. A strong surface current pushed us out as we descended nervously out away from the vertical wall to avoid the luxuriant outgrowth of invertebrates: scleractinians, gorgonians, alcyonaceans, sponges, anemones, ascidians, sipunculids, crinoids, urchins, oysters. A school of small tunas, probably skipjack, passed quickly in the fringes of our vision. We reached thirty feet, and Stan gave a shot of air to his vest to neutralize his descent. From the blue, a seven foot white-fringed shark appeared, swimming in toward us from about 2:00 o'clock. As it neared, it gave a quick flick of its tail, glided and rolled, showing us its fat white belly as it peeled off and circled back out into open ocean. The shark passed again twenty feet out, and Stan snapped several shots. It came closer on the next pass, its size more impressive than before and I held my spear out. Then two smaller gray sharks joined in. Swimming faster than the big white-fringed shark, they came closer, slowly at first, then with quick bursts, shot off away. We slowly kicked our fins, making for the surface. From the blue, a third gray about four feet long came from the left of Stan and rushed straight for him. Stan threw up the Giddings to block it and it veered off, coming around again, from the other side, my side. I stuck my gun up and punched it once; it jerked sideways and darted off. We reached the surface and as I watched for sharks, Stan clipped his camera to the overboard rope and climbed into the skiff. I saw no sign of the big shark, but the smaller grays swam in mixed patterns under the boat. I tossed my gun in the boat and heaved myself in. Stan pulled in his camera, and we saw the little gray come zooming by as if to take a bite out of the Giddings. We looked at each other quizzically. Stan smiled, showing crooked teeth.

"Well Pat," he said. "Think he wanted my Giddings?"

"Yellow!" I answered.

---

may take about twenty years to grow to a length of one meter. Significantly, on that trip two abandoned Japanese long-line boats lay grounded on the northeastern reef.

The wind had come up during our dive and we had a nine-mile, two-hour trip back across the lagoon to the *Frigate*. I started the engine, and we started beating our way upwind through one and two foot waves generated by a stiff northerly breeze fetching across the lagoon. The little aluminum boat, much too overloaded, pounded and pounded; and we bounced and jarred, and swore and cussed, and wiped salt water from our eyes, and bailed, and bailed some more. At dusk we reached *Frigate* on a fuel tank nearly dry. Had we ran out of fuel or broke down, they never would have seen us. Nor could they have reached us, since we were using the only dinghy and navigating the *Frigate* at night in the lagoon was out of the question. We talked it over with George and decided to move the *Frigate* to the southern end until Stan and I completed our work there.

After several days of diving the southern reefs, we moved back up to the northern end where Bob spent his days on the island. The TT ship had picked up the arrested poachers and headed back to Koror, leaving Bob in peace to study the vegetation and birds, trap rats, and count turtle nests.

The beach on Helen Island was covered with thousands of eggs and baby chicks. Small blacktip sharks, dorsal fins cutting the surface, cruised the shoreline looking for the occasional chick washed in by a tidal surge. Hundreds of birds flew around, walked around, and sat around, their relentless calls adding to the apparent disorder. This small little sand island—mid-ocean incubator, bird metropolis—with its congestion and apparent confusion, seemed out of control, like so much chaos. An observer might well ask how a parent bird could ever recognize its own out of this madness. But to the seabird residents of this island, this was neither chaos nor madness nor confusion. This was normal. This was life on Helen Reef.

Terns, tropic birds, shearwaters, petrels, boobies; all make their living from the sea by diving on baitfish. But the larger seabird species, the frigates or "man-of-war," play a different game. With wingspans over seven feet, they are highly adapted to gliding and soaring the thermal airstreams. Because they are unable to regain flight except from an elevated position, they must avoid alighting on land or on water and so they roost high in the trees. Each morning, the frigates fly out to sea along with the other seabirds in search of fish schools. Soaring high in the air, far above the other birds, frigates swoop down like dive bombers on the seabirds below, chasing and harassing them until they drop or regurgitate their food whereupon the skillful frigates catch it for themselves. Ironically, at dusk, all the birds, frigates included, fly back to the island and roost together in peace for the night.

On our last day at Helen Reef, Stan wanted to make a night dive in the channel area. George wanted to depart after our dive and, being unable to negotiate the channel safely at night, we snuck outside in midafternoon and hove to near the channel entrance. The Australian crocodile hunters had given me a twelve-gauge shark prod that I wanted to take along. I had become wary of channels, especially at night.

At dusk, Stan and I took the dinghy and motored in, anchoring on a slope adjoining the channel. We suited up and made our descent, our six-volt lights throwing concentrated beams through the turquoise to the sandy bottom. At sixty feet we encountered an enormous brain coral head, its gray-green polyps extended, each polyp ringed with tiny arms, minute tentacles grasping for zooplankters. Brush your tender tummy across this coral and get welted. Between the sand bottom and the live polyps was the dead zone, a massive calcareous foundation colonized by algae, sponges, mollusks, worms, and crustaceans. Red and white banded shrimp equipped with gangly appendages crawled delicately over the rough. From a vertical crevice within the coral, spiny antennae protruded, moving like chopsticks to thwart off intruders. The beady eyes of the lobsters glowed bright red in the light beam as Stan shot off a roll of film.

We made our way around the base of the coral head, our lights now and then piercing the darkness around us in search of visitors. Several feet from the coral head, a school of red snappers hovered just above the rippled sand. A stingray lay buried, only its eyes peering up. It bolted in a cloud of sand and fled on giant wings when Stan's camera flashed it. Then Stan, swimming along in front of me, suddenly stopped and went vertical. Accelerated pulses of bubbles flowed from his mouthpiece, causing me to swing my light in a great arc around and behind us, looking for whatever had startled him. When my light came around in front again, I saw the creature. A giant grouper, the largest grouper I had ever seen underwater, faced us. The big fish hovered several feet above the sand, its fanlike pectoral fins, dorsal fin, and tail fin performing rhythmic undulating sweeps to maintain equilibrium. From the sides of its huge gray-brown mottled head, each black eye rotated independently of the other, watching us. Prominent pointed white teeth shown from its lower jaw as it opened its mouth to suck water over its gills. This thing weighs three hundred pounds, I thought. So caught up was I that when Stan shot his first frame, he had to grab me to change the bulb.

George had been bugging me the whole trip to bring back a big grouper. Large groupers are excellent eating, the flesh having a consistency similar to lobster. So when Stan finished the roll, he motioned me to bang the grouper with the prod. Now George would get his fish. I had reservations about doing it, but on the other hand, it would be a thrill to bring up a three-hundred pounder. I took a last look around with my light for sharks and moved directly in front of the monster, tucking my light between my knees so it illuminated the big fish's head. With some hesitancy, I slipped out the safety pin, pulled back hard on the sling, and sighted down my arm to the flat portion between the fish's eyes. I let it fly . . . *Thud.* The prod bounced back and fell to the sand, unexploded. Unmoved, the monster fish opened its mouth and flared its gill covers, its big eyes giving me a funny look. It easily could have inhaled me. Low on air and unwilling to press my luck with another shot, I carefully retrieved my defunct prod and we ascended to the dinghy. As Stan climbed into the boat, I shined my light down for a quick look around but saw only sand and a few fish; no sharks.

Aboard the *Frigate*, George, on hearing our story, voiced his displeasure that I missed catching the grouper. But later, after rethinking my actions, I considered the misfire an act of God. First, I had no business killing such a magnificent animal and second, nighttime, at sixty feet, in a deep channel on a tropical atoll, had the prod fired, who knows what might have come in.

As a waypoint, George set our course to Merir Island, 120 miles to the northeast and almost in a direct line with our course home. In the bright sunshine of noon the following day, we sighted coconut trees and by early afternoon, we motored slowly along the east side of the island. Toward the northern end, a shallow shelf reached out to sea, setting up a strong pattern of currents. Along the current rip, schools of small tuna foamed on the surface in pursuit of small baitfish while above, hungry terns and shearwaters dove and dipped noisily at the fleeing bait. Numerous green turtles swam near the island, some paired and copulating, others waiting for nightfall to crawl up the white sand beach, dig a hole, and lay their load of eggs.

As we rounded the northern end and started down the west side, we saw several people waving white flags on the beach.

"But it's not supposed to be inhabited," I said.

George checked it out through binoculars.

"Strange," he said, "there are six of them, and they don't look like islanders. Maybe we've got more poachers."

A hundred yards offshore George brought the *Frigate* to a stop in the absolute calm of the lee. Then he went below and emerged with his Smith & Wesson. Stan readied his camera, and we lined the rail watching three of them paddle out in a long dingy. When they climbed aboard from the stern ladder we could see they were emaciated. Their clothes were rotten, torn, and shredded; and they stunk. The leader, whose head was wrapped in a soiled towel, spoke broken English, enough to get it across that they had shipwrecked. En route from Indonesia to Australia, their ship had caught fire, the crew setting out in lifeboats, themselves in the one they had paddled out in.

He lifted his hand and showed us three fingers. "Three weeks then see here." Then two fingers: "Two weeks already stay here. You take us, okay."

"Uh uh," George shook his head. "No room. Sorry."

We didn't know what to make of that story, but we had nothing else to go on. Their appearance seemed to bear them out. They indicated that they were in no danger, had water, and had little need of medical assistance. I gave them some matches and a pack of cigarettes. While they puffed on their cigarettes, George radioed Koror. Then he gave them several blankets, a machete, and some canned food—wished them luck, and told them a ship would arrive to pick them up in a couple of days. We found out later, after the TT ship had brought them back to Koror, that they *really* had been shipwreck victims from Indonesia.

After we departed Merir for Koror, I got off watch one morning at six just as we passed the southeast tip of Angaur about a quarter mile offshore. Out of the eastern horizon, the sun had just popped up through the serene ocean, burning off the coolness of the night as another sweltering day began. The *Frigate* motored along peacefully, gliding over the ground swells sweeping the passage, the diesel providing a monotonous, almost hypnotic cadence.

Lee Marvin had made a standing offer of one thousand dollars to the first person in Palau (excluding Ray) to land a marlin on a rod and reel. In a rod holder clasped to the stern railing, George kept an unlimited 180-pound class rod equipped with a 14/0 Gold Fenor reel. I had brought along a big eight ounce lead-head with black and red feathers that Ray had rigged up for me and now, thinking thousand dollar bills, I fetched it and went aft. I snapped the end of the lure's stainless steel twisted wire leader into the ball-bearing swivel on the end of the line, dropped the lure into the water, pulled back on the drag release lever to release line, then pushed forward to adjust the drag. The lure trolled along just beneath the surface and alongside the path of the prop bubbles about two hundred feet back. Satisfied with this, I stepped back from the rod just as the spool started spinning like the wheels of a dragster at the start of a race. It sang, "... *Wharrrrrl, wharrrrrl, wharrrrrl*..." Few sounds are as distinctive on a fishing boat, and few sounds generate so much excitement.

About a hundred yards off our stern and to starboard, a big marlin jumped and tail-walked, ripping line off the spool at sizzling speed. My heart pounded as I took control of the rod. I looked over my shoulder and behind me at the bridge—George, his back to me, held the wheel, unable to hear the screaming reel over the engine noise. Stan and Bobbie sat up from their bed on the afterdeck.

"Look Stan," I yelled, pointing at the marlin.

His eyes bulged, and he scrambled below decks for his camera. Turning my attention to the reel, I saw the spindle shaking wildly back and forth on its axle, the spool diameter decreasing as I watched. Bad bearings. I touched the side plate, immediately pulling my hand back, my fingers seared. Licking my scorched fingers, I watched the spool size decrease as the line neared its end.

"Son-of-a-bitch won't stop!" I screamed to anyone who would listen. Then the reel stopped, a wisp of smoke rising from the spool's margin. I grabbed a bucket of salt water sitting on the deck and doused it, the reel hissing as the water cooled its burnt bearings. Afflicted with marlin fever, I cranked the reel wildly. Stan positioned himself beside me with his Nikon F and telephoto lens. Way back, the marlin broke water, jumping again, and again.

"Look at it! Look at it!" I screamed while Stan snapped off shots.

The big fish sounded, stripping off what little line I'd gained. George, finally having noticed the activity on the stern, yelled from the wheel:

"Set the hook! Set the hook!"

Set the hook? How, I wondered, yanking up on the rod, unable to budge it. Friction held the rod butt firmly in the holder, like it had been epoxied.

Now most of the line was out again. I settled down a little and decided to tighten up on the drag just a bit lest the fish strip the reel in another second or two. I pushed the brake lever forward; the spool slowed and stopped. *Uh oh.* Too much. I jerked the lever back. The line grew limp. Far behind, the marlin broke water again. Grief overwhelmed me. Few events can generate so much disappointment so quickly as when a fishing line goes slack. I turned and looked up pathetically at George on the wheel, his forthcoming words already registering in my head.

"Should have set the hook," he said emphatically.

Two days later, I walked into Ray's office and told him my fish story. He sat at his work bench, busy tying up a lure, his bifocals down on his nose.

"Why'd you lose it?" he asked.

"He had me stripped," I said. "I tightened up a wee bit on the drag to slow him down. I don't know—just spit out the lure I guess. Anyway, I could have been a grand richer today, son-of-a-bitch."

Ray turned slightly and looked up at me out of the corner of his eye. "Should'a set the hook," he mumbled.

—

Stan left Palau a few days later explaining that he had to get back to review his slides and meet with *Life* editors. He left his camera and diving equipment with Bob Owen. Bobbie left with him on the same plane. He'd be back, he said, to fill in any holes in his work. I told him I'd be waiting.

Chapter 13

Wildness

Peter flew to the mainland on business, and he returned talking of bringing out several American purse seiners to attempt seining tuna in the clear tropical waters around Palau. A month later, three beautiful new seiners docked in Malakal Harbor. The seven-hundred-ton state-of-the-art boats, built specifically for purse seining, sported high bows, tall crow's nests, and sweeping angular lines. The crew's quarters slept two to a room, each containing wall-to-wall carpeting and a stereo system. The galleys were big and roomy with adjacent crew lounges and libraries. And for spiritual comfort, each vessel contained a small chapel. They fished in class, first class.

This was a unique experiment. No one had ever attempted to seine tuna in the western tropical Pacific. Consequently, the boats set on tuna schools around Palau with little success, their shallow nets and the clear water allowing the swift tuna to escape beneath the seines. Purse seiners based in San Pedro and San Diego traditionally fished in the Eastern Pacific off the coasts of Mexico and South America. The water is less clear than in the Western Pacific and tuna, mostly yellowfin, are associated with surface swimming porpoise, the boats setting their nets around the porpoise, capturing the fish below.[14]

---

[14] This 1968 pilot fishing attempt by American purse seiners in the Western Pacific failed, but not for long. The emergence of Latin America two-hundred

The new boats were family owned by Portuguese-Americans, and they brought with them a long tradition of fishing—and wealth derived from the industry. The young crew members, new elements in town, spent their free time in the bars, flaunting their money and charming the night ladies.

One Friday night a bunch of them stopped by the Peleliu Club, which was located shore side on the Koror side of the Malakal Bridge. Three locals with a couple of electric guitars and a drum set were playing Palauan music while several couples danced. The crewmen made several loud remarks about the dancing and the music. About an hour later, they left in a U-Drive. As their car reached the main road, a hail of rocks pelted it, shattering the rear window. The car slid to a halt and the men jumped out, ready for battle. Stones rocketed in from the dark, banging off the car and thumping one man in the chest. The men scrambled back inside and the driver floored it, spinning the tires and leaving a rooster tail of coral gravel. The Datsun sped across the bridge, its taillights fading in the dust, rocks streaking after it.

Each purse seiner carried two high-performance boats equipped with 120-horsepower Mercury outboards for chasing porpoise. Crew members often used them for water skiing in the bay out in front of fisheries. Gene Helfman made friends with the crew and often skied with them. He asked me to join them but I never did. Gene enjoyed their dope, liquor, and recreational activities. Rumor had it that he was quitting Peace Corps and going back to the States on one of the boats.

---

mile exclusive economic zones, the exodus of U.S. canneries to the Territories, declining yellowfin stocks, and the effects of the Marine Mammal Protection Act on restricting dolphin kills forced the Eastern Pacific fleet to move westward. In the mid-1970s, American seiners, equipped with deep-setting nets and beefed-up deck winches, began fishing successfully in the South Pacific off New Zealand and New Guinea. By 1983, almost the entire Eastern Pacific purse seine fleet had relocated to the Western Pacific. Then, in 1990, Starkist, Bumblebee, and Van Camp, suppliers of 75 percent of the canned tuna consumed in the U.S., adopted a "dolphin safe" policy, effectively forcing the remaining Eastern Pacific seiners to either tie up or move westward. Other canneries soon followed suit. Rather than an effort to preserve dolphins, however, most fishermen and environmentalists consider "dolphin safe" a political and marketing strategy, a calculated move to win the hearts and dollars of the fickle U.S. consumer.

Before the seiners departed for California, one of the boats held an open house. Peter had the *Emeraech* stay in port that day so the crew members could visit the seiner. That evening, I walked with the *Emeraech* crew over to the seiner at the Van Camp dock. We walked up the stairs and onto the afterdeck, got a beer from the bar on deck, and eased our way down some stairs toward the galley for the buffet. As I walked through the companionway, the cook, a fat Portuguese with greasy black hair and hairy tattooed arms, took me aside. He wiped his hands on his soiled apron and spoke to me in an aborted whisper.

"If those black bastards ever give you any trouble, just let us know. We'll take care of those fuckers." His garlic breath caused me to step back. I blinked, unbelieving.

"What makes you think they'd give me any trouble?" I said.

"Those fuckers stoned my buddies. They're all assholes. They're just lucky we didn't get our guns that night or it'd been all over for those fuckers," he said, referring to the trouble at the Peleliu Club. The cook obviously felt violated by the presence of these island savages on his ship.

Feeling tight inside, I thanked him for his concern and sauntered into the galley, where, like a starved dog, I stuffed myself with hors d'oeuvres: little hamburger balls on sticks covered with ketchup sauce; sections of grilled hot dogs on sticks; greasy lumpia; oily sautéed chicken parts. Grimacing, I steered clear of the mushy, gray-green sashimi prepared from mishandled frozen tuna.

A few minutes later, Steven, a soft-spoken Nukuoroan from the *Emeraech*, came over and whispered to me: "Trouble with Deisen, outside."

We heard shouting and scampered through the small companionway leading out to the deck, Peter right behind us. On the afterdeck, Deisen stood toe to toe with the cook, punching the cook's chest, backing him up. Peter and the ship's captain grabbed Deisen and pulled him back.

Deisen, 170 pounds of muscle, screamed at the cook: "You called me a black bastard! You called me a black bastard!"

Peter struggled to restrain him. The cook wiped blood from his nose with his apron, then staggered down into the companionway. Embarrassed, the captain apologized to Deisen. The seiner boys stood around the deck watching, their faces set in revenge. Peter led Deisen off the boat with me and the other *Emeraech* members following.

Peter drove Deisen back to the *Emeraech*, which was docked in front of the co-op across from Van Camp. The rest of us walked, saying little, our thoughts to ourselves. Once again, I felt a particular shame over being American. American pride was a thing of the past.

Back on the boat, Deisen was unable to settle down. After Peter left, he paced the deck, swearing in Kapingamarangan. A little later, Kailang and the co-op boys, Mekreos, Albert, and Masahiro, who had also been on the seiner, came aboard the *Emeraech* with several cases of Schlitz and Kirin. We drank and discussed the purse seine incident. The Palauan, Moko, with his one-and-a-half ears, pow-wowed with Kailang. They talked of a reprisal in Palauan. Later on, Peter came back. He wanted to keep the peace, and he talked down what had happened. Peter knew the ingredients for trouble were simmering on the *Emeraech* that evening. Deisen's pride, as well as the other crew member's, had been offended; Kailang stood ready for a good fight; and alcohol had emboldened everyone. Peter took Deisen into the cabin and talked quietly with him. When they came out on deck, Mekreos, always one to argue, especially when filled up on beer, challenged Peter: "What are we supposed to do, Pete? Let those *chad er a ngebard* call us names like that?"

Peter answered loudly: "I'm just asking you guys to stay cool. It's over. They'll be leaving tomorrow, so let it be. We all know it was bad, but it's over."

The crew nodded affirmatively, the simple islander response to the white man's enlightenment. Peter walked off the gangplank, turned and snapped: "Remember. No trouble!" Everyone nodded in agreement again; sure Pete, no trouble.

No sooner had Peter left than the cops cruised through the co-op, on patrol. News of the mishap had already reached the station. Palauans respected the police like they respected *belice* (dogs). Kailang lobbed a bottle over the roof of the co-op, the bottle shattering on the ground behind the police car as it drove out. Too timid to acknowledge the affront, the police continued down the road toward Van Camp.

In the darkness, I wondered how I could pull the "great disappearing act." I had little desire to participate in a drunken brawl between irate Portuguese sailors and outraged islanders. From the *Emeraech*, we could see the purse seiner, its deck lit up like Times Square. The super bright floodlight glowing from its masthead spread out in a reflective sheen across the satin night waters of the bay. Crewmen milled about on the deck drinking beer. I looked over at Deisen standing on the afterdeck staring out at the seiner, his eyes bloodshot. Kailang talked explicitly in Palauan to his comrades.

Suddenly, all at once, everyone filed off the *Emeraech*, a mixture of Nukuoroans, Kapingamarangans, and Palauans. Armed with Schlitz and Kirin, they began the short hike over to Van Camp to wage war. Only myself and Tengadink, the Palauan bait man who was too old for such nonsense, stayed back. I walked down the dock and into the co-op office, telling Masahiro, on watch, I'd be sleeping in the loft, a small attic over the co-op shop where the *Emeraech* stored its bait nets. Too hot during the day because of the tin roof, the loft served as a comfortable sleeping place at night. Rats liked it too.

Only a few minutes had passed when I heard shouting from across the bay. Masahiro stood on the dock watching, and he called me to come look. I scampered down in time to see Kailang dash across the Van Camp dock, chuck a bottle, then race back. Immediately the others charged in and pelted the seiner with rocks and bottles. I heard cars coming and turned around in time to see the cops roar by the co-op in their two little Datsuns, kicking up a lung-clogging cloud of dust. A minute later, with red lights flashing, they drove onto the Van Camp dock, causing the rock throwers to disperse like chickens. Some ran back through the Van Camp plant and jumped the fence; others ran down the dock, jumped the fence, and disappeared into the boonies. Several minutes later they straggled in and congregated on the *Emeraech*, breathing heavily from their sprint, drinking and laughing and watching the cops across the bay argue with the enraged crewmen on the seiner. The island black bastards had evinced their mettle, demeaning the proud Portuguese fishermen.

Invisible behind the glare of the bright floodlight shining down from the roof, I sat in the loft watching the boys on the *Emeraech* through the roof overhang and listening to their talk. Kailang, drunk and ornery, was "going to get those guys if they come over." I thought: As soon as the cops leave Van Camp, those Portuguese sailors will be coming over all right, probably with guns. Then what will Kailang and the gang do? Brandish spears?

It was 10:00 p.m., and Kailang sent Mekreos into town in the co-op truck for more beer. The cops left Van Camp and cruised slowly by the co-op, never stopping. They were scared; scared of the situation, and scared of Kailang. Five drunks from the Peleliu Club drove up with beer. Kailang welcomed them aboard.

"Bring your *biang* (beer)," he commanded.

Mekreos returned with several cases of warm Kirin which added considerable stock to the inventory. Kailang and the Palauans sang songs while some of the others lay on the gunwale storage covers, dozing. Maybe it was over. I flopped back on the nets and dozed.

Boom! Boom! Shots, right in front of the co-op, woke me. I sat up in time to see the seiner boys jump from two cars and run out on the dock, firing pistols and rifles in the air.

"Come on you black mothas!" "Get out here, you chickenshits."

Those on the *Emeraech* charged forward into the cabin, some going around and hiding behind it. Only Kailang stood his ground. He pulled out a switchblade, a souvenir from Japan, and waved it in front of him, beckoning the aggressors to come aboard as he jumped from hatch cover to hatch cover. The purse seiner members tossed bottles, shattering them on the deck and bouncing them off the cabin. Kailang danced and screamed, his face red, his blood-gorged veins bulging from his neck.

The seiner boys dashed back to their cars and drove off. Kailang, his voice raspy and unintelligible, ran down the gangplank, sprinted through the co-op, and lobed a Schlitz bottle at the receding taillights of their cars. Kailang turned to Masahiro standing nearby, his crippled body bent laterally toward his short leg and demanded the keys to the co-op truck. Masahiro tossed him the keys, and Kailang and two of his friends tore off toward town.

On the *Emeraech*, the crew silently swept up the mess and tossed it overboard. They were outclassed, and they knew it. Rocks and bottles were one thing, guns another. Mekreos and Albert climbed up into the loft and fell asleep. The crew hit their bunks. The *Emeraech* fell silent. It was 1:00 a.m., late, even for drunken sailors. Soon only the occasional *tuk, tuk, tuk* of a gecko and the invariable droning of the reefer compressors could be heard.

I awoke again to the sound of Kailang down below talking in Palauan to his friends; something about taking a boat over to the seiner at Van Camp. Peering out from beneath the rafters, I saw Kailang. He held a rifle, a.22/.410 over and under.

Kailang kept his runabout down at the end of the dock next to the *Ngerengchol* along with several other small boats. When I heard the outboard start up, I shook Mekreos and Albert but neither would wake. I climbed down and walked over to Masahiro on the dock watching. Masahiro shook his head in disbelief.

"*Kmal meknid a chad* (They are very bad)," he proclaimed.

I nodded in agreement. It wasn't funny anymore.

"Go call the police," I said to Masahiro.

He limped over and dialed the three-digit police number, but it failed to ring.

Down at the end of the dock, the thirty-three-horsepower Johnson idled softly. *Clunck*! The shift lever engaged forward. Kailang and his friends zoomed off, the runabout cutting through the surface glare of the Van Camp flood lights and leaving a stinky trail of blue-gray exhaust smoke clinging to the water. They headed straight out across the bay, disappearing into the darkness. I could hear the engine whining as the boat made a long sweeping turn. It came out of the darkness and passed close to the seiner, Kailang and his friends appearing as puppets in a toy boat. The sound of breaking bottles echoed across the bay. The seiner's crew, out on deck now, peered over the railing. On the upper deck, several men came out of their cabins with guns. As the little boat came around for another pass, Kailang fired the.410 into the air and screamed: "Get out of Palau!"

We saw fire flash from a gun on the seiner and water splash up around the runabout, heard the shots a second later. The whole show seemed to be happening in slow motion. Kailang sped homeward, back toward the co-op and safety. Sirens wailed from up the road. I climbed back up to the loft.

Three blue and white Datsuns pulled up in front of the co-op, and eight police officers jumped out. Several cops, having been rousted from their sleeping mats, were bare-chested. They rushed down the dock and confronted Kailang and his friends as they docked the boat. After a brief scuffle, the police wrestled Kailang's friends into a car and drove off. Kailang, gun in hand, argued bitterly with the police in Palauan. He pointed to the seiner.

"It's their fault," he yelped. "They started it. Go get them!"

But the police were unimpressed. They wrestled him to the cement and handcuffed him. From the back seat, Kailang shouted indignities about their mothers as they drove off. Masahiro looked up at me with a relieved expression on his face. Mekreos and Albert snored blissfully. I finally passed out.

About 6:30 a.m., the district attorney came down to Van Camp and placed the three seiners under house arrest. Several policemen stood guard on the dock to prevent anyone from disembarking. That ended the conflict.

In the afternoon, the seiner's captain and Kailang appeared before the judge. They apologized to each other on behalf of themselves and their affiliates. The judge fined both men then suspended the fines. Case closed. The seiners pulled out that evening, Gene Helfman sailing with them.

The next day I ran into Marcello, the Van Camp engineer, at WCTC store.

"Hey, Pat," he said. "You know, *Emeraech* boys make trouble other night. Oh, plenty trouble. I don know why. Kailang too, he was there. They throw rocks. I don-a-know. Then they shoot. Why you think, eh, Pat?" His hands went palms up and he smiled.

"Those guys on the purse seiners don't have any manners," I offered.

"Why they don-a make-a friend? We get along, eh, Pat? I mean, we make good here, eh?"

"Yeah, I guess so, Marcello."

"I don know. I just don-a know, eh, Pat?"

"Yeah, I know."

—

Editor Valentine Suguino of the *Didl a Chais* made good copy of the story. Headlined "Racist American Fishing Boats Cause Riot, Leave Island in Disgrace," Valentine's story compared the Portuguese sailors with the Klu Klux Klan. Most Palauans had never heard of the KKK and were unmindful that their own attitudes toward the southwest islanders paralleled those of the racist KKK.

The story was hashed, rehashed, and embellished during the week by gossipy Palauans (everyone). "KKK" had struck a Palauan nerve. "KKK" was heard on the path, in the bar, in the store, in the co-op, in the office, in church, in hospital, and in school. Kids loved it. "Hey you! KKK," they'd yell. And if your name happened to be Kaleb, it now was "K-K-Kaleb."

—

Kintaro, owner of the store on the upper road where Terresa worked at night, opened a bar on lower road. He named it the Caterpillar Inn after an old derelict Caterpillar tractor which sat out in front of the place. Kintaro and his brother also ran the Royal Palauan Hotel, and these businesses made up Kintaro Enterprises.

Kintaro submitted a request to Peace Corps for a business advisor, a PCV who could straighten out the books and boost the ailing Royal Palauan Hotel. Peace Corps sometimes used less than good judgment in its volunteer assignments. The RP Hotel had some problems, but the Kintaro's were wealthy businessmen and could well afford to hire an accountant. Palau had many struggling businesses which *really* needed help. But Peace Corps went ahead and assigned Kintaro a volunteer named Freddie to help out with the Royal Palauan Hotel.

Soon after Freddie started work on the Royal Palauan Hotel, Kintaro eased Freddie into managing the Caterpillar Inn. He built Freddie a small living area in the back of the bar which kept Freddie close to his work. Freddie lived there with his girlfriend, Rufi, a likable local girl who enjoyed Peace Corps volunteers. Freddie was happy managing the bar. It was just the sort of thing he liked to do. A mole, Freddie's blond hair, blue eyes, and pale white skin were too delicate for the harsh tropical sun, and he rarely ventured out before sunset. He ate like a bird, smoked two to three packs of Winstons each day, and sipped Johnny Walker Red Label over ice from opening until closing. His major exercise consisted of the walk from behind the bar across the floor to open and close and whatever he and Rufi came up with in the back room. Freddie's cryptic lifestyle kept him out of sight and out of trouble.

Freddie fixed up the Caterpillar Inn by giving it atmosphere. He air conditioned the place and made it dark. A long bar sat opposite the front door across an open dance floor. Tables and chairs were positioned around the periphery. Freddy stuffed the new Wurlitzer jukebox with slow, slow music: Bob Dylan, Jose Feliciano, Johnny Rivers, Patsy Cline. *Lay Lady Lay*, the Caterpillar Inn's theme song, played at least five times on any given night. Peace Corps volunteers patronized the place and so did anyone else looking for something on the quiet side. Freddie opened the Caterpillar around 7:00 in the evening and shut it down around midnight. When Freddie hosted his poker games in the back room behind the bar about twice a month, the back door stayed discreetly unlocked all night. Supposedly on the sly, everyone in Peace Corps knew about the gambling except Terry Clancy, the director. Regulars included Palauan businessmen, American contract workers, and two PCVs. One volunteer consistently lost his ninety dollar pay check each month and owed money to many PCVs and several contract workers as well. Freddie's smoothly run gaming operations quickly promoted his status to VIP in Koror.

But the big night in Palau was Saturday night of payday weekend—and that night always belonged to the Peleliu Club. The Peleliu Club wound up about 10:00 p.m., when the local band began playing. By 10:30, all seats would be taken, leaving standing room only. Smoke would get thick enough to cut with a machete; the floor would turn to a swirl of spilled beer and dirt, the muddy goo forming a slippery interface between feet and zorries and squeezing up between toes. The later it got, the louder the music; the denser the smoke; the muddier the floor; the jerkier the dancing.

When the Peleliu Club closed at 1:00 a.m., a party often followed, especially when the moon was big, at one of the favorite spots (never at anyone's house): down at T-Dock, or at the Airai ferry dock, or at Meyungs *skokee* (seaplane) ramp, or at Icebox. People would bring beer, Apollo, and food and sit in a circle, drinking, dancing, eating, and singing until dawn. At sunup the party was over, and everyone would disperse like cockroaches caught in a flashlight beam, leaving beer cans, bottles, and other refuse, for the prisoners to clean up, perhaps.

On Sundays, people went to church, ate, and slept. Stores stayed boarded up, and everything stayed closed down. Sometimes, if you woke up the manager of the local boony store, you could get a case of warm Kirin for six bucks (normal price was five). Only flies, mosquitoes, cockroaches, and PCVs operated on Sundays.

—

When I met Kline, she was hanging with Carl, a PCV who lived in Yebukl, just down the road from me. Kline was a senior in Mindszenty High School just across the road from Yebukl. Sometimes she came to the village to see Carl, and when I'd see her on the road I'd stop and talk to her. Her dark skin, bright smile, and sculptured body intrigued me. Carl had been in an earlier group than I and when he terminated, I moved in. Sometimes at night, I'd go to Kline's house, knock on her window and we'd sneak off to the Boom Boom Room. I knew her father because he was a member of the co-op, and I always helped him unload when he brought his catch in. I felt a little awkward because I was twenty-three at the time, and Kline was only eighteen. But her parents seemed to like me; Kline told me they considered me *ungil buik* (a good boy). I never understood why because one night, a bit drunk, I mistakenly banged on her father's window. When Kline failed to respond, I banged again, calling out "Kline, Kline." He threw the shutter open and ordered me to go far, far away. Too embarrassed to speak, I half-ran, half-stumbled off into the darkness. The next time I saw him at the co-op, I timidly apologized. He acted like it had never happened.

Around Christmas time, 1968, Peace Corps brought out a new assistant to Terry Clancy by the name of Bruce Cole. Terry threw a welcoming party for him one Saturday night at a restaurant down on T-Dock. Every PCV in Koror showed up, of course; free food and booze. I went as well, and for some reason, I wore long Levi's.

A short time after the party started, Florie, Kline's sidekick, called to me from the door and told me someone outside wanted to see me. At the time, Carl had just left the island and I had only made a few moves on Kline. I walked outside with Florie and saw Kline across the road.

"Hi Kline," I said.

She was a unique young girl—unique because she only rarely chewed betel nut and was uniquely fine looking.

"I have a Christmas present for you," she said.

"Honest. What is it?"

"*Ngak* (me)," she answered.

My face reddened and Florie giggled. We walked over to a coconut tree with a grassy area beneath it and shadowed from the lights across the way. I gave Florie a dollar and asked her to go buy us some soft drinks. Kline and I sat cross-legged facing each other. I put my hands on her bare knees, leaned forward, and kissed her full sweet lips. A curious warmth spread through my crotch—as if I had sat in a giant jar of Tiger Balm. My gonads felt on fire. They *were* on fire.

"Yeeoow!" I squealed. "Son-of-a-bitch!" I uncoiled upward and hopped around, struggling out of my Levi's.

Discarding them, I ran around the backside of the coconut tree in my underwear and ripped off my shirt. While I whipped at my back with my shirt, Kline laughed and slapped the ants on my legs. Big red welts popped up on my white buttocks and thighs.

When Florie came back and saw me springing around in my underwear she squealed and doubled over.

"Only *chad er a ngebard* would sit on *bembangch*," she joked to Kline.

Ha ha, I thought. Kline shook out my pants as I picked off the stragglers. After I put my pants back on, with Kline and Florie in tow, I waddled back across the road into the party and drank my pain away. Palauans got rid of red ant nests by peeing on them. When the party ended, I walked across the road and pissed on *bembangch*.

—

Palau had many beautiful girls. I loved the dark skin, the full red lips, the white teeth (in the younger girls; red teeth in the older girls), and the big brown eyes above those prominent cheeks. And the way they carried themselves, in a slow shuffle, head held high, shoulders squared away. They talked without saying a word. A simple raising of their eyebrows marked an affirmative. *Esilch*, a girl's word for disgust, made a man want to crawl away if used by a woman in anger. Palauan girls differed radically from the California girls I'd grown up with. California girls smelled of Chanel No. 9; Palauan girls smelled of nature. California girls painted their faces with makeup; Palauan girls didn't bother. California girls ate with knife, fork, and spoon; Palauan girls ate with fingers. California girls manicured their nails; Palauan girls cleaned their nails with machetes. California girls bleached, dyed, colored, ratted, and tatted their hair; Palauan girls combed their hair occasionally with a turtle shell comb which rode in their hair. California girls chomped gum and blew bubbles; Palauan girls chewed betel nut and spat. California girls smoked cigarettes; Palauan girls chewed cigarettes. California girls wore bikinis to the beach; Palauan girls wore cutoffs and T-shirts. I found wet T-shirts much more attractive than bikinis.

One pretty Palauan girl was Teo, the nurse, who liked Jerry Facey. Teo topped Jerry's rather short height by half an inch. She drank heavily at times and was known for her shrill, ultra high-pitched scream when under the influence. Dumae had called her *kebelung* at the picnic, and since then, I'd heard several stories about her.

Jerry lived and worked at Trust Territory Headquarters in Saipan but often travelled to Palau on business or otherwise. He enjoyed Palau and liked to whoop it up in the Palau bars. Only a few years older than I, he was blond, strong, and handsome. When Jerry came to Palau, Teo was his girl.

One Friday night at the Boom Boom Room, while I sat with Kline, Florie, and Dale Jackson, Jerry came in alone and sat down with us. When I asked him about Teo, he implied that she was on duty at the hospital. Later on, Jerry picked up a girl and the six of us took Jerry's U-drive down to the Caterpillar Inn.

The Caterpillar Inn that night was empty and quiet. We sat down at a table near the door, ordered drinks from Freddie, and plugged quarters into the jukebox. Several minutes later, the door opened and Teo walked in. Wearing a tight-fitting white summer dress and high heels, she presented a stunning profile in the reduced light, appearing to me every bit a high fashion *Vogue* model. I stared unbelieving, having never seen a Palauan in high heels. Jerry's mouth fell open, and his eyes glassed over. Teo paused, glanced quickly at our table through fiery eyes, then walked to the bar and sat on a stool next to Rufi, who sat chatting with Freddie working behind the bar.

Without saying a word, Jerry's friend rose and slipped out the door. Patsy Cline finished her rendition of "Crazy" on the jukebox. The air conditioner hummed on, but the room seemed suddenly hot. No one spoke. I looked at Jerry, his face a sickly white. Jerry got up and played *Lay Lady Lay* on the jukebox, then walked to the bar and sat on a stool next to Teo. Teo faced Jerry and then shoved him off the stool. He staggered backward.

"You motherfucker! Go get your *katuu* (cat, meaning 'girlfriend'), you son-of-a-bitch!" she shouted.

Jerry squirmed back onto his stool. "Listen Teo, I'm sorry. We were only sitting together," he explained.

"*Esilch*! You-son-of-a-bitch," Teo growled.

They argued over the sounds of the jukebox which we kept playing as if nothing was happening. Rufi, always the cool *katuu*, shuffled over and sat down with us. Freddie stood fixed behind the bar trying to mediate, which, if anything, added fuel to the situation. Abruptly, Teo let out an intense scream, sending chills down my back and stirring Jerry to stand off his stool. She picked up her empty glass, wound up, and threw it at Jerry. He jumped to the side as the glass flew by and shattered on the back wall just beneath the 2000-btu air conditioner.

Freddie ducked down behind the bar and ran to the far end, then stood up and yelled out to Teo, "That's enough, Teo!"

"*Adelam* (your mother)!" she retorted, as the Wurlitzer shut down Bob Dylan.

She turned to Jerry, who now stood shaking by her side, his arm across her dark shoulders.

Politely she whispered: "Jerry, I need a drink," causing Dale and I to burst out laughing.

Teo glared at us, and I lowered my head trying to control my giggles. Kline punched me in the ribs to "shut up."

Meanwhile, Freddie, whispered to Jerry to "get her out of here." Teo heard it and flew into a rage.

"*Adelam* Fred! Give me a drink, you motherfucker!"

Freddie hurriedly fixed her a drink in a paper cup and handed it to her. She sucked half of it down, then tossed it at him, bouncing it off his shoulder and drenching his shirt with vodka and tonic. He dabbed his shirt nervously with a towel.

"I want it in a glass, motherfucker!" she said. Jerry whispered to her, trying to calm her, to soothe her, to get her out before she destroyed the place and everyone in it.

Then Teo placed both hands on the bar, pushed herself up off the stool, and, turning a half revolution, sat on the bar. She pivoted on her shapely rear, swung her legs across and jumped down behind. Checking out the liquor shelf, she snatched a full fifth of vodka by the neck and flung it at Freddie, who stood motionless, paralyzed. The bottle somersaulted through the air, missing Freddie's head by inches, and smashed into the back wall to the side of the air con, showering the floor with glass fragments and Smirnoff. Grabbing a butcher knife from the sink, she yelled, "*Adelam* Jerry!" and started for him. Jerry turned and headed for the door with Teo, knife in the Alfred Hitchcock position, hot on his heels. They circled the room once, Jerry dodging behind tables, then crashed out the door one after the other. Kline, Florie, and Rufi all began talking at once in breakneck speed Palauan. Freddie, behind the bar, babbled unintelligibly to himself. Suddenly he ran across the floor and locked the door. He turned and leaned back against it, looking up toward the ceiling in relief.

The muffled voice of Teo swearing at Jerry outside filtered in. The Caterpillar had no windows, so I sneaked out the back door and made my way around to the front. Peeking around the corner, I saw Jerry perched on top of the old Caterpillar tractor. Teo circled the Caterpillar, Indian style, holding him at bay with her knife. Jerry pleaded with her to calm down, but she swore at him in Palauan, letting him know his mother was a wide-open whore. The only cure for Teo, I knew, was twenty-four hours on a cool mat with a jumbo bottle of extra strength Bayer.

I slipped along the side to the back door and went into the bar where Freddie and Rufi were mopping up the floor and sweeping glass. We sat at the bar and sipped beer, talking about the incredible show we'd just witnessed. Then Jerry and Teo marched in through the back door, Jerry tossing the knife into the sink. They sat down at the bar. Teo's nice white dress was badly soiled and she was barefoot, her heels bonded somewhere in the soft mud outside. The wrestling match appeared to have been a draw.

Quite now inside the room, Teo sobbed softly. Jerry, his eyes also teary, sat with his arm around Teo's waist.

"Freddie," Jerry said, "how 'bout a cup of coffee?"

Teo raised her head and straightened up. With her left hand, she threw her long black hair back over her shoulder. Her tears had dried.

"Vodka tonic, you son-of-a-bitch," she growled, her hand banging down hard on the bar causing Freddie to flinch.

Turning to look at Jerry, her eyes rolled back and her head fell to her shoulder. She pitched sideways into Jerry and slid from her stool. Jerry reached out to grab her, but too late. Teo crashed to the floor, down and out on her back, her hair fanned on the floor, her muddied white dress up above those pretty knees.

CHAPTER 14

Underwater

About once a month Lee Marvin would throw a Saturday night open house party on the *Oriental Hero*. A local band always played, and the ballroom floor would overflow with dancers. The bar featured free Singapore slings, which got you drunk and then got you sick, and everyone drank them. Lots of dope went up in smoke at those parties. The Hollywood crew would light up out on the companionway and the smoke would drift in, giving the ballroom a distinct odor of you-know-what. Most of the PCVs knew about that, but few others did.

When the filmmakers finished shooting in the rock islands, they moved the set over to Airai, filming the last segment of the movie at the old Japanese communications building near the airport. Much of the production was done at night, and sometimes a gang of us would go over and watch the filming. The old building, with its real-life scars, the derelict tanks, and the antiaircraft guns, provided an overwhelming sense of realism.

And then, suddenly, it was all over; the filming completed, the gear packed up, and the *Oriental Hero* prepared to ship out. Six months of hectic work, conflict, frustration, and fun for the American and Japanese filmmakers in Palau had come to an end. In appreciation of the Selmur Productions endeavor, the Palau Administration hosted a tremendous farewell party on the dock. Once again, grass-skirted women and breech-clothed men, their faces dabbed with red dye, performed traditional dances. Long tables covered with banana leaves held all the traditional foods: sashimi, sea cucumber, sea urchin, squid, octopus, fish, turtle, clam, oyster, mangrove crab, coconut crab, land crab, fruit bat, pigeon, taro, tapioca, yam, greens in coconut milk; and roasted pig, chicken, and, even Spam—Micronesian steak. People came from Babeldaob, Peleliu, and Angaur, to eat, drink, dance, have fun.

Well into the party, Lee Marvin's "second," Bob Gee, announced over the loudspeaker that his Palauan girlfriend would accompany him to Hollywood where they would marry. The matchup seemed a bit outlandish, even for Hollywood, Bob in his late thirties and the girl, exceptionally beautiful but, nevertheless, a subpubescent twelve. The girl's parents, overjoyed at having a Hollywood "stand-in" for a son-in-law, clapped and raved.

A short time later, Doc got up and wobbled onto the platform. Grabbing the microphone, Doc announced that he, as well, would take his girlfriend to California where they would tie up at the same time as Bob and his twelve-year-old. It would, he said, be a double ceremony and everyone in Palau was invited. Doc's fiancée, a not-so-well respected Palauan lady categorized locally as a "U-drive," after the rental car, probably in her late forties, although it was difficult to tell, could match Doc drink for drink and probably outlast him as well. The crowd cheered.

Lee stepped up and thanked the people of Palau for their hospitality while Michelle and Dick, all smiles, stood below. Later, while Lee celebrated, Michelle and Dick disappeared.

—

Dick Doughty stayed at the T-Dock Hotel, a small roach-infested shack situated above a store midway down T-Dock road. A couple of days before Lee was to leave Palau, Doughty scuffled with the hotel manager, knocking him down the stairs and giving him a black eye. Humiliated, the manager went to Peace Corps Director Terry Clancy, and Terry, without hesitation, terminated Doughty. But Doughty was unfazed. He had planned to quit Peace Corps anyway and accompany Lee and Michelle back to Hollywood. Michelle had convinced Lee to help Doughty become an actor, set him up in TV or in the movies. Doughty, it seemed, had pulled a double whammy. He had Michelle, or Michelle had her Dick, and now Lee had committed to help get Dick into showbiz. Few people understood why Lee tolerated Doughty, let alone why he would help him. Michelle was intimate with Dick and if she projected the mother image, then their relationship could only be described as incestuous. Triangles are usually dishonorable, and this one reeked excessively.[15]

—

The vacuum left by the departure of the *Oriental Hero* was quickly filled by island routine. I renewed my efforts to get next to Terresa, and she continued to check me off.

Meanwhile, Mechas, ailing for some time, entered the hospital for some tests. To fill her responsibilities, *rubak* Techur came down from Ngkeklau and tended house. I spent a lot of time sitting around with him chewing betel nut and gabbing in Palauan. He wore only a *thu* to cover the midsection of his slight brown body, and his short white hair stuck straight up. Faded blue tattoos of triangles and bars ran from his ankles up the outsides of his legs to his hips; then up his sides and across his back. With Melanna by his side, he would slowly and methodically pound his betel nut while relating old stories of Palau and his youth. He spoke the old Palauan dialect, true Palauan, not the evolved Palauan that the younger generation spoke, already bastardized by Japanese, English, and fad slang. I struggled with his words and Kilad would come over and translate, help me grasp the meaning while Melanna would grin and say, "Oh, Patrriiiick, wheeeee." The old man ate it up.

—

Melanna continued to be the blossom of the household. Interested in whatever I did, she radiated happiness and energy.

---

[15] In 1979, while working in Samoa, one of Lee Marvin's lawyers called me and asked if I would come to Los Angeles to testify as a witness in the Marvin-Triola (palimony) trial then underway, all expenses paid, of course, plus remuneration for work lost. Particularly, he wanted to know what I knew about Doughty and Michelle in Palau. I knew everything that Doughty had bragged to me about, which was plenty. I declined the offer.

Kailang's kids roamed around out of control, and when I caught the oldest boy stealing betel nut from our tree one night, Kailang beat his shorts off. I felt bad about it, but it seemed to moderate the little rascal. And Kilad, always around, fun and games, and nice to look at. I loved Kilad, but not as I loved Terresa.

Down at fisheries, I told Kailang I was leaving, explaining that with his return from Japan I had completed my job at the co-op; that I was not a business person, I was a biologist and I wanted to work on the *ruusch* (starfish) problem. Kailang balked, pleaded with me to stay, told me so much was left to be done, how could I think of leaving; made me feel like dirt. He couldn't understand how I possibly would rather work on *ruusch*. But my mind was set and I told Peter that a deal was a deal, that I'd fulfilled my job at the co-op and he'd better tell Kailang he was pulling me off to work on starfish. He did, and Kailang said, "okay," and got over it.

—

Late in 1967 and during 1968, a fantastic environmental scare generated in the Pacific on both sides of the equator. Exploding populations of the "Crown-of-Thorns" starfish, scientifically known as *Acanthaster planci*, were discovered on the Great Barrier Reef of Australia, and scientists reported similar phenomena in Guam. Lately Peter's office had received reports of starfish infestations from several Trust Territory Districts while locally, fishermen complained about the increased numbers of *ruusch* on the reefs. Armed with long aciculated spines coated with toxic mucus, *ruusch* presented considerable danger to fishermen. To the reef ecosystems, their population explosions posed an even greater threat since they fed on live corals. At maturity they reached a diameter of eighteen inches or more, and killing them was not easy. Possessed with incredible regenerative powers, if you tore one in half you had two starfish, and so on. And they had few natural enemies. Only *maml* (a large wrasse) and a gastropod, the Triton trumpet, were known to eat them, although some people claimed a small "painted shrimp" also fed on them.

Because the starfish fed on living corals, some scientists theorized that the animals would destroy the coral reefs, exposing the islands to wave and wind action which would erode the coastal environments and cause widespread ecological havoc.

University of Guam scientist, Dr. Richard Cheser, quickly jumped on the starfish bandwagon. He spearheaded a population study of the starfish in Micronesia by Westinghouse Ocean Research Laboratory under contract with the U.S. Department of Interior. Peter embraced the starfish phenomenon as an opportunity to secure funds through the Trust Territory and began lobbying for money to begin a starfish control program in Palau. He invited Cheser to survey Palau and map starfish population centers. In addition, Westinghouse filmed a documentary on the starfish situation in Palau and Micronesia.

Based on the results of Cheser's Westinghouse report, Peter obtained funds from Department of Interior to set up a monitoring and control program throughout the Trust Territory, but excluding the Marshalls where starfish populations remained at normal levels. He hired an expatriate named Milton McDonald to set up diving shops in the districts, train divers, and locate and destroy starfish. An excellent diver, Milton had participated in University of Guam starfish control efforts in Guam. He would oversee Ponape, Saipan, Yap, and Truk, and I would take care of Palau.

Marine Resources employee Becky Madraisau and I started diving for starfish in the rock islands around Koror. We used oversized hypodermic injectors attached by a rubber tube to a douse bag filled with formaldehyde, injecting the starfish around the central disk to pickle the nerve ring, the starfish equivalent to a brain. If any part of the nerve ring survived, it would regenerate into a new animal, and several carefully placed injections were needed to destroy an animal. It was imperative to avoid the spines. Getting stuck produced unbelievable pain, intense pain that caused chills and salivation, pain that could send you into shock. The wounds usually turned septic, healed slowly, and the effects were cumulative, the symptoms getting worse with each new wound. No fun.[16]

---

[16] Once, a starfish severely pierced me on the side of my thumb beneath the fingernail. The pain made me nauseous, nearly causing me to throw up through my regulator. My thumb swelled to twice normal size and stayed septic for weeks, constantly oozing pus. Today, over twenty years later, that area of my thumb where the spine penetrated remains numb, the flesh depressed.

The Palauans utilized the entrails of sea cucumber to protect their feet when walking on the reef. They would stimulate certain species of sea cucumbers, causing them to evert long, sticky, wormlike cords which readily adhered to the bottom of their feet, thereby offering protection against sharp corals. But this offered negligible protection against the pungent spines of *ruusch*. When a Palauan steps on a *ruusch*, the antidote is to turn the animal over and place the punctured foot on the underside of the starfish. As part of its water vascular system, *Ruusch* has rows of suckers or tube feet along the midline of each arm, and these tube feet suck the poisons from the wounds.

Sometimes I took out groups of school kids to collect starfish. On one of these trips, Teruo and I took PCV Kerry Fitzgibbons and his students over to the Airai channel to collect starfish on some patch reefs. About twenty kids were diving and bringing up starfish on stringers, while two students motored around in the bait skiff picking up the stringers of starfish and loading them onto the back of the *Milotk* and *Ngermeyaus*. About a hundred starfish lay in a pile on the stern deck of the *Ngermeyaus*, partly shielded by the hatch covers. The starfish, gray-blue in color, blended in with the gray deck of the vessel.

Kerry and I were standing up forward in the wheelhouse talking when the bait skiff motored up and its engine died.

"Whooo!" I yelled, seeing that the skiff would smash into our stern.

Kerry, in bare feet, ran back to fend it off and landed on the pile of starfish with both feet. He turned and looked back at me, his face contorting in pain. Falling to one side, he gripped his knees to his chest and rolled back and forth on the deck, screaming in pain. His face morgue white, saliva ran from his mouth and he trembled violently. Then he vomited. The boys in the skiff came aboard, and we pulled Kerry forward and covered him with a tarp, attempting to make him as comfortable as possible.

Kerry, sweating now, his eyes closed, whimpered and moaned, overwhelmed with pain. On the Marine Band, I called Marine Resources and told Peter to have an ambulance waiting at T-Dock, about thirty minutes away. With several students aboard to help, we pulled anchor and steamed off toward T-Dock, leaving a trail of black smoke in the sky.

The ambulance sat waiting for us at T-Dock along with a crowd of around 150 gawkers. Kerry lay still, moaning pitifully while gritting his teeth and taking shallow breaths. His feet had already swollen to football size. We eased him onto a stretcher, passed him up to the dock, and slipped him into the back of the World War II weapons carrier which served as Palau's ambulance. The old ambulance rumbled off up the bumpy road toward MacDonald Hospital, its big military tires kicking up coral and dust, the driver blasting its horn.

At the hospital, the doctors sliced open Kerry's feet to extract spines. Kerry spent a week convalescing in hospital; then used a wheelchair and crutches for several months fighting off infection. He told me he had never experienced such pain. I empathized with him, having been punctured a few times myself. Like red ants, *Ruusch* were nothing to fool with.

—

Peter recruited some young Palauan divers, and I began training them in SCUBA. This would be the core group for the Palau starfish control and monitoring program. When funds were finally allocated for the program, it was like Christmas. I ordered several thousand dollars worth of diving gear and other equipment. Additionally, Peter wanted to buy the jet boat from the movie people to use in the program, reasoning that the jet boat, with its 427 Corvette engine and Holly four-barrel carburetor, could reach long distance areas, such as Kossol Reef, quickly, relative to the slow diesels.

"It's got a shallow draft so you can get in close over those coral heads," he explained to me, his tongue protruding from the side of his mouth, holding back a smile. I raised my eyebrows at that. With six—or seven-foot tides, you didn't dare get into shallow water on an outgoing tide, shallow draft or not, or you'd have a six-hour wait to get off, that is if you escaped poking a hole in the bottom.

"Sure, Pete," I said. "Good idea."

If Peter wanted to give me an expensive hog like that to cruise around in, it was fine with me. The jet boat was a great ski boat, though. He must be thinking the same thing, I thought. I asked him to order me a yachting cap so I'd look the part.

But meanwhile, from under Peter's nose, Don Henly snuck in and bought the jet boat. Ostensibly to be used by Public Works for work-related activities, in reality Don used it for rock island picnics and pleasure cruises. No one seemed to care, however, for Don, as director of Public Works, the most important government department, was beyond "open" contention.

Several weeks later, Don and his family drove to the little floating dock in boatyard bay where Don kept the boat. Don, in a hurry to get out to the rock islands, rushed down the dirt path and jumped into the boat, leaving his wife and kids to carry gear down to the dock. Neglecting to run the blower to clear the bilge of gas fumes, Don turned the ignition key to crank her up. The boat exploded into a fireball, throwing Don some twenty feet over the bow and into the water. Don treaded water while he watched the boat burn to a charred mass of fiberglass, ashes, and melted 427, then sink to the bottom. Later, Don convalesced with nasty burns over a significant portion of his face, chest, and arms, the rest of his torso having escaped the scorch because he'd been fully clothed. All of this meant that Peter could forget about the jet boat for the starfish patrol. The *Ngermeyaus* and *Milotk* would do just fine; never fast, but reliable, comfortable, and—diesel. Neither boat would ever blow up.

—

Over in Truk, Norman, Rupp, Ives, and Maloney had come upon a very useful piece of equipment. Truk Office of Marine Resources possessed SCUBA gear but no compressor. Air for diving had to be obtained from the Public Works paint locker compressor, a hazardous and inconvenient situation. When a visiting underwater photographer from California offered to sell his portable Mako compressor, Norman and the boys pooled their money and bought it for their own use. This opened up considerable opportunities for them to dive the World War II Japanese shipwrecks in Truk Lagoon.[17]

---

[17] . On February 17 and 18, 1944, U.S. Navy planes had strafed and bombed Truk in what later was dubbed the Truk Duck shoot, destroying 270 aircraft and sinking nine warships and thirty-four transports. Greg "Papa" Boyington, about whom *Baa Baa Black Sheep* was written, but prisoner of

Peter had been the first to dive with SCUBA on the wrecks. After the war, the navy had surveyed some of the wrecks with hard-hat divers, but close inspection could not be accomplished with hard hat. Nor were the locations of many of the wrecks known. Some of the ships had been unmanned, but many of them held artifacts and remnants of once living persons.

Peter spotted one wreck while flying into Truk one day. Looking out the window of the Pan Am DC-4 as it swooped in low over the water for a landing, he spotted an oil slick on the glassy surface of the lagoon near Udot. When the plane landed, he hustled over to Public Works, commandeered a boat and driver, and went out to the slick. Because of the calm conditions, they were able to follow the oil slick to its origin. Peter jumped in and found what appeared to be a patch reef down about thirty feet. Puzzled by the absence of a ship, he snorkeled around until he saw a drop of oil float slowly up from the reef to the surface. At the end of the reef he found a huge propeller and rudder. The "reef" was the bottom of a ship, later dubbed the "upside-down" ship by Norman and the boys.

Over the years, Peter had been searching for a sunken Japanese submarine. Through his research on the bombing of Truk, he had come across a full intelligence report on the sub's sinking, including an account of the Japanese efforts to raise her and save the crew. During the American bombing raids, the I-169 Class submarine had sounded to wait out the bombing, but in the confusion, the crew had left a hatch open which flooded the engine room. When the alarms went off, the crew was able to salvage the batteries, but the sub lay crippled on the bottom "not under command," her sixty crew members still alive and able to converse over radio with headquarters on Dublon. After the air raid, with little time left, divers from a salvage vessel fastened cables to her and lifted her toward the surface. Just as the sub reached the surface, the cables snapped and the sub and her crew plunged back down to the bottom, this time for good. Now the submarine had become the undiscovered treasure of Truk Lagoon. Early on, Peter had instructed Norman and the others to find it if they could.

---

war at the time, sat in a pit on Moen with two other Americans while the bombing took place.

Wreck diving is dangerous business, requiring caution and control. When Norman and the others dove on the "upside-down" ship, they discovered dishes and coal in the galley, and the remains of someone's boots buried in silt in one of the rooms. Norman got separated and inadvertently swam into what was probably the captain's quarters on the bridge. Inside he found a safe, but in his excitement he stirred up the silt and became suddenly disoriented, unable to find his way out. At ninety feet, his air diminished, he sat quietly in the room, taking controlled, slow breaths, until the silt settled enough to allow him to find the doorway. They never went back for the safe.

On another ship, Norman collected a seaman's chest which contained a shell collection; sake bottles with live shells inside already grown too large to get out—dishes, tools, and a set of keys. They once recovered a safe, but it was empty. Peter Wilson brought up a Japanese hard hat (diving helmet) from one ship, restored it, and presented it to the Truk museum.

One day out diving on the "upside-down" ship, John Rupp brought up something which resembled a suitcase. On the deck of the *Wogut*, John Rupp and John Ives stood looking at it, speculating; booby trapped? When Norman and Maloney started fiddling with it, Rupp and Ives ran forward into the engine room. But it didn't explode. It was a surgeon's kit, and the contents remained in excellent condition. They took a few items as souvenirs and Norman repacked the kit, carefully inserting an empty Hawaiian Punch can. On their next dive, Norman planted the kit inside one of the rooms deep in the bowels of the ship. He figured it would get a laugh twenty years or so down the line when some happy diver rediscovered it.

Several weeks later, some visiting scientists came to Truk to do some diving. One of them was Jack Randall, the well-known ichthyologist from Bishop Museum. Jack wanted to collect fish around one of the wrecks so Norman towed a skiff out to the "upside-down" ship, about ten miles out of Moen, and dropped off Randall and his diving partner with the skiff. Norman and the others then took the *Wogut* to another wreck a few miles away, leaving instructions with Jack to come over when they were finished.

Several hours later as Norman and the others sat on the deck of the *Wogut* after diving, Randall and his partner cruised up in the skiff, Randall yelling out, "Hey, you'll never believe what I found. I found a surgeon's kit in that ship!"

The three PCVs looked at each other and laughed. Randall jumped aboard the *Wogut* with his suitcase, and he laid it on the deck.

"Look here," he said, opening the case. "It's a fucking Hawaiian Punch can!"

Norman, Rupp, and Maloney were rolling on the deck laughing. The other scientists looked at each other and chuckled, unaware of the inside joke and hardly interested at any rate. Randall, a bit puzzled, packed up his prize and they returned to Moen. That night, the PCVs met Randall and the other scientists at the Truk Community Club for drinks. Randall, sitting hunched over a Kirin, reflected: "I wonder how that Hawaiian Punch can got in there?"

Norman choked in his drink. "You, you put it there!" Jack said.

"You mean you really didn't know?" Norman asked. "We put that can in there two weeks ago just for you."

—

Norman and crew dove on the wrecks at every opportunity, mapping their locations relative to land bearings. They knew more about the wrecks than anyone at the time. Then Phillipe Cousteau and his all French crew showed up to do a documentary on the wrecks. Phillipe spoke only once with Norman and Rupp, never asking the PCVs to accompany them on any of their filming trips. The French operation was completely independent. They carried their own equipment, functioned within their own closed system, and produced no publicity. They left Truk several weeks later as stealthily as they had arrived.

Some time later, while in California on business, Peter attended a Man and Sea Symposium in San Francisco sponsored by underwater photographer and inventor, Al Giddings. Several films were shown, including one by Paul Tzimoulis, publisher of *Skin Diver* magazine, and another by Phillipe Cousteau on the Truk wrecks. The downbeat Cousteau film emphasized World War II death and destruction while highlighting the bravery of the French filming crew. Unhappy with Cousteau's film, after the showing Peter approached Tzimoulis and Giddings about producing another film of the Truk wrecks, one that would portray the wrecks as a treasure, rather than just a graveyard. Peter offered them boat support and to show them the locations of the wrecks which had been mapped thus far. They showed immediate interest. Peter went on: "And there's the ultimate bonus—the submarine—if we can find it."

Three months later, Paul Tzimoulis, Al Giddings, and a filming crew of about ten showed up to produce the film. AMF Voit had fully outfitted them with diving gear and Continental Airlines had flown them out—all for free. Peter worked with them for two days, showing them the wreck sites and leading a concerted search for the sub. From his documents, Peter knew the submarine lay somewhere near Dublon but they still were unable to find it. Then Peter flew off to attend a meeting in Noumea.

The next day, an old Trukese fellow came to the hotel and told Tzimoulis he would take them to the submarine for fifty dollars. During the war, the old man said, he had driven a ferry boat between Dublon and Moen, passing by the moored submarine every day. The next day the old man took them to a spot off Dublon and they found it, full of skeletons, in ninety feet of water.

In those early days of Truk Lagoon exploration, Peter understood at once how vulnerable the wrecks were to divers and collectors. He wanted to set aside the wrecks as "historic sites." But his attempts at this went unheeded. Local lawmakers gave little consideration toward preserving the wrecks as a national treasure. Finally, after Cousteau's filming endeavor which documented the sunken Japanese fleet, and then the film of Tzimoulis and Giddings that explored the submarine, it became apparent that Truk Lagoon held historical and commercial significance. Local interest suddenly flourished over the uniqueness of the underwater hulks, leading local legislators to establish them as national historic sites and making it illegal to remove anything from them.

In the early part of 1970, Frank Hester, a big shot with National Marine Fisheries Service in Hawaii, and Bob Moncrief, journeyed to Truk on a scientific expedition aboard the National Marine Fisheries Service research vessel, *Townsend Cromwell*. Previous to their arrival, Peter had told Frank to check out a Japanese twin engine Betty Bomber which had crashed off Eten and lay on the bottom intact with a twin barreled round-magazine machine gun mounted just behind the cockpit. When Peter visited Truk sometime after the *Cromwell's* visit, Kimio Aisek, Truk's only local SCUBA diver and an authority on the wrecks, jumped all over Peter for allowing Hester to take the machine gun off the Eten airplane. Peter blew his stack over that, having never given Hester nor anyone else permission to take anything from Truk Lagoon. Under Trust Territory letterhead, he fired off a letter to Hester, thanking him for restoring the artifact and rendering it to the Truk Museum. Captured, Hester cleaned up the gun, mounted it on a wooden backing with a plaque, and sent it off to the Truk Museum. The plaque read:

> This is the gun from the Second World War
> which FH stole and made Peter sore.
> Now here it is back all shiny and neater;
> and now he can function without a sore Peter.

The gun and plaque grace the Truk Museum.

—

When Stan Wayman came back, we went out in search of Triton trumpets to see if we might get some shots of a Triton attacking *ruusch*. Tritons, large gastropods (snails) with conical shells used as horns by the ancients, are natural predators of *Acanthaster*. They possess a calcified proboscis which they use to tear open the starfish for feeding. We found a couple of them in the rock islands and staged a shooting session down about thirty feet, positioning the withdrawn tritons on some coral near several starfish. We waited underwater for an hour, then changed tanks. On our second tank of air, one of the Tritons finally poked its head out of its shell. After a short period of sensing its surroundings with its retractable antennae, the Triton slid straight to an adjacent starfish, and its foot sliding easily over the spines, crawled up on the *ruusch's* dorsum and everted its proboscis. No match for the Triton, the starfish tried to creep away, the tips of its arms curled up as if feeling for the monster on its back. The water turned cloudy from escaping body fluids and bits of tissue as the Triton bored into the *ruusch*. We could almost hear the Triton chomping away. With each flash of Stan's camera, the Triton would recede momentarily into its shell, then resume its work; but after several photographs it continued its feeding unabated, ignoring the intermittent flashes altogether. Soon the other Triton slid over and, apparently stimulated, chased a *ruusch* for several feet before catching it. Then it too went to work with its proboscis. Stan shot two full roles, and I shot a role with the Nikonos. After taking a break and warming up, we watched and photographed through a third tank of air which brought me dangerously close to hypothermia. In the end, little remained of the first *ruusch*; only bits and pieces of arms, spines, and tube feet. The other Triton continued its feast.

—

One of Bob Owen's employees was John Koichi, a Palauan conservation officer. An excellent diver, John took his job seriously, functioning in the marine environment out of a little twelve-foot aluminum skiff with a twenty-five-horsepower Johnson outboard. At Bob's request, I taught John how to dive with SCUBA. Short, chubby, and unimpressive looking, John possessed intrinsic natural knowledge and incredible skills. He knew his plants. He could husk a coconut on a sharpened stake in two seconds flat. He could scoot up a betel nut or coconut tree like an Angaur monkey. He could use a machete like an ax or like a scalpel, depending on need. He could catch wild chickens in the forest by making a snare trap out of twigs and bark. He knew where and when turtles would lay their eggs. He knew the spawning habits of coconut crabs, mangrove crabs, and land crabs. He knew fish and shark behavior. He could smell the breath of a dugong on a calm evening. He knew weather, tides, and moon phases. John was close to nature, and sometimes he even smelled a bit gamey.

Stan wanted to photograph sea snakes in the water as they swam.
"Let me see what I can do," I told him.
I went up to Entomology.
"Ollei, John. Where can we get some *mengerenger* so Stan can get some shots of them swimming in the water?" I asked.
"Don't worry, I know where," he said. I wasn't worried.
The next day, Stan and I met John down at fisheries. He had a fifty-pound rice bag half full of *mengerenger* in the back of his truck.

"Think you have enough there John?" I said a little sarcastically. Stan's attitude toward snakes paralleled mine—fear and loathing. I didn't mind these banded sea snakes as long as they stayed in the bag, and the bag stayed somewhere else. I certainly wasn't looking forward to being in the water with them, again.

We loaded our gear in the fisheries runabout and John threw the bag of snakes up in the bow under the deck. Going out the channel entrance we hit choppy water, and the boat pounded—enough to shake the rope around the top of the bag loose. The next thing I knew, snakes were slithering around on the bottom of the boat. Instantly I throttled back, killed the engine, and jumped up on the deck with Stan, who had wasted no time himself.

Stan had always reminded me of Marlin Perkins, star of the TV show *Wild Kingdom*. Now, with the snakes out of the bag, he acted like anyone but Marlin. The sloppy chop put us in danger of taking on water and sinking with both of us up forward on the deck. John, groped around in the bilge, laughing openly as he grabbed snakes and threw them in the bag.

"Catch those mothers," I yelled.

Water broke over the bow and drenched us.

Stan giggled: "Come on John, catch those suckers before we sink."

John was finally able to bag them all and we continued on our way, anchoring in a small cove near Ngerengchol Beach to do the filming.

We were in about thirty feet of water, and Stan wanted John to take the snakes down to the bottom and release them one at a time as he shot photographs. He handed me the Nikonos telling me to "shoot away."

Stan wore his usual outfit: loose blue pajamas and a Buoy Fenzy life vest. When we got down to the sand bottom, John opened the bag to release a snake. About five *mengerenger* squiggled out, four of them swimming off. Stan, focusing through his camera at the four snakes, failed to notice the loner swim up his pant leg. Feeling the slick skin of the cold-blooded reptile up around his gonads, he lurched back and dropped his camera. Tearing at his pajamas leg and kicking violently to free the snake, he wailed through his regulator in sheer terror: *Auugghhh! Auugh!* I choked from laughing.

At last Stan stretched his pajamas out at the waist allowing the snake to poke its head out and look at Stan who was peering down at the snake—a stare-down. Several seconds later, the snake swam up in front of Stan's mask and casually snaked off. Stan puffed on his regulator like a locomotive while performing a body search to be sure no other serpents lurked in his pajamas.

After we had all regained our composure, Stan got set again and John backed away, releasing the other snakes one by one, just as we'd planned. Stan got his photographs, and I shot off a roll with the Nikonos. Back in the boat, Stan mumbled, "Sonabitch, I could'a been killed." We laughed like hell.

—

Stan chartered the *Ngerengchol*, and we went back up to the Kossol Reef area. We dove on the outer drop off of the Northwest Reef taking shots of huge Tridacnid (giant) clams, their mantels embedded with striking patterns of zoozanthellae, unicellular aglal colonies living symbiotically with the clams. The algae, photosynthetic producers of sugars, supplement the food intake already obtained by the filtering apparatus of the clams.

On our third day out, inclement weather engulfed us and we made our way down off the northern coast of Babeldaob to find anchorage. Navigating through Kossol passage with its myriad patch reefs and coral heads was hair raising. For an hour, torrential rain kept us from seeing the island, but Captain Oerbelau picked his way through without a hitch, anchoring in the lee of the small island which sits off Ollei. That evening, we watched Ray catch one fish after another as he spin fished off the deck. After midnight, the storm passed and the wind abated.

The next morning found us hard to the bottom by the anchor, and no amount of maneuvering could unhook us. The storm had churned the water into a puke green-brown color with visibility about three feet. I donned a tank and made my way down the anchor rope to about seventy feet, fearful of the unknown in that dark water and wishing I'd worn Stan's pajamas. The half-inch diameter anchor chain, about twenty feet of it, had wrapped on a huge coral head and the flukes and shank of the eighty-pound

Danforth anchor were lodged beneath the coral head, buried in sand. With Oerbelau maneuvering the boat to relieve tension from the anchor rope, I struggled with the anchor, digging and pulling, sucking air from my mouthpiece. Nearing the end of my second tank of air and with my decompression meter on redline, I finally freed it and rose to the surface, inhaling hard on my last cubic foot of air. I yelled for another tank, then hung off the anchor rope down at twenty feet for twenty minutes, attempting to rid my tissues of nitrogen. I'd pushed myself to the limits of nitrogen abuse, and I feared getting bent. That evening, back in Koror, my shoulders ached and burned, and my head throbbed. I slept fitfully and worried about the bends, but the next morning I felt fine, and Stan and I went out again for another day of diving and shooting.

On our last day out, Doug Faulkner showed up in Palau. He stood on the dock in shorts, his legs fresh from lack of sun, as we pulled up in the *Ngerengchol*. After we had tied up and were unloading, he asked me: "Where've you been shooting?"

"Oh, here and there," I said, sensing underlying tension between he and Stan.

"You going to be able to help me?" he said. I knew that was a dig at Stan.

"Probably," I answered.

Life had sent Stan a series of reject slides, and he wanted to show us his work before he left Palau. That night he staged a slide show up at the Entomology dormitory at Bob Owen's place. I was there; so was Bob and Hera, Peter and Ann, Ray, Tosh, John Koichi, and several others. Stan had furnished beer, several bottles of hooch, and a big block of ice; the mood was festive. Having completed his work, he had reason to celebrate. And so did I. Stan had "gifted" me several hundred dollars for my help, effectively taking me out of debt to the co-op.

"No—thanks anyway, Stan, but I can't accept money as a volunteer. Against the rules," I told him when he offered it.

"Listen, Pat, it's a gift. Besides, no one'll ever know." Unable to refuse Stan, I accepted his gift. Anyway, I deserved it. I really did, I think.

Doug Faulkner walked in just as Stan showed his first slide.

"Umm, not too good," he said.

"What is it? Looks too light, washed out," he mumbled about the second.

"I've got a better one of that if you want to borrow it, Stan," about the third.

"Lights, please," Stan yelled out. I walked over to the door and flipped the light switch.

"What's your problem?" Peter growled at Doug.

"Nothing. I was just trying to be helpful," Doug said grinning.

"These are rejects, Doug," said Stan. "If you want good slides, maybe you'd better go look at your own."

Bob spoke up in his low, even voice. "Look Doug. If you don't like the show, maybe you should leave. The rest of us want to watch without hearing your comments."

"Yeah, okay. Sorry," he mumbled.

Stan started the show again. A Triton sat on the back of a large *ruusch*, the Triton's proboscis arching down into the starfish like the trunk of an elephant—an exquisite shot of invertebrate drama.

"Did you set that up?" piped Doug. Stan turned off the projector, and we sat in darkness.

"Please leave, Doug," Bob's low gnarly voice bellowed.

I turned on the lights. Stan, his face red with anger, got up and mixed a drink. Doug, who was lodging in the Entomology dormitory, got up and sauntered down the hall, closing the door to his room. Faulkner, the independent, resented the fact that Stan was in Palau shooting for *Life*. Relieved, everyone refurbished their drinks and Stan, himself perked up, continued with the slide show. After the show, the drinks flowed and the party enlivened, the noise forcing Doug to move himself across the lawn to Bob's house to sleep in the spare room.

Not long after Stan's departure from Palau, Bob got word that Stan had died of heart failure. Stan's work on Palau was published in *Life*.

CHAPTER 15

Wildlife

About twice a year the Coast Guard Cutter USS *Basswood* would call on Palau, presumably to undertake buoy tending and navigational marker chores in Malakal Channel and the West Passage. More important to the crew, however, was the quality of R&R which Palau offered. The *Basswood* usually stayed in port for two or three days, long enough for the crew to stir up a bit of trouble here and there. Coast Guard crews generally, in Palau anyway, had reputations for being rowdy and obnoxious, and feelings of dislike and distrust reciprocated between PCVs and the "coastees." I always wanted to go down late at night and cut the *Basswood's* mooring lines. No one would ever know, I figured, until the ship grounded on a patch reef or drifted into a rock island. But I could never tempt anyone to help me with the escapade, so the plan never saw action.

About a week after the purse seiner incident, the *Basswood* came into port one Friday afternoon. That evening, Kilad and I went to the Boom Boom Room to meet Dale Jackson and his girlfriend. Kilad rarely visited bars, but when I left my house that night she had called to me as I walked up the path. "Patriick! *Ke mo er ker* (Where are you going)?"

"The Boom Boom," I answered, adding. *'mei ki merael* (come, let's go)."

"*Hal* (wait)!" she yelled.

I stopped and looked back at her little house, kerosene lamp in the doorway glowing dully, a swarm of termites serenading the single flame before losing wings, a hatch induced by this windless, balmy night. She shut the window board, snuffed the lamp, and stepped onto the step, a dark figurine with arm stretched overhead grasping the door frame for balance as she struggled to slip into her zorries, she ran up the path to join me. A loose-fitting dress, pink with white flowers, covered her curves.

"You look nice, Kilad," I offered.

"Eeh, Pateriick, tee hee," she said.

We walked silently up the road to the bar.

When we entered the Boom Boom Room, six or seven coastees were sitting at the bar. Already pumped up on booze, they talked loudly and plugged the jukebox with quarters, playing the Moody Blues and the Beatles. We sat in a booth with Dale and friend sipping our rum and Cokes, listening to the music, discussing what a sorry bunch the coastees were. Several Palauan guys sat on the bench at the back of the dance floor, and two others stood at the bar. In the booth behind us sat four girls, government secretaries on their way home, the long way. Now tight on vodka tonics, they took turns dancing with the coastees, giggling and laughing at the gyrating seamen. I glanced over at the local boys leaning on the bar; they looked displeased, and I raised my eyebrows at Dale. He nodded in acknowledgment.

Bang! Bang! Bang! A coastee worked on the jukebox with his fist to dislodge his stuck quarter. *Crunch!* He kicked it. *Crunch!* He kicked it again. One of the local boys reprimanded him in Palauan.

"Speak in English, motha," said the coastee, seconds before a Schlitz bottle ricocheted off his temple. He dropped in a heap.

"Hey, fucker!" growled a coastee, shoving the Palauan who'd winged the bottle.

Several bottles whistled through the air from the back dance floor, smashing into the mirror behind the bar. Barmaids Rose and Pauline dove for cover. The Palauans, suddenly mobile, threw bottles from everywhere. Another coastee fell down, blood flowing from his head. At the end of our table, a bottle shattered on the wall, showering us with bits of glass.

"Hit the deck," Dale yapped.

We ducked down and squirmed under the table. Bottles winged back and forth; glass shattered, sending frothing beer and bits of brown glass raining down on the floor. A bottle of Asahi smashed into the shelf behind the bar, spewing grain alcohol and shattered glass over the backs of Rose and Pauline squatting on their haunches. They squealed and scooted across the hallway and out the back door. The coastees yelled and screamed and swore and groaned.

The Palauans had suddenly vanished. From outside, rocks punched through the screen windows, bouncing off the walls and falling on the floor. Now the frustrated coastees crouched behind the bar, the only protection from the rocks and bottles flying through the windows, through the door, through the screens, through everything. Pinned beneath the table of our little booth on our hands and knees, it felt as if we'd been caught in a close quarters firefight between warring platoons of combat troops.

Kilad said suddenly, "follow me," and began crawling down the short hallway toward the door. In single file, we crawled along behind Kilad. A rock smashed into the door just as Kilad opened it, sending her reeling back on my shoulder. She yelled out to the street, "*Msall uetech! Kemam chad er a Belau!* (Stop throwing! We are Palauan!)"

The flurry stopped. We sprinted out onto the dirt road, and the barrage started again. About ten Palauans stood out on the street throwing everything they could pick up at the Boom Boom Room. The screams and profanity from inside could barely be heard over the concussions of rocks and bottles. Then the lights went out.

We heard the dim wail of sirens coming up the hill and ran across the street into a growing crowd just as the police roared up in two cars. Before the police could exit their cars, the Palauan warriors disappeared into the surrounding darkness. From inside the Boom Boom came sounds of breaking bottles and the crunching sounds of someone smashing the jukebox. We followed the cops into the Boom Boom behind their flashlights to retrieve Kilad's *tet* from under the table, broken glass crunching under our zorries. The cops quickly herded the coastees out in single file. Under siege, and frustrated by their inability to vacate the place without injury or perhaps, loss of life, the coastees had "run amuck," kicking in the bar, breaking bottles, pulverizing the old Rock-Ola jukebox—destroying the place from within—as the Palauans destroyed it from without. Back outside the ambulance arrived and carted off two bleeding coastees. The police took the rest of them down to the station.

We took a last look at the Boom Boom Room as we walked down the road. In the diffused light of the nearby street lamp, it looked grossly unlike the cheerful place it had been minutes before. Nothing more now than an old decrepit abandoned building, leaning out over the cliff on stilts, ready to collapse. Nor did it reflect the site of the raging battle of only minutes before, perhaps because the scene lacked smoke. It would have been more fitting had the Boom Boom gone up in smoke, a giant cliffside bonfire fueled by rum, gin and vodka, plywood, Christmas decorations, and a jukebox full of 45s.

While the cops busied themselves with the errant group of coastees, the native sons acquired a couple of cases of beer from Kintaro's Store just down the road. On the steps of the Mindszenty High School administration building, they formulated plans to attack the *Basswood*. Minutes later, armed with bottles and rocks, and nourished by Schlitz and Asahi, a pickup-load of warriors made its way down to Malakal Dock, where, in the calm night, the black hulled ship with the orange band across its bow, tugged gently on its moorings. As the truck slid to a stop on the dock in front of the ship, the boys plastered the *Basswood* with everything in their arsenal, sending the officer on deck scrambling for cover as bottles smashed the deck and rocks twanged the bulwarks. One Palauan jumped from the truck and hacked through the ship's three-inch stern mooring hawser with a machete. A minute later, having exhausted their arsenal of rocks and bottles, the war party clamored back into the truck and sped off into the darkness. Just past the co-op, they turned left on boatyard road and parked in the boonies—until the cops passed by; then they drove back into town, winners.

Blessed with another great story, the *Didl a Chais* blasted the Coast Guard from cover to cover, both pages. And in Guam, the story, heavily biased in favor of the Coast Guard, made front page copy of the *Pacific Daily News*. The owner of the Boom Boom Room, his business demolished, filed charges against the United States government and Coast Guard. From that time on, when on shore leave, personnel on the Coast Guard ship *Basswood* came under strict orders to act civilized rather than impetuously as tradition would have it.

But the Boom Boom Room was finished. The coastees had instigated the destruction of a Palauan and PCV institution. The termite riddled, dry rotted Boom Boom Room, once a proud canteen at the gateway to Koror, stood (barely) in shambles—totaled; done, gone, dead. We would never again shuffle zorries on its pink floor to the rhythm of "Hey Jude" or flirt with sweet Rose behind the bar; or shield our drinks from termite shit trickling down from the rafters.

—

Several months later, the word went out: The *Basswood* was steaming toward Palau. Excitement filled the air. Rumors permeated town—the coastees were coming back to kick ass; trouble was brewing.

After the demise of the Boom Boom Room, the Caterpillar Inn became the favored hangout. One night, while four of us stood at the bar gabbing with Rufi and Freddie, two coastees came in. They took seats at the far end of the bar, and we made our way over to a table and got comfortable. Only Bob Dylan on the jukebox made a sound as he sung "Lay Lady Lay." One of the coastees came over and apologized for the trouble they had caused on their previous trip. Feeling noble, we invited the two to join us at our table, and they did. Then they bought us round after round of drinks. As they were leaving, they invited us to come down to the ship for breakfast the following morning: "Seven sharp, "Coast Guard time," they joked.

After they left, Valentine, Kathy, JoAnn, Ann, Sandy, and several other PCVs showed up; the place filled up. We danced and partied and extended the coastee's breakfast invitation to everyone who came. "They want to make amends," we lied. "Everyone's invited, seven sharp."

The next morning I made the rounds in the Marine Resources truck, picking up ten people. At exactly 7:00 sharp, four trucks pulled up in front of the *Basswood*. Thirty ravenous bodies, a mixed bag of Palauans and PCVs, marched up the gangplank to the foredeck, all looking for orange juice, steak, bacon, ham, eggs, omelets, french toast, and pancakes—delicacies unavailable to us except on the *Basswood*. On deck, an alarmed watch captain greeted us.

"We were invited for breakfast last night by Bob and Carl," said our designated spokesman, Valentine. He held his skinny arm up and arched it in front of us in introduction. "Here we are," he smiled.

Just then, Bob and Carl appeared from out of the companionway. Looking quite unglad to see us, they showed us into the galley where the cook did a double take, then turned away and shook his head in disgust. We ate in shifts, some of us standing, drinking coffee while others gobbled scrambled eggs, bacon, and toast. The frustrated cook sweated over the hot stove, giving us dirty looks and probably spitting in our scrambled eggs. When the captain came in for coffee, he assured us that the Coast Guard had only honorable intentions and that the events of the previous trip would never be repeated. Valentine furiously scribbled notes for his next issue of *Didl a Chais*.

The *Basswood* hauled up and left that afternoon, more likely than not to get back to Guam and refurbish the galley. After the great breakfast, no crew member ever again invited a PCV aboard the *Basswood* while in Palau.

—

Peter had his fingers in the Coast Guard pie. Good friends with the Coast Guard pilots, they flew in goodies for him on their trips; goodies like steak, wine, and Black Label scotch. For these favors, Peter wined and dined the crews, the C-130 pilots taking delight in buzzing Peter's house when they flew in, which meant, "get the drinks ready." Once, buzzing just a bit too low, they lost the plane's trailing antenna to Peter's backyard stand of *Casuarina* trees.

Sometimes Peter would fly to Guam with the Coast Guard. One time I took Peter and the Coast Guard crew out to the airport in the Marine Resources' truck. The coastees guzzled beer all the way to Airai, a one-and-a-half-hour trip, and I drove right up to the C-130 Hercules and parked beside it. As we exited the truck, one of the pilots finished his beer and tossed the empty.

"What's this rule about no drinking within twenty-four hours of flight time," Peter asked in a serious tone.

"You got it all wrong, Pete," the pilot answered. "The rule says 'no drinking within twenty-four feet of the airplane.'"

When the *Emeraech's* engine blew up, Peter called on the Coast Guard to fly in a new crankshaft from Hawaii. They arrived early one morning flying low over Peter's house. On his way in to work, Peter picked me up and quickly lined me up to take the flight officers out fishing on the *Milotk*. At fisheries, I borrowed a couple of eighty-pound test rods from Ray. Ray told me he'd seen big yellowfin about an hour west of Malakal Channel, so I headed west. The three Coast Guard pilots had their wives along, the ladies having flown down on Air Micronesia to meet their hubbies for some R&R. Their gear included a Coast Guard-issue stainless steel cooler full of beer and ice.

The weather was superb, no wind and hot and glassy. About an hour and fifteen minutes out, a big fish hit one of the lines. They'd been dragging a small lure called a "Crocodile," and whatever had crunched it was quickly stripping the little 6/0 Penn Senator reel of its fifty-pound test dacron line. I yelled to the coastees to bring in the other lines and began backing the boat down. The Coast Guard pilots, unaccustomed to taking orders but quite proficient at giving them, gave me steerage instructions, which included going forward and turning around. When I reminded them that I was the captain of the vessel, they rolled their eyes at one another, but I ignored them and concentrated on backing down.

It was work. In reverse, the clockwise prop rotation made the boat track to starboard. Over and over I'd have to crank the wheel to starboard, throw it in forward to straighten out, then crank the wheel to port while reversing again. The old Yanmar diesel huffed and puffed, billowing a column of black smoke with each burst of throttle.

The coastee on the rod sat on the fish box, his back bent forward pushing out his beer belly, the butt of the rod jammed into a gimbal. Panting and sweating in the early afternoon sun, he pumped the rod and cranked the reel. I made it clear that no one should touch the rod, lest any chance of a record be negated under the rules of the International Game Fish Association; not that I cared at all—I just wanted to keep the excitement up. The coastees, well attuned to authority and rules, refrained from helping their wilted friend except to feed him more Olympia.

The supercharged fish would come to the surface and circle toward the front of the boat keeping me busy swinging the stern. Then it would sound, and I would have to back down. I backed down and maneuvered for nearly three hours, the fish several times stripping the line down to the red backing on the reel's spool. With the coastee on the rod near fainting, the fish at last came to the boat. I threw the boat into neutral, put on a glove, and ran back grabbing the gaff. Leaning over the gunwale, I took a wrap on the wire leader with my gloved hand while easing the big gaff into position under the fish. Then I yanked up, the big hook gaffing the animal through the pectoral fin, and horsed it alongside. The beaten mako shark, a thick seven footer with wicked teeth, lay on its side looking up at me inquisitively.

"You want it?" I asked the coastees.

"Naw, we don't want no shark," one of them answered.

While a coastee held the gaff, I leaned over the rail and with my Super Pete, roughly sliced through the tough skin of its mouth around the bent and twisted treble hook. The exhausted shark thrashed, then fell off the gaff, rolled once in the crystal clear blue water, and sank slowly downward, its size diminishing with its descent. The sapped coastee, thoroughly overcome by the mako battle, laid out on the deck like a wet slug for the remainder of the trip.

The next day I returned the rods to Ray and told him the story. He looked at me excitedly.

"Why didn't you bring it in, for crying out loud! It was probably a world's record."

I felt as if I'd committed a nasty crime or something. "Next time," I said.

Unlike Ray, I was unimpressed by world fish records.

—

Out fishing one time on the *Milotk*, I jumped from the roof to the afterdeck and scraped the skin off my shin on the edge of the fish box. When it got infected, I took antibiotics and the wound finally scabbed over. Then I slipped on a step and ripped the scab off. More infection set in, and a red streak developed on my thigh and leg. When my groin swelled up I went to see the Peace Corps doctor who happened to be in town. He gave me a shot and put me on another regime of antibiotics. I hated the wound-infection-antibiotic syndrome. Antibiotics always made me feel sluggish and rendered my eyes sensitive to light. I had taken so much penicillin since coming to Palau that the drug was ineffective.

During dark moon, I often accompanied Teruo on the *Milotk* to fish for *terekrik* (big-eye scad). We'd fill up the four bait wells with fish and bring them into the co-op at first light to sell, the money going into a Marine Resources account for equipment needs and boat maintenance.

On one of these fishing trips I got cold and tired and went down forward into the engine room to catch some sleep next to the Yanmar three-cylinder engine which still radiated heat from the trip out. Although still fighting the infection in my leg, after my shot the pussy wound had partially scabbed over again, and I felt on the road to recovery. Lying comfortably on my back, my head propped on a Mae West, I fell into a deep sleep and dreamed. In the dream, a rat began gnawing the wound on my leg, hurting me. As the pain increased, I slowly awoke. Groping for the flashlight next to me, I aimed it toward my wound and switched it on. A jumbo-sized cockroach perched on my shin, its ugly little head submerged in my infection, like a horse sucking water from a trough. The big brown roach was eating me.

"You motha," I hollered and kicked my leg out straight. The three-inch scavenger scrambled across the floorboards, and I whipped the flashlight at it, the flashlight smashing into the side of the hull sending the batteries flying. I turned on the overhead lamp and tore up the floorboards. But the little bastard had gotten away. Teruo poked his head in and asked what all the ruckus was about. I recounted the story, and he chuckled.

"Life in Palau, *ollei*," he said.

"Yeah," I said, thinking, Woody got eaten by a rat, now I get eaten by a fucking cockroach.

"Which do you hate most, Teruo, rats or cockroaches?" I asked.

"Rats are the worst, *ollei*. They take big bites and make big mess." He laughed and went back up on deck.

Feeling violated, I doused my wound in diesel fuel to wash away any cockroach germs. After that, I considered cockroaches my worst enemy, a step above flies and mosquitoes.

When Richard Cheser and Dick Randall from the University of Guam visited Palau, I told them my cockroach story. Not to be outdone, Cheser told one of his own. He and a friend had gone on a diving trip off Guam. His friend, a novice diver at the time, used a double-hose regulator that had been in his garage for several months. They donned their gear, and just before going overboard, his friend sucked in deeply on his regulator to test it out. He yanked out his mouthpiece and coughed harshly, spewing out cockroach wings and legs. Realizing what had happened, he tossed his lunch up over his life vest. Back home, Cheser's friend coughed up bits and pieces of wings and legs for a month, and his breath reeked of decaying bugs. Nothing he could do would neutralize the odor. His wife consigned him to the couch, and his friends and coworkers gave him the cold shoulder. I suppose Cheser was one-upping me, but I didn't care. I relished the thought that at least someone else had been tormented by those abhorrent critters.

—

"Alii! Pateriiick, bekiis!" Melanna jumped around outside my door one Saturday morning, yelling at me to wake up. I'd been out drinking and roistering the night before and was in no mood for an early wake-up.

"Nga ra soam, eh Melanna? (What do you want?)" I asked irritably.

"Husto is coming! Husto is coming! Wheeee," she sang out in English.

I couldn't imagine who Husto was. But Mechas had sometimes mentioned his name.

Later that day, I went over and chewed betel nut with Kilad. Husto was her cousin, she told me, and the real son of Mechas. Husto had been in Guam attending college but had decided to quit and return to Palau. I wondered how this would affect me as the adopted son.

The next day Husto arrived. Melanna was ecstatic to see her brother, and Mechas seemed overjoyed. Rubak had come down from Ngkeklau, and a lot of people from the village wandered in to see the college boy from the big island of Guam. He looked a lot like Mechas, a little oriental in the face and with lighter skin than the average Palauan. I sat and talked with him about Guam,

Palau, the family, and a bunch of things. Later I went down to fisheries and spent the afternoon swimming with some friends over at Icebox. When I arrived home in the evening, Husto lay sleeping in Vini's room amidst a bunch of empty beer cans.

Sometime during that night I awoke by a rock hitting my roof. First one rock hit, then another, and another. Lying on my back, I heard Husto, drunk, yelling my name, cursing me in Palauan, telling me to go home and I could hear Mechas trying to talk him down. But the stones kept coming, bouncing off the tin roof. Not wanting to walk out into the line of fire, I just lay there, nervous, waiting for him to stop. Then I heard Kailang arguing with Husto, their voices becoming fainter as they walked toward Kailang's house. I fell back asleep.

In the morning when I got up, Mechas spoke to me while Melanna fixed me coffee. Husto didn't mean anything, she said. He was sick from the beerso don't be upset But I was upset. Perhaps Husto had just been keyed up, and it wouldn't happen again.

That evening when I returned home from work Husto apologized to me. It was the beer, he said. Melanna and Vini slinked around timidly, embarrassed over the situation.

Two nights later, Husto staged a repeat performance. Again I stayed put in my room, not wishing to confront a drunken Husto. The barrage continued at intervals throughout the night, interspersed with Mechas's pleas to stop. I lay there on my pandanus mat, drifting in and out of sleep between attacks. I felt sorry for Mechas and for the neighbors.

At the crack of dawn, I put on my shorts and walked out to confront Husto. Incredibly, he lay asleep in Vini's room, right outside my door. I shook him awake and asked him what his problem was, why he hated me. He looked up bleary eyed, at first not comprehending who I was nor where he was. Ashamed, he whined and whimpered apologies. What a smuck, I thought. Should I punch him in the nose? Disgusted and mad, instead, I bounced back out through my window to avoid Mechas and walked up the trail to the road where I caught a ride to Malakal.

That evening when I arrived from work, Husto was out somewhere. If he had gone out drinking, I knew I could expect trouble later. I looked around the household. Mechas looked exhausted as she sat in the kitchen combing Melanna's hair, and

Melanna had a sad look on her face. I sauntered over to see Kilad, who, of course, had already talked to Mechas about the problem.
"He is jealous," she said.
"I know that, Kilad. But is he *kebelung* (crazy)?"
"Only when he drinks," she answered. "Don't worry about it Patrick. Soon he will go back to Guam, and it will be *ungil* (good) again." Fat chance of that, I thought.

I left Kilad's, walked down to the Caterpillar Inn, and came back smashed. But I slept well that night. I was tired. Tired of this stupid rock-throwing business. Tired of Palauan leniency; the "it's okay, he was drunk" business. Tired of everything. I wanted to ask Mechas why she put up with Husto's behavior; but I knew the answer lurked beyond my realm of understanding. I was not Palauan.

The next night, the instant I heard Husto milling around outside, beebling and babbling, I dressed and slipped out the back window opening. As I walked quickly up the path, I heard the distinctive *whack*! of a rock hitting the roof. I hustled up the road to Jay's house and spent the night on the rug.

At fisheries the following morning, I told Peter my troubles. He loaned me the government truck, and I drove back up to Yebukl. Kilad sat talking to Mechas as I walked up, and I could hear Husto snoring away in Vini's room, overcome by another night of alcohol and delusion.

"Mechas," I said as I slipped off my zorries, crossed my legs, and sat on the plywood floor. I spoke slowly in Palauan so that my meaning would ring clear. "Husto does not want me here and I must leave. I don't wish to leave, I'm very happy here. But there will only be more trouble if I stay. So I must leave so that Husto and everyone can be happy."

Mechas pleaded with me in Palauan. "Husto does not know what he is doing. He drinks too much. He learned this in Guam. He was never this way before. He will get better." Kilad looked at me and reiterated Mechas's words. But I'd had it with Husto. Poor ol' Husto could find another scapegoat to stone. I hated to leave. I loved the family, and I loved Terresa and Kilad. I loved the village. But this thing with Husto could never be resolved. As long as I remained, Husto would continue his drunken rampages. I had to get out of there.

My belongings in the shack consisted of an old rotting Samsonite suitcase, my sleeping mat, pillow, sheet, a pair of Levi's, two shirts, one pair of cutoffs, two pairs of shorts, underwear, toothbrush, and razor. Several books and some personal papers sat on a shelf and when I lifted them, they fell apart in my hand. Insect food. I stuffed my things in the suitcase and threw it in the back of the pickup. Then I walked back to Mechas's room where she sat with tears on her cheeks. I told her I would be around to see her and Melanna and not to worry; then I headed for the truck feeling like gecko dung. Kilad ran out as I got in. I'd miss Kilad, my confidant. Teary-eyed, she made me promise to come back when Husto left. I knew Husto wasn't leaving; having flunked out of college, he was an alien in Guam. He wasn't going anywhere.

"Bye, Kilad," I said, holding back tears of my own.

My friend, Greg Halstead, had asked me several weeks previous if I might be interested in finding a place to stay with him. Like me, he was extending for a third year. He wanted to leave his family and be on his own, and he'd rented a small shack down on lower road near the Smiling Cafe, just down the road from the Caterpillar Inn. At thirty bucks a month, he seemed happy to have me share the rent.

The little house consisted of one room about 15 x 15 with a small, closetlike kitchen in the back containing a one-burner kerosene stove atop a rickety old wooden table. Greg had several dishes and a pot or two so we could at least cook sometimes. A cardboard wall separated our room from the room next door, the owner's way of creating a duplex. An impoverished mother, her teenage daughter, and an infant lived just beyond the cardboard wall. The infant cried constantly, and we often overcame the wailing by cranking up some music on the Akai tape deck which I had inherited from Dale. Out back, a single *benjo* and shower served both us and the neighbors.

Greg had his share of girlfriend problems. Almost from the day he arrived in Palau, Greg had taken up with a young Palauan girl named Sepe who lived in the village of Ngarbeched located down-slope from the upper road toward Iwayama Channel. Ngarbeched had a reputation for being a rough place, and Sepe was Palau's equivalent to a Harlem street girl. Cute Sepe, a sweetheart at sixteen years old, harbored a temper which matched Teo's in both spontaneity and violence. Her young firm body was astoundingly strong and no one gave her shit, not even

Greg. Rumor had it that it was she who had bitten the ear off Moko, the *Emeraech* fisherman.

Over a Kirin in the Texas Saloon one night, Greg related to me how Sepe's increasing sexual appetite intimidated him. If he had a headache, which he often had these days, she would beat the hell out of him. Greg had a proclivity for black eyes and more than once he sported one. He wanted to break away from Sepe, but she wouldn't take the hints. Greg was her man, her *rubak*. Sepe failed to understand that Greg secretly loved another.

The first night I stayed in the new place I was by myself. Greg had left to spend a week in Babeldaob as part of his job with the Education Department. Asleep on my mat, I awoke to the tactile pressure of tiny feet sprinting across my chest. Noises: *Squeak squeak, eek eek*. Startled, I sat up and turned on the lamp. In the middle of the floor, about fifteen rats fought over a loaf of bread that Greg had left on the shelf. When I tossed a flimsy *Time* magazine at them, they casually scampered off to their hideaways. I swept out the crumbs and threw the bread out back, then laid back down, unable to sleep. I was not going to share my new house with a bunch of rats; at least not with that many. War plans.

Next morning I told Peter my rat story. "Go see Neal at Ag," he said. "And go see Public Health. They'll give you some traps."

At Agriculture, Neal gave me ten traps. "Bait them with scorched coconut," Neal said. "They love it."

Over at Public Health, the man gave me another five. "Bait with cheese," he said. "Rats love cheese."

"Cheese? Where am I going to get cheese?" I asked the man.

"*Consume*. In the can. WCTC got it. They got everything," he said, full of knowledge.

"Oh," I answered and took my traps.

The traps, big and strong, had oversized springs—finger breakers, if you weren't careful. That night, fully armed, I carefully cocked and baited all fifteen traps with scorched coconut meat. Then I turned off the light and laid down to sleep, figuring it would be an hour or so before the little varmints came out.

Several minutes later . . . *Thud!* . . . *Bang!* . . . *Whack!* . . . *Thud!* . . . *Wham!* . . . Too easy, I thought. That initial salvo netted nine rats, not including a couple that crawled away, mortally wounded. I threw the bodies in a bag, wiped up blood, and reset the traps.

Wap! . . . Thud! . . . Bang! . . . Thump! Four more bodies. The massacre continued during the night, until all the traps sat loaded and waiting, but without takers. I got 'em all. Well, almost.

—

I soon found that I missed my family and village life immensely. The little things that they did for me and which I took for granted became regrettable chores for me as I settled into my new routine. Melanna no longer woke me up and brought me lukewarm sugared coffee in the mornings. I missed having her around, her cute radiant smile, her slipshod English with the *Wheee* ending, and her adultlike mannerisms. Melanna had washed my clothes, fetched my food, cleaned my room, and done any favor I asked of her. And Vini, the teenage gentleman, always helping out. I missed Mechas's scoldings, missed watching her groom Melanna, and missed chewing betel nut with her and *rubak* Techur. Kilad was irreplaceable, and I thought of Terresa often, the old fire still burning.

At Mechas's house, Melanna had always prepared my food. Now I had to fix my own. I had lost about twenty-five pounds these last two years, most of it college fat. Now, living on my own this third year, I would certainly lose a few more pounds. Perhaps I'd fatten up when I went home on leave.

—

About two weeks after moving into the new place I was in the Peace Corps Office talking with Dale Jackson who had finished his Peace Corps stint and was heading back to the States. "I'm going through Saipan to see the Micronesian Olympics," he said.

"Hey, that's great. Wish I could go," I chirped.

"Well, let's do it," he said.

The first Micronesian Olympics, as they were called, would bring together athletics from each of the six districts to compete in different sports events, much like the "real" Olympic games. My mind raced for an excuse to get to Saipan. I walked in to see my friend Shiro, a good fisherman and the PC secretary and accountant.

"Shiro," I said. "Can I go to Saipan to get my physical?" Peace Corps policy ordained that volunteers take a physical every two years.

"Aren't you extending?" he asked. "The doctor will be here in two weeks. You can take it then."

"Ah, I'd rather take it now. It might make a difference in whether or not I extend. There's a job opportunity and if my physical has me under the weather, I'll probably take the job back home. It starts in a couple of weeks, so I have to decide for sure," I explained lamely.

"You mean you might not extend?" he asked.

"Depends on the physical results," I said.

He looked at me grinning. "Oh, and the Olympics too," he said.

"Yeah, hadn't thought of that," I said, trying to act serious.

"Let me talk to Terry, and I'll let you know," he said.

So Dale and I flew off to Saipan where we had some unfinished business from our previous trip with two floozies we'd met in a Palauan bar known as Da Place. Needing a place to stay, when we landed in Saipan I called up Jerry Facey at the Social Security Office.

"Hello, Jerry? We're back," I said over the airport telephone which actually worked.

There was a long pause. "Already? What for this time?" He sounded displeased.

"We came to see the Micro Olympics, what else. Can we camp on your floor?" I sensed him squirming, so I added; "We'll only be here over the weekend."

"Ah, yeah, I guess, but—"

"Thanks Jerry. We know where the key is. See you tonight."

Palau dominated the games, winning the majority of medals. I never did get my physical.[18]

---

[18] Unlike the International Olympic Games which are held every four years, the Micronesian Olympics were held again in summer of 1990, twenty-one years later.

Chapter 16

California

On the *Ngermeyaus* one afternoon, I took Ray Accord across the channel from Icebox to some rock islands for some light spin fishing. Ray was the finest light tackle fisherman I'd ever seen. He enjoyed an uncanny ability to sniff out fish.

"Huge barracuda live around here," he yelled as the diesel chugged along.

It was one of those unusual tropical days; slightly overcast and dead calm. In the rock islands, I could maneuver perfectly—backing down, swinging the stern around here and there—positioning the vessel to better facilitate Ray's fishing. He used an ultralight Mitchell spinning reel and Fenwick rod with four-pound test line. I'd been diving around these islands numerous times and I'd never seen any "huge" barracuda. A few small ones, yes. But none I would classify as "huge." Perhaps Ray had been drinking.

Whipping and retrieving a small flashing spoon, Ray caught several jacks, each weighing about five pounds. When he reeled in a larger jack and eased it alongside the boat, I bent over with a scoop net to bag it. From under the boat, a "huge" barracuda appeared and sliced the jack in half. With the jack's head in its mouth, the chunky cuda rifled out for blue water, smoking out the monofilament on Ray's reel. Ray used light wire leader on his hook and as the cuda stripped line, Ray lightened the drag on the Mitchell to lessen resistance.

"He's gotta swallow it," he said. I nodded in agreement, wondering how Ray would handle this one.

Forty-five minutes later, Ray had battled the life out of that "huge" cuda. His shirt soaked with sweat, Ray coaxed the giant fish alongside.

"I'd release it in a second if I didn't think it was a record," he explained.

I gaffed the now docile brute carefully through the underside of the lower jaw and hefted it aboard where it lay gasping across the hatch covers, its enormous lower canine teeth protruding up in front of its snout. After Ray knocked the fish out, we took it back across the bay and hung it on the scales in front of Ray's office. With the jack inside its stomach, it legally weighed in at just over fifty pounds, a new world record for Ray on four-pound test. Then I cut out the jack from the stomach of the big fish. The "huge" cuda weighed in under the record.

I spent a lot of time helping Ray make lures and tie up tackle, learning as much as I could from him. When I wasn't out diving for starfish I made trips with Ray on the *Ngerengchol* or went out fishing for tuna on the *Emeraech*. Peter scolded me.

"All you do is go fishing," he grumbled.

But I was addicted; addicted to boats, the water, the reef, and fishing. Not since my surfing days had I had so much fun. And like my surfing days, these were the times of my life.

Most of my Peace Corps friends had left that summer of 1969 or previously. The Truk group had long gone. My old pal Dale Jackson was gone; so was Jay Klinck. Only Greg and a few others remained from Group VI. The new PCVs of Group VII I found stuffy and bourgeois, a testament to a new generation of kids and a changing Peace Corps.

The world was changing and so was Palau, except for the roads. They remained the same, unpaved. Continental Airlines broke ground in Ngerkeseuaol for a new hotel overlooking Iwayama Bay. Continental Air Micronesia now flew DC-6s into Palau twice a week. A new ferry service between Koror and Airai—featuring a cable-pulled barge capable of transporting up to ten vehicles at a time across the Airai Channel—cut the four-hour round trip to the airport and back to three hours. A new "traditionally" constructed *bai* was dedicated at the Entomology

Laboratory as part of the Palau Museum. In downtown Koror, George Ngirasoal opened a new theater. Billed as state of the art, it boasted a prodigious curved screen, which the obsolete projector could never fill out, and an incomprehensible sound system. Cheap George accoutered his cement hot house with tiny Japanese plastic seats. Hollywood's Selmur Productions appropriately rejected *The Cowards* as the title of their movie, but chose instead the title *Hell in the Pacific*, which may have been why the movie only broke even. *Life* magazine featured a story on the production, and Lee Marvin appeared on the *Tonight Show* where host Johnny Carson showed a film clip of the movie, all of which helped put Palau on the map but did little for the movie. Lee Marvin, having finished his next movie, *Paint Your Wagon*, returned to Palau alone to do some fishing on the *Ngerengchol*. When I asked Lee what Dick Doughty was up to, he shrugged and said only, "acting, I guess." Bob Owen underwent major back surgery, his condition remaining tenuous. Peace Corps Director Terry Clancy burned out and went home, Bruce Cole taking his place. Olympia was fast displacing Schlitz as Palau's number one beer. Dale left me with the Yap radio station's grandiose Akai tape deck which played resplendently but tended to think for itself. Someone gave me tapes of albums by Blood, Sweat and Tears, Moody Blues, The Band, and the Beatles. When NASA's Apollo mission put the Americans on the moon, a *Didl a Chais* cartoon portrayed the astronauts being welcomed on the moon by Palauans clad in loincloths, a *bai* in the background. Kline left for Guam to live with her sister and start college. I was scheduled to go home on leave in October but felt ho-hum about it.

One Saturday, several weeks after I had moved out of Yebukl, I took a stringer of fish up to Mechas and the family. As I walked down the path toward the house, Melanna came running out and grabbed my hand:

"Oh Pateriick—Wheee!" she yelled, dancing around in circles.

My eyes flooded. Mechas scolded me for being gone so long, then laughed. Kilad came over, and we chewed betel nut and talked all afternoon. When I left, Kilad walked with me up the path and told me that Terresa missed me. That perked me up and I decided I should visit on a regular basis, keep myself visible. Kailang had been working on me about moving back, claiming Mechas fell ill by my departure. But I refused to move back as long as Husto lived there. I would stay away, except for visits, that's all.

Greg and I were partying hard every night in our little shack, blasting out tapes on the big Akai. Sepe hung around constantly, ignoring Greg's efforts to absolve the relationship. Then one night Sepe brought over her friend, a cute, young girl from Ngarbeched named Clarinda. The two girls were hard to handle. They could guzzle as much as Greg and I, and they loved dancing, their newfound hormones fueling them with energy. They ran us into the ground, night after night, never ending wild flings through the darkness and into the dawn—burning us both out.

One night Greg came home from Ngarbeched and told me he'd finally had it out with Sepe. "I told her flat out it was over, done, no more, ever. Finished. Then she went berserk. She started punching me out," he exclaimed. Despondent, he sat cross-legged on the pandanus floor mat and fixed a chew. His necklace of red, white, and gray seeds garnered from some tropical legume hung off the side of his bare shoulder, across red scratches from Sepe's fingernails.

I loaded a tape on the Akai and pressed "Play" just as someone rapped on the door. "*Alii*, Greg, let me in! Let me in Greg, please let me in."

"Oh shit—it's Sepe," Greg whispered. Sepe banged on the door, wailing and sobbing, making us both unnerved. I lit up a water-stained Winston watching my hands shake. Greg lit up one of his own, then stood and paced the room, yelling out to her: "Go home, Sepe. It's over. Finished!"

"Noooo, Greg! It can't!" she screamed, pounding hard on the door and shaking the whole house. Then it got quiet.

"Did she leave?" whispered Greg.

Blam! The door flew open leaving the hasp hanging by a splinter of wood. Sepe, her wet face full of rage, burst into the room screaming, "You motherfucker Greg!" She charged him with closed fists, punching him in the face and chest. Greg tripped backward, and they both tumbled to the floor. "Fuck you, Greg. Motherfucker. Fuck you!"

I watched them grabble on the floor, Greg on his back, Sepe straddling his stomach. *Whaap*! Sepe slapped Greg hard across the face, knocking his glasses across the room. Greg cocked his right arm and slugged Sepe square in the face, snapping her head back. Blood gushed from her nose. Spooked by the blood, I jumped in and pulled Sepe off. She sobbed hysterically, the fight gone from her. Greg rose and dabbed at her nose with his shirt, mumbling apologies, ashamed of himself.

I grabbed my *tet*, threw on a T-shirt, and flew out the door. Then I stopped and looked back in. They sat on the floor holding hands, Sepe sobbing hysterically, cursing at Greg, Greg staring at the floor. At the Caterpillar Inn, my hands shook while I downed a rum and Coke.

Arriving home later, I found the house empty and the hasp reattached. I fished the key out of the hiding place beneath the step, went in, and fell asleep. Next morning Greg came down to fisheries in the Education truck to talk with me. He would be going to Babeldaob for a week, he said, to escape Sepe's wrath. I told him I'd hold down the shack.

When I got home that evening, Clarinda was waiting for me with a box of clothes and some other stuff. "What's that?" I asked, knowingly.

"I want to stay with you," she said.

Uh oh. No good. Now my turn had come to end a relationship. I let it go until morning when I told her that she couldn't stay there because Greg wouldn't like it. She argued but I held my ground. Not wanting to deal with the problem, the next day after work I got on the *Emeraech* and fished for three days. Jumping off at Van Camp when we off-loaded our catch the third evening, I took several tuna up to Yebukl to give to Mechas and the family. When I arrived home later, I found all my clothes missing, along with a twenty dollar bill I had stashed in my shorts. Clarinda had wiped me out. What I wore was what I had—a slimy pair of fish-stink shorts and a blood-fouled T-shirt. Under the cold shower I washed the clothes I had on and then went to bed, silently cursing my misfortune.

Clarinda refused to return my stuff, and I had no use for the little thief anyway. Happy to be rid of her, I didn't press. Peter gave me two pairs of oversized shorts, and Ray gave me a shirt belonging to Lee Marvin. I knew I could get some new clothes when I went home on leave.

Greg returned from Babeldaob in good spirits. While he was away, Sepe had been around bugging me to talk to him, to get him to see the light. She told me that if he didn't take her back, she would put a curse on him with Palauan magic. *That* scared me, even though I wasn't the target; but when I told Greg, he only laughed. Greg had seen the light, he said, the warm glow of his new friend—and Sepe's magic would never work on him. I figured I'd had enough excitement in my life these last few weeks and so I had Shiro, the Peace Corps secretary, get my plane tickets home for a vacation. Two days later, carrying a *tet* full of betel nut and dressed in a pair of new almost clean white cargo shorts I'd found at Western Caroline Trading Company and Lee Marvin's orange shirt, I boarded Air Mike at Airai International Airport for a flight back to my beginnings.

But when I arrived in Guam, Pan American informed me that I had no reservation for the Guam to Hawaii segment of the trip, and that the flight was full up. I figured I'd wait around the airport until flight time that evening to see if I could get on as a standby. While standing against the wall killing time, John Sakie from Palau came up and asked me where I was going.

"San Francisco," I said, informing him of the reservation screwup.

"Give me your ticket and your passport, and I'll see what I can do," he said. I watched him take my ticket up to the counter and converse with the Pan Am airline agent for several minutes. When he came back, I had confirmed seating on that evening's flight to Hawaii, the same flight he was on.

"Hey thanks, John."

"No trouble," he said. We walked over to the Blue Marlin for a beer.

As we sat in the bar drinking our beer, I kept thinking: John Sakie—CIA? Why's he so interested in me? He worked for Education, but not as a teacher, and not as an administrator. As what? Every month, he flew off island, to where, no one knew. Rumors had him working Asia; Japan, Korea, Taiwan, Philippines, Malaysia, Indonesia; using Palau as a home base. Other rumors placed him as CIA military intelligence, keeping his finger on the pulse of Palau. John Sakie, mystery man. John Sakie, CIA. If you projected the myth of conundrum in Micronesia, you were CIA.

Sakie had business in downtown Agana, and he asked me if I wanted to come along. With several hours to kill before the flight, he rented a car and we took off. No James Bond, Sakie was, nevertheless, tall and fit. With his neatly cropped blond hair and dark shades, he looked the part. He wore a loose-fitting cotton aloha shirt and I kept stealing glances, looking for the telltale bulge of his agency-issue, Beretta? My curiosity heightened when he parked the car and walked into the downtown Post Office with his briefcase. Then he spent twenty minutes in the RCA communications center across the street.

Flying to Hawaii on the Pan Am 707, we sat in adjacent seats, Sakie in the aisle, myself in the middle, and a quiet middle-aged women at the window to my right. When we reached cruising altitude, Sakie ordered us a beer then began probing me about my background and about Peace Corps in particular.

"What do you think the *real* objectives are of Peace Corps in Micronesia?" he asked.

"It's hard to put a finger on, but I suppose it has to do with keeping the Micronesians friendly. I mean, the TT is strategic. We want it as a buffer to our western flank. We don't want any other nation to have it, and we won't *let* anyone else have it. We don't want internal problems so we're trying to make friends. And I believe we're also supposed to be preparing the people for self-government, whatever that means. So why else would they pump so many bodies into these islands?"

"Do you think it's effective?"

"What? Peace Corps?"

"Yeah, Peace Corps."

"In a way it is, in a way it's not. Look at the disparity between contract workers and PCVs. They distrust each other, and the Micronesians know it. So what are Micronesians supposed to think? Dumb Americans, that's what they think. I don't think PCVs are spreading subversive ideas or anything like that, but the fact is they're much closer to the people than contract employees. We know more about what the Palauans think than anyone else. The Palauans can't understand why the Americans don't do something useful—like fix the roads, fix the power system, fix the water system. I mean the Americans destroyed the infrastructure after the war and now, as trustees, they're ignoring it. What the hell are the Palauans supposed to think? Are they supposed to love America just because the Americans kicked out the Japanese? No way. They expect something tangible out of this Trust, I think, and they're not getting anything, except education."

"The Americans probably think that the best way to win Micronesians over is through education and the institution of democratic ideals," he said. I knew he referred to the Solomon Report, a 1963 Kennedy administration, three volumes, six-hundred-page report on the political, economic, and social status of Micronesia, including recommendations for policy reform.

"That's another problem area—education," I said. "Where are the jobs for all these young people we're educating? Government can only take so many, and the wages aren't up to par. Educated Micronesians want to live in the new world. They want the goodies, just like the Americans. In the old days, before the Trust, young kids were taught the old ways to preserve tradition. Now the young kids are taught by western standards. Then the kids introduce western ideas into the culture, and the whole thing gets screwy. Traditional values deteriorate. Culture is lost. Then, when the educated generation comes back from college, western ways and standards replace the older, more practical ways. But economically the islands can't stand alone, especially by western standards; western standards, that's what's being instilled in the young people."

"Yeah, tin verses thatch."

"Yeah. Air-con verses open air."

Sakie pointed out that the Americans were just another group of outsiders in the long history of Micronesia's domination by outsiders. "First came the Spanish. Then the Germans, and then Japan. The Japanese saw Micronesia as a tremendous resource to supplement their little island back home. They were hardly interested in the welfare of the Micronesians. They worked the locals and utilized the land and marine resources to strengthen their own economy back in Japan. They gave the Micronesians substandard educations, forced them to prepare the islands for war, and pummeled them when they got out of line. And they killed them if they suspected allegiance to the Americans."

"That's true," I said, "but many of the older Palauans, those brought up under the Japanese mandate, remember the good things, the infrastructure, and the order. Now they see a free economy, but the Americans don't seem to give a rat's ass about the pathetic state of Koror, the crummy roads, the water hours, the power outages every day and night. They have a right to be pissed. I've seen the prewar pictures. Koror was a beautiful place until we razed it. Sure, some of the infrastructure was destroyed by bombs during the course of the war. But after the surrender, the navy came in and leveled Koror out of pure arrogance. And they did the same to Dublon in Truk. Dirk Balendorf, during training, told us that after the war, anything 'Jap' got bulldozed. That was a military order. It had nothing to do with *why* the Japanese built it. And now twenty-nine years later, the TT Government buys new trucks—from Japan—every year because of the roads. Now that doesn't make sense to me, and it sure as hell makes little sense to the Palauans.

"How can the Americans justify this sham?" I went on. "They can't. And you don't have to be educated to resent it. Everyone breathes that fucking dust from the roads. Everyone suffers because of the arrogance of the Americans."

Sakie seemed to be enjoying himself, and he ordered us another Olympia. "The road and infrastructure problem really is shameful, and I don't know what to say about it except that my understanding is that the limited funds available to Public Works through the Trust Territory is not sufficient for improvement."

"Bullshit!" I bellowed, causing the lady next to me to look over. "The money they've thrown away replacing broken equipment and maintaining equipment caused by those shitty roads could have paved them several times over. Think of the costs to the citizens. They buy a car knowing they'll get a year or so out of it when, if the road was paved, it might last five or six years. Isn't that something to be concerned about? A lot of the TT budget money goes into improving the standard of living for American contract people—new housing projects, new furniture, washing machines, better comforts, stuff like that. The money's there, it's just going for other things.

"And another thing," I continued. "I don't really think most of these contract types take their positions seriously. How could they? What are they doing? Nothing but maintaining a facade of government, keeping a lot of locals in jobs, shuffling paper," I said.

"What about Peace Corps? Aren't they a joke also? I mean they're really just a free source of labor, aren't they?" he said, hitting base camp. "Free teachers, free nurses, free lawyers; and you, you're a marine biologist."

He was right. The Palauans respected wealth and power. They may have resented the Americans in many ways, but they respected TT contract personnel, bureaucrats, those who made money. Deep down, I had the feeling that many Palauans thought that maybe Peace Corps was something the Americans introduced as an aversion, to distract from the serious business of the Trust. What other nation would be so bold (silly?) as to throw in a bunch of "low clan" Peace Corps rebel rousers to act, in many instances, divergently to its own trumped-up administration of "high clan" bureaucrats? We were, after all, just free labor. But we were educated and trained, and the locals at least respected us for that. But that's probably as far as it went. Americans often used the phrase "only in Palau" for island ironies. Perhaps the Palauans thought, "only in America" for the way the Americans operated.

"You're right," I answered, "we are free labor. But we do a job and most of us live with families. And in most cases, I believe, we're treated not as something special, but as sons and daughters, and we're expected to contribute to the households in which we live. That also means that there is an exchange of cultures. I mean, in my case I bring home the fish to eat, it's expected of me. If I don't, no one says anything to me, but I know I've screwed up. My Palauan mother will send my little sister to the store to charge a can of tuna so we can have *odoim*, protein, something other than just rice or taro. So now, if I can't get any fresh fish, I make sure I bring home something else. It's my duty as first son. And when I've done something wrong or when something is expected of me, the word gets to me through the neighbors or relatives. It's part of the 'beat around the bush' syndrome, *melengmes*."

"So what do they get from you other than handouts?" he chuckled but with some misanthrope.

"I think they enjoy having me around, a white man, *chad er a ngebard*. I've certainly enjoyed staying with my family, except for recently. A family member from Guam is giving me trouble."

"What's that?" he asked.

"One thing I've learned is that islanders lack discipline among themselves. Maybe there was no need for punishment in the original culture. Usually when alcohol is involved, misbehavior is shrugged off as just a manifestation of drink. It's like, 'Oh, he was drunk, so it's okay.' I can't understand that logic, but I guess it works for them." I lit up a Winston, and the woman in the window seat next to me gave me another dirty look.

Then Sakie said: "Alcohol is bad enough but I think you'll see drug traffic in Palau in the next several years. All that stuff from Nam and the orient. It's already having an impact on Guam. I mean look at the drug-related crime on Guam. It's out of control, and it's going to get worse." He seemed to know a lot about Guam affairs. I didn't know what he was talking about. The closest I'd been to drugs in Palau was smoking some Hollywood grass on the *Oriental Hero*. "Are volunteers bringing in much dope?" he popped. He *really* was CIA, wasn't he?

Caught off guard, I took a sip of beer. I knew several volunteers who sometimes got stash through the mail, but only for their own use.

"I don't know," I said. "I really doubt it, but if so it's just for personal use."

"What about other drugs, the hard stuff, heroin and cocaine, LSD? Ever see it around Palau?" he asked.

"Ho," I laughed. "Never seen anything like that. Couldn't recognize it even if I did see it. Unless that white stuff we use for betel nut is really cocaine."

I'd never been so vocal in my life. It must have been the beer and altitude. We talked on about education, economics, and marine resources in Palau. Finally, unable to contain myself any longer, I asked him outright: "John, are you really a spook?"

He choked on his beer, chuckled, then turned his head toward me. With his hand cuffing his mouth, he uttered: "Doesn't every district have an agent?"

Taking it all in, the lady next to me gawked at us in disbelief. Embarrassed, I crawled over Sakie and headed for the *benjo*. Funny thing, after we said goodbye in Hawaii, I never saw John Sakie again. To my knowledge, he never returned to Palau. He just disappeared; as if he'd been deselected.

Those trans-Pacific flights were long. Eight hours from Guam to Hawaii, a two-and-one-half-hour layover, then another five and a half hours to the West Coast. When we landed in San Francisco at 6:00 p.m., the weather was cold and miserable. I felt uncomfortably naked in my shorts, all those people staring at me, and stepped up to the first pay phone I came to and called my old friend Eddie Brooks in San Jose.

"Come and get me, Eddie. I'm freezing over here."

Eddie and his wife Kathy found me in the bar drinking a beer and shivering. When we got to San Jose, Eddie gave me a pair of long pants and a sweatshirt. His oversized clothes hung off me like a scarecrow, but I didn't care. My tropical thin blood needed heat, and the only thing that mattered to me was that I stay warm.

The next day I went over to Santa Clara to see our mutual Lompoc friend R. B. Lilley. Married now, and holder of a recently acquired law degree, he was interning as defendant's council in a pornography trial involving a live act sex show in downtown Santa Clara. I spent a few days running with him, enjoying the trial and swilling free beer at his client's bar while topless dancers performed erotic overtures to a complacent ten-foot python. RB, right at home with the case, proudly defended the pompous Jewish owner—who only operated his bar, he claimed, under the sanction of the city code—against a group of outraged citizens.

I'd brought a bunch of betel nut and *kebui* along with me, the Hawaii customs official, apparently confused by the strange looking nut, waving me on through, but I had neglected to bring lime. *Chaus* looked so much like cocaine I feared getting hassled going through customs. When I showed RB my stash and elaborated on the betel nut effect, he became obsessed about trying it. We hustled down to a pharmacy.

"It's lime," I told the spectacled gentleman behind the counter. "They make it out of coral."

"Coral?" he said. "That's just calcium carbonate, isn't it?"

"Yeah, that's the stuff," I said. It was coming back to me now, all those chemistry courses I almost flunked. "We'll take a half pound."

Back home, as RB watched in fascination, I fixed a chew and crunched it, then quickly spit the green and white mass into the palm of my hand before I puked. It was intolerable. We looked all over town for the chemical equivalent of coral but failed to come up with the right stuff. When we chewed it without lime, the bitterness sickened us.

"Shit Bryan, this stuff is terrible," blurted Lilley, his hands flying.

"Damn it, Bryan," he continued, "next time bring the complete kit."

On and on, he chided me. I felt stupid.[19]

Eddie's parents from Lompoc came up to San Jose for a visit, so after a couple of days I drove down to Lompoc with them. After spending two years in Palau where top speed in an auto is about 15 mph, cruising along on H-101 at 65 mph had me in a state of controlled panic. Sitting in the front passenger seat, I slinked down low and punched my foot hard into the firewall trying to slow the car down. Finally, a nervous wreck, I jumped into the back seat and slept the remainder of the trip home.

In Lompoc, I visited with my parents a couple of days and then started looking up old friends. But things had changed. Old friends had new concerns: jobs, wives, kids, homes, responsibilities; things I held little interest in yet. Nor did my friends seem interested in my life style. I felt disappointed, almost betrayed.

I dug my old surfboard, a 9-6 Ike, out of the garage and went to the beach. I felt obsolete. Most surfers now used little boards six feet long or under. Surfing had evolved into a "plant and squat" style with some shoulder swinging for effect. Big boards were out and so were the graceful days of walking the board, hanging ten, and kicking out. But my problem had little to do with the new style. Accustomed now to eighty-five-degree water, my body repulsed the harsh temperate California ocean. With my feet purple and aching, I gave up. I once could surf California all winter long without a wet suit. Not now. Not as a tropo. Two years seemed like such a short time, but so much had changed.

Norman Vas had recently returned home from his trip around the world with the rest of the Truk guys. I called him up in Long Beach, and he told me to come on down. Taking a Greyhound bus, I viewed the sights of my old surfing grounds, the beaches along 101 north of Santa Barbara and south to Rincon. Norman met me at the Long Beach Greyhound depot in a Vespa motor scooter. Riding tandem, Norman maneuvered through heavy Long Beach traffic down to his mother's house, a frightening ride for me. From Long Beach, we went to Newport, borrowed his brother's VW bus, and headed down into Mexico looking for warmer weather. Norman seemed as lost as I in California.

---

[19] I saw R. B. Lilley again twenty years later at our thirty-year high school class reunion. He resumed castigating me for neglecting to bring the "damn" lime.

In Mazatlan, we drank beer and ate crab and shrimp for a few days, then drove back up to Long Beach. I stayed a few more days, driving around, eating, and drinking. Starved for red meat, we bought lean round steak, sliced it thin, then would eat it *sashimi*, making a sauce out of soy sauce, fresh lemon, and Tabasco. Already I had gained back some of the weight I had shed while surviving on fish and rice in Palau. I felt bloated.

Norman took me to Los Angeles where my old surfing friend Rennie Adam and his wife Sally were living while Rennie attended USC. Rennie was driving up to Lompoc for the weekend, and I wanted to catch a ride with him. Before Norman left for Long Beach, I asked him what his future plans were.

"I really don't know," he said. "Maybe get a job as a fireman. They get a lot of time off, so I can do some fishing out of San Pedro. Or maybe I'll join Peace Corps again and go to Tonga. There's a fisheries program down there that sounds interesting." I wished him luck.

Like Eddie Brooks, Rennie had married his high school sweetheart. Now, as we drove along the Ventura Freeway, Rennie seemed engrossed with his Russian wolfhound sitting in the back seat of his Mercedes.

"Still surfing, Ren?" I asked.

"Yeah, sometimes," he answered, "when I have time. School takes up most of my time." He wasn't really into it anymore, I could tell. Perhaps we both were too old for the new boards, and the new hot dog style. The new boards were the shits, all right.

"Nice car, Ren."

"Thanks, Peege. It's pretty bitchin'."

Rennie had always been "in" engaged. When we graduated from high school, I got my first car, a '57 Chevy. A month later, Rennie had a '57 Chevy. But Rennie wanted the fastest car. He put in a 327 full race engine and bolted on a four-speed transmission his friends had dropped out of a Los Angeles Corvette, jacked the car up high for racing, then spent his weekends in his garage, fixing blown head gaskets and replacing gears, clutches, and rear ends—while the rest of us were out dating and cruising. When he got into hunting, he used an expensive Russian rifle. When wing-tip shoes became fashionable, he had several pairs. Rennie hadn't changed in this respect. Now, Russian wolfhounds were "in"; he had one. Mercedes-Benz, always "in"; he had one. Dressy leather jackets? Rennie wore a nice one. We were best friends growing up, and we had pioneered surfing around Lompoc. But he seemed distant now. Maybe it was just me, but he seemed disinterested in my story.

My good friend, Tony Centeno, recently back from the navy, worked for a Lompoc loan company. Most of his navy savings had gone to a new Corvette. Seemingly possessed now by an unprecedented rush of hormonal activity, Tony's lifestyle revolved around loose women, bars, and fast cars. One night we hit the bars, then took his Corvette out on Central Avenue for some speed trials. Central ran from Lompoc's main street, west, through the flower fields, toward the ocean for about eight straight miles. Over the years, Lompoc youths had traditionally used Central as an impromptu drag strip. And Centeno, now an aging young adult, was feeling young again.

Tony's Chumash Indian blood had thinned considerably by the Jim Beam he'd been downing all night. We pulled on to Central and stopped. He looked over at me, staring out through huge bloodshot eyes.

"Fasten your seatbelt, Peege," he said.

Through the roar of the 427-cubic inch engine, he ground through the four gears, each speed shift snapping our heads back, the sleek Corvette propelling us like a rocket down Central at 120 mph. My palms sweated, and I gripped the sides of the bucket seat. Then we hit the shoulder, and Tony lost control. The Vet spun around several times, its tires squealing pathetically and plowed sideways into a recently planted poppy field. Suddenly we were bouncing backward across the furrows, the alcohol in my stomach slurping up into my throat with each bounce. We stopped. Santa Ynez River floodplain dust crept in through the vents.

Tony yelled out, "*Aiieeoo!*" a Chumash expletive meaning "Oh shit!"

"No lie Tony—great," I said, shaking. Fast cars didn't do it for me anymore; fast sharks did.

I spent another couple of days in Lompoc visiting with my folks and watching the war on TV. The Viet Nam War made me sick and the cold, uncomfortable weather made me anxious to get back to the Pacific, back to Palau where I felt I belonged. Then my old college friend, Fred Buss, called me up from Ojai. We agreed to meet down at Refugio Beach north of Santa Barbara.

At Refugio, we sat on the grass under a palm tree in back of the beach sipping bottles of Coors beer, watching the waves form up and roll around the point where Rennie and I had learned to surf. Soon after I had joined Peace Corps and left for Palau that summer of 1967, Fred had joined up and gone out to Yap. He'd quickly decided it wasn't his thing.

"You didn't like Yap, eh Fred?"

"Nope. I couldn't believe it, Peege. They were in loincloths, dirty. They had red teeth. I couldn't live in a place like that. I had visions of, like, Hawaii."

"It ain't like Hawaii, Fred."

"No shit. You really like it out there, Peege? I mean, all that stuff?"

"I love it. It's great. Can't wait to get back. What're you going to do, Fred?"

"Go back to school. Get my MBA. Make money. I'm tired of being poor."

"What about the draft," I said.

"They tried. I just didn't step forward. Everyone's doing it. They can't prosecute. Too many. I'm not worried. Fuck that war."

"Yeah," I said. "How's Charolette?"

"We broke up last year. Think she's getting married to some rich executive in San Fran. I'm going with a girl working for Merrill Lynch in LA. She's a broker. We might get married. She can put me through school."

"Sounds good, Fred."

I drove back down to Lompoc knowing I'd probably never see Fred again. And I felt empty.

Then I drove over to Santa Maria and saw Eileen Engle, her husband, Steve Will, and Jim and Sandy Princeton. We had all paled around together in junior college and in the years after. I sat with a beer in a fluffy chair in Eileen's middle-class tract home trying to explain a little about life in the islands. I got blank looks, and I squirmed. They have no idea what I'm talking about, I thought. They think I'm nuts—they really do. Are these really the same people I knew before? "How can you go back out there and live like that?" Jimmy asked incredulously.

I said goodbye and left, depressed now more than ever. All my middle class cultured friends, with everything in their world fine and squared away. But me? They'd given me funny looks, like maybe I was *wacko*. Perhaps I was. Perhaps. One thing was certain—I could hardly wait to get back out there and live like that again.

I bid my folks farewell and flew up to San Jose, said goodbye to Eddie and RB, then flew back out to the islands, not caring if I ever saw the States, or at least the mainland, again.

CHAPTER 17

And Polynesia

I must have been twenty pounds overweight when I arrived back in Guam. I felt roly-poly and bleached out. My skin had dried and cracked from the dry California air, and each time I blew my nose it bled. When I exited the DC-6, the hot, moisture-laden air hit me like steam from an overstoked sauna, just like it did on my arrival two years earlier. How readily we adapt to different climates. The cold dry air of California had left me unprepared for the tropical heat and humidity. I would have to get reacclimated and lose some weight before I felt comfortable again.

I left the terminal and walked down to Tamuning to look up Harson. Still living with his sponsors, he had quit school and was spending his days shooting pool and drinking beer at a Palauan bar in Tumon, the same bar where a Palauan gang called the Stingers hung out. Associating with that bunch could only mean trouble for Harson. Even I had heard of the Stingers. They carried a reputation for fighting in Guam, and local Chamorro hoods had it in for them. The Stingers' leader was a guy named Damon. When Harson introduced us, Damon proudly showed me his weapon—a midnight special he carried deep in the pocket of his black leather jacket.

"Far out," I said, in my coolest voice.

That night Harson and I went to a Palauan disco joint called the Tigers Den in Tamuning just off Marine Drive. When it closed, we accompanied a group of Palauans down to Tumon Bay where we sat on the beach and drank and sang all night, Palauan style.

Early in the morning, groggy from alcohol, I caught a plane for Palau. I worried about Harson. Sandy and I had each given him a hundred dollars for school. We expected better of him. Before leaving Guam, I encouraged him to stay away from the Stingers and to get back into school. He assured me that he would return the next semester, but I left feeling doubtful.

After I landed in Palau, I stopped by Yebukl on my way in to give Mechas and Melanna some gifts from the mainland. In Palau, it's considered a sign of well-being to be overweight. Mechas kidded me that I looked good, nice and round, and Melanna teased me as well. Then, when Kilad came running over and asked me how I got so fat, I felt like shit. The heat and humidity gripped me uncomfortably and being overweight made it that much worse. I got out of there before Terresa could see me.

Peter growled at me when I walked into his office on Monday morning. "Where the hell have you been?" he chided.

"Hey, Pete, I've only been gone a month, and I had six weeks' vacation time. I'm two weeks early, and you're bitching at me. I'm leaving," I said.

He chuckled, his tongue sticking out the side of his mouth. "No, you're not. Look in the back room." I walked into the library and peered at boxes of equipment I'd ordered several months ago: new tanks, regulators, vests, decompression meters, and a lot of other diving gear. Christmas.

Peter wanted to get going with the starfish program so we planned out some multiday trips to northern Babeldaob. I had trained four divers for the program, and their legal papers had been processed. Young guys, right out of high school; they waited, ready to go.

For the next several months, I led the starfish team on a murderous crusade of starfish extermination. We worked the west coast of Babeldaob, camping on the village docks and working out of the *Ngermeyaus,* diving on the barrier reef and on the myriad patch reefs within the lagoon. We found fronts of starfish everywhere except on the outside of the barrier reef, *Ruusch* for some reason never crossing the surf zone. We killed them by the thousands, injecting them with formalin or ammonia-based industrial cleaners. And we speared tons of fish. The weight I'd carried back from California quickly vanished, and even with my Winston habit I could free-dive to seventy feet and spear alongside the best of them.

After I lost my watch while water-skiing, Peter convinced me that the new Blancpains were superior to the earlier models. He sold one to each of us on the starfish team, letting us make payments each payday. One by one the watches failed. First they fogged, then they ran intermittently, then they quit. If we dove with SCUBA below seventy feet or so they flooded. Fed up, I returned them to Peter and demanded that he refund our money. He did, but grumbled grudgingly about it.

"You guys don't take care of anything," he barked, "that's why your watches don't work."

I pointed out that the watches were billed as "diver's" watches, waterproof to one hundred feet.

"Well, *my* watch never gives me problems," he countered.

"That's because you always take it off before you shower," I said. He poked his tongue at the inside of his cheek.

"Wise ass," he mumbled.

—

Time had flown; 1969 had vanished and only a few short months remained for me as a Peace Corps volunteer. I kept asking myself what I would do when it was over. Going back "home" was out. Get a job? Where? I thought about school, reluctantly, and looked into graduate school at the University of Hawaii which informed me I had to make up some deficiencies. Then Dick Randall from the University of Guam came to Palau to assess starfish damage. I mentioned I would soon be leaving Palau, and that I had no idea what I would do. He encouraged me to apply at the University of Guam Marine Laboratory.

"It's a brand new facility, and we need graduate students for the master's program in marine biology. With your experience, you'll be tailor made for it," he said.

Going back to academe would be hard after three years of undisciplined play, but it clearly seemed the best alternative.

As summer approached, Peter talked about performing a starfish survey down in lower Ponape on the atolls of Nukuoro and Kapingamarangi. Located a degree above the equator, Kapingamarangi had been surveyed the previous year by a team from the University of Guam. The team had been flown in on a navy aircraft, the Grumman UH-16A tearing open its undercarriage on a shallow coral head as it landed in Kapingamarangi lagoon.[20]

The survey found few starfish in Kapingamarangi, supporting one theory that held atolls as unproductive grounds for *ruusch*. Low coral islands lacked the nutrient transfusion into the surrounding waters necessary to enhance starfish larval survival. Kapingamarangi had been the only atoll in Micronesia surveyed for the starfish, and University of Guam scientists wanted a follow-up survey to substantiate the theory. They asked Peter to provide manpower for the survey.

Since the navy now considered landing in Kapingamarangi lagoon too risky except in an emergency, the only alternative transportation for a survey team was by boat. The team would consist of Peter's assistant, Tosh Paulis, himself a Kapingamarangan; Milton McDonald, the TT starfish expert based in Saipan; Ken Davico, a navy diver from Guam; and myself. In May, a privately owned, sixty-foot trimaran stopped in Ponape. Milton approached the captain about chartering the vessel for the expedition and arranged for a June departure.

Ponape had the best airport in Micronesia, a new runway capable of handling *JuJu*, the new Boeing 727 that Air Micronesia had pressed into service. Milton and Ken had flown to Ponape the previous day and they met Tosh and I at the airport when we landed on the sleek jet. When my diving bag failed to appear in

---

[20] When the plane stopped, the divers hurriedly donned their masks and fins and plugged the hole from underneath with clothing, which allowed the pilot to beach the plane before it sank. After radioing Guam for help, the following day a Navy C-130 flew over. The plane circled and, in naval precedence, parachuted a chest full of beer and ice. On the second go-around, the plane dropped a bundle of toilet paper and a navy survival manual. The final drop contained the materials for patching up the plane.

baggage claim, I sprinted out to the 727 and crawled up into the cargo bay searching for my diving bag. I chucked down luggage to a Ponapean ground crewman but only found other people's bags, my bag apparently having flown instead to Truk on the DC-6.

At the terminal, we sweltered in the Ponape heat and after I put a tracer on my diving gear, Milt suggested we go for a swim at the Nanpil River road crossing, a popular area for swimming and washing clothes. The Nanpil was but one of several rivers which funneled water down from Ponape's high mountainous rain forest. Perennially shrouded in clouds, the mountain receives over four hundred inches of rain a year, reportedly the highest annual rainfall in the northern hemisphere.

We arrived at the river and found it rushing over the crossing at about a two-foot depth. The cement road crossing the river contained five, round, two and a half foot diameter pipe culverts which channeled the water beneath the road crossing. It had rained heavily all night, and the culverts could not contain the volume of water carried by the river.

Unable to cross the river, we parked the truck and I walked upstream for a swim. The hot tropical sunshine had attracted many villagers to the river. Along the banks, children jumped from overhanging trees into the water. Down below the road, topless women lined the bank, gabbing, laughing, and carrying on as they scrubbed and pounded their laundry on rounded river boulders.[21] I slipped into a deep pool and swam out, the cool water recharging my body. Looking downstream, I saw Milt sitting on the backside edge of the road near the opposite side of the river and decided to drift down in the current to where he sat. Lying relaxed on my back, I floated feet first downriver toward the road. Nearing the crossing, I sensed the velocity of the water increase and as I lifted my head to get oriented, the water sucked my feet downward. As if some superforce had grabbed me by the ankles and yanked me under, my head submerged in midbreath. I gagged. My forehead slammed into the edge of the culvert, and my elbows banged the edges as my arms trailed behind. Careening through the pipe, I felt the suction tear at my shorts. Is the outlet open?

---

[21] "Topless" was the traditional way for women to wash clothes in Ponape.

I shot out the other end and plummeted into a churning pool below the falls. Tons of falling river water buffeted me around like a leaf, seemed to hold me under, bringing me to an anoxic panic. Clawing my way to the surface, I gasped for sweet air. The river swept me along and I stroked my arms cross-current toward the women washing clothes. Ten feet from the edge, in knee-deep water, I stood up, coughing. I cleared the mucus from my nose, wiped the blood from my forehead, and inspected my bloody elbows. Then I looked up. Why are they staring like that, I thought.

I heard Milt yelling at me from the road upstream: "You okay? You're naked! Wait, I'll be right there."

Naked? No wonder they're staring. In front of them stood a bloodied American exposing himself. Embarrassed and upset over the loss of my shorts, I turned and sat in the water to cover myself. An old Ponapean women waded over and handed me a lavalava. I stood back side to them, wrapped up, then walked to the river's edge where the women donned blouses and descended on me, dabbing my wounds.

When the police arrived, they insisted I go to the hospital but I politely refused. I needed stitches for the gash in my forehead, but I opted for a lifetime scar instead. Later, the captain of the trimaran patched up my forehead with a butterfly bandage. I held the proud distinction of being the only person ever to have shot the tube at Nanpil River.

However, about a week later, under similar circumstances, one of the pipes sucked in an overweight Ponapean man. Too rotund to squeeze through, he nearly drowned before friends could pull him out. Alarmed by these incidents, the district administrator banned swimming upstream of the crossing until Public Works could install heavy steel grids over the inlets.

Kolonia, the district center of Ponape, looked every bit as forlorn as Koror. The potholed coral road that was the main drag was lined with a hodgepodge of buildings made of old shipping crates, cement, or tin roofing material. A few functional but heat gathering Quonset huts, their overworked air conditioners groaning torturously, served as government offices. Down by the dock, the Community Club occupied another Quonset. Several small general stores, with a sprinkling of everything and not much of anything, baked under tin roofs, while bugs and cockroaches bloated inside aged dusty boxes of cornflakes, pancake mix, and bags of flour. A few shabby bars sat here and there, their jukeboxes wailing out country-western tunes. Outside of town, the traditional thatched outer island village of Porakiet was occupied by Nukuoroans and Kapingamarangans, some of them Tosh's relatives.

Walking through town, I ran into Matt Mix, the Peace Corps hippy and free spirit of Group VI who had caused all the fuss in Guam on our way out to Micronesia three years previous. After Peace Corps had kicked him out, he'd gone home to upstate New York, made some money, and come back out. Married now to a local girl, he worked for the Ponape Cooperative Federation. Matt seemed overjoyed to see me, even though I had only briefly met him during staging three years before. He wanted to go with us to Kapinga, but I knew Tosh wouldn't let him. Over a beer, we talked about Palau and Ponape. With his cleanly shaven face and his short cropped brown hair, he could have been a lawyer. Ponape, apparently, had mellowed him.

The trimaran had plenty of deck space and was named the *Azi Kazi*. The boat crew consisted of the captain, his wife, two children, and a helper named Tom. The family pet, a large tomcat, also accompanied the vessel. They had voyaged from Hawaii and were cruising Micronesia.

We loaded and stowed our equipment, including a Zodiac, outboard engine, air compressor, and tanks. The spacious trimaran quickly became burdened with gear and belongings. The next morning my diving bag arrived, and the captain set our departure at four o'clock pm.

With several hours to kill, I walked up to the Community Club and watched a couple of locals play Ping-Pong. No Mickey Mouse game, they stood about twelve feet back from the table, banging the ball back and forth at breakneck speed. After the game, I struck up a conversation with one of them. His name was Ponciano Rasa, an impressive-looking guy with slightly curly jet black hair and a sculptured muscular physique. Ponce was a mixture of Ponapean, Spanish, and German, and his family owned a small hotel on the hillside called the Rainbow Inn. He attended the University of Hawaii at Manoa where he was a standout track-and-field athlete. We talked about surfing and about how the new, smaller boards had revolutionized the sport. Ponce had been a world-class big wave surfer in the early 1960s and had once doubled for Fabian in the Hollywood surfing movie, *Ride the Wild Surf* (1964), riding the North Shore heavies for the filmmakers as Fabian and costar Tab Hunter looked on from the beach.

Ponce told me he crewed on some of the pole-and-line tuna boats operating out of Honolulu's Kewalo basin during summers, one of these a boat called the *Electra* which sunk between Kauai and Niihau. Loaded with twelve tons of tuna, the *Electra* had been steaming back to Honolulu one night when she ran between a tug and barge, snagging on the tow cable and foundering, taking on water but not sinking immediately. The tug, unaware of the mishap, continued on. The *Electra's* captain and most of the crew decided to stay with the partially submerged boat, but Ponce and four others set out for Niihau. Using hatch covers for flotation, they swam in triangular formation to present the largest profile possible to predators, making the island of Niihau the following morning. Their decision to swim for it paid off—the rest of the crew perished.

After that incident, Ponce went to work on another boat. One night as the vessel returned to Kewalo Basin from fishing, it took on water and sunk. This time, however, a nearby fishing boat rescued all the crew members. After that, Ponce gave up tuna fishing.[22]

Milton had taken up with a Ponape PCV named Kim. Kim, with her angular figure and long waist-length brown hair, rarely hesitated to strip to the waist like the natives when washing clothes. And when Milt introduced us, she was bent over scrubbing clothes. Kim came along as a crew person, bedding down every night with Milton in the starboard hull lower bunk.

Negligible wind blew as we departed Ponape, and we motored most of the way through the doldrums at a slow three or four knots. The sun beat down on the white decks without mercy, and the still air did little to cool our sweating bodies. We stretched a canvas across the boom and spent the afternoon hours lying in

---

[22] Ponce later married and settled in Saipan where he entered politics and became the Senate president. Later he ran for governor of the Northern Marianas. A tennis buff, we played together for years while I lived in Saipan during the 1980s.

its shade, mesmerized by the constant droning of the engine. We took turns standing on the stern dousing ourselves with buckets of cool sea water. The ocean, an infinite expanse of glassy desert, reflected the sun's rays like a mirror and drove us to interminable thirst. Sometimes we saw distant cumulus clouds dropping loads of rain as fluently as a shower, but we never hit one, and after two days we were forced to ration water.

We made Nukuoro one morning right on the money, slipping in through the angular passage between two southern islands. Remnants of an old Japanese fishing boat sat on the reef, awash in the surf. Inside the lagoon, Tosh sat on the bow, pointing the way around coral heads for the captain, and an hour later we dropped anchor in front of the village which lay back behind the beach. This was an outpost, a traditional Polynesian village without power, fuel, or other amenities found in the district centers. The Nukuoroans and Kapingamarangans are of Polynesian descent, the only people in Micronesia who are.

That evening we brought ashore a slide projector and small generator. In the open air village meeting house, which had an angular thatch roof and coral floor, the captain showed slides of other islands, mostly Hawaii, while the noisy little Honda generator pumped life into the projector. The villagers loved it, and afterward they provided us a feast of island food. Later Ken walked down the beach with a young girl, and I made off with a girl so well-developed, but oh, so young, that I hesitated, but not for long. Down the beach, we slipped beneath the strand vegetation, in the soft sand, on her lavalava, under a bright moon.

We surveyed Nukuoro for two days, finding nothing significant but beautiful blue water, extravagant coral, and lots of sharks. Milt brought along two Bang Sticks, the newest underwater protective devices available. They fired .357 magnums, lethal to sharks, and generated considerable concussion on your ear drums.

The morning before departing, we made a deep dive over the lee outside barrier reef, a steep drop to over 200 feet. Curious fish, unaccustomed to divers, swam in from everywhere, and several gray sharks roamed about. Milton and I glided down to 150 feet where coral growth gives way to sand. We found no starfish. On our ascent, several sharks followed us and I pulled back the rubber sling of the Bang Stick and shot a four-foot gray shark which came too close. It stopped, dead, its back arched, green blood flowing from its gill slits. We continued upslope and watched from under the Zodiac as excited sharks from the fringes pounced on their dead buddy and tore him apart. Later, Tosh mumbled something about sharks being sacred in Kapingamarangi.

Two days later we entered Kapingamarangi lagoon and dropped anchor off the main village. The village lay split between the islands of Soho and Ueru, the two islands connected by a high arching cement footbridge which spanned the dividing reef flat. Built the previous year by the Army Corps of Engineers, the bridge looked out of place in the unadulterated thatched village nestled along the beach and in the coconut trees.

Tosh took us in to his family's household where grass-skirted aunties, loinclothed uncles, and naked nephews smothered him with affection. The open air huts of thatched pandanus had removable walls of woven thatch used only during inclement weather. Built on beds of crushed coral, the main room was a combination living and eating room. Off to the side sat two sleeping huts built of long straight sticks spaced about an inch apart and arranged vertically from the coral floor. A thatch roof, made of pandanus, covered the hut, and the doorway was a simple thatch lean-to. Kapingamarangi was plagued by flies, but they would not stay inside the sleeping huts. One could enjoy a midday sleep in the relative cool, darkness of the hut without being nuisanced by flies.

During the war, the Japanese had used Kapingamarangi as a lookout station and antiaircraft guns still stood on one of the islands. Down near the southern end of the lagoon, several wrecked Japanese Zekes, modified for lagoon takeoffs and landings, lay along the beach. American planes had strafed them as they sat in the lagoon, the Japanese unable to scramble fast enough to take off. Even Kapingamarangi, perhaps Micronesia's most obscure terrain, had been influenced by the war.

This time of year, scarcity of water presented hardships for the villagers. Tosh's family owned a Japanese built World War II cement cistern, and Tosh allowed each of us one bucket of water to rinse ourselves at the end of the day. That bucket of freshwater proved the most refreshing stimulant imaginable. Saltwater is a threat to metals, plants, and human skin.

Several days after our arrival, the villagers staged a ceremonial feast for us. Moray eel is cherished by the Kapingamarangans and is highly sought after for festivities. Morays, large reef dwelling eels, are top carnivores and have a reputation for carrying ciguatoxin in many areas of the Pacific. Apparently "clean" in Kapingamarangi, we tasted roasted eel, boiled eel, and fried eel. And taro, tapioca, breadfruit, pandanus, flying fish, and "aged" yellowfin sashimi, another Kapingamarangan and Nukuoroan favorite. I stuffed myself, cramming my food down to outcompete the flies.

An old man who spoke only one English word, a relative of Tosh I learned (all Kapingas were related to Tosh), invited me down to the beach where about ten other old men sat in a circle on the coral floor of the canoe shed, the traditional Polynesian gathering place for men at work or play. We eased ourselves in among the other loinclothed gentlemen and waited our turn to take a slug from the Clorox jug of tuba they were passing around. Curious about the contents, when they passed the jug to me I peered inside, taking note of the ants and moths floating around, then cringed as I drank. The old men roared with laughter, then insisted I take another slug, just to catch up. Holding the jug with both hands, a dribble of tuba on my chin, I looked at my partner and he nodded.

"Yes," he rasped, grinning without teeth, his white hair flowing gracefully over his ears.

The acidic brew burned going down, then churned in my stomach.

"Ahhh," I commented and looked again at my friend. "Yes," he said again, the grin larger than before. Again I raised the jug to my lips—definitely smoother this time. I glanced around the circle. Broad dark faces grinned out at me, nodding in approval. I took another greedy gulp. Later I awoke under a canoe, my head feeling full of tuba.

My old friend, the "yes" man, took a liking to me. After we returned from our survey each evening just before dark, the old man would wander down to the boathouse with his jug and wave to me on the *Azi Kazi* to come ashore. I'd jump into the Zodiac and zoom ashore to share his harvest. Sitting on the beach watching the sun dissolve into the horizon, he would pass me the jug: "Yes," he'd say. And yes, I'd drink. And he'd speak to me in Kapingan.

And I'd laugh and feel dumb. And he'd laugh, take another swig and say, "yes." And we'd drink the whole thing. Then I'd get a stomachache and a headache too. But the old man enjoyed it, and I suppose I did as well.

The adored pet of the boat family, Frank, the big gray and white tomcat, had successfully alienated most of us—everyone, that is, but myself. Milt complained bitterly to me about "that fucking cat," and Tosh talked quietly about feeding Frank to the sharks. Evidently sensing security from the protective shield of its adopted family, Frank had pranced around the boat spraying cat stink on everyone. Then one placid night as I sat on deck with Tom talking story after having consumed a half gallon of tuba with my friend on shore, the cat came up and sprayed my leg and shorts. Without hesitation, I reached out, grabbed the cat by the neck, and tossed it overboard

"*Yeeooow*," old Frank said as he flew through the air and landed with a splash. Tom and I stood up and watched the cat dog-paddle for its life around the boat, and I chuckled insidiously over my revenge. The wife bounced up from below decks.

"What's going on?" she asked, suspiciously.

"Oh, uh, the cat sprayed me and I, uh, knocked it overboard. I'm going to get it out."

"Oh no," she cried, "you didn't!" I tried to explain to her that I only reacted instinctively when I grabbed the cat, wrung its neck, and threw it to the sharks.

I dropped the rope ladder over the side and Frank scampered up, looking like a wet cat, which threw the wife into a tizzy. Just then the captain stormed up and took over the discussion.

"That cat is part of our family and you had no right to do that," said the captain as he picked up Frank and stroked his wet fur.

"But the son-a-bitch peed on me. He's been peeing on everyone, and the whole boat smells like cat piss," I countered, perturbed.

"The cat is our pet, and this boat is its home. It's defenseless. It has our trust; and now—you've destroyed that trust. You could have killed it. Don't ever do that again."

"Okay. I'm sorry. It just made me mad, that's all. I won't do it again," I promised, my head hanging.

I felt rather ashamed. The captain could have called me a louse, or a shithead, or a turd; anything he might have called me would have been right. He might well have told me to swim back to Ponape—I deserved it. That night I had degenerated to maggot.

Which put *me* at the head of the boat families' shitlist. Which put the *cat* at the head of mine. Frank seemed to know; he kept his distance, fully aware that I'd chuck him to the sharks again if he even *looked* suspicious.

—

Each morning, we had to run several miles down to the southern end of the lagoon to go out the channel. Once outside, we headed north, along the eastern reef or around to the western reef to the point where we had finished our survey the previous day. During the surveys, one or two of us would hang on to the handles of the Zodiac, watching the reef bottom for starfish while the boat towed us slowly along. If we saw something interesting, we would anchor and free-dive or use SCUBA to check it out. We kept notes on the condition of the reef, numbers of starfish sighted, feeding areas, and any other pertinent observations.

The fourteen-foot Zodiac had nearly a hundred patches on it, and most of them leaked. Several times a day we'd have to add air, and each day when we returned from our survey, we'd patch up new holes and repatch old holes. The hole situation got worse and worse, but the Zodiac would never sink. It was impossible to get all the air out of one unless you really worked at it. Sometimes we'd limp in, the boat low in the water, but we always made it.

Kapingamarangi possessed the clearest water I had ever seen. Just outside the channel, along the outside lee reef, the view was staggering. The reef flourished with lush coral growth and diversity. Angling gently down from the surf zone, it shelved onto a plateau at thirty feet, then dropped off at a steep angle to about 175 feet where it dropped off vertically to the abyss. Seaward lay a dark blue panorama, like outer space. This reef contained all the elements of a great adventure.

Our last day out, we anchored on the thirty-foot shelf and suited up for our last dive on Kapingamarangi. In the Zodiac, we developed a quick diving plan, then fell in. Tosh and I wielded spear guns, and Milt and Ken carried bang sticks and cameras. My partner Milt and I, equalizing our ears, descended immediately to the ledge at 175 feet, while Tosh and Ken meandered along the slope above us, watching. The crystal clear water diminished the feeling of depth; only the high-pitched bubbling of our exhaled CO_2 and the nitrogen-induced euphoria suggested depth. Like eagles over El Capitan, we hung just above the drop-off, taking in the giddy view of the cliff and blue water. Rainbow runners glided past, in formation, like a flock of geese. Then several schools of tunas. Several times we glimpsed a large outline in the apogee of the distant blue, just beyond recognition. Gray reefs glided along the slope and wall, their nictitating membranes flicking across their eyes as they checked us out. Then, from the blue, a mammoth white-fringed shark swam toward us and veered off, its fat white belly almost glowing against the dark blue background. Our breathing rates increased immediately. At that depth, we had little bottom time, and the big creature gave us inspiration to head back upslope. Milton grabbed my arm, gave me thumbs-up, and we kicked upward staying close to the slope, our exhaled bubbles whistling in the depth. Up above, Ken and Tosh appeared as black silhouettes against the incredibly bright backlight of the sun. A school of large midwater surgeon fish hung off in the blue, and, like a fool, I turned and pushed off the reef, gliding out, holding my breath, spear gun out front. I squeezed the trigger: *Clack*! The spear punched through a fish, and I gripped the stock tightly as the fish jerked and struggled, spewing blood. Turning back to the reef, I kicked hard, dragging the speared fish behind me. Excited gray sharks appeared from nowhere. Like a windmill, the big fish spun on the spear, giving me trouble. *Boom!* The whole ocean seemed to shake when Milt fired his stick. A gray spun out into the blue trailing blood. Now Milton and I backed up the slope, watching the blue water. My fish kept swimming out with my spear while the sharks zoomed around, getting closer and closer.

Tosh and Ken climbed into the Zodiac while Milt and I waited at the anchor watching the sharks. Decompression would have to take second place to getting into the Zodiac. We started up. Not too fast, bubble speed only. Milt ripped off his tank and flew into the Zodiak. The sharks, too many and too close now, converged on my fish. I dropped the gun. First things first, I thought. My ass first. I reached the surface and, with the tank still on my back, porpoised into the boat. Wriggling out of my backpack, I lay on the floorboards gasping for air. Milt put his mask on, leaned over and stuck his face in the water. He pulled back up and yelled, "Hey! No sharks."

Looking up at him, I said, "Get my gun, will you?"

He rolled in and dove down to retrieve my gun. Seconds later he flew into the Zodiac like a hooked *mahi mahi* and landed on my stomach, knocking the wind from me and almost bouncing Ken and Tosh, who were sitting on the side pontoons, into the water. Ripping off his mask, he pointed into the water and shrieked: "*Car-char-hinus motha-fuckii!*" A reference to the animal we'd seen earlier off the wall—the big white-fringed shark had been lurking near the boat, waiting for him.

Kim was sick. Her stomach hurt her, she said, and when she ate her food came up. Her temperature read normal and she looked okay, but she felt terrible, she said. We speculated on her condition, wondering if perhaps she just didn't want to make the trip home on the boat. Or maybe she'd lost her virginity and felt down about it. After the third day of her sickness, the captain called Ponape on the radio and described the symptoms. The next day he called again. The navy would send down a sea-plane from Guam for a medevac the following day, they said.

The next morning at high tide the whole village watched the stubby little Grumman Albatross make a low fly-over, then land in the lagoon and taxi up to the beach. The crew, aware of the receding tide, hurriedly got Kim inside and situated. We said goodbye, and the plane taxied out. As the plane roared across the lagoon, they ignited a *jato*, an auxiliary rocket attached to one wing to give them extra power on takeoff. The plane lifted quickly off and flew in a wide circle. Coming in at coconut tree level just off the beach, they released the empty *jato* tank and it tumbled into the water. Every kid in Kapingamarangi, swimmer or sinker, hit the water to be the first to reach it.

The following day, we cruised out the channel for the last time and headed for Ponape. In the doldrums again, we motored for two days before finally catching mild southwesterlies which gently pushed us into Ponape.

Kim met us at the dock when we pulled in. She was fine after all, not even pregnant. Milt went back to Saipan, Ken left for Guam, and Tosh and I flew back to Palau. Before he left, Milt told me that he knew of a couple in Guam who, for a pittance, would put me up for a few weeks until I found a place to stay and got settled in for school. "Great," I said. I'd be leaving Palau in a month for Guam and graduate school.

—

When I got back to Palau, I was surprised to see Harson back from Guam. He came by one evening with his friend, a young Palauan girl from the University of Guam. You could tell she had been away from Palau; her lips glistened with lipstick, her nails sparkled pink from polish, and she wore a sleek jumpsuit and sandals. She was gorgeous.

Harson had changed. Gone were his boyish good looks. His hair had grown long, brushed back over his ears, and he wore a slight mustache which made him look handsomely older. We walked down to the Caterpillar Inn and chatted over some beers, while his girlfriend talked with a friend across the street.

"Are you going back to school, Hars?"

"*Cho choi*, but I want to sit out one semester first and make some money."

"Who's the girl," I asked. "Does she have a sister?"

"I met her in Guam. She's a student. We're going up to Ngaraard to stay for the summer. What about you, *ollei*? When are you leaving?"

"A few weeks. Are you hanging out with the Stingers?" I asked. I wondered if this was the real reason he was home, the Stingers.

"They want me to join with them, but I can't do that. All they do is fight and *melamech* (smoke—pot)," he chuckled.

"Maybe it is better you sit out a semester. You live too close to their turf in Tamuning. Let them sting someone else."

"*Cho choi. Te mekngit a chad* (Yes. They are bad). Are you still going to the University of Guam?"

"Yeah, sure am. So I'll see you there for sure."

"*Cho choi.* See you there, *ollei.*"

—

Peter wanted me to take the starfish team down to the Seventy Islands conservation area before I left.

"One last trip," he said. "We really need to clean out the Seventies."

I was less than thrilled about it because I wanted to spend my last days out fishing on the *Ngerengchol* and the *Emeraech*. But Peter was squeezing the last bit of mileage out of me, so we packed up the *Ngermeyaus* and went down to spend a week.

I wouldn't let the starfish guys spear anything in the Seventy Islands. That was a "no-no" that they seemed to comprehend. So for compensation, every day about 3:00 p.m., we'd take off and go fishing somewhere, spearing fish and lobster and catching coconut crabs for the night's barbecue at the base camp in the Seventies. We ate good.

One afternoon, Boogi, one of the starfish divers, guided us to a spot he said had big fish. "We use SCUBA there," he said.

Boogi anchored us between two small rock islands very close to the Seventys. The water, fifty feet deep and a turbid green, looked barren. I saw no reef.

"*Ngdiok ngikel er tiang* (No fish here)," I proclaimed.

Boogi flashed me a cagey smile which caused me to grin. I knew these guys knew the fishing grounds, and obviously Boogi knew something I didn't.

The other guys jumped in to free-dive around the islands, and Boogi and I suited up with SCUBA. Boogi told me to take my big gun.

"*Kot klou ngikel er tiang* (The biggest fish are here)," he said, a wild grin on his face.

I grinned back and raised my eyebrows. Maybe, but I couldn't imagine what, unless shark.

Boogi and I fell in and about twenty feet down we hit a reef, unapparent from the surface because of the turbid water. With visibility less than ten feet, I quickly lost sight of Boogi. I heard fluttering sounds and felt high frequency vibrations from something large passing close by, like a jet. *Vroom. Vroom.* I couldn't see anything but knew big fish swam close—either fish or sharks. Sharks? Never heard sharks make sounds like that.

I looked out and down and saw Boogi appear through the murk from deeper water, dragging a big hunker *eropk* on his spear. Jacks! Dropping down deeper, I passed through a thermocline, the water getting colder and clearer. Now I could see the jacks, swimming rapidly in paired formations, making distinct coordinated turns, hunting. Big fish. Silver and white fish, laterally compressed and deep-bodied, fish the Palauans claimed would attack sharks by ramming them in their abdomens, until they bled from their gill slits and sank, dying. I tucked myself back between two massive coral heads, my big seven-foot gun sticking out, and sucked air deeply, holding each breath (an excellent way to get a migraine headache, or pass out, or both), waiting for a fish to come in close. A pair came in, swimming straight at me, then veered off several feet out. I aimed at one and shot, hitting it behind the eye, the spear driving through the fish but missing the brain. As I increased the grip on the stock, it took off with the spear, yanking me along like a piece of spaghetti. After a twenty-foot pull, the fish tired and started circling. Tethered by the string and spear, the fish orbited me as I held out the stock to my spear gun and slowly finned my way to the surface.

Boogi sat in the boat watching my bubbles and at the surface I handed him the stock of my spear gun, then I pulled in the spear and grabbed the fish, trying to get a grip on its gills. On the surface now, the fish thrashed wildly, out of control, throwing water with its tail and beating me up as I struggled to manhandle it. Then its tail whacked me in the side of the face, gashing my cheek with its scutes and flipping my mask off. I held the big fish tight against my chest, my diving vest protecting my skin against the sharp scutes while Boogi jumped in and wrapped a rope around the fish's peduncle. He jumped back aboard and pulled it up over the side, the big fish still thrashing vigorously. I dove back down to retrieve my mask, and when I climbed aboard Boogi laughed at me while I panted from my ordeal.

"*Klou ngikel*" (big fish), he pointed, in mock admiration of my fish. I looked at my fish, then glanced at his fish. His was larger than mine.

Peter wanted me to make radio contact with him each morning but sometimes I'd forget, or I couldn't raise him. The day before we were to go home, the weather turned foul. The sky clouded over and the air cooled. Squalls rolled through with increased frequency. I tried to contact Peter on the radio without success. Probably not even on, I thought. By noon, the lagoon had kicked up like open ocean, and we headed for our camp to take cover. A big cave sat in the limestone island behind the beach, perfect shelter for foul weather.

Late in the afternoon, Melisebes showed up with word that a typhoon was east of us and would hit Palau that night. He decided he'd better stay with us rather than try the fifteen-mile trip back to Koror with the lagoon now as convulsed as soapy water in a giant Maytag and visibility approaching zero in the squalls. The *Ngermeyaus* was firmly anchored directly in front of our cave, and Melisebes decided to tail his boat off the stern of the *Ngermeyaus* rather than anchor it independently and risk having one crash into the other.

We collected fire wood and settled into the cave to await the storm. Outside, the wind picked up tempo and squall after squall whizzed by in flurries of forty-five-degree rain. Just inside the entrance we built a fire, the smoke getting sucked out by the passing wind, but sometimes getting blown back in by deviant wind currents. On shore twenty feet away, waves crashed ceaselessly and rain whipped across the cave's entrance, now and then the wind sending in a flurry of drops, enough to dampen us as we huddled in the sand on pandanus mats.

Around midnight, the storm reached full intensity. As it passed, the wind swung 180 degrees, and by first light the weather had cleared to a dull gray with dark rain filled squalls rolling in from the west, bringing in torrents of rain at the entrance and dowsing the fire. As the light gathered outside, we looked out to check the boats; there were no boats. Melisebes, much concerned about his racy conservation boat, ventured out for a look.

Minutes later he was back.

"*Indebus a bilas* (The boats are gone)," he said.

We looked straight across from us, about a half mile away, at two islands but saw only white beaches. The geography of our rock island with its limestone outcroppings at either end limited our north and south views of the lagoon, so two of the boys waded around the fringe of the island to get a better view. Soon they yelled out for us to come. We sprinted down the beach and as we neared the tip saw the boats sitting far out in the lagoon toward the barrier reef, a mile or more away. They bobbed steadily in the choppy waters, appearing to be stationary.

Boogi and I geared up in fins and masks and set out swimming, the western fetch across the lagoon sending a stiff two-foot chop busting headlong into us. We battled the waves for a half hour, only making good about a hundred yards. This is stupid, I thought, exhausted; those boats aren't going anywhere. I signaled Boogi, and we started back on a broad reach, swimming and surfing the little storm waves. Back on the beach, there was nothing to do but wait.

Peter must have had fits. Not only was his starfish crew missing, now Melisebes had not returned.

Late in the morning we heard the distinctive sound of a diesel and ran down to the end of the island to see who it was. Peter and Tosh steamed around the corner in the *Milotk*, and we screamed and hollered. They had found the other boats, unmanned but anchored in the lagoon, so they'd headed for the Seventies. Koror had been lucky, they said, no damage.

They had brought the skiff in tow, and we used it to load our gear while Peter motored the *Milotk* off the beach keeping her bow into the wind. Then we recovered the *Ngermeyaus* and the conservation boat and started off toward Koror in a procession: Melisebes out front, his head sticking through the cabin hatch as he steered with his feet, then the *Milotk*, Tosh's head and shoulders poking through the top hatch, and the *Ngermeyaus* following, my head and shoulders also sticking through the hatch as I stood on one foot and steered with the other. We travelled east across six miles of open lagoon water, avoided the dangerous patch reefs along the rock islands north of Eil Malk, and rocked and rolled our way into the bottlenecked passage between Ashakasengu Island and Ngaiangas Island behind the keen eyes of Melisebes in the lead. Sliding east with the wind and waves across the several mile expanse of open lagoon east of Ngaiangas, we snaked northward around the tip of Ngermidiu Reef, gliding along in the flat calm offered by its lee. At the limestone cliffs of Urukthapel, which disappeared into the indigo, we veered northeast for a mile, rounded the white lighthouse marking the tip of the reef, and began the last twenty-five-minute leg through the curvy Malakal Passage to fisheries.

Safely back home, that night Peter and Tosh hosted a party on the lawn in front of the Marine Resources Office. I shoved Peter off the wall into the water before he could get his watch off; later he got me. My work was done; I could only think of Guam now, and school.

—

Before I left Palau, Lee Marvin had a falling out with the Palauans. Several high clan politicos, unhappy over his charter boat operation, probably because no handouts were forthcoming, openly complained to Lee. So Lee told them: "Fine; I'll leave."

While I prepared to depart Palau, Ray had already started folding up shop, making arrangements to ship the *Ngerengchol* to Guam.[23] Sinichi Wong, the fishing master, put his learning experience on the *Ngerengchol* to good use. He bought a sleek twenty-six-foot boat, outfitted it for big game sports fishing, and began a profitable charter fishing operation in Palau.

—

The afternoon before leaving Palau, I went up to Yebukl to say goodbye to the family. Husto was out somewhere, and Terresa and Kilad came over. We sat around with Mechas and Melanna, talked and chewed, then chewed some more. Kailang showed up with some beer, and we talked and drank and chewed. Finally I said goodbye and started up the path. Just before reaching the road, I heard, "Patriick!"

Turning, I saw Terresa and Kilad walking up the path behind me. Kilad stopped under a mango tree, but Terresa hastened up to me holding out her closed fist.

"Patrick," she said, "here."

I held my hand out, and she grabbed it, placing a betel nut into my palm. Quickly I closed my hand around the nut, trying to take her hand at the same time, but she pulled away.

"*Meigung*, Patrick." She turned and ran down the path to Kilad, leaving me all choked up.

"*Meigung*, Pateriick," Kilad yelled out, waving, a red hibiscus flower glowing from her black hair.

---

[23] I later skippered the *Ngerengchol* in Guam after Ray succumbed to a heart attack. I would take the Coast Guard guys fishing; in exchange, they maintained the boat and gave me free fuel. I was making money from fish sales to boot. After I left Guam in 1974, however, someone torched it; a sad end.

I waved back, turned, and walked up the path to the road. My nose ran, and I blew it the Palauan way, one nostril at a time, then wiped my eyes with the backs of my hands. At the corner, I paused for a last look around. On the left, enclosed by a low hedge, was Mindszenty High; Kintaro's little green shanty store stood on the right; and across the street loomed Maris Stella Elementary School, a thick crop of grass reaching out from its single brick building to the road. *Mechas'*, returning from the taro and tapioca patches, walked steadily along the roadside path, their baskets of starch balanced on their heads, while Datsuns and Toyotas rumbled along the coral road, kicking up dust.

I wondered what it had all been about.

A barefoot youngster in shorts popped out from nowhere and stood next to me. He looked out at the road and up at me.

"*Ollei*, Peace Corps," he said and took my hand.

I breathed in deeply. "*Ngdiok*," I said then popped the nut in my mouth and crunched it. It was the complete kit.

The End

INDEX

Note: Locators marked with *n* refer to notes.

A

Accord, Ray, 192-93, 201-2, 238-39, 290-91
Adam, Rennie, 12, 303-5
Adams, Jack, 120-21, 140-41, 143
Aetkin, Steve, 182
Alphonso (president of the boatyard), 39, 50-51, 201
"And Polynesia," 307-28
Ann (Peace Corps volunteer nurse), 111
Asuma. *See* Mechas (head of Kailang's household)
Aten, Dildo, 167-68, 183
"The 'Ax'," 75-88

B

Basswood, 274, 279
Benhart (Harson's friend), 206-7
"Bird, a Bomb, and Camping Out, A," 164
Black, Peter, 53-55, 149-50
Bliok (worker at co-op), 100
Boogi (starfish diver), 323-26
Boorman, John, 196-98
Bourne, Don, 24-26, 43-51, 65-66
Brock, Vernon, 216
Brooks, Eddie, 12-13, 301, 303
Bryan, Patrick G.
 application for the Peace Corps, 19-20, 22-23
 in Babeldaob, 203-5, 207-9
 back in California, 301-5
 at the Boom Boom Room, 275-76
 college years of, 13-16
 co-op work for, 93-94, 100-102, 105, 107
 diving test taken by, 73
 on the Emeraech, 119-25, 127-37
 first few days in Palau for, 30-32, 34-36
 fishing in Uchelbeluu, 171-72, 174-75, 177-78

329

in Guam, 27
in Hawaii, 24-26
in Helen Reef, 150, 229-31, 233-36
hunting sharks at Ngemelis, 219-21
Kailang's family's adoption of, 85-87
in Kapingamarangi, 315-19, 321
in Koror, 90
leaving Palau, 327
memo to Peter Wilson, 150-53
on Morei's send-off party, 103
move to Greg Halstead's place, 286-87
in Ngaiangas, 80, 82-83
obsession with Terresa, 115-17
Peace Corps training for, 41-44, 46-48, 64, 75-78
as photographer's assistant, 269-70
project in Ngchesar, 65, 67-70
in Saipan, 160-62
in Truk, 155-60
visit to Melekeok, 69-70
Buss, Freddie, 13, 15, 17-18, 305

C

"California," 306
Callaghan, Paul, 85, 94
Cally (Bud Fuchs's wife), 22
Carol-ungil (girl from Palau), 37-39
Centeno, Tony, 304
Cheser, Richard, 260, 283
Clancy, Terry, 52-53, 75-76, 180
Clarinda (girl from Ngarbeched), 293-94
Constein, Mike, 55, 84

D

Damon (leader of the Stingers), 307
Davis, Gene, 53, 149
Deisen (crew on the Emeraech), 124-27, 129-30, 133, 135, 242-43
diving, 82
Doughty, Dick, 40, 55-56, 163, 199-200, 257-58
Dumae (babysitter), 145

E

Emeraech, 35-36, 119-27, 129-31, 133-40, 178-79
"The Emeraech," 119-45
Erica (Harson's sister), 110

F

Faulkner, Doug, 102, 218-22, 224, 272-73
Fitzgibbons, Kerry, 261-62
Fluharty, Sandra, 109-11
Freddie (volunteer), 248-49, 252-54
Frigate, 229-30
Fuchs, Bud, 22-23

G

Gail (ex-girlfriend), 13-14, 17
Glover, Tom, 147
"Group VI," 23

H

Halstead, Greg, 286-87, 291, 293-95
Hardy, Jack, 73-74

Harson (Palauan native), 61-64, 95, 110, 116, 203-10, 227-28, 307-8, 322
"Helen Reef," 146-63
Helfman, Gene, 62, 84-85, 88, 95, 241, 247
Henly, Don, 7, 263
Hester, Frank, 267-68
Hillanger, Charles, 159
Hoar (priest), 89, 98, 154
Hodges, Dave, 84-85, 88, 99
"Hollywood Comes to Palau," 191
Howle, Richard, 71-72
Husto (Mechas's cousin), 283-86

I

Imes, Dave, 79, 132, 209
Imes, Jan, 22, 209
"In Palau," 37-58

J

JoAnn (Peace Corps volunteer nurse), 111

K

Kailang (co-op manager), 84-85, 88, 93-94, 99-101, 103-5, 117-18, 137-38, 155, 161, 168, 243-47, 259
Keel, Tony, 14-15
Kilad (Terresa's friend), 113-16, 118, 274-76, 283, 285-86, 327
Kim (Peace Corps volunteer), 314, 321
Kinney, Richard, 35, 120, 133-34
Kintaro (store owner), 248

Klinck, Jay, 48-49, 78, 156, 209-12
Kline (Patrick's friend), 250-51
Koichi, John, 269

L

Leary, Dan, 22, 51-52, 54
"Life in Koror," 89-118
Lujan, Rufo, 81

M

Madraisau, Becky, 132-33, 260
Marcello (Van Camp mechanic), 184-86, 247
Marvin, Lee, 119-20, 179-80, 192-200, 202, 256-58, 292, 327
Masahiro (co-op worker), 103, 122, 173-75, 197, 245-46
Matsumoto (boat builder), 35, 99, 193
Mechas (head of Kailang's household), 85-88, 111-16, 191-92, 210, 212, 283-86, 292, 308
Mekreos (co-op worker), 103-6, 199, 243, 245
Melanna (Mechas's granddaughter), 86-87, 111-12, 114-15, 191, 258, 283, 288, 292, 308
Melisebes (conservation officer), 61-63, 88, 95, 199, 213-14, 325
Michelle (Lee's friend), 119-20, 192-94, 198-202, 257-58
Micronesia, 18-19
Mike (Sabed's husband), 109
Mitsuo (co-op worker), 107-8

Mix, Matt, 26, 313
Moko (fisherman), 126, 129-30
Moncrief, Bob, 171-72, 174, 176, 184, 186
Morei (judge), 103, 108
"More Training," 59-74
Morris, Neal, 71, 97, 287

N

Nemi, Rudi, 133, 135
Ngerengchol, 200-202, 327

O

Oerbelau (skipper), 201
Oriental Hero, 194, 256
Owen, Bob, 7, 58, 95-97, 175-76, 231-32

P

"Palau Graffiti," 203-24
Paulis, Toshiro, 36, 94-95, 159, 169-71, 178-79, 181-82, 310, 316-20
Peace Corps, 19-20, 91-92
Pedro, Don, 154-55
Peleliu Club, 249
Powell, Ron, 84, 156, 167

Q

Quell (pet booby), 164-67

R

Randall, Jack, 217, 265-66
Rasa, Ponciano, 313

Rebluud (fisherman), 59-61
Rose (worker at the bar), 112
Rupp, John, 54, 159-60
ruusch, 42, 259, 261-62

S

Sabed (Harson's sister), 109
Sablan, Henry, 49
Sakie, John, 97-98, 295-98, 300
Sepe (Greg Halstead's girlfriend), 286-87, 293-95
Smouse, Scott, 48, 54-56, 63, 73-74, 76, 78-80, 83
Stark, Walter, 222-24
Steven (crew on the Emeraech), 127, 242
Suguino, Valentino, 247
Sumong (Bob Moncrief's assistant), 185-87
Swey (doctor), 179

T

Techur (Mechas's husband), 192, 258
Tengadink (bait man), 124, 127-28
Teo (nurse), 145, 252-55
Terresa (Kailang's niece), 86-87, 113, 115-18, 192, 209-11, 327
Teruo (boat captain), 180, 282
Toshiro Mifune, 195
"To the Carolines," 24-36
Trudy (Bob Moncrief's wife), 171, 173-75
Trust Territory Air Service (TTAS), 27
Trust Territory of the Pacific Islands, 19, 91, 94

U

Uab (Polynesian god), 11
Uchledong, Sabo, 43, 63–64
"Underwater," 256

V

Vas, Norman, 21, 46, 72–73,
    76–79, 121, 123, 135–44,
    156–57, 159–60, 264–66, 302
Vini (Mechas's grandson),
    112–13, 115
Von Schute, 225–26
"Voyages," 225–39

W

Wadsworth, Chet, 22
Wayman, Stan, 216–19, 228–30,
    233–39, 268–73
Weir, Tatiechi, 49–50
White (comptroller), 100
White, Rusty, 227–28
"Wildlife," 274
"Wildness," 240–55
Wilson, Ann, 25, 119, 143
Wilson, Peter, 93–99, 119–21,
    131–32, 136, 138, 140–44,
    146–48, 153–54, 167–69,
    181–82, 196, 199–200, 215–18,
    222–24, 261–64, 266–68
Wogut, 159–60
Wong, Sinichi, 201, 327
Woody (woodsman), 40, 48

Y

Yap Islander, 148, 150

Made in the USA
Lexington, KY
31 July 2012